'Black T<

Manchester University Press

Politics, culture and society in early modern Britain

General editors

PROFESSOR ANN HUGHES
DR ANTHONY MILTON
PROFESSOR PETER LAKE

This important series publishes monographs that take a fresh and challenging look at the interactions between politics, culture and society in Britain between 1500 and the mid-eighteenth century. It counteracts the fragmentation of current historiography through encouraging a variety of approaches which attempt to redefine the political, social and cultural worlds, and to explore their interconnection in a flexible and creative fashion. All the volumes in the series question and transcend traditional interdisciplinary boundaries, such as those between political history and literary studies, social history and divinity, urban history and anthropology. They contribute to a broader understanding of crucial developments in early modern Britain.

Already published in the series

'Black Tom'

Sir Thomas Fairfax
and the English Revolution

ANDREW HOPPER

Manchester
University Press
Manchester and New York

distributed exclusively in the USA by Palgrave

Published by Manchester University Press
Oxford Road, Manchester M13 9NR, UK
and Room 400, 175 Fifth Avenue, New York, NY 10010, USA
www.manchesteruniversitypress.co.uk

Distributed in the United States exclusively by
Palgrave Macmillan, 175 Fifth Avenue,
New York, NY 10010, USA

Distributed in Canada exclusively by
UBC Press, University of British Columbia, 2029 West Mall,
Vancouver, BC, Canada V6T 1Z2

British Library Cataloguing-in-Publication Data is available

Library of Congress Cataloging-in-Publication Data is available

ISBN 978 0 7190 7109 6 paperback

First published by Manchester University Press in hardback 2007

This paperback edition first published 2013

The publisher has no responsibility for the persistence or accuracy of URLs for any external or third-party internet websites referred to in this book, and does not guarantee that any content on such websites is, or will remain, accurate or appropriate.

Printed by Lightning Source

Contents

List of maps, tables and figures

Preface and acknowledgements

The initial research for this book began as a BA dissertation in the Department of History at the University of York in 1992 and the work intermittently proceeded alongside other projects ever since. I am indebted to James Sharpe and Andy Wood for encouraging me in this research and reminding me that a new study of this nature was necessary and important. I am also particularly grateful to Richard Cust both for his valuable criticisms and for allowing me time to finish the book during my postdoctoral fellowship on his High Court of Chivalry project at the University of Birmingham. I would also like to thank the School of Historical Studies of the University of Birmingham for supporting my archival research at Yale and the Folger with a research grant.

I am grateful for the supportive and stimulating environments that I have been fortunate enough to enjoy during my time at the Universities of York, East Anglia and Birmingham. I would also like to thank Gerry Webb, Norman Fairfax and John Thomson of the Fairfax Society for their kind interest, advice and helpful support. John Adamson, J. T. Cliffe, Ian Gentles, Ronald Hutton, Mark Jenner, David Johnson, Philip Major, Jason Peacey, David Scott and William Sheils have also provided illuminating and thoughtful discussion. I am indebted for my youthful discussions to the late P. R. Newman. Never among Fairfax's fondest admirers, Dr Newman's refreshingly partisan approach to the topic has already been sorely missed.

I have received much generous assistance from archivists at the British Library, the National Archive, the Bodleian Library, the West Yorkshire Archive Service, and in particular my thanks are due to Clive Wilkins-Jones at Norwich City Library, Amanda Capern at the Brynmor Jones Library at the University of Hull, and Deirdre Mortimer and John Powell at York Minster Library. I am also grateful for the enthusiastic help from the kind archivists at the Beinecke Rare Book and Manuscript Library at Yale University and the Folger Shakespeare Library in Washington DC. I would like to thank Alison Welsby and Jonathan Bevan at Manchester University Press for their efficiency and patience. I am also particularly grateful to the series editors and the anonymous reader for their valuable suggestions for revisions and improvements to an earlier draft of the book. Any remaining errors are entirely my own. It is fitting that a study of Black Tom be published by a university in northern England, as the Fairfaxes would have dearly loved to establish such an institution during the

1640s. Finally, I would like to dedicate this work to my wife, Vicky Hall, who has not only endured my ramblings with patience, but whose example always fortifies me with strength and inspiration, my 'Rider of the White Horse'.

Abbreviations

BL	British Library, London
BL, Add. MS	British Library, London, Additional Manuscript
BL, E	British Library, London, Thomason Tracts Collection
Bod.	Bodleian Library, Oxford
CSP dom.	*Calendar of state papers domestic*
EHR	*English Historical Review*
HMC	Historical Manuscripts Commission
HRO	City of Hull Record Office
HULA	Brynmor Jones Library and Archive, University of Hull
JBS	*Journal of British Studies*
JHC	*Journals of the House of Commons*
JHL	*Journals of the House of Lords*
Markham	C. R. Markham, *A life of the great lord Fairfax* (London, 1870)
Oxford DNB	*The Oxford Dictionary of National Biography* (Oxford, 2004)
SP	State Papers
THAS	*Transactions of the Halifax Antiquarian Society*
TNA	The National Archive, Kew, London
TRHS	*Transactions of the Royal Historical Society*
WYRO	West Yorkshire Record Office
YAJ	*Yorkshire Archaeological Journal*
YASRS	Yorkshire Archaeological Society, Records Series
YML, CWT	York Minster Library, Civil War Tract

Introduction

On 3 June 1642, a great gathering of the ministers, yeomen and husband-
men of England's largest county took place on Heworth moor, an open,
windswept meeting ground two miles east of the city of York. The crowds,
perhaps as many as 40,000 strong, were exasperated at the many grievances
their county had endured during the past three years, especially the burden
of billeting soldiers for their king's failed wars against the Scots. With the
outbreak of civil war just weeks away, whom most of the throng would choose
to blame for their sufferings remained unclear. Charles, always uneasy about
such mass demonstrations, had long nurtured a debilitating fear that his own
people were in conspiracy against him. Crowds alarmed him, reminding
him of the tumults that had recently frightened him out of London. It was a
measure of his desperation that he had summoned the meeting at all. It was
indeed the only occasion on which Charles I sanctioned such an assembly and
it was not intended as a consultative exercise.

Having failed to arrest the five members of the House of Commons who
were at the centre of opposition to his rule, the King had fled from London,
fearing for his life and family. He established his new court at York in March
1642. His presence forced the northern gentry to confront the political divisions opening among them as he sought their armed support to capture the
critical arms magazine at Hull. When Sir John Hotham, the parliamentary
governor, denied him admission to Hull on 23 April 1642, Charles hoped the
northern gentry would restore his full powers by force. To do this, he grudg-
ingly realised that these gentry would have to appeal to the common people for
support, at least as effectively as his parliamentarian enemies were doing in
the south. Therefore the meeting on Heworth moor was specifically intended
to remind Yorkshire's lesser landowners, freeholders, copyholders and clergymen of the due obedience they owed their sovereign. Few gentry attended,
save those in the royal guard.[1] The King rode on to the moor with his sons
the Prince of Wales and the duke of York, and his nephew the Prince Elector,
escorted by 140 gentlemen horse-guards and 800 trained bandsmen. Some of
the crowd cheered him, but others declared for the Parliament. Shouts of 'God
bless the King' mixed with clamours of 'God turn the King's heart'.[2] According
to the King's secretary, Sir Edward Nicholas, Charles orated a 'pertinent and
gracious preface' himself and then ordered Sir Thomas Gower, Yorkshire's

high sheriff, to read the royal declaration several times so that all the people might hear.[3]

The meeting was too vast for Gower to accomplish this personally, so loyal gentlemen dispersed themselves across the moor to read the royal declaration to the throng, copies of which were circulated in print. In the confusion Charles perceived a small group of gentry soliciting signatures among the common people. Among them was a young soldier whom he had knighted the previous year for military service against the Scots in the second bishops' war. The soldier approached holding some papers in his hand, but at first could not penetrate the guard of mounted gentlemen and courtiers whose horses encircled the King's. Undeterred, he persisted and forced his way past them, firmly planting his petition upon the pommel of the King's saddle. Charles pretended not to have noticed him and spurred his mount forward, nearly trampling the fellow under his charger's hooves.[4] This affront was for a long time indignantly remembered in Yorkshire and was retold in Joshua Sprigge's *Anglia rediviva* in 1647. The King then 'rode about the field, stayed a little, and so departed'.[5]

The young man was Sir Thomas Fairfax, the eldest son of Ferdinando, second baron Fairfax of Cameron, and he would soon become Charles I's most formidable battlefield opponent. Their next meeting was three years later at Naseby, when the man snubbed at Heworth would trample upon the King's last decent chance for victory over his rebellious subjects. Yet that day on Heworth moor, the Fairfax family was still far from armed rebellion. Fairfax's petition was moderate in tone. Lamenting the poor condition of the county after the bishops' wars, it 'attempted to exploit neutralist sentiment'.[6] Its opening words were:

> This particular county, most affectionate to your Majesties service, hath well nigh for three years past been the stage whereon the tragicall miseries, which necessarily accompany War and Armies, have been presented and acted, whereby the generall wealth and plenty of this Country is exhausted and brought very low: Which weight of miseries are sensibly become much more heavy, by reason of your Majesties distance in residence and difference in Counsells from your Great Councell the Parliament, begetting great distempers and distractions throughout the Kingdome, and have especially amongst us produced factions and divisions.[7]

The petition complained about the illegality of the King's newly raised guards, and the alleged flocking of armed Roman catholics to the royal court at York. Those freeholders on the moor who sympathised with Parliament selected Fairfax to deliver the petition, and having discharged his trust he returned to them to report his efforts. While the petition's language seemed conciliatory enough, the venue and manner of its delivery were not.

Fairfax's action made him conspicuous among the King's opponents. The petition, later published in London, told Charles to reject all other counsel but Parliament's, and drew on the politics of country tradition to complain of the King's malicious courtiers gathering at York: 'their Language and Behaviour speaking nothing but Division and Wars, and their Advantage consisting in that which is most destructive to others'. Some of these courtiers, including the earl of Lindsey and Lord Savile, had obstructed the circulation of Fairfax's petition on the moor, sending swordsmen to goad and provoke leading parliamentary sympathisers.[8]

Recent historiography has questioned polarised views of elite and popular politics in early modern England.[9] Elite and popular politics certainly collided in the fracas on Heworth moor. Here the elites of both emerging sides literally grappled with the people in their efforts to engage popular support. Rival petitions circulated. Pledges, handshakes, exhortations, pleadings, predictions, curses, warnings and threats were exchanged between men of varying status in negotiation of their allegiance. Lord Savile reflected that the leaders of the parliamentarian sympathisers that day were not county gentry, but two lesser gentlemen, John Reyner and John Farrer, along with Robert Todd, minister of St John's church, Leeds. These men were closer to the people, but they knew the Fairfaxes personally and soon became committed intermediaries in mobilising popular parliamentarianism.[10] The emerging popular press played a new and revolutionary role in attempting to shape this process, with print penetrating deep into popular culture. Within three weeks of Heworth, a newsbook claimed that Yorkshire's tenantry would refuse to pay rent to landlords who supported the King.[11] Although the royalist gentry would later successfully raise a large force in Yorkshire, the King's attempt at a popular strategy on Heworth moor backfired. Many thousands attended the royal summons, but nothing was propounded that sought an answer from them. Edward, Lord Howard contended it was impossible to judge the mood of the county from the meeting while Sir John Bourchier recalled 'they went away much unsatisfied and discontent, because they knew not wherefore they were summoned'.[12] Charles would soon appreciate that enlisting support and thereby shaping popular allegiance would be a more complex process than issuing proclamations demanding obedience.

The King's reaction to Heworth moor highlighted his difficulties in fashioning consistent responses to parliamentary propaganda. He announced that the petition Fairfax presented was supported by none but himself, and that the amount and quality of the signatories 'was not in truth so great as is pretended'. He dismissed Fairfax and his supporters as 'a few mean inconsiderable Persons, and disliked and visibly discountenanced by the great Body of the known Gentry, Clergy and inhabitants of this whole County'. Yet Charles's apparent conviction of his subjects' loyalty was soon shaken when Parliament condemned Savile and Lindsey as 'enemies of the State' for having been active in suppressing parliamentary sympathisers on the moor. He quickly admonished Parliament for having exposed these two peers 'to the Rage and Fury of the People'.[13]

Above all, the Heworth moor meeting reveals a mass engagement with national popular politics that had the potential to challenge localist or neutral sentiment. Charles rightly feared that opposition in Yorkshire was connected to his enemies at London and that those disaffected from his church would be foremost among the rebels. Among these, Sir Thomas Fairfax and his father would prove well-connected and tenacious opponents in heading the parliamentary cause in the north. Although their estates and family were largely restricted to Yorkshire, they were part of a national network of famous puritan families that included the Veres and Sheffields, while their own keen interest and involvement in the thirty years' war reflected a deep commitment to international Calvinism. They were quite capable of connecting local matters with national politics and even international affairs. Their contacts and correspondence with Westminster kept them well informed of developments and eventually integrated them into a national parliamentarian war effort.

II

If Fairfax's engagement with popular parliamentarianism is a recurring theme in this book, then so too is his relationship with his deputy, Oliver Cromwell. The latter has proved a difficult topic because the English people's search for heroes in the early modern period has idolised Elizabeth I and Oliver Cromwell, leaving little room for any who divert the limelight. Cromwell has become perhaps the most intensively studied Englishman in the early modern world. Despite dozens of biographies and scores of other studies examining aspects of Cromwell's life, Cromwell has remained the subject of many recent reinterpretations.[14] To this purpose, in both popular literature and Cromwell-centric studies of the civil war, Fairfax has been marginalised into a dull-witted, supporting role, if mentioned at all.

A timely reassessment of Fairfax is necessary, a revision that seeks to embrace a variety of historical approaches that will widen the confines of high politics and military narrative that have heretofore dominated considerations of Fairfax. For these reasons this work does not set out to provide a conventional, exhaustive, narrative biography. Three biographies have already been published, by Clements Markham in 1870, Mildred Ann Gibb in 1938 and John Wilson in 1985. Although Markham's account is tremendously detailed, all verge on hagiography, with Markham acclaiming: 'There are few names in history so spotless as that of the great Lord Fairfax.'[15] Incredibly for such a major figure in the civil wars, Fairfax has lacked an academic biographical monograph from a modern historian. Historians have tended to avoid Fairfax, partly because of the complications that taking him seriously generates for seventeenth-century historiography.

This study begins the work of filling that gap, confronting the problems and issues in interpreting his life. Chief among these is that Fairfax was often reticent about voicing his religious and political views during the civil wars and interregnum. His only reflections on his public career, the 'Short memorials', were never intended for publication and written in the transformed political atmosphere of the 1660s.[16] Written by a tired and troubled mind, he was unable or unwilling to recall his role in specific events and offered excuses for his conduct rather than explanations. Further glimpses of his religion, politics and temperament survive in his many letters held in the British and Bodleian Libraries, some of which were published in four volumes in 1848 and 1849.[17] Although much of the Fairfax family archive and library has been dispersed and sold,[18] many of his political declarations survive in printed tracts in York Minster Library and the Thomason collection at the British Library, especially for the years 1645–50. An important problem in interpreting these tracts is the question of how far these were Fairfax's own declarations, or whether they were penned for him by his council of officers or his secretary, John Rushworth. Indeed it has been suggested that by 1648 his army's council were 'in the habit of acting in his name without much regard to his feelings'.[19] The questions of Fairfax's involvement in army politics during 1647–9, his role in the promotion of radical officers and his part in bringing the King to trial all remain vexed questions largely due to the contradictions and tensions within his character. Fairfax remains something of an enigma: a committed parliamentarian, untroubled by championing popular support and willing for a time to accept the republic, yet racked with guilt over the King's execution and uncomfortable with all the non-traditional forms of government during the interregnum. He favoured greater religious toleration, disliking denominational conflict among godly protestants and yet his wife was devoutly Presbyterian. Furthermore, his reputation for moderation and lenience seems at odds with his severity at Colchester and the strict discipline he maintained over his own soldiers. This study hopes to tackle these paradoxes, and address Fairfax's wider political significance, thereby avoiding another rehash of the military history of the civil war.

Part I provides an analytical chronological account of Fairfax's life, taking care to employ new sources and minimise repetition of material found in the works of Markham, Gibb and Wilson. Chapters 1 and 2 will show how at the outbreak of war, Fairfax moved from heading his county's movement for neutrality, to championing the common people's right to defend themselves from their local gentry. His response to this fracturing of hierarchical authority in the West Riding was to join with what he called 'the readiness of the people' and to lead an army of ill-equipped, unpaid volunteers, with remarkable success against overwhelming odds. The national recognition he achieved for this dogged tenacity forged a reputation described by one royalist historian as 'the Roundhead answer to Rupert'.[20] This experience, combined with his religious conviction and faith in God's providence, enabled him to travel far further than other Englishmen of comparable status in a political alliance with revolutionary forces drawn from among his 'social inferiors'. Through the work of Ian Gentles and Austin Woolrych,[21] Fairfax's personal significance in the creation of the New Model Army and its first campaigns has become increasingly recognised, yet comparatively little is known about his experiences before 1645 and after 1650.

Chapter 3 will reveal Fairfax's importance in the formation of the New Model Army and his role in bringing the first civil war to a swift conclusion. It will challenge the view that Fairfax was chosen as general because he was a safe, apolitical choice. His father's extensive connections in the House of Commons and his family's known connections with the war party suggest otherwise as do the formidable political obstacles Fairfax was faced with in forging the New Model Army. Chapter 4 focuses upon the period between the end of the first civil war and the violent conclusion of the second, showing how Fairfax's political standpoint was transformed by Parliament's ill treatment of his army, and the growing assertiveness of his soldiers. His low profile in both the negotiations with the King and in the Putney debates with the agitators and Levellers, suggests that he allowed his ill health to respite him from tackling thorny political problems. The crucial importance of his strategic decision-making in the second civil war will be revealed, along with his frequently overlooked success in safeguarding London from the Kent and Essex rebels.

Chapter 5 will examine the trial and execution of Charles I from Fairfax's perspective, discussing how his repeated efforts to spare the King were derailed by an incorrigible monarch and a vengeful army. Despite his withdrawal from regicide being much reported, Fairfax was still depicted as the King's headsman in several prints and paintings. This chapter challenges depictions of the regicide that portray Fairfax as a halfwit tricked or coerced by an omnipotent Cromwell, establishing a more balanced perspective of Fairfax's complex dilemma. Chapter 6 provides a broad overview of Fairfax's life after the regicide until his death in 1671. His participation in the foundation of the English republic will be discussed, along with the background to his resignation as general. The period from Fairfax's return to prominence in 1659–60 up to his embarrassment at the 1661 Yorkshire county elections will receive close attention. The chapter will show how his hopes for the restored monarchy were swiftly dashed, widening into a discussion of how defeat and disillusion among former parliamentarians during the 1660s provide a dark contrast to the joviality traditionally held to characterise Restoration political culture.

The series of essays in Part II utilises Fairfax's experiences to explain the transformative impact of the English revolution from a new direction and illuminate topics of particular concern in current historiography: the social depth of politics, civil war allegiance, godly providentialism, honour, gender and authority, and the changing nature of the relationship between the gentry and the people. More might be learned by considering the English revolution from Fairfax's fresh perspective, than from further studies of Cromwell.

Chapter 7 will focus on the Fairfaxes and the causes of civil war, focusing attention upon the religious and political culture of Pennine parishes such as Bradford, Halifax and other centres of popular parliamentarianism in the north. An examination of the West Riding's cloth trade then illustrates how economic and agrarian crises influenced local allegiance. Suggesting that areas of popular parliamentarian politics did not always correlate with the estates of parliamentarian gentry, this study will explore ways in which a 'post-revisionist' approach to the civil war's causes might be extended and developed. Chapter 8 will examine why Fairfax's providential puritanism, temperament and notions of honour were so intertwined, revealing how religious and political differences were often articulated in changing conceptions of honour. Fairfax's broadly tolerant approach to religious practice and his family's concept of honour, rooted in godliness, service and humility, deepened conflict within parliamentarianism. His family clashed first with the Hothams and then with Parliament's Presbyterians, suggesting that Fairfax was more of a political figure than historians have hitherto realised.

Drawing upon material from plays, literature, propaganda and print, Chapter 9 discusses Fairfax's image and reputation in relation to the cult of personality among civil war generals. His elevation to the apocalyptic 'Rider of the White Horse' (Revelation 19:11) during January 1643 raised unrealistic expectations of his troops and enshrined him in the propaganda of those who viewed the conflict in religious terms. His cultivated modest image as the lowly, humble general was immensely attractive to the godly, and featured heavily in parliamentary propaganda. Chapter 10 examines the importance of Fairfax's strong-willed wife, Anne Vere, to make a fresh contribution to the debates on gender relations during the English revolution. Anne Fairfax's patronage of Presbyterian ministers who criticised her husband and his army flouted the gender hierarchy, while her defiant interruptions during the King's trial led to a propaganda portrayal of their marriage which inverted gender roles. Anne Fairfax provides an excellent case study from which to approach Sara Mendelson and Patricia Crawford's conclusions that women were actively engaged in politics despite their theoretical exclusion from such matters. This chapter then turns to Fairfax's scholarly and literary achievements, and his employment of Andrew Marvell as tutor to his daughter Mary. Marvell's poem 'Upon Appleton House' is analysed in the context of a political defence of the general's withdrawal into retirement in 1650. Marvell's praising of the honour of a quiet private life anticipated the 'country' identity that emerged in the 1690s, while his lauding of Fairfax's modesty and humility as 'the lowliest but the highest of all Christian qualifications' gave literary form to Fairfax's ideals of honour.[22] Here, a linguistic turn among historians has coincided with a growing acknowledgement among literary scholars of the necessity of interpreting seventeenth-century poetry within the context of a broader cultural analysis that takes closer account of contemporary historical events.

The focus of Chapter 11 is the relationship between Fairfax and Cromwell, examining why Fairfax advanced Cromwell's career, and why Cromwell became more forthright in dealing with Parliament and in articulating the soldiers' political concerns. The chapter also examines the emergence and longevity of claims that Fairfax was the unwitting tool of Cromwell's ambition, focusing on the changing power relationships between them and on the key occasions when they experienced serious disagreements.

Fairfax was a notable absentee from Blair Worden's recent book *Round-head Reputations*.[23] My conclusion adopts his techniques by beginning with a discussion of how and why Fairfax's post-Restoration memoirs, the 'Short memorials', despite being intended to remain private, were refashioned and published to appeal to a 1690s' audience. Excised of his providential puritanism and criticisms of kingship, Fairfax was reinvented as a 1690s' Whig patriot, an acceptable face of the Roundhead cause, concerned with the more secular issues of liberty, constitutionalism and parliamentary rule. His refashioning endeavoured to personify an earlier, more agreeable phase of the struggle before the purge and regicide. The conclusion then pursues the memory of Fairfax from his retirement to the present, revealing how opinions of him have been driven by rival memories of the civil wars and contrasting political and religious allegiances.

This book aims to restore Fairfax to his rightful place in civil war historiography and the ongoing debate on the English revolution. It will establish how northern England was not a secondary theatre in the civil wars but critical to Parliament's victory. The Fairfax family, politically as well as militarily, played an important role in Charles I's overthrow and the restoration of his son. Rather than retiring after the regicide as many accounts have maintained, Fairfax played a key part in establishing the republic, not resigning his command until 26 June 1650. His engagement with popular politics and his puritan religious zeal made a lasting impact, the memory of which was long cherished by protestant dissenters in his Yorkshire heartlands. The familiar assertions that he was a political failure and promoted beyond his abilities seem strange when directed at one of England's most successful generals. Such charges seem to reflect historians' frustrations at his inability to fulfil Parliament's role for them and his failure to save Charles I's life. He was not appointed as general to accomplish either of these tasks and this has been too readily forgotten. Transitions from soldier to statesman were rarely unblemished successes in the seventeenth century. Fairfax's mild temperament and his lack of ambition for personal political power have never been sufficient causes to undervalue his perspective on the English revolution.

NOTES

1 *The parliamentary or constitutional history of England, being a faithful account of all the most remarkable transactions in parliament from the earliest times to the Restoration of King Charles II, by several hands* (London, 1753), vol. 11, pp. 163–5.

2 D. Parsons (ed.), *The diary of Sir Henry Slingsby of Scriven, bart.* (London, 1836), p. 77; BL, E150(5), *A letter being sent by a Yorkshire gentleman to a friend in London, being a full and true relation of the proceedings between his Majesty and county of York, at Heworth Moor, upon Friday, June 3* (London, 1642), pp. 1–2; A. Woolrych, 'Yorkshire's treaty of neutrality', *History Today*, 6 (1956), 697.

3 *CSP dom. 1641–3*, p. 336.

4 J. R. Boyle (ed.), *Memoirs of master John Shawe, sometime vicar of Rotherham, minister of St Mary's, lecturer at Holy Trinity Church, and Master of the Charterhouse, at Kingston-upon-Hull. Written by himself in the year 1663–4* (Hull, 1882), p. 25; BL, E150(5), *A letter being sent by a Yorkshire gentleman*, p. 3.

5 J. Sprigge, *Anglia rediviva* (London, 1647), p. 8; *JHL*, vol. 5, p. 107.

6 A. Fletcher, *The Outbreak of the English Civil War* (London, 1981), p. 317.

7 Harvard University Library, Wing / C2411, Wing / 1546:24, *His majesties letter to the lords of his privy councell of Scotland. As also the humble petition of the gentry, ministers, freeholders and other inhabitants of the county of York, assembled by his majesties summons at Heworth moore, June 3 1642. 8 June* (London 1642).

8 *Ibid., The parliamentary or constitutional history of England*, vol. 11, pp. 169–75.

9 K. Sharpe, *Remapping Early Modern England: The Culture of Seventeenth-Century Politics* (Cambridge, 2000), pp. 458–9.

10 *CSP dom. 1641–3*, p. 413.

11 YML, CWT, 42–06–22, *An extract of several letters sent from Yorke, Hull, France and Holland* (1642).

12 *JHL*, vol. 5, p. 107; BL, E150(5), *A letter being sent by a Yorkshire gentleman*, p. 3.

13 *The parliamentary or constitutional history of England*, vol. 11, pp. 246–7.

14 P. Gaunt, *Oliver Cromwell* (Oxford, 1996), pp. 239–46; A. Marshall, *Oliver Cromwell, Soldier: The Military Life of a Revolutionary at War* (London, 2004); J. C. Davis, *Oliver Cromwell* (London, 2001); B. Coward, *Oliver Cromwell* (Harlow, 1991); J. Morrill (ed.), *Oliver Cromwell and the English Revolution* (London, 1990).

15 C. R. Markham, *A life of the great lord Fairfax* (London, 1870), p. 399; M. A. Gibb, *The Lord General: A Life of Thomas Fairfax* (London, 1938); J. Wilson, *Fairfax* (New York, 1985).

16 Bod., MS Fairfax 36; B. Fairfax (ed.), *Short memorials of Thomas, lord Fairfax* (London, 1699).

17 Bod., MS Fairfax 30–7; BL, Add. MS 18979, G. W. Johnson (ed.), *The Fairfax correspond-ence: memoirs of the reign of Charles I* (2 vols, London, 1848); R. Bell (ed.), *The Fairfax correspondence: memorials of the civil wars* (2 vols, London, 1849).

18 W. J. Connor, 'The Fairfax archives: a study in dispersal', *Archives*, 11 (1973–4); 76–85; *The Fairfax Library and Archive*, Sale Catalogue, Sotheby's, London, 14 December 1993.

19 D. Underdown, *Pride's Purge: Politics in the Puritan Revolution* (Oxford, 1971), p. 115.

20 G. Trease, *Portrait of a Cavalier: William Cavendish, First Duke of Newcastle* (London, 1979), p. 98.

21 I. Gentles, *The New Model Army in England, Ireland and Scotland, 1645–1653* (Oxford, 1992); A. Woolrych, *Britain in Revolution, 1625–1660* (Oxford, 2002).

22 C. Hill, *A Turbulent, Seditious, and Factious People: John Bunyan and his Church* (Oxford, 1988), p. 279.

23 B. Worden, *Roundhead Reputations: The English Civil Wars and the Passions of Posterity* (London, 2001).

Part I

A life of Fairfax

Chapter 1

The Yorkshire Fairfaxes
and the outbreak of war

Thomas Fairfax was born on 17 January 1612 at Denton, near Otley, in Wharfedale, the eldest son of Sir Ferdinando Fairfax and Mary Sheffield. The Fairfax family were among Yorkshire's oldest gentry families and closely connected to the highest level of the county's elite. They enjoyed aristocratic connections and were steeped in martial tradition. Thomas's grandfather, Sir Thomas Fairfax, purchased the Scottish barony of Cameron in 1627, while Sir Ferdinando's wife was the daughter of Edmund, third baron Sheffield, Lord Lieutenant of Yorkshire and President of the Council of the North from 1603 to 1619. An impressive mansion house had been built by Sir Thomas Fairfax at Denton from around 1600, and the family held extensive estates including the nearby manor of Menston and the manors of Nun Appleton and Bilbrough in the vale of York. Notes copied from the family's great Bible at Denton reveal that Henry Hastings, third earl of Huntingdon was the godfather of Sir Ferdinando's brother Henry. Lord Sheffield and the wife of Toby Matthew, Archbishop of York, were among the impressive array of godparents for Sir Ferdinando's eight children. Other godparents were drawn from the richest county gentry, including the Askes, Vavasours, Hawksworths and Belasyses.[1]

Much of Thomas Fairfax's upbringing was presided over by his grandfather, Sir Thomas, later first baron Fairfax. During the 1580s this Sir Thomas Fairfax was employed on several diplomatic missions to Scotland for Elizabeth I, during which he tactfully declined James I's offer of a Scottish peerage. Around 1589 he served under Sir Francis Vere in the Low Countries and was knighted by the earl of Essex at the siege of Rouen in 1591. Although he was knight of the shire for Yorkshire in 1601 and 1625, he preferred the military life and breeding horses. With Sir Ferdinando often away at Westminster during the 1620s, Sir Thomas brought up his grandson at Denton in a strict household, run with military efficiency. After having assisted in collecting the forced loan, in 1627 Sir Thomas Fairfax was permitted to purchase the Scottish barony of Cameron, for £1500, from Scottish heralds who came to wait upon him at Denton.[2]

The Fairfax family were proud of their martial traditions, serving the protestant cause on mainland Europe. The first baron's military service included 'various duties of war among the French, Germans and the Dutch', while his military virtues were commemorated in the Latin inscription at his tomb in Otley parish church.[3] His brother Sir Charles Fairfax had been killed fighting alongside Sir Francis Vere at the siege of Ostend in 1604. Three of the first baron's sons, John, William and Peregrine, were slain overseas, the former two fell defending the Palatinate in 1621. John Fairfax had been trapped with sixteen others in an outwork defending Frankenthal, and, refusing quarter, they had been 'cutt in pieces'. William Fairfax had been in the trenches there, where a 'Cannon shot took his legg & part of his thigh from him'. Sir Ferdinando consoled his brother Henry: 'Good brother lett nott this grieve you, butt rayse your spirits to prayse him who is so good unto us to inable his servants with good gifts & graces, & takes them in no evill courses, butt in their best endeavors of a just & honest profession.'[4] As we shall see, this stoic forbearance became a constant feature of the Fairfaxes' temperament, even it seems in their most private and personal spheres.

In 1622 Sir Thomas Fairfax channelled his grief at the loss of his sons into writing 'The highway to Heidelberg', a warning to protestant princes of the dangers of Spanish expansionism.[5] This work condemned the Pope for maintaining his power by force and behaving too much like a temporal prince, yet above all Fairfax blamed Philip IV, king of Spain, and his predecessors. As the king of Spain was 'reputed the greatest prince in the world', Fairfax maintained that Philip IV was 'puffed with pride', 'overwhelmed with crewelty' and the cause of Christendom's troubles. Fairfax argued that the European wars were 'not occasioned by the differences in religion but the swelling pride of this mighty monarch still thirsting after new conquests'. He called for a general alliance of protestant states with France against Spain, remarking that there was 'nothing that can quench the Jesuits fire but bloud'. Nostalgic for the supposed glory days of Elizabethan privateering, he fondly recalled when 'our court and camps did glitter in Spanish gould and silver cloaths soe as then it seemed that the mines of Peru were ours and the Spanyard did but dig them for our uses'. Therefore in addition to a continental land war, he advocated a naval blockade of Spain's coast and a plantation in the West Indies to disrupt New Spain's trade. Believing that Spain's enemies were strongest at sea, he recommended the Palatinate's recovery by utilising this naval strategy to compel Spain to negotiate.[6]

'The highway to Heidelberg' constituted fairly orthodox English Calvinist Hispanophobia, but in places it included criticisms of monarchy in general, albeit guarded ones. Fairfax condemned 'tyrannous kings, whose wills be ther

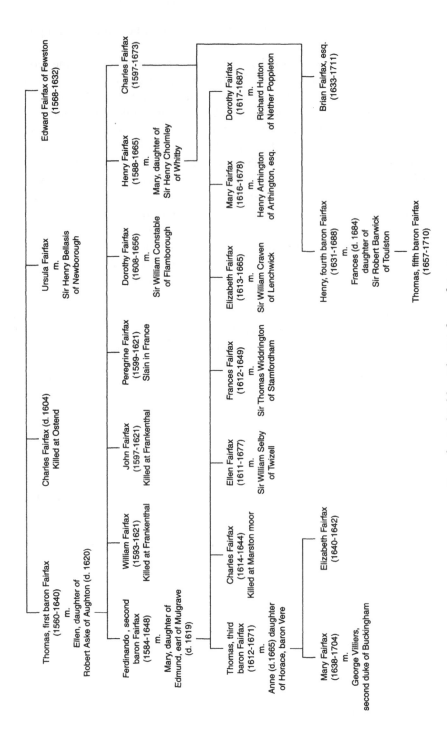

Genealogical Table: *The Fairfaxes of Denton*

Edward Fairfax of Fewston
(1568-1632)

Charles Fairfax
(1597-1673)

Ursula Fairfax
m.
Sir Henry Bellasis
of Newborough

Henry Fairfax
(1588-1665)
m.
Mary, daughter of
Sir Henry Cholmley
of Whitby

Dorothy Fairfax
(1617-1687)
m.
Richard Hutton
of Nether Poppleton

Charles Fairfax (d. 1604)
Killed at Ostend

Dorothy Fairfax
(1608-1656)
m.
Sir William Constable
of Flamborough

Mary Fairfax
(1616-1678)
m.
Henry Arthington
of Arthington, esq.

Brian Fairfax, esq.
(1633-1711)

Thomas, first baron Fairfax
(1560-1640)
m.
Ellen, daughter of
Robert Aske of Aughton (d. 1620)

Peregrine Fairfax
(1599-1621)
Slain in France

Elizabeth Fairfax
(1613-1665)
m.
Sir William Craven
of Lenchwick

John Fairfax
(1597-1621)
Killed at Frankenthal

Frances Fairfax
(1612-1649)
m.
Sir Thomas Widdrington
of Stamfordham

Henry, fourth baron Fairfax
(1631-1688)
m.
Frances (d. 1684)
daughter of
Sir Robert Barwick
of Toulston

William Fairfax
(1593-1621)
Killed at Frankenthal

Ellen Fairfax
(1611-1677)
m.
Sir William Selby
of Twizell

Thomas, fifth baron Fairfax
(1657-1710)

**Ferdinando, second
baron Fairfax**
(1584-1648)
m.
Mary, daughter of
Edmund, earl of Mulgrave
(d. 1619)

Charles Fairfax
(1614-1644)
Killed at Marston moor

Elizabeth Fairfax
(1640-1642)

**Thomas, third
baron Fairfax**
(1612-1671)
m.
Anne (d.1665) daughter
of Horace, baron Vere

Mary Fairfax
(1638-1704)
m.
George Villiers,
second duke of Buckingham

lawes and policies ther Religions'. Although he praised James I for having 'a goodly septer, and Solomons wisdome to wield it in peace', he wished 'he would let them see he has a sharp sword, and Davids valour to handle it in war'. He argued this would abate Spanish pride, relieve England's allies, promote the Gospel and please God 'which is the end for which he hath ordained and doth preserve Kings'.[7] The 'highway to Heidelberg' was intended to reflect the Fairfaxes' place among the foremost of England's godly military families, a family identity that proved an enduring one.

In 1633, the first baron Fairfax developed his political views further in his manuscript 'Discourse of court and courtiers' dedicated to James Stuart, duke of Lennox, and later duke of Richmond. Fairfax had not broken with his habit of offering advice to his social 'superiors', and although he humbly admitted he did 'offer theis like the pissinge of the wrenne, in the sea of your experience', this lengthy work instructed Lennox exactly how to behave as Charles I's foremost courtier. He recommended the rejection of flatterers, unbridled pleasures, self-love and vainglory, and rather 'an humble and Debonayre behaviour, and turning faces about from vice'.[8] This work ran to eighty-five folios. It included chapters advising courtiers on how to serve as ambassadors, how to become skilful at war and how to counsel kings. Fairfax exhorted them to 'augment the coffers of their Sovereigne with discretion and moderation'. He praised Charles I for his personal integrity, abstention from vice and preservation of Britain from the ravages of war, but he criticised courtiers for their supposed idleness, inconstancy, fraud, atheism and ambition, maintaining that a good courtier should 'build all of his Accons upon Religion'. Robert Cecil, earl of Salisbury and Sir Francis Walsingham were among Fairfax's model courtiers. He recommended the establishment of martial seminaries and noble academies in England to train the gentry and nobility and keep them from idleness and debauchery.[9] The 'Discourse of court and courtiers' sought to enhance the Fairfaxes' reputation for the 'country' interests of unblemished religion, honesty and plain-dealing, a self-fashioning as good commonwealth men distanced from the self-seeking sycophants and flattering courtiers.

The first baron had an uneasy relationship with his eldest son, Sir Ferdinando, especially during 1626 when the old patriarch, a widower for six years, was considering remarriage. He blamed his son for preventing this, which Sir Ferdinando indignantly denied, adding 'when I shall know my accuser, wch all just courts do allow, & fathers usually permit to their children, I think I shall not be found guilty of so foul a crime'.[10] Around this time the old lord reportedly told Archbishop Matthew that he sent Ferdinando 'into the Netherlands to train him up a soldier, and he makes a tolerable country justice, but is a mere coward at fighting'.[11] He would not live to see how mistaken he was in his eldest son, who became the finest of Parliament's noble generals from 1642 to 1644.[12] The old lord placed his hopes in his grandson, Thomas.

The antiquarian Ralph Thoresby recalled that his neighbour William Atkinson of Leeds, gunsmith to the Fairfaxes, once said he heard Fairfax calling to his grandson: 'Tom, Tom, mind thou the battle; thy father is a good man, but a mere coward at fighting. All the good I expect is from thee.'[13]

I

Evidently, Thomas grew up in a masculine environment in a family choked with martial traditions and expectations. In 1626 he matriculated at St John's College, Cambridge, and entered Gray's Inn in 1628.[14] A military education swiftly followed, with Sir Ferdinando deferring to his father in the arrangements. Having himself served with the late Sir Francis Vere, Fairfax agreed to his grandson serving under Vere's brother, Horace, baron Vere of Tilbury. Sir Ferdinando informed his father on 13 February 1629:

> My Lord of Clare adviseth to send my son to my Lord Vere's company, at Dort; he saith he may there practise arms, fencing, dancing, and study mathematics; and my Lord Houghton promiseth his best care over him whilst he is there. He goes over about six weeks hence, and all the companies have order to be ready the 1st of April. I could not resolve anything herein until I knew your lordship's pleasure, and therefore what you shall be pleased to command I shall carefully observe.[15]

Thomas joined Lord Vere in spring 1629. Vere's company was essentially England's foremost military academy, and Fairfax learnt alongside other future commanders such as John Hotham and Philip Skippon. Thomas was his family's third generation to enter Dutch service, and he wrote to his grandfather on 12 May that he had been fired upon by enemy artillery while besieging Busse (Bois-le-Duc). The tedium of protracted, indecisive warfare and long garrison duties followed.[16] He soon exceeded his allowance and became 'oppressed with melancholy'. Lord Fauconberg interceded with his grandfather on 3 April 1632, writing that 'it were great pity yt this condition should be altered with discontent or this spirit dejected with want'.[17] Thomas returned to England unexpectedly and pleaded in vain for his grandfather's permission to join the Swedish army, 'for whilst I lived in France I only learned the language, and knew ware only by an uncertaine relation'.[18] His military education was scarcely covered in martial glory, but it fulfilled most contemporary requirements including knowledge of arms, drill, fencing, fortifications and Europe's foremost military language – French. It remains doubtful if he saw action before 1640 but Austin Woolrych's judgement that he 'had no pre-war military experience' is true only in the narrowest sense.[19]

Thomas was denied martial endeavour for seven more years, but he was able to learn from his grandfather's expertise in horse breeding. Despite the seventy-six-year–old lord's pain from gout, the stone and purging, in 1636 he still made 'shift in his slippers to walk to ye stable'. Thomas inherited his grandfather's passion, and later wrote a treatise on horse breeding.[20] In June 1637, the first baron instructed Sir Ferdinando to have Thomas appointed a justice of the peace, and Thomas attended his first sessions at Knaresborough on 5 October 1637.[21]

Thomas met his bride, Anne Vere, while serving abroad under her father, Lord Vere. The families were already closely linked as Thomas's grandfather had served with Sir Francis Vere, and his uncles John and William Fairfax had died under Horace Vere's command. In addition to the Veres' martial virtues, the Fairfaxes also esteemed their puritan religion. Although the families were well acquainted, the negotiations for Thomas's arranged marriage to Anne were long and protracted. Horace Vere died in 1635, so the negotiations fell to his widow, Mary, and Sir William Constable, who had been authorised by Sir Ferdinando Fairfax to pursue the match.[22] When the couple finally wed on 20 June 1637 the Fairfaxes' links with England's premier military family were cemented. Sir Ferdinando wrote to his father from Hackney that 'I hope she will prove a good wife her affection to her husband & demeanour in these few hours promiseth well.'[23]

The couple were both struck with illness soon after their marriage and they did not enjoy peace together for long as Charles I's ill-fated attempt to impose the English prayer book on Scotland called the Fairfaxes to return to arms.[24] Little is known of their service in the royal army during the bishops' wars, but like the rest of the English forces, they can scarcely have emerged with much credit. On 10 March 1639, Sir Ferdinando Fairfax was commissioned colonel of a regiment of 1000 drawn from the West Riding trained bands in the wapentakes of Claro, Skiracke, Staincliff and Ewcross. He mustered his regiment by 24 May and marched to Richmond.[25] He wrote to his father on 18 June that he had received £500 to pay the troops in advance at Ripon, but nothing since:

> If supply come not before Saterday next we are in danger to disband. I must think this regiment the most miserable of all others & myself unhappy in itt to be removed so far from his Majesty & the other regiments of my country & to be the first putt upon such straites as must either undoe or dishonor ourselves ... I cannott keepe them together.[26]

Denied pay until they left Yorkshire, Ferdinando's regiment was ordered towards Carlisle, a secondary theatre away from the main army. Consequently they languished at the bottom of the administration's priorities for pay and supply, a foretaste of the Fairfaxes' experience in the first civil war. Thomas himself commanded a company of 160 Yorkshire dragoons that were probably part of the earl of Holland's unsuccessful forays across the Scots border. The first bishops' war ended without a major engagement and on 24 June the royal army was dismissed.[27] Thomas Fairfax was glad of the treaty negotiated at Berwick and looked forward to Parliament meeting.[28]

Sir Ferdinando Fairfax was returned as MP for Boroughbridge in the 'Short Parliament' of April 1640, defeating a candidate backed by the King's leading counsellor, the fellow Yorkshireman Thomas Wentworth, earl of Strafford.[29] Wentworth had been President of Charles I's Council of the North from 1628. The first baron Fairfax had partnered Wentworth as knight of the shire for Yorkshire in 1625, and Wentworth had previously been a critic of royal policy, championing the Petition of Right in the House of Commons in 1628. Yet by 1632 the Fairfaxes' relationship with Wentworth was deteriorating. Wentworth was involved in a property dispute with the first baron Fairfax, and he censured Sir Ferdinando for mishandling an investigation into the misuse of public funds by a local chief constable. Sir Ferdinando saw himself as defending the traditional government of the north and the office of justice of the peace against Wentworth's undue attempts to increase royal prerogative power. Although the Fairfaxes were probably not involved in the Belasyse family's intrigues against Wentworth, Sir Ferdinando sympathised with the grievances of his cousin Thomas Belasyse, Lord Fauconberg, who became a vocal critic of Wentworth's presidency. Fauconberg and his son Henry Belasyse were imprisoned for petitioning the King against Wentworth in 1630. An influential grouping of Yorkshire families linked by Fauconberg and distrustful of Wentworth emerged, which included the Listers, Slingsbys, Belasyses and Fairfaxes. Yet there were clearly limits to the Fairfaxes' disaffection as they contributed to the forced loan.[30] Unlike many future parliamentarians in 1639, the Fairfaxes had served the King loyally, suggesting that behaviour during the bishops' wars is not always an indicator of civil war allegiance. In doing so they were driven in part by their anti-Scottish prejudices, hints of which survive in their correspondence.[31]

Sir Ferdinando had only recently returned to Yorkshire when Charles I commenced the second bishops' war in June. Although Sir Ferdinando's loyalism had become questionable, Thomas was restored to command, this time of cavalry. He commanded 150 horse – two troops – under Edward, viscount Conway, general of the horse. He was probably part of Conway's force that failed to prevent the Scots crossing the Tyne at Newburn on 28 August 1640.[32] The English forces were outnumbered three to one and outgunned by the Scots artillery, but some English cavalry under Henry Wilmot fought bravely before being routed. Fairfax may have been part of Wilmot's force. According to Gilbert Burnet, after this defeat, 'the whole army did run with so great precipitation, that sir Thomas Fairfax, who had a command in it, did not stick to own, that till he passed the Tees his legs trembled under him'.[33] If this was true it is surprising that Charles knighted Fairfax at Whitehall for his military service on 28 January 1641.[34] Immediately after Newburn, the English evacuated Newcastle and the royal war effort collapsed. The Scots had been better organised, better led and better equipped than the English,

Figure 1 The father of 'Black Tom': Ferdinando, second baron Fairfax, by Edward Bower

but, according to Mark Charles Fissel, the English had lost primarily because Charles I had chosen to make war without the money to finance it.[35]

When the first baron Fairfax died on 1 May 1640, Sir Ferdinando succeeded him as second baron Fairfax (Figure 1). With his father gone, Ferdinando became less inhibited in his politics. David Scott has contended that during 1640 several leading Yorkshiremen frustrated the royal war effort from within, and that the new Lord Fairfax, but not Sir Thomas, were among them.[36] On 28

July 1640 Lord Fairfax was among the leaders of the fifty Yorkshire gentry who drafted a petition to the King complaining that the county had been ruined by the contributions, coat and conduct money, and forced billeting brought by the war. Charles regarded the petition with suspicion and was encouraged to do so by Strafford, who knew many of the petitioners personally. Strafford and Charles alleged that with the Scots about to invade, the petition smacked of mutiny. Sir Hugh Cholmley later reflected that this petition was of such critical importance that it encouraged the Scots to invade and prompted the twelve opposition peers to petition the King for a Parliament. As one of these peers was Lord Fairfax's father-in-law, Edmund Sheffield, earl of Mulgrave, it is possible that Fairfax acted as one of a number of conduits between the peers and the Yorkshire gentry to co-ordinate opposition.[37]

Only four days before the defeat at Newburn, on 24 August 1640, the Yorkshire gentry petitioned the King again, and Lord Fairfax was chosen to deliver it.[38] They stipulated that they would lead their trained bands no further than the river Tees, and that they would march only once the King had granted them a fortnight's pay, a demand which they knew was beyond his means. Lord Fairfax knew that the delay in mobilising the Yorkshire militia would isolate the English forces around Newcastle, which included his son. The King grew so doubtful of Lord Fairfax and the other Yorkshire trained-band colonels that he issued commissions of array on 28 August to raise men without them.[39]

The Scots victory at Newburn allowed the twelve peers to present their petition to the King at York on 2 September, requesting him to summon Parliament. On 12 September 1640, Lord Fairfax again helped to organise another petition of Yorkshire gentry in support of the peers and openly calling for a Parliament.[40] His Scottish peerage did not prevent his return to the House of Commons as knight of the shire for Yorkshire alongside his kinsman Henry Belasyse in October 1640. By now Lord Fairfax, although not his son, was thoroughly identified with opposition to royal policies. He was soon accompanied by his brother-in-law, Sir William Constable, who had been imprisoned as a loan refuser in 1627, and who had recently returned from three years of religious exile at Arnhem.[41]

II

The full extent of Lord Fairfax's activism at Westminster from 1641 to 1642 remains unknown, but it seems likely he was pushed in a parliamentarian direction by several initial factors: the earl of Newcastle's involvement in the first army plot against Parliament, Newcastle's proximity to the Queen, and the notion that evil counsel at court was preventing the relief of a Yorkshire population still suffering at the hands of an unruly soldiery yet to be disbanded after the second bishops' war.[42] A remarkable series of letters addressed to

Ferdinando survives, penned by his friend and neighbour Thomas Stockdale of Bilton Park, Knaresborough. These letters were initially concerned with communicating the county's grievances, but they soon became embroiled in commenting upon and shaping national events, providing a rich source for the political and religious attitudes of the kind of men the Fairfaxes relied upon at the outbreak of war. The measures that Stockdale urged Fairfax to advocate in the House of Commons courted popular support for the parliamentary opposition and became deeply provocative towards the King. Stockdale suggested Parliament publish a declaration against ship money '& all the like charges hereafter' to please the people. He suggested that the estates of the recently arrested earl of Strafford might be used to pay the Scots army and warned that if Strafford was reprieved of the charge of treason 'the people will be extreamly discontent & murmur against it'. He advocated to Lord Fairfax:

> It will be no small encouragement to the subject to see justice done upon that great Engine the Lo: Strafford, who hath in a manner battered downe their laws & liberties, & leveled them with the most servile Nations. His friends are all hopeful and almost confident of his deliverance; yet methinks it is impossible that good language & Elocution, can wipe off the gilt of his crymes; Rich apparel makes not beauty, it only dazells weak sights.[43]

Lord Fairfax was closely involved in the proceedings against Strafford, despite the earl's championing of Yorkshire's 'country' interests during the early 1620s and Strafford's friendship with his late father. On 5 March 1641 Lord Fairfax was named alongside Pym and Hampden on the Commons' committee liaising with the House of Lords over Strafford's trial. He was also on the committee that framed Strafford's indictment. On 20 April, he informed his brother Henry Fairfax that 'we have framed a short Bill to convict him of treason'. Lord Fairfax voted for this attainder and Strafford was beheaded at Tower Hill on 12 May.[44]

On 3 May 1641 Parliament passed the Protestation oath, and Lord Fairfax took it immediately.[45] Stockdale responded with joy, informing Fairfax on 27 May 1641 that he 'was allwaies of opinion that such an Association must be made ... both to preserve the breach of the Parliament; and also to distinguish the subjects affections'. Stockdale added that it should be 'publiquely tendered to all manner of people in Churches or some other such assemblyes', certain that 'it would be generally embraced'. Perhaps drawing inspiration from the list of MPs voting against Strafford's attainder, headed 'Enemies of Justice and Straffordians' that had been posted up at the Exchange, Stockdale suggested that the names of Protestation refusers should be similarly exhibited, so the people might know their enemies.[46] Many of those MPs who had voted against Strafford's execution were dubbed 'Straffordians' and as such derided as supporters of arbitrary government. Many later became committed royalists.

Later that year, news of the outbreak of rebellion among the native catholic Irish against the protestant settlers in November 1641 hardened Stockdale's views and extended his engagement with popular politics. He suggested to Lord Fairfax ways of fusing popular anti-catholicism with an emerging politics of popular parliamentarianism. On 3 December 1641 he stirred Fairfax's fears: 'I perceive there is some expectation that the King will pardon the Recusant Rebells of Ireland.' Perhaps knowing that Fairfax had been on the committee that presented the Grand Remonstrance to the King, Stockdale suggested publishing all the names that voted for and against its printing, so that 'the contry may take notice of their friends & know to elect better Patriots there-after'.[47] Soon after the King's failure to arrest the five members, on 7 January 1642 Stockdale commented upon the rioting in London; although he admitted that the 'insurrections of the prentices (as all other ungoverned multitudes) are of very dangerous consequence', he remarked:

> But God that workes myracles can out of such violent actions, bring comfortable effects, which I besich him grant to this much distracted Empyre; and truly the like and much more violent tumults in Ireland for unjust & irreligious pretences; seeme to give warrant & president to an opposite irregularity of the same nature, which is for just and Religious endes in this kingdom.[48]

This allowance of disorder would have confirmed Charles I's suspicions of a popular puritan conspiracy against him, while Stockdale's conviction that a Jesuit plot was hindering the relief of Ireland's protestants diminished the King's majesty. Perhaps with an emulation of John Foxe's *Acts and Monuments* in mind, Stockdale suggested to Lord Fairfax that a book be published for the people containing all the reports brought to Parliament concerning the murders of protestants in Ireland: 'for I find that the dayly resort of the distressed Protestants of Ireland that come hither driven from their habitations by the Papists; do animate the People here against the Popish partie, and make them distaste them exceedingly; which is one good effect of many evils'.[49] Evidently Stockdale's anti-catholicism and puritan providentialism had overtaken his fear for the social order.

Stockdale proved himself a man of action. In Lord Fairfax's continued absence from Yorkshire during February 1642 he secured the high sheriff's agreement to summon the Claro trained bands 'to suppress unlawful assemblies', and ordered searches for priests and recusants' arms. Reflecting the power of parliamentary propaganda, he told Lord Fairfax that he had recently heard from Chester 'the papists have murthered and destroyed in Ulster 50 thousand protestants, men, women and children, which is a most horrid cruelty, hardly to be paralleled and it concernes all to endeavour the prevention of the like in this kingdom'.[50] On 25 March 1642 he implicated English catholics in the Irish rebellion by reporting to Lord Fairfax that he had been informed that 300 priests and Jesuits had arrived in Ireland from England the previous year, specifically to prepare the rebellion.[51]

Sir Thomas Fairfax was more cautious than Stockdale about expressing opposition to royal policies in letters to his father, and may have harboured misgivings over Stockdale's populist opportunism. Sir Thomas had another audience with Charles I in York in November 1641 upon the King's return from Scotland, and he reported to his father at Westminster that he had represented the county gentry's request for a new council of the north at York, 'but qualified & not of so large a power'. The King had answered him 'we had better have that then none', and seeking to highlight royal grievances said to Sir Thomas that Parliament 'did think it too great a Prerogative for him to place a President there'.[52]

By this time the shocking news of the Irish rebellion had affected Sir Thomas deeply. Despite recurring illness, he restlessly sought an opportunity of 'serving the commonwealth', writing to his father that he would do so, 'even to the hazard of my life'. He requested his father's permission to fight the rebels in Ireland, but Lord Fairfax's subsequent refusal was also supported by Lady Vere who realised Thomas's health was too fragile.[53] Instead, Sir Thomas wintered in York, while Lord Fairfax became embroiled in the political crisis at Westminster. Sir Thomas kept his father informed of northern affairs in a series of letters that were dominated by the perceived catholic threat. He demonstrated restraint and scepticism in his reports; on 10 December 1641 he wrote that although it was commonly held that catholics were preparing an uprising, he believed they were too few and such suspicions were ungrounded. Nevertheless he added that 'a seacret enimy is more dangerous then a discovered one & seing occations sutes so wel with their discontents I believe they break their sleepe for something'. He also believed that there were so many catholics in York that the Ainsty's trained bands should be quartered in the city.[54] By 7 January he believed there were so many swordsmen walking York's streets, that there was 'cause enough to suspect secreate practices' in the city, although he believed the countryside was safer 'as not being so subject to a sudden surprise'.[55] With news of the King's attempt to arrest the five members, his fears of a popish plot became more developed. On 14 January he remarked: 'Though noe strength of papist apeare in this Contry yitt ther is such an activeness observed amongst them as is noe doubt but they al joyne in one centre the wch once moved give motion to the rest.' This supposed catholic activity included three families of Howards who had joined Lord Evers at Malton. York's mayor ordered that catholics and strangers in every constablery should be listed and their removal from the city considered. Even then, Sir Thomas was not overly fearful, determining that Yorkshire's trained bands would be too strong for any local catholic rising.[56] At York on 18 February he informed his father that local catholics had been 'very insolent in their behaviour', and that there had been a general search for catholic arms throughout the county. He added that although the people were heavily charged in maintaining the trained bands, so great were their fears, that they were 'glad to take upon them that burden'.[57]

III

Having failed to arrest 'the Five Members' at the heart of Parliament's opposition, and menaced by tumultuous crowds, Charles I, fearing for his person and family, fled from London on 10 January 1642. He chose to travel northwards, intending to build his own party of armed supporters among the northern gentry. His arrival in York on 17 March 1642 dramatically altered Sir Thomas Fairfax's position from a correspondent of local affairs to a man well placed to observe Charles I with his embryonic new court attending him. The King was considering seizing the arms magazine at Hull to equip a northern army with which to quell the Irish rebellion. However, he did not receive an auspicious welcome in York. Edmund Cowper, the mayor, made a speech urging Charles to concur with Parliament, and several city preachers, including Samuel Wintour, preached defiant sermons. On 18 March, Sir Thomas Widdrington, Sir Thomas Fairfax's brother-in-law and Recorder of York, urged the King once more to 'hearken unto and condescend unto Parliament'.[58] In the meantime, Sir Thomas Fairfax's brother-in-law, Henry Arthington, and his uncle, Charles Fairfax, prepared the populace to stand by Parliament by tendering the Protestation to the people at Leeds.[59]

On 23 April the King appeared before Hull's Beverley gate and requested admission, which the parliamentary governor, Sir John Hotham, refused. Warned of his approach, Hotham had made extensive preparations, drawing up the bridges, shutting the gates, confining the inhabitants to their houses and manning the walls with his recently paid soldiery.[60] The King had Hotham declared a traitor and rode off enraged at the affront to his dignity. The lengthy paper war that was sparked by this remarkable confrontation made a deep impression in Yorkshire, with anti-Hotham feeling playing a large part in the emergence of a royalist party. Hotham later reflected, with characteristic self-regard, that although he did not seek to have 'a part to play unpresidented by any', he nevertheless 'satt down with joy under the name and hazard of a Traytor'.[61]

The House of Commons sent four Yorkshire MPs as commissioners to relieve the pressure upon Hotham and negotiate with Charles at York. As knight of the shire, Lord Fairfax headed this delegation, arriving in the northern capital on 8 May 1642 with Sir Hugh Cholmley, Sir Henry Cholmley and Sir Philip Stapleton. When the King ordered them to leave the county they disobeyed, declaring they were a committee ordered by Parliament.[62]

The risks of such disobedience were tempered by the King's need to act with restraint; with such a small following at York, Charles could ill afford to antagonise the Yorkshire gentry by maltreating them. At this point it was still doubted whether the King could raise any Yorkshire forces at all.[63] Lord Fairfax and his colleagues reported how Charles claimed they preached a 'doctrine of disobedience to the people', necessitating the raising of a royal guard. When they advised Charles that it would be dangerous to summon in the county's trained-band cavalry he threatened to 'clap them up' if they tried to raise a party against him.[64]

Charles summoned the Yorkshire nobility and gentry to him at York, delivering a speech to them on 12 May. Thousands of freeholders attended to press their grievance at being excluded. The embattled high sheriff, Sir Thomas Gower, observed that: 'The freeholders not being called with the gentry, have delivered a protestation that nothing done without their consents shall bind them.' He added that the King's neglect to summon them had caused over a thousand gentry and freeholders to petition against forming a royal guard.[65] Ainsty freeholders had petitioned for a voice in elections at York in 1641, and royalist attempts to exclude yeomen from grand juries was unlikely to win over trust or deference from such groups.[66] These groups might even have empathised when by 1 July 1642, Lord Fairfax and nineteen more of the 'well affected' had been ejected from Yorkshire's commission of the peace.[67] The King's realisation of his mistake in not summoning the freeholders to York prompted his uncharacteristic calling of the county meeting at Heworth moor.

Soon after Heworth, Lord Fairfax fell from his horse in York, and, breaking two ribs, he retired to Denton to recover, declining his fellow commissioners' invitation to return with them to London.[68] Leaving Sir Thomas to gauge events at York, Ferdinando sponsored anti-royalist sermons in his West Riding heartlands and conferred with his gentry and clergy neighbours over the advisability of armed rebellion.[69] In retrospect the King's decision to leave the Fairfaxes unmolested during his failed siege of Hull in July and when he marched south to Nottingham in August proved a costly blunder. Although Ferdinando had headed Parliament's delegation at York, and Sir Thomas had presented the petition on Heworth moor, Charles still believed that they would not appear in arms. Unlike Sir John Hotham, they had no fortress to protect them and no means of escape by sea to London. Clarendon recalled that Charles was 'so far from expecting any notable mischief' from the Fairfaxes, that 'he left them at their own Houses'. He overruled those who urged their arrest, thinking they 'were rather desirous to look on than engage themselves in the War'. Sir Thomas Fairfax later recalled that despite rumours of royalist intentions to arrest his father, Ferdinando 'Resolved not to stir from his own House'. Sir Thomas then remembered how his father was importuned by the local people 'to joyne with them in defence of themselves & Country' which were 'sadly oppressed by those of ye Array'.[70]

After the houses of George Marwood and Sir Henry Cholmley were plundered by cavalier horsemen, the West Riding's parliamentary sympathisers organised for action, listing nominees to raise and command men in Yorkshire for parliamentary approval.[71] They met at Otley, the Fairfaxes' home parish. Their declaration on 29 August 1642 was signed by many of the Fairfaxes' future officers including Sir Thomas Mauleverer, Sir John Savile, John Bright, John Farrer, William Lister, John Mauleverer, Thomas Stockdale and William White. Although printed in London, it was intended for circulation in all Yorkshire's churches and markets. It protested strongly against the disarming of the trained bands and the formation of an armed royalist party at York, but pledged to 'keep the Peace of the county entire'. Although it approved of Hotham's garrison in Hull it would not abandon the language of peace, reconciliation and unity.[72] This was probably the petition that Sir Henry Slingsby recalled Sir Thomas Fairfax carrying when he followed the King south with a petition 'about ye latter end of August 1642', suggesting that Fairfax remained bold enough to continue presenting petitions after the King had raised his standard. Subsequently, Sir Thomas Fairfax remained at his house in York, even after commissions of array had been issued. When he remonstrated with Slingsby against the King's raising of forces, Slingsby replied 'that neither himself nor any of his had any cause of fear, seeing as then he had [not] appear'd in Armes, & what was intend'd was against Hotham, who rang'd ye Country & would not keep in Hull'.[73] Overlooking the Otley declaration's commitment to peace, Parliament thanked Lord Fairfax and discussed sending him troops.[74] Yet Lord Fairfax and Sir Thomas still refrained from taking up arms, even when Ferdinando's brother-in-law, Sir William Constable, and his nephew, Sir William Fairfax, were raising their regiments around London. When these forces were ready to leave for Yorkshire the earl of Essex demanded they reinforce his field army and both regiments subsequently fought in Sir John Meldrum's brigade at Edgehill.[75]

In early September it was reported that Lord Fairfax had garrisoned Denton in response to royalist threats to pillage the place. The same newsbook declared that 'all the Country about him, for 15 or 16 miles stands for him, and will protect him against any violence, they are wel-affected to the King and Parliament, and especially the great Townes thereabouts, as Wakefield, Leedes, Hallifax, Bradford and Otley'.[76] On 7 September Ferdinando and Sir Thomas Fairfax wrote to Sir John Hotham from Denton complaining of a 'desert of Armes', requesting arms for 500 foot, thirty barrels of powder, match and arms for 100 cavalry.[77] On 19 September a general meeting of parliamentary sympathisers was held at Leeds. They ruled that they would stand with Lord Fairfax as their knight of the shire, proclaiming him their leader.[78] It was probably around then, soon after Sir Thomas Fairfax's withdrawal from York, that the Fairfaxes' house in Bishophill was plundered by royalists.[79]

The West Riding parliamentarians now had a wealthy, respected leader, with trained bands and volunteers arriving in Leeds daily. Orders were sent to West Riding parishes commanding their trained bands to appear at Leeds before Lord Fairfax and Sir John Savile. One such order came to Emley on Sunday 25 September 1642, and Ralph Assheton noted in his commonplace book that 'manie about Bradford went thither'.[80] Yet Lord Fairfax himself had still not appeared in arms. Within ten days, backed by many of his gentry supporters, he signed a peace treaty with the earl of Cumberland's royalists at Rothwell. The treaty suspended the commissions of array and militia ordinance in the county, by which King and Parliament had been raising forces. It stipulated that if any troops invaded Yorkshire, they would face a rising of the whole county, and that all arms confiscated from the county trained bands since 21 September should be returned. With Sir Thomas Fairfax's cousin Henry Belasyse leading the royalist delegation, the treaty may have represented an attempt to resurrect the consensus among Lord Fauconberg's grouping of the 1630s. It certainly demonstrated the Fairfaxes' reluctance to fight their kinfolk, friends and neighbours such as the Belasyses, Gowers and Slingsbys, who despite having shared in the Fairfaxes' opposition to royal policies from 1640 to 1642 were now lining up on the royalist side.[81]

Thus far, the Hothams had clearly served Parliament's war effort far more effectively than the Fairfaxes. Denying the King entry to Hull on 23 April, they had held out during the siege in July. Since the King's departure southward, the governor's son, John Hotham, led two troops of horse and 500 foot out of Hull, capturing Howden and Doncaster without a fight and raising money by fining royalist gentry. Leaving Doncaster on 29 September, John Hotham rode through Hatfield for a rendezvous with more Hull forces under Sergeant-Major John Gifford, when he heard that the Fairfaxes had abandoned him by their treaty of neutrality.[82]

The treaty left the Hothams and their supporters isolated. Any prospect of early peace negotiations placed Sir John Hotham in a precarious position for his refusal of the King's person at Hull. The treaty had been negotiated without the Hothams' knowledge and dictated terms to them, ordering the withdrawal of John Hotham's troops into Hull. Furthermore, the leading parliamentary gentry in the North Riding were seeking Lord Fairfax's advice about how to negotiate a similar 'preservation of peace' in their part of the county.[83] The Hothams responded by launching a combined political and military campaign to destroy the treaty. Both Hothams published declarations against the treaty, accusing Fairfax of dictating terms to Parliament and leaving the county naked of defence. In support of his declaration John Hotham procured the signatures of Sir John Bourchier, Sir Matthew Boynton, Sir Henry Foulis, Sir Thomas

Remington, Sir Thomas Norcliffe, Francis Boynton and Francis Lascelles.[84] On 1 October John Hotham captured Selby and on 4 October his forces took Cawood castle. This completed his stranglehold on the river network upon which York depended for its trade. From these riverside bases, his troops struck out at royalist estates and convoys, provoking them into breaking the treaty.[85] The royalist high sheriff, Sir Thomas Gower, remarked that Hotham 'will much trouble us by being master of the water, whereby he can take and leave when he pleaseth'.[86] With the treaty condemned in London and rendered unworkable locally, the Fairfaxes returned to raising forces. They had left recruitment very late and antagonised their allies in the East Riding with a failed treaty.

With Charles I resident in York from March to August 1642, Yorkshire had been a crucial county in the outbreak of war. The King's failure to raise an army there led him south to seek better fortune in the north Midlands and the Welsh marches. His departure gave the county's parliamentarians a brief opportunity of domination which they failed to take. In October 1642 the Fairfaxes were a long way from proving themselves as popular war leaders. Yet Lord Fairfax's abandonment of the treaty set his family on a path of championing the West Riding godly. Standing for the interests of their home region and neighbours, against the perceived interests of their fellow nobility, the Fairfaxes embarked on a collision course with the traditional ruling order and social hierarchy.

NOTES

1   Bod., MS Fairfax 30, fos. 25–6.

2   L. Stone, *The Crisis of the Aristocracy, 1558–1641* (Oxford, 1965), p. 117; Markham, p. 14; J. Binns, 'Thomas Fairfax, first lord Fairfax of Cameron', *Oxford DNB*.

3   H. Speight, *Upper Wharfedale* (London, 1900), p. 65.

4   Bod., MS Fairfax 30, fo. 152.

5   BL, Add. MS 28326, fos. 3v–5r; Simon Adams incorrectly identified Ferdinando, second baron Fairfax as the author: S. Adams, 'Foreign policy and the parliaments of 1621 and 1624', in K. Sharpe (ed.), *Faction and Parliament: Essays on Early Stuart History* (Oxford, 1978), p. 151.

6   BL, Add. MS 28326, fos. 10v, 21r–23r.

7   *Ibid.*, fos. 2r, 25v.

8   Beinecke Rare Book and Manuscript Library, Yale University, Osborn shelves b165, Thomas, 1st baron Fairfax, 'A discourse of court and courtiers digested into sundrie heads and chapters written in the year of our Lord 1633', fos. 1r–3v.

9   *Ibid.*, fos. 4r–v, 31v–33v, 39v–41v, 44r, 55r–v, 69v–70r.

10 Bod., MS Fairfax 30, fo. 175.

11 Markham, p. 12.

12 I. Gentles, 'The civil wars in England', in J. Kenyon and J. Ohlmeyer (eds), *The Civil Wars: A Military History of England, Scotland and Ireland, 1638–1660* (Oxford, 2002), p. 124.

13 D. H. Atkinson, *Ralph Thoresby, the topographer; his town and times* (Leeds, 1885), vol. 1, p. 165; R. Thoresby, *Ducatus Leodiensis*, ed. T. Dunham Whitaker (Leeds, 2nd edn, 1816), appendix, pp. 147–8.

14 J. Venn (ed.), *Alumni Cantabrigienses, Part 1, From the Earliest Times to 1751* (Cambridge, 1922), vol. 2, p. 118; J. Foster (ed.), *The register of admissions to Gray's Inn, 1521–1889* (London, 1889), p. 185.

15 G. W. Johnson (ed.), *The Fairfax correspondence: memoirs of the reign of Charles I* (London, 1848), vol. 1, p. 160.

16 *Ibid.*, vol. 1, pp. 160–2.

17 Bod., MS Fairfax 31, fo. 15.

18 *Ibid.*, fo. 40; R. B. Manning, *Swordsmen: The Martial Ethos in the Three Kingdoms* (Oxford, 2003), pp. 8, 33.

19 A. Woolrych, *Britain in Revolution, 1625–1660* (Oxford, 2002), p. 304.

20 Bod., MS Fairfax 31, fo. 74; YML, modern typescript of Thomas Fairfax's 'A treatise touching the breeding of horses' (c.1660).

21 Thomas's service as a justice was interrupted from 1639 to 1640 by his engagement in the bishops' wars: Bod., MS Fairfax 31, fo. 106; J. Lister (ed.), *West Riding Sessions Records: Orders 1611–1642, Indictments, 1637–1642* (YASRS, 53, 1915), pp. 32, 42, 57, 313, 363.

22 Bod., MS Fairfax 31, fos. 78, 96–104.

23 *Ibid.*, fo. 108.

24 *Ibid.*, fos. 112, 114, 118, 126.

25 *Ibid.*, fo. 134; *Cowper MS*, HMC, 12th report, appendix, part II (London, 1888), vol. 2, pp. 228–9.

26 BL, Add. MS 18979, fo. 58.

27 Markham, pp. 29–31.

28 Johnson (ed.), *The Fairfax correspondence*, vol. 1, p. 386.

29 J. K. Gruenfelder, 'Yorkshire borough elections, 1603–1640', *YAJ*, 49 (1977), 113.

30 J. T. Cliffe, *The Yorkshire Gentry from the Reformation to the Civil War* (London, 1969), pp. 299, 314; D. Farr, *John Lambert, Parliamentary Soldier and Cromwellian Major-General, 1619–1684* (Woodbridge, 2003), pp. 18–22.

31 The first baron refered to the Scots as 'the common enemy', while Sir Ferdinando Fairfax wrote that the 'impure hands' of the Scots had 'carried away the crown, scepter and other regal ensigns, to places of their own': D. Scott, ' "Hannibal at our gates": loyalists and fifth-columnists during the Bishops' Wars – the case of Yorkshire', *Historical Research*, 70:173 (1997), 289–90; Johnson (ed.), *The Fairfax correspondence*, vol. 1, pp. 352, 357.

32 Markham, p. 37.

33 G. Burnet, *History of his own time*, 6 vols (Oxford, 2nd edn, 1833), vol. 1, p. 51.

34 BL, Harleian MS 6832, fo. 75v.

35 M. C. Fissel, *The Bishops' Wars: Charles I's Campaigns against Scotland* (Cambridge, 1994), pp. 53–60.

36 Scott, 'Hannibal at our gates', 277–80, 290–1.

37 *Ibid.*, 271, 274–7, 280; C. H. Firth (ed.), 'Papers relating to Thomas Wentworth, first earl of Strafford', in *Camden miscellany*, vol. 9 (Camden Society, 3rd series, 53, 1895), p. 29; J. Rushworth, *The trial of Thomas, earl of Strafford* (London, 1721), vol. 8, pp. 602–5; J. Binns (ed.), *The Memoirs and Memorials of Sir Hugh Chomley of Whitby, 1600–1657* (YASRS, 153, 2000), p. 101.

38 Binns (ed.), *The Memoirs and Memorials of Sir Hugh Chomley*, p. 102.

39 Scott, 'Hannibal at our gates', 283–4.

40 *Ibid.*, 287.

41 D. Scott, 'Sir William Constable', *Oxford DNB*.

42 Farr, *John Lambert*, p. 23.

43 BL, Add. MS 18979, fos. 73r–75r.

44 Cliffe, *The Yorkshire Gentry*, pp. 327–8; Rushworth, *The trial of Strafford*, vol. 8, p. 33; Bod., MS Fairfax 32, fo. 5.

45 Rushworth, *The trial of Strafford*, vol. 8, pp. 736–40.

46 BL, Add. MS 18979, fos. 78r–79v; T. Kilburn and A. Milton, 'The public context of the trial and execution of Strafford', in J. F. Merritt (ed.), *The Political World of Thomas Wentworth, Earl of Strafford, 1621–1641* (Cambridge, 1996), p. 241.

47 BL, Add. MS 18979, fos. 99r–100v.

48 *Ibid.*, fo. 108v.

49 *Ibid.*, fo. 109r–v.

50 *Ibid.*, fos. 120r–121v.

51 *Ibid.*, fo. 135r–v.

52 Bod., MS Fairfax 32, fo. 41.

53 *Ibid.*, fos. 19, 43.

54 *Ibid.*, fo. 49.

55 *Ibid.*, fo. 21.

56 *Ibid.*, fo. 23.

57 *Ibid.*, fo. 24.

58 W. Sheils, 'Provincial preaching on the eve of the civil war: some West Riding fast sermons', in A. Fletcher and P. Roberts (eds), *Religion, Culture and Society in Early Modern Britain: Essays in Honour of Patrick Collinson* (Cambridge, 1994), pp. 290–2.

59 Bod., MS Fairfax 32, fo. 77.

60 TNA, SP 28/138/4; T. Gent, *Gent's history of Hull, reprinted in fac-simile of the original of 1735* (Hull, 1869), p. 145.

61 HULA, Hotham MS, DDHO/1/34.

62 Cliffe, *The Yorkshire Gentry*, p. 332.

63 C. Russell, *The Fall of the British Monarchies, 1637–1642* (Oxford, 1991), p. 497.

64 YML, CWT, 42–05–13, *A letter from the right honourable Ferdinando Lord Fairfax, Sir Hugh Cholmley, Sir Philip Stapleton, Sir Henry Cholmley, committee of the commons house of Parliament, residing at Yorke* (London, 1642), p. 4; YML, CWT, 42–05–17, *Some special passages from London, Westminster, Yorke. Hull, Ireland, Scotland, France, Holland and other parts* (London, 1642); *CSP dom. 1641–3*, p. 322.

65 *House of Lords MS*, HMC, 5th report, appendix (London, 1876), p. 197.

66 R. Carroll, 'Yorkshire parliamentary boroughs in the seventeenth century', *Northern History*, 3 (1968), 89; B. Manning, 'Religion and politics: the godly people', in B. Manning (ed.), *Politics, Religion and the English Civil War* (London, 1973), p. 115.

67 YML, CWT, 42–07–05, *Some speciall passages from Westminster, London, Yorke and other parts*, no. 6 (London, 1642).

68 *Sutherland MS*, HMC, 5th report, appendix, p. 141; BL, Harleian MS 7001, fo. 155.

69 G. Duckett, 'Civil war proceedings in Yorkshire', *YAJ*, 7 (1882), 75.

70 Clarendon, *The history of the rebellion and civil wars in England* (Oxford, 1717), vol. 2, part 1, p. 138; Bod., MS Fairfax 36, fo. 1r.

71 YML, CWT, 42–08–19, *A full relation of all the late proceedings of his majesties army in the county of Yorke* (London, 1642).

72 YML, CWT, 42–09–08, *The reall protestation of manie and very eminent persons in the county of Yorke declaring their resolution concerning the present distractions; some of whose names are subscribed* (London, 1642).

73 D. Parsons (ed.), *The diary of Sir Henry Slingsby of Scriven, bart* (London, 1836), pp. 77, 80–1.

74 BL, E239(16), *A perfect diurnall*, 5–12 September (London, 1642).

75 BL, E240(12), *England's memorable accidents*, 19–26 September (London, 1642), p. 15; P. Young, *Edgehill, 1642: The Campaign and the Battle* (Moreton-in-Marsh, 1998), p. 99.

76 BL, E116(9), *The last true newes from Yorke, Nottingham, Coventry and Warwicke*, 24 August–4 September (London, 1642).

77 HULA, Hotham MS, DDHO/1/9.

78 A. Woolrych, 'Yorkshire's treaty of neutrality', *History Today*, 6 (1956), 700; BL, E240(20), *A perfect diurnall of the passages in parliament*, 26 September–3 October (London, 1642).

79 BL, Egerton MS 2146, fo. 24r.

80 Beinecke Rare Book and Manuscript Library, Yale University, Osborn shelves b101, fo. 130.

81 Farr, *John Lambert*, p. 28; Woolrych, 'Yorkshire's treaty of neutrality', 696–704; BL, E119(29), *Fourteen articles of peace propounded to the King and Parliament by the gentry and commonalty of the county of York*, 4 October (London, 1642).

82 BL, E119(24), *Speciall passages*, 27 September–4 October (London, 1642).

83 BL, Add. MS 15858, fo. 215.

84 YML, CWT, 1642–3(2), *Reasons why Sir John Hotham, trusted by the Parliament, cannot in honour agree to the treaty of pacification made by some gentlemen of York-shire at Rothwell, Sept. 29. 1642* (London, 1642); BL, E121(32), *The declaration of Captaine Hotham sent to*

the Parliament, wherein he sheweth the reasons of his marching into the county of York, 6–11 October (London, 1642).

85 Parsons (ed.), *The diary of Sir Henry Slingsby*, pp. 78–9; BL, E123(5), *Speciall passages*, 11–18 October (London, 1642), p. 88; BL, E124(14), *Speciall passages*, 18–25 October (London, 1642), p. 96.

86 *Sutherland MS*, HMC, 5th report, appendix, p. 191.

Chapter 2

'The rude malice of the people': Fairfax and popular parliamentarianism

This chapter will demonstrate how Lord Fairfax and Sir Thomas Fairfax adapted themselves to become popular war leaders in the north from October 1642 to September 1644. With the arrival of the earl of Newcastle's large royalist army in Yorkshire in December 1642, the Fairfaxes faced a daunting task to field a parliamentarian counterpart. They had no fortified towns or castles to defend. They received little money or effective assistance from Parliament. They had only a slim base of support among Yorkshire's leading gentry, and their foremost ally, Sir John Hotham at Hull, eagerly awaited their destruction. To conduct a military campaign against a numerically superior foe in these conditions forced them into heading popular insurgency at a time when most parliamentarian leaders were distancing themselves from such movements. The Fairfaxes turned to the inhabitants of the West Riding's clothing districts, a populous, industrial region with an established and unruly reputation for popular politics.

I

The failed neutrality treaty had not damaged the Fairfaxes' reputations irretrievably, and Parliament, which could ill afford recriminations, soon encouraged them to return to their allegiance. One newsbook obligingly proclaimed that if Lord Fairfax had known the enemy's 'dangerous and mischievous' motivations for the treaty, he would never have consented. The parliamentary propagandist John Vicars later claimed the treaty was a royalist plot to beguile the 'good and honestly meaning Lord Fairfax'.[1] Lord Fairfax ordered musters early in October, in response to mounting pressure from his West Riding supporters who were anxious for their safety. Sir Thomas recalled that 'my Father was called forth by ye Importunity of ye Country to joine with them in Defence of ymselves'. When Martin Iles of Leeds remembered 1642,

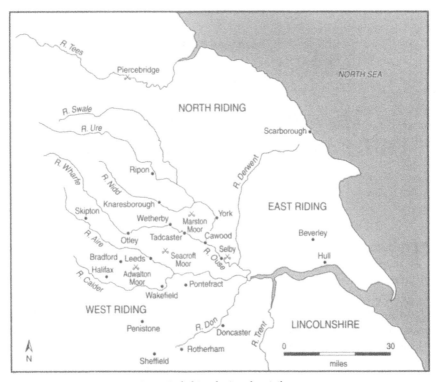

Map 1 Yorkshire during the civil wars

he recalled how 'many hundreds' in his neighbourhood clubbed together to protect themselves from cavalier plunderers, and 'so armed themselves'.[2] Halifax constables dated payments for watchmen from August 1642 and their parish's armed parliamentarianism from when 'Lord Fairefaxe first tooke upp armes at Bradford'. Local parliamentarians had been arming for weeks when Lord Fairfax finally 'gave an invitation for the country to come in'.[3] This news spread to Westminster and on 21 October 1642 the earl of Northumberland had heard Fairfax was 'in the field with five hundred foote, and are encreasing dayly'.[4] He could scarcely have known that on that very day, the Fairfaxes were fighting for their lives.

Having enjoyed a mere fortnight to muster support, their headquarters at Bradford were attacked by a royalist force of 240 horse and 500 foot under Sir William Savile and Sir Thomas Glemham. The town was unfortified and thinly defended by 300 men in four weak infantry companies under Sir John Savile, William Lister, John Farrer and Henry Atkinson, with only half a troop of horse under Sir Thomas Fairfax. With Lord Fairfax's closest advisers, Thomas Stockdale, Thomas Lister and William White, also present, the royalists had a golden opportunity to capture the parliamentarian leadership in a single stroke. To offset the Fairfaxes' lack of cavalry, Bradford's streets were protected by barricades, so that the royalist horsemen 'could not enter though they went near the ends of the streetes wch were blocked upp wth harrowes, waynes & the Ld Fayrfaxe & they within the towne wth burning strawe & such stuffe caused that scarse any of their men could be seene for the smoake'. The royalists withdrew in failure and abandoned Leeds, where the parliamentarians soon raised £2000 by borrowing or composition.[5]

Rather than consolidating their grip on the clothing districts, the Fairfaxes pressed the royalists back towards York and established new quarters at Wetherby, Cawood and Tadcaster. Lord Fairfax expected reinforcement by 500 Lincolnshire dragoons, the horse troops of Sir Henry Foulis, John Alured and Captain Mildmay, and by the foot regiments of Sir Matthew Boynton and Sir Hugh Cholmley drawn from the trained bands of Cleveland, Scarborough and Whitby. In theory, Fairfax anticipated commanding 3000 men, most of whom his family had not mustered. Although some of these forces were soon diverted by other local concerns, this evidence questions Clements Markham's assumption that the Fairfaxes' first army was raised from their Wharfedale tenantry.[6]

Within a week the Fairfaxes' position was completely transformed. On 21 October their minuscule force was struggling to evade capture, but by 28 October, alongside John Hotham and Sir Hugh Cholmley, they were threatening York itself. It is rarely recognised how close York came to being besieged in November 1642, and the citizens panicked as the parliamentarians approached. One inhabitant wrote on 26 October 1642: 'We are all in an uprore in the Citty of York, for it is reported that Mr Hotham with his forces are within 3 miles of York, all the westridinge, except the Castle and Towne of Pontefract are at his command and of the Lord Fairfaxe.'[7] Three days later the city corporation appointed seven men to reply to a letter from Lord Fairfax and on 8 November York's common council ordered these men to negotiate with the royalist general, the earl of Cumberland: 'to shew unto him that in respect what danger this Cittie now standeth whether it be fitteinge to move a treaty with my Lord Fairfax & the Rest'.[8] On 11 November, another frightened inhabitant wrote: 'We are here in a manner blockt up by the Parliament's forces, insomuch that not any provisions can be suffered to be brought into us.' With Lord Fairfax at Tadcaster, Sir Thomas Fairfax at Wetherby, Sir Hugh Cholmley at Stamford Bridge and John Hotham at Cawood, only the north side of York lay open. Hotham's cavalry rode up to the walls to jeer at the defenders, and a townsman was shot at Micklegate bar. The city's aldermen complained of the costs of tending watchfires and digging trenches, and one London newsbook confidently predicted that Fairfax and Hotham 'will have York in fourteen dayes siege'.[9] By December two newsbooks reported that Cumberland had offered terms for surrender.[10]

Until now Yorkshire's parliamentarians had mobilised their forces more effectively than their royalist counterparts, but the earl of Newcastle was raising a large royalist army in Northumberland and Durham, which pressured the parliamentarians to take York swiftly. On 9 November, Lord Fairfax sent a force under John Hotham to rally the handful of North Riding parliamentarian gentry against Newcastle. Hotham was unimpressed by the North Riding's forces at Northallerton and Yarm. Nevertheless, the local royalists retreated northward and Hotham wrote to Lord Fairfax from Darlington on 23 November that he had seized Piercebridge, the main crossing of the river Tees. He assured Fairfax that by holding the bridge he could prevent Newcastle's southward march, writing 'for the wayes now grow so ill as will be soone unpassable'.[11]

On 1 December, Newcastle's large army confronted Hotham's force of around 1000 men at Piercebridge. Emulating the Scots' tactics at Newburn, the royalist artillery enabled their troops to force a crossing and the parliamentarian war effort in the North Riding collapsed.[12] Only Scarborough held out and within four days Newcastle's army was in York. Of the 1000 North Riding men supposedly mustered only 130 foot under Sir Matthew Boynton accompanied Hotham's forces south, along with two troops of horse under Sir Henry Foulis and Captain Henry Anderson.[13] Another North Riding captain, John Dodsworth of Watlas, was captured and marched through the streets of York by royalist troopers who allegedly 'threatened to Pistoll him'.[14] Other North Riding gentry that joined Fairfax did so without their commands; with their estates in enemy hands, they enlisted as troopers and corporals.[15]

As Newcastle approached, Lord Fairfax withdrew from blockading York and concentrated his forces at Tadcaster. To face Newcastle's army of 8000 men, he mustered eighteen companies of foot and seven troops of horse, scarcely 2000 men. On 6 December Newcastle assaulted Tadcaster but the parliamentarians drew up their musketeers in breastworks and held the town until nightfall. Around 40,000 shots were exchanged and Sir Henry Foulis wrote 'you cannot imagine how hot service it was'. As at Bradford, the engagement was fought defending an urban area, hampering the royalists from deploying their superior cavalry. Fairfax's army quitted Tadcaster that night, because, as Foulis explained, 'we wanted victual and ammunition, for I dare well say that in 48 hours not a Commander eate a bit, much lesse a Common Souldier'. Lord Fairfax retreated to Selby and John Hotham to Cawood.[16] The parliamentarians had been fortunate; the royalists could not easily pursue them because of the narrow lanes and low, boggy terrain, while the earl of Newport's cavalry that were intended to prevent their retreat never arrived.[17]

Lord Fairfax fortified his new Selby headquarters, hoping to obstruct the royalists from marching southward. With royalist forces within twelve miles at York and Pontefract, both sides launched cavalry raids against outlying quarters. On 13 December, John Hotham and Sir Thomas Fairfax beat up royalist quarters at Sherburn-in-Elmet with five troops of horse. This successful attack foreshadowed much of the conflict's cavalry raiding, and, for a second time, Fairfax was lucky to escape alive when his mount was killed.[18] Newcastle's army still outnumbered the Fairfaxes by at least four to one, and Charles I confidently wrote to Newcastle on 15 December: 'The business of Yorkshire I account almost done.'[19] Lord Fairfax received no money from Parliament to pay his forces despite warning them that they were disintegrating through desertion.[20] Forced to quarter his soldiers upon Selby's inhabitants, he was unable to protect the clothing districts, without whom his forces would have collapsed. He warned Parliament:

> I have hitherto supported this army with the loans and contributions, for the most part, of the parishes of Leeds, Halifax and Bradford, and some other small towns adjacent, being the only well-affected people of the country, who I much feare may now suffer by this popish army of the North merely for their good affection to the Religion and Publike Liberty.[21]

Lord Fairfax attempted to send Sir Thomas with forces to protect the clothing districts, but their passage was blocked by royalists at Pontefract and Ferrybridge.[22]

On 18 December Bradford's inhabitants reinvigorated the Fairfaxes' flagging cause, by demonstrating they would fight without them. As the royalists approached, one observer recalled that Bradford's wealthier parishioners fled, leaving 'not a gentleman to command us'. Although Fairfax had already recruited the town's trained bands and volunteers, the remaining inhabitants 'blocked up every avenue leading into the town, sent out spies, and watched every move of the enemy'. Eighty men armed with 'muskets and long guns' defended the church, where local wool was hung to protect the steeple. Other inhabitants were armed with 'clubs, scythes, spits, flails, halberds, sickles laid in long poles and such like rustic weapons'.[23] On 21 December a letter was allegedly written at Bradford for the London press describing the episode, much of which was echoed in the later accounts by John Hodgson and Joseph Lister:

> The last Lords day 13 Colours came against us, under the command of Col: Goring, Col. Evers a Papist, Sir William Savill, Sir Marmad: Langdale, and Sir John Gothricke, a Papist, & c. They appeared in Barker End about 9 a clocke, when we had not in towne above 40. Musquetiers; planted their Ordnance in William Cookes Barne, marched down the Causey with their foote, whilest their horse coasted about the towne to hinder ayde from coming in, possesst themselves of those houses under the Church, and from thence played hotly upon our Musquetiers in the Church till 11 a clock, about which time Hallifax men, and other neighbours came in to our help; the fight before was hot, was then hotter: our men impatient to be coopt up

in the Church, rusht out, forced a passage into the foresaid houses, and there our Club-men did good execution upon them.[24]

The attack on Bradford sparked a wider insurrection, drawing men in from Halifax, Bingley and the surrounding townships. Isaac Baume brought the news to Coley chapel where John Hodgson was among the congregation at prayer. At the urging of the minister, Andrew Latham, they armed themselves and marched on Bradford where Hodgson witnessed scenes of frenzied violence. Furious poorly armed townsmen routed and pursued royalist cavalry. Marksmen armed with fowling pieces singled out the royalist gentry, holding fire until 'any buffe or scarlet coat appeared'. Sir John Goodricke was dismounted by a scytheman, captured and thrashed with cudgels. Another officer, perhaps the earl of Newport's son, was unhorsed and despite calling for quarter was murdered by locals who supposedly cried 'aye they would quarter him'.[25] Barbara Donagan has asserted that the subsequent feeble excuse that this brutality arose from Bradford men's ignorance of military language rather than intent 'reflected a need to assert that Bradford men were not outlaws from the customs of war, and did not merit the retributive penalties of such outlawry'.[26] This killing resembled the dispatching of Lord Sheffield by Kett's rebels in 1549,[27] but despite being reminiscent of Tudor popular rebellion, Bradford became a national symbol of defiance towards royalism. With a shortage of other good news the parliamentarian press invested Bradford with Herculean status. Earlier that year a Lincolnshire crowd demonstrating against enclosures threatened 'that if the parliament would not help them, they would help themselves by club law'. London polemicists now adopted the term, urging all England to 'rise and execute Bradford Club Law upon the Cavaliers'.[28] This advocated the common people executing judgement against their social 'superiors', albeit along prescribed lines. Another pamphlet celebrated that 'the inhabitants of Bradforth and Halifax have united themselves and raised some thousands of men, whereof many of them are for the old Club Law',[29] and that they were driving Newcastle's soldiers from the county.[30] Other tracts echoed the language of Stephen Marshall's sermon 'Meroz Cursed' to emphasise Bradford's defenders as 'the Lamb's followers and servants', the 'poor and off scouring of the world', when the 'Kings and captains, merchants and wise men, give all their strength to the Beast.'[31]

Bradford's success placed the Fairfaxes in a dilemma. Could they identify themselves with an armed rising of clothworkers against the county gentry? In a world where the gentry were supposed to have withdrawn from armed political demonstration in alliance with the common people, it would be difficult for them to do so without appearing to subvert the social order. Lord Maynard had recently written to Sir Thomas Barrington: 'I shall not easily suffer my self her[e]after upon the perswasions of others to appear in any popular assemblies whear fellows without shirts challenge as good a voice as myself.'[32]

Across England popular anti-royalist insurgency was being curbed by anxious parliamentarian gentry. After Rupert sacked Cirencester in February 1643, captured parliamentarian soldiers lamented that their gentry and ministers had 'undone them'. Another rising at Lewes crumbled because no gentlemen would lead it. The Staffordshire moorlanders, led by the mysterious 'Grand Juryman', abandoned their attack on Stafford after Sir William Brereton and Sir John Gell both refused them aid.[33] Yet having failed to field an army capable of engaging the northern royalists, Lord Fairfax could scarcely turn away support. Nor would he let fear of popular activism undermine his trust in his neighbours and countrymen. On 29 December he answered Bradford's call for aid, sending his son and Sir Henry Foulis to them with three troops of horse and 120 dragoons.[34]

II

Bradford club-law was the making of Sir Thomas Fairfax. It provided him with his first army and brought national fame: 'Sir Thomas Fairfaxe with Bradford Clubs' were celebrated by the London press.[35] Soon after his arrival, he promised to arm the entire town, and by 9 January 1643, he anticipated mustering 600 musketeers and 3000 with other arms; double his father's numbers at Selby. He warned Lord Fairfax: 'These parts grow very impatient of our delay in beating them out of Leeds and Wakefield, for by them all trade and provisions are stopped, so that the people in these parts are not able to subsist, and, indeed, so pressing are these wants as some have told me, if I would not stir with them, they must of necessity rise of themselves.' He requested permission to take the offensive and 'join with the readiness of the people'.[36] Pennine clothworkers had endured two years of plague, taxation and forced billeting, and now denied transport of their cloth to Hull by the royalists, many would starve if they failed to secure foodstuffs from the royalist-occupied vale of York. Cloth was easy to plunder on open roads and by the summer of 1643 one Leeds clothier lamented that all trade to London had been stopped. Necessity forced these recruits to enlist faster than Sir Thomas could arm or organise them.[37] On 17 January Lord Fairfax sent Sir William Fairfax with more officers, horse and dragoons to aid Sir Thomas in recapturing Leeds.[38] Popular support was now dictating parliamentarian strategy. In the face of superior enemy forces, Lord Fairfax riskily divided his army, weakening his main force at Selby to nurture the clubmen insurrection.

On 23 January 1643, Sir William Savile's royalist garrison of 1500 men in Leeds found Sir Thomas's new army drawn up on Woodhouse moor. An eyewitness account from one of Fairfax's chaplains, Thomas Crompton, stated that Fairfax deployed six troops of horse under Sir Henry Foulis, three companies of dragoons under Sir Thomas Norcliffe, 600 musketeers and 1200 clubmen under Sir William Fairfax. Their word was 'Emmanuel', and 'most of them were but unexperienced fresh-water Souldiers taken up about Bradford and Hallifax but upon the Saturday before'.[39] Fairfax sent forward his best companies along the waterside, commanded by the Scot, Sergeant-Major William Forbes. The future Quaker James Nayler distinguished himself in the assault, and Jonathan Scholefield, a minister from Todmorden, bellowed the sixty-eighth Psalm while overrunning enemy artillery.[40] London's newsbooks relished this victory, praising the 'Bradford men, with their Clubs and Forks'. Consequently, Newcastle withdrew all his garrisons south of York, except Pontefract, which Sir Thomas intended to capture to 'open a free passage to Hull' to save the clothing towns.[41]

The day before Leeds was recaptured, the club-law rose in Rotherham when the royalists rode into town on a Sunday, as at Bradford five weeks earlier. Once more they were defeated by poorly armed civilians rallying to their church and defending their homes from feared plunderers. One London newsbook described an 'Ambuscado of 60 Musquettiers who fired upon them so that divers fell and the rest run away'.[42] The town's vicar, John Shaw, recalled that six or seven hundred royalists launched their attack during his sermon, but were repelled after a fierce encounter by only twenty-five men armed with muskets.[43] The episode no doubt furnished Shaw with plentiful material for subsequent sermons.

Similar insurgency erupted in Penistone. After Sir Thomas Fairfax refused them aid, local inhabitants rose in arms regardless. Sir Francis Wortley was the detested figure of this locality. He was the first Yorkshireman to draw his sword for the King in April 1642 and was notorious for having plundered the moorlanders of north Staffordshire in November 1642, a locality which 'harboured a thriving plebeian population'.[44] His ancestor Sir Thomas Wortley had levelled a town to make way for Wortley park during the reign of Henry VIII. Popular memory of this ensured that a century later Sir Francis's park suffered mass deer stealing by co-ordinated gangs. When one of Sir Francis's servants discovered venison for sale in Barnsley market he was assaulted and his master traduced. Sir Francis suffered similar verbal abuse in the quarter sessions, one yeoman declaring 'I worship him with my arse.' The poaching in Wortley park could be construed as an act of havoc, and Roger Manning has suggested that such organised violence lubricated the movement towards war in 1642.[45] Led by three parochial gentry, William Rich of Bullhouse, Adam Eyre of Haslehead and George Shirt of Cawthorne, the Penistone insurgents established their church as a garrisoned strongpoint, just as at Bradford and Rotherham. All three were later commissioned as captains by Lord Fairfax, while a local husbandman was commissioned as Eyre's lieutenant.[46]

The club-law unleashed a wave of popular violence against the estates of royalist landowners. On 17 January 1643 three local men on the margins of gentry status, Joshua, Thomas and Nicholas Greathead, led 250 insurgents into Lord Savile's mansion at Howley, a monument of conspicuous wealth in the heart of the impoverished cloth districts. They were entertained by the absent Savile's tenants and servants, which Savile complained were so notoriously parliamentarian that they paid his rents to the Fairfaxes.[47] Savile had invited popular hostility in 1638 when he attempted to enclose land on the highway from West Ardsley to the clothing towns of Bradford, Halifax, Huddersfield and Birstall. He was punished accordingly by plebeian poaching and robbery on his estates at Lindle Hill and New Park, Wakefield. Howley was transformed into a parliamentarian garrison of 'raw soldiers, menial servants, and volunteers out of the clothing district'.[48]

On 27 January 1643 Sir Thomas Fairfax wrote to his father for more weapons to 'arm the country with them, for strangers being very restrained of their will are very mutinous'.[49] He sent letters to the constables of Mirfield, Shipley and Bingley to lead all able-bodied men aged between sixteen and sixty to his muster on 29 January at Almondbury. This township had been surrounded and dominated by the royalist landowners, the Beaumonts, Ramsdens and Kays, whose mansions at Whitley, Longley Old Hall and Woodsome were now targets.[50] Sir William Savile was also warned of the danger posed to his estates by the parliamentarians at Bradford.[51] He was particularly anxious over his reputation for rack-renting his family's twelve Yorkshire manors, and from 1640 his deer parks at Bradfield and Brearley both suffered from well armed plebeian poachers. His house at Thornhill was rased by the clubmen to wreak vengeance upon him.[52] On 31 December 1642, insurgents under Sir Henry Foulis pillaged £1000 worth of goods from another Savile manor at Emley. On 21 January 1643 1000 newly raised clubmen visited Emley where they shredded bonds and evidences, stole sheep, horses and plate, and slaughtered deer in the park.[53] Much of this violence appears similar to that inflicted upon Roman catholic and Laudian landowners in Essex and Suffolk the previous August, during the notorious 'Stour valley riots' recently explored by John Walter.[54] Roving crowds of armed clothworkers enduring a subsistence crisis must have been a fearsome spectacle at any gentleman's gate. Such looting challenged hierarchical order far more than cavalier gentry plundering the poor commons, and Ann Hughes has pointed out that 'gentlemen were not accustomed to being ordered to relinquish their property in this fashion'.[55] These features of popular violence were familiar in the gentry's nightmare memories of 1549, and scarcely widened the Fairfaxes' slim base of county gentry support.

In March 1643 Sir Thomas Fairfax reinforced his father's troubled position at Selby. Their army remained unpaid and short of supplies, the very even- tuality that Selby's river links with Hull should have prevented. Immediate pressure on Selby was relieved when the Queen landed at Bridlington on 22

February and Newcastle's army advanced into the East Riding to guarantee her convoy safe passage to York. Far too late to hinder the Queen's passage, on 9 March, Parliament ordered Lord Fairfax to send at least 1000 men, half his entire force, into the East Riding to aid the Hothams, thereby isolating the West Riding and removing the only obstacle to Newcastle's army marching south.[56] Lord Fairfax disobeyed, placing his trust in the clothing districts that had supported and supplied him where Parliament and the Hothams had failed. Swayed by the clubmen's successes, on 30 March Lord Fairfax's army abandoned Selby, the headquarters they had spent months fortifying, and marched to Leeds, thereby surrendering Newcastle a passage southward. Sir Thomas Fairfax commanded the vulnerable rearguard, which included John Hodgson of Coley, an ensign in Captain Bower's company. Hodgson recalled that Sir Thomas, 'exceeding his commission at the request of the clubmen', marched to Tadcaster to destroy royalist defence works. This time Sir Thomas's soldiers paid for his pliability to popular demand; Sir George Goring with twenty troops of horse caught them on Seacroft moor, just east of Leeds. Fairfax's three troops of horse were insufficient to protect his foot, most of whom were captured. Rather than accept responsibility, Fairfax later blamed his disorderly men, craving drink on an unseasonably hot day: 'the Countrymen, presently cast downe their Armes and fledd ... The Foote (soon after which) for Want of Pikes, was not able to withstand their Horse; some were slaine and many taken Prisoners.'[57] Sir Henry Foulis and John Hodgson were wounded, and the few foot that escaped Goring's troopers hid in Killingbeck woods until nightfall. It was reported in Parliament that the Fairfaxes blamed the absence of Hotham's cavalry for their defeat, further worsening relations between the two families.[58]

With the Queen in York, Cholmley at Scarborough turned royalist, and with John Hotham in Lincolnshire plotting his defection, Newcastle's army was free to field over 10,000 men against the Fairfaxes. Lord Fairfax mustered six troops of horse and 1800 foot against them at Leeds. On 9 April 1643 the Queen wrote: 'Our army is gone to Leeds, and at this time are beating down the town.'[59] Her optimism was ill founded. Leeds was a town of over 5000 inhabitants. Its circumference was too large even for Newcastle's army to surround. Its blurred urban–rural divide and outlying townships made the ground difficult for the royalist cavalry. After much skirmishing in the suburbs, the defenders held out, Lord Fairfax himself reportedly leading one sally.[60] James King, the royalist lieutenant-general, remembered wisely that all parliamentarian victories in Yorkshire thus far had been fought on urban battlefields. He warned Newcastle that a direct assault would ruin the army, 'by too severe a slaughter'.[61]

Newcastle raised the siege and marched south, capturing Rotherham and Sheffield in early May.[62] While Sir Thomas complained to his father of their continued failure to recruit cavalry, Lord Fairfax lamented to Parliament that the 'loss of these two places hath much elated the Enemy, and cast down the Spirits of the People in these Parts, who daily see the Enemy encrease in Power, and to gain Ground, and no Succours come to them from any part'.[63] Yet Newcastle miscalculated in leaving the Fairfaxes undefeated in his rear and Sir Thomas Fairfax's strategy was determined by popular pressure for a third time. The wives and children of the Seacroft prisoners urged him to secure their release, but negotiations failed. Sir Thomas recalled 'their Continuall Cryes & Teares & Importunitys compelled us to thinke of some way to Redeeme these men, so as, we thought of Attempting Wakefield'.[64] Fairfax hoped to capture enough royalist prisoners to exchange for his men taken at Seacroft.

Sir George Goring commanded Wakefield's garrison of 3000 men. His father had recently written that the royalists would soon be 'sweeping away ye rubbedge crowded in two or three holes of this Country, yt only obstruct noe way indanger us'.[65] On Saturday 20 May Goring was drinking and bowling with his officers at Heath Hall while Sir Thomas Fairfax gathered forces drawn from Leeds, Bradford and Halifax at Howley Hall. Early Whitsunday morning, with eight troops of horse, three companies of dragoons and 1000 foot, about 1500 men in all, Fairfax set off, mistakenly believing the garrison was only 900 strong.[66] During the confused street-fighting that followed in Wakefield's streets, Fairfax was cut off from his men and almost captured but Sergeant-Major-General John Gifford and the infantry secured the town. Three thousand arms and 1500 prisoners were taken, while Lieutenant Matthew Alured captured Goring himself.[67] Wakefield ranks among the most astounding actions of the entire civil wars. Outnumbered two to one by a royalist garrison enjoying defensive positions, Fairfax's men nevertheless prevailed. A tract entitled *The Pindar of Wakefield*, supposedly penned by one of his infantry officers, reported:

> S[h]all I tell you the Story of an awde wife in Wakefield as she was sitting on the midding wringing her hands and greeting after the feight was done, that she had lived sea lang, and she had heard of the Pindar of Wakefield, Geordy Greene and Little John, but never thought sike [such] doings had been in the world, and never since was borne did she, and she thinks nene else in the Towne observe the Song of Geordy Greene before now.[68]

Geordy Green, the pindar of Wakefield, was a hero comparable to Robin Hood, a champion of the town's freemen and yeomanry, guarding against the foul designs of a corrupt nobility. A ballad and play celebrating his heroic deeds had existed since the 1590s and this language of legend and folk memory was now channelled into a popular parliamentarian politics that was exalting plebeian liberties.[69]

Wakefield saved the West Riding parliamentarians from despair, but unfor-

The Right Worshipfull Sr Iohn
Hotham Kt Gouernour of Kingston
vpon HVLL

Figure 2 The Fairfaxes' rival: Sir John Hotham, Governor of Hull

tunately for them, it inspired Parliament and press into placing higher expectations upon them. In contrast the royalist *Mercurius aulicus* correctly predicted
Wakefield was 'a lightning before death' for the Fairfaxes' army.[70] Lord Fairfax
warned Parliament that 'this Overthrow hath much enraged the Enemy, who
threaten a present Revenge, and are drawing all their forces this way to effect
it'. The Fairfaxes requested reinforcements, especially cavalry, and warned that
'if such succours come not timely to us, we cannot long subsist, but must be

forced to accept of dishonourable conditions'.[71] Sir John Hotham (Figure 2) had not supplied the Fairfaxes with ammunition for nineteen weeks, although he spared twenty barrels of gunpowder for the 100 musketeers garrisoning his seat at Scorborough.[72] On 2 June, his son, John Hotham, treacherously persuaded the parliamentarians gathered at Nottingham, which included Oliver Cromwell, that 'Lord Newcastle's army, so weak and in such a distraction' was in no condition to defeat the Fairfaxes. This provoked an angry response from Lord Fairfax to reinforce him at once or risk the whole kingdom falling to Newcastle's army. It went unheeded.[73]

In April 1643, Goring predicted that the way to defeat the Fairfaxes was to march into the clothing districts and force them to battle: 'wherefore if you can get between Bradford and Leeds, you will so annoy, divert and separate them in all their Designs'.[74] Newcastle's army now did so, beginning by capturing Howley Hall on 22 June, whose governor, Sir John Savile of Lupset, was fortunate to be spared execution.[75] Newcastle now punished the districts that had maintained the Fairfaxes' army, forcing the Fairfaxes to risk the open battle they had always striven to avoid. Early on 30 June, the Fairfaxes attempted to regain the initiative. They launched a surprise attack from Bradford against Newcastle's forces on Adwalton moor. They mustered ten troops of horse, described in Thomas Stockdale's eyewitness account 'as for the most part weak', 1200 men from Leeds, seven companies from Bradford and 500 men from Halifax and the Pennine townships. They also deployed recent reinforcements of twelve companies of foot and three troops of horse from Lancashire. These soldiers, perhaps 4000 strong, were supported by an unknown number of clubmen.[76] The royalists fielded at least 4000 horse and 8000 foot in a host which Stockdale believed outnumbered them by at least five to one.

In the first academic study of the battle, David Johnson has shown that the battlefield's terrain, littered with lanes, ditches, hedges, enclosures and coal pits, suited the Fairfaxes as it was difficult for the feared royalist cavalry to negotiate.[77] After their initial assault drove the royalists back, the Fairfaxes' forces were eventually outflanked and overwhelmed by superior numbers. The battle was not won through the courage of royalist commanders, but because the royalists were eventually able to employ their heavy numerical superiority.[78] This was of course later denied by Newcastle's daughter, Jane Cavendish, whose poem, 'On the 30th June; to God', disguised how it had taken her father's 'little flock' seven months to defeat a much smaller foe:

> And it was true Fairfax was then more great
> But yet Newcastle made him sure retreat.[79]

Sir Thomas withdrew to Halifax, while Lord Fairfax escaped to Bradford.[80] The defeat was a crushing one: 790 prisoners were taken, and Stockdale lamented 'the fear and distraction it hath gotten in the country'. Bradford and Halifax swiftly surrendered and John Brearcliffe, a Halifax apothecary, noted on 3 July 'I clok morn Bradford taken & I into Lancashire.' Lancashire's parliamentarians garrisoned the Pennine passes at Rochdale and Blackstone edge, through which many of the clothing districts' inhabitants fled, fearing retribution from the triumphant royalists. Lancashire parish registers at this time abound with deaths of Yorkshire refugees.[81]

Lord Fairfax withdrew his shattered forces to Leeds where 'a boy came just in the nick of time, like the case of Mordecai, or the Shunamite ... with a letter from the major and aldermen of Hull, acquainting his honour that Hull was open for him if he would come thither'.[82] Hull's townsmen had arrested the Hothams and their officers on suspicion of treachery on 29 June, establishing a haven for the Fairfaxes' withdrawal. Lord Fairfax arrived in Hull on 3 or 4 July where his exhausted son joined him after a legendary forty-hour ride from Leeds on 4 July. The fugitives had suffered such depredations that the corporation 'could not choose but lament their sad condition'. Robert Burton foreboded 'the clouds are so exceeding dark and thicke', while Nicholas Pearson noted in the registers of St Mary's, Beverley: 'War in our gates ... All our lives now at ye stake. Lord deliver us for Xt his saike.'[83]

III

Given the bleak outlook for the parliamentary cause, the Fairfaxes' success in raising a new army at Hull so soon after Adwalton moor was astonishing. For the first time they now enjoyed a secure, defensible base, plentiful ammunition, massed artillery, naval support, a swift maritime link with London, assessment revenues from the less ravaged East Riding, access to Sir John Hotham's treasury and his network of parliamentarians among the county gentry. This last point became apparent when troops formerly under the Hothams were reorganised and reinforced. Sir Thomas assembled the new cavalry at Sutton and Stoneferry, which by mid-August constituted twenty troops, double the numbers deployed at Adwalton. With this force they threatened Stamford Bridge and raided close to York.[84] This was a critical moment in the war because Newcastle's Yorkshire officers now forced his army's return northward to besiege Hull. Sir Thomas commanded a fighting withdrawal from Beverley, and Lord Fairfax ordered the sluices in Hull's defences opened to flood the besiegers. On 26 September Sir Thomas ferried twenty troops of horse across the Humber to rendezvous with Cromwell in Lincolnshire and bring Newcastle's cavalry to battle.[85]

On 11 October 1643, Lord Fairfax launched a decisive sally from Hull, and Sir Thomas, commanding over 1000 troopers, led his first massed cavalry charge at Winceby. The next day, Sir William Widdrington informed Newcastle of the royalist defeat, commenting: 'Their horse are very good, and extraordinarily well armed; and may be reported to be betwixt 50 and 60 troops, being very strong ... your Lordship will be much streightned for the Preservation of York-shire.' On 12 October the earl of Manchester reported to Parliament that Sir Thomas Fairfax was 'a Person that exceeds any Expressions as a Commendation of his Resolution and Valour'. Peter Gaunt has conceded that it was Fairfax, not Cromwell, who deserved most credit for the victory at Winceby.[86]

With the Fairfaxes campaigning far to the east, some of their supporters in the royalist-occupied clothing districts fought on without them. John Hodgson had fled into Lancashire, and then into Craven 'where we gathered together three or four companies of such as had fled away or got out of prisons'. On 14 October it was agreed at Manchester that Captain Bradshaw would lead a rising at the hilltop village of Heptonstall and notes were sent to sixteen local churches to raise men. This region's chapelries provided the organisational apparatus for parliamentarian activists to raise men without gentry leadership, as they had done formerly in response to the Bradford club-law. By 17 October around 60 horse, 280 musketeers and 500 clubmen had been mustered. They soon raided down Calderdale towards Halifax, but locals were punished for their activism when the royalists burned the villages of Heptonstall and Haworth in retaliation. Once again this region demonstrated its capacity to wage war without leadership from county gentry.[87]

After Winceby Sir Thomas Fairfax campaigned in Nottinghamshire and Derbyshire before being called upon by Parliament to relieve the siege of Nantwich and defeat Sir John Byron's army, swollen by royalist troops recalled from Ireland. Crossing the snowy Pennines in January 1644, Fairfax anticipated his first field battle as commander-in-chief. He placed his cavalry under Sir William Fairfax on one wing, with John Lambert and Christopher Copley on the other. The thawing river Weaver turned the battlefield into a mudbath, enabling Fairfax to capture all of Byron's guns and baggage. This victory negated much of the King's advantage won by the cessation in Ireland. Fifteen hundred prisoners were taken, half of whom joined Fairfax, and thanksgivings were ordered in London's churches.[88]

The entry of the Scots army of the Covenant, 20,000 strong, into the northern war on Parliament's side in January 1644 dramatically altered the strategic situation, forcing Newcastle's main army northwards to defend the north-east and permitting the Fairfaxes to resume offensive operations. While Sir Thomas reduced royalist garrisons in Cheshire and Lancashire, in mid-February he sent a force under John Lambert into the West Riding. In Hull, Lord Fairfax sent out Sir William Constable to recover the East Riding. Newcastle warned the King on 13 February 1644 that they were 'all threatening to march towards us, which will make them a great body'. Lambert retook Halifax, Bradford and Howley Hall, and on 25 March repelled a royalist assault on Bradford.[89] By 8 April the Fairfaxes and Lambert were reunited south of

Selby, mustering 2000 horse and dragoons, and 2000 foot. They stormed Selby on 11 April, defeating a large garrison under John Belasyse, governor of York. The capture of Belasyse and much of his army was decisive and forced Newcastle's army to hastily return southwards to save York.[90]

On 23 April the Fairfaxes combined with the Scots and besieged York. On 3 June the Eastern Association joined them, swelling the allied army to perhaps 28,000 men. Prince Rupert marched north through Lancashire and crossed the Pennines to raise the siege, and, in conjunction with Newcastle, he fielded almost 20,000 men. The largest battle of the civil wars, and possibly on English soil, commenced on Marston moor, seven miles west of York, on the long evening of 2 July 1644. Sir Thomas Fairfax commanded the allied right wing of cavalry, some 4000 strong, but suffered heavy losses from royalist musketeers in an advance slowed by difficult terrain. Most were routed by the royalist northern horse under Sir George Goring and Sir Marmaduke Langdale. Many of the officers in Fairfax's wing were injured or slain, including his only brother, Charles Fairfax, who was mortally wounded. Fairfax himself recalled that 'as many were Hurt & Killed, as in ye whole Army besides'.[91] Although Fairfax's right wing was broken, several Scots infantry regiments in the centre held firm, who, along with Cromwell's successful cavalry on the left wing, eventually delivered victory for the allies.

Manchester's chaplain, Simeon Ash, reported that although Fairfax had 'the heart of a Lion, stout and undaunted', he was dismounted, wounded in the face and 'brought off by a Souldier'. Manchester's scoutmaster, Leon Watson, agreed that Fairfax 'was unhorst', and 'lay upon the ground' until he was rescued by Cromwell's troops. Fairfax's 'Short memorials' selectively preferred to remember how he led his own regiment's successful charge before he crossed the field to aid Cromwell in directing the left wing.[92] Sir James Lumsden remarked that although Fairfax was 'a brave commander', 'his horse answered not our expectation nor his worth'. Another Scots officer explained that Fairfax mistakenly placed his new regiments in the van, and when they broke, they trampled over Lord Fairfax's foot and the Scots reserves.[93] P. R. Newman asserted that many 'commanders on both sides fought better at Marston Moor than Fairfax did'. Nevertheless, English accounts played down the Scots' importance, and the defeat of Fairfax's cavalry did not prevent him from sharing with Cromwell the credit for the victory in London.[94]

After the battle and York's subsequent surrender, Sir Thomas was sent to besiege Helmsley castle in August 1644, where he strayed too close to the walls and was shot in the shoulder by a royalist sharpshooter.[95] He spent the next months convalescing in York. His body was prematurely infirm and weakened with wounds, but he had won renown for daring, resolution and tenacity, and, above all, forged a reputation for recovering from defeat. It soon brought him command of Parliament's newly amalgamated southern army.

NOTES

1 YML, CWT, 42–10–05, *The declaration and votes of the lords and commons assembled in parliament concerning the late treaty of peace in Yorkshire* (London, 1642); J. Vicars, *God in the mount or England's parliamentarie-chronicle* (London, 1644), p. 179.

2 BL, Add. MS 21417, fo. 46; Bod., MS Fairfax 36, fo. 5r.

3 WYRO, Calderdale: Papers of Nathaniel Waterhouse of Halifax, 1559–1650, MIC:7, fo. 142; J. H. Turner (ed.), *The autobiography of Captain John Hodgson of Coley Hall, near Halifax* (Brighouse, 1882), p. 23.

4 BL, Add. MS 18979, fo. 127r.

5 YML, CWT, 42–11–03, *A true and perfect relation of a victorious battell obtained against the earl of Cumberland and his cavaliers, by the Lo; Fairfax and Capt: Hotham* (London, 1642), pp. 3–4; Beinecke Rare Book and Manuscript Library, Yale University, Osborn shelves b101, fo. 141.

6 YML, CWT, 42–11–03, *A true and perfect relation*, pp. 5–6; BL, E126(1), *Speciall passages*, 25 October–1 November (London, 1642), p. 103; Markham, p. 51.

7 Durham University Library, Mickleton-Spearman MS 46/7/61.

8 City of York Archives, House Books B36, fo. 77a–b.

9 W. Page (ed.), *The Victoria History of the County of York* (London, 1913), vol. 3, p. 420; D. Parsons (ed.), *The diary of Sir Henry Slingsby of Scriven, bart* (London, 1836), p. 82; City of York Archives, House Books, B36, fo. 78b; YML, CWT, 42–11–03, *A true and perfect relation*, pp. 5–6.

10 BL, E129(2), *Diurnall occurrences*, 28 November–5 December (London, 1642), p. 5; BL, E129(21), *A true and full relation of the troubles in Lancashiere*, 9 December (London, 1642), p. 7.

11 *Portland MS*, HMC, 29, 13th report, appendix, part 1 (London, 1891), vol. 1, pp. 68–9; HULA, Hotham MS, DDHO/1/13.

12 J. Rushworth, *Historical collections* (London, 1721), part 3, vol. 2, p. 78; YML, CWT, 42–12–20, *An exact and true relation of a bloody fight* (London, 1642), p. 3.

13 BL, Add. MS 18979, fo. 129r.

14 TNA, SP 19/120/128.

15 TNA, SP 28/129/6, fo. 9; TNA, E121/5/5, no. 1; TNA, E121/1/7, no. 59.

16 YML, CWT, 42–12–20, *An exact and true relation of a bloody fight*, pp. 6–7; J. Vicars, *England's worthies under whom all the civill and bloudy warres since anno 1642 to anno 1647 are related* (London, 2nd edn, 1845), p. 35; BL, Add. MS 18979, fo. 129r–v.

17 M. Cavendish, *The life of the thrice noble, high and puissant Prince William Cavendishe, duke, marquess and earl of Newcastle* (London, 1667), p. 21; Parsons (ed.), *The diary of Sir Henry Slingsby*, p. 86.

18 YML, CWT, 42–12–16, *A true relation of the fight at Sherburn in the county of Yorke* (London, 1642), p. 1.

19 S. R. Gardiner, *A History of the Great Civil Wars* (London, 1904), vol. 1, p. 71.

20 YML, CWT 43–01–05, *A second letter from the right honourable the Lord Fairfax* (London, 1643); *Portland MS*, HMC, 29, 13th report, appendix, part 1, vol. 1, pp. 79–80.

21 BL, Add. MS 18979, fo. 130r.

22 Bod., MS Fairfax 36, fo. 6r.

23 BL, E88(23), *The rider of the white horse and his army, their late good successe in Yorke-shiere* (London, 1643).

24 YML, CWT, 42–12–30, *Brave newes of the taking of the city of Chichester by the parliaments forces under the command of Sir William Waller... and of the maintaining of Bradford in Yorkshire by 40. musquetiers against 1300 cavaliers* (London, 1642).

25 BL, E88(23), *The rider of the white horse*; Turner (ed.), *The autobiography of Captain John Hodgson*, p. 23; T. Wright (ed.), *The autobiography of Joseph Lister of Bradford in Yorkshire* (London, 1842), p. 17.

26 B. Donagan, 'Codes and conduct in the English civil war', *Past and Present*, 118 (1988), 82.

27 B. L. Beer (ed.), ' "The Commoyson in Norfolk, 1549": a narrative of popular rebellion in sixteenth-century England', *Journal of Medieval and Renaissance Studies*, 6 (1976), I, 91.

28 A. Woolrych, *Britain in Revolution, 1625–1660* (Oxford, 2002), p. 229; BL, E86(5), *The kingdoms weekly intelligencer*, 17–24 January (London, 1643), p. 29.

29 Club-law is defined as: 'The use of the club to enforce obedience; physical force as contrasted with argument; law or rule of the physically stronger.' The term was in print by 1597 and 1612: J. A. Simpson and E. S. C. Weiner (eds), *The Oxford English Dictionary* (Oxford, 2nd edn, 1991), vol. 3, p. 369.

30 BL, E244(46), *Englands memorable accidents*, 2–9 January (London, 1643), p. 144.

31 C. Hill, *Antichrist in Seventeenth-Century England* (London, 1971), p. 81.

32 J. Walter, *Understanding Popular Violence in the English Revolution: The Colchester Plunderers* (Cambridge, 1999), p. 119.

33 A. R. Warmington, *Civil War, Interregnum and Restoration in Gloucestershire, 1640–1672* (Royal Historical Society, studies in history, new series, 1997), p. 38; J. T. Cliffe, *Puritans in Conflict: The Puritan Gentry During and After the Civil Wars* (London, 1988), p. 48; B. Manning, *The English People and the English Revolution* (London, 2nd edn, 1991), p. 304; D. H. Pennington and I. A. Roots (eds), *The Committee at Stafford* (Manchester, 1957), p. lxii; BL, E246(30), *A perfect diurnall of the passages in parliament*, 20–27 February (London, 1643).

34 YML, CWT 43–01–05, *A second letter from the right honourable the Lord Fairfax*.

35 BL, E86(40), *The kingdoms weekly intelligencer: or speciall passages*, 24–31 January (London, 1643).

36 R. Bell (ed.), *The Fairfax correspondence: memorials of the civil war* (London, 1849), vol. 1, p. 33.

37 M. James, *Social Problems and Policy during the English Revolution, 1640–1660* (London, 1966), p. 56; TNA, SP 19/113/118; YML, CWT, 43–01–28, *An exact and perfect relation of the proceedings of Sir Hugh Cholmley* (London, 1643).

38 Rushworth, *Historical collections*, part 3, vol. 2, pp. 125–7.

39 BL, E88(19), *A true and plenary relation of the great defeat given by my Lord Fairfax forces unto my Lord of Newcastles forces in Yorkshire, January 23: which was the absolutest and considerablest victory that was obtained since the beginning of these unhappy warres*, 6

February (London, 1643), pp. 4–5.

40 BL, E88(23), The rider of the white horse.

41 Ibid.; BL, E86(40), The kingdoms weekly intelligencer: or speciall passages, 24–31 January (London, 1643), p. 39; Bell (ed.), The Fairfax correspondence, vol. 1, p. 35.

42 BL, E88(20), The kingdoms weekly intelligencer, 31 January–7 February (London, 1643), p. 43.

43 J. R. Boyle (ed.), Memoirs of Master John Shawe (Hull, 1882), p. 132.

44 P. R. Newman, The Old Service: Royalist Regimental Colonels and the Civil War, 1642–6 (Manchester, 1993), p. 22; BL, E127(12), Speciall passages, 8–15 November (London, 1642); R. Hutton, The Royalist War Effort, 1642–1646 (London, 2nd edn, 1999), pp. 39–40.

45 College of Arms, Curia Militaris, Cur Mil II, fos. 134–5, 138–9; J. Lister (ed.), West Riding Sessions Records: Orders 1611–1642, Indictments 1637–1642 (YASRS, 53, 1915), vol. 2, pp. xi–xii, 60, 159–60; F. Barber (ed.), 'West Riding sessions rolls', YAJ, 5 (1879), 381; R. B. Manning, Hunters and Poachers: A Social and Cultural History of Unlawful Hunting in England, 1485–1640 (Oxford, 1993), pp. 48, 67, 124, 235–6; D. Hey, Yorkshire from A.D. 1000 (London, 1986), p. 123.

46 J. N. Dransfield, History of Penistone (Penistone, 1906), p. 65; Lister (ed.), West Riding Sessions Records, vol. 2, p. 304; C. Jackson (ed.), Yorkshire diaries and autobiographies in the seventeenth and eighteenth centuries (Surtees Society, 65, 1877), pp. 2, 21, 353.

47 M. Sheard (ed.), Records of the parish of Batley in the county of York (Worksop, 1894), p. 277; J. J. Cartwright (ed.), 'Papers relating to the delinquency of the Lord Savile, 1642–1646', Camden Miscellany, vol. 8 (Camden Society, 2nd series, 31, 1883), p. 10.

48 Lister (ed.), West Riding Sessions Records, vol. 2, pp. 107, 322, 347; Barber (ed.), 'West Riding sessions rolls', 389; N. Scatcherd, The history of Morley, in the parish of Batley, and the West-Riding of Yorkshire (Leeds, 1830), pp. 248–9.

49 Bell (ed.), The Fairfax correspondence, vol. 1, p. 36.

50 E. Peacock, 'On some civil war documents relating to Yorkshire', YAJ, 1 (1870), 97; Yorkshire Archaeological Society Library and Archive, Leeds: letter to the constable of Mirfield, MS 205a; J. H. Turner, Historical notices of Shipley, Saltaire, Idle, Windhill, Wrose, Baildon, Hawksworth, Eccleshill, Calverley, Rawdon and Horsforth (Idle, 1901), p. 15.

51 TNA, SP 19/17/157.

52 Hey, Yorkshire from A.D. 1000, p. 123; Lister (ed.), West Riding Sessions Records, vol. 2, pp. 189, 321, 329; Calderdale Central Library, Halifax: 'Our local portfolio' (cuttings from the Halifax Guardian, 1856–62, collected by J. W. Walker), p. 18.

53 Beinecke Rare Book and Manuscript Library, Yale University, Osborn shelves b101, fos. 143–5.

54 Walter, Understanding Popular Violence in the English Revolution.

55 A. Hughes, 'Parliamentary tyranny? Indemnity proceedings and the impact of the civil war: a case study from Warwickshire', Midland History, 11 (1986), 58.

56 The parliamentary or constitutional history of England, being a faithful account of all the most remarkable transactions in Parliament from the earliest times to the restoration of King Charles II, by several hands (London, 1753), vol. 12, pp. 190–1; Yorkshire Archaeological Society Library and Archive: YAS MS 1033, K.P., vol. 98, art. 2.

57 John Brearcliffe of Halifax noted 688 men were captured at Seacroft: WYRO, Calderdale: Brearcliffe MS, MISC: 182; Bod., MS Fairfax 36, fo. 6r.

58 Turner (ed.), *The autobiography of Captain John Hodgson*, p. 24; W. Wheater, *A history of Sherburn and Cawood* (London, 2nd edn, 1882), p. 249; BL, Add. MS 31116, fo. 42v.

59 BL, Add MS 31116, fo. 46r; M. A. E. Green (ed.), *The letters of Queen Henrietta Maria* (London, 1857), pp. 183–4.

60 BL, E97(9), *The kingdoms weekly intelligencer*, 11–18 April (London, 1643), p. 124.

61 G. Trease, *Portrait of a Cavalier: William Cavendish, First Duke of Newcastle* (London, 1979), p. 115.

62 Jackson (ed.), *Yorkshire diaries and autobiographies*, p. 136; C. H. Firth (ed.), *The life of William Cavendish, duke of Newcastle, to which is added the true relation of my birth and life by Margaret, duchess of Newcastle* (London, 1906), p. x.

63 Bell (ed.), *The Fairfax correspondence*, vol. 1, pp. 44–5; Rushworth, *Historical collections*, part 3, vol. 2, p. 269.

64 Bod., MS Fairfax 36, fo. 7v.

65 BL, Add. MS 18980, fo. 48r.

66 J. W. Walker, *Wakefield: Its History and People* (Wakefield, 2nd edn, 1966), vol. 2, pp. 431–2.

67 BL, E249(10), *A perfect diurnall of the passages in parliament, 22–9 May* (London, 1643); YML, CWT, 43–05–29, *A fuller relation of that miraculous victory which it pleased God to give unto the parliaments forces under the command of the right honourable Lord Fairefax* (London, 1643).

68 Worcester College, Oxford, Wing 2251A: *The pindar of Wakefield, or a true narration of the unparallell'd victory obtained against the popish army at the taking in of Wakefield in Yorkshire by the Lord Fairefaxe his forces, May 20. 1643* (London, 1643), p. 5.

69 J. W. Hales (ed.), *Bishop Percy's folio manuscript ballads and romances* (London, 1867), vol. 1, pp. 32–5; F. J. Child (ed.), *The English and Scottish Popular Ballads* (New York, 1957), vol. 3, pp. 129–32; J. Q. Adams (ed.), *Chief Pre-Shakespearean Dramas: A Selection of Plays Illustrating the History of the English Drama from its Origin Down to Shakespeare* (London, 1917), pp. 691–712.

70 P. W. Thomas (ed.), *The English Revolution III, Newsbooks I, Oxford Royalist* (London, 1971), vol. 1, p. 289.

71 *The parliamentary or constitutional history of England*, vol. 12, p. 272; Peacock, 'On some civil war documents relating to Yorkshire', 103.

72 BL, E61(16), *Certaine informations*, 17–24 July (London, 1643), p. 209; BL, Harleian MS 165, fo. 107.

73 BL, Add. MS 18979, fos. 141r–142v.

74 Rushworth, *Historical collections*, part 3, vol. 2, p. 270.

75 G. Fox, *The Three Sieges of Pontefract Castle* (Leeds, 1987), p. 6; G. Wood, *The Story of Morley* (London, 1916), p. 134.

76 *Portland MS*, HMC, 29, 13th report, appendix, part I, vol. 1, supplement, pp. 717–19; T. W. Hanson, 'Three civil war notes', *THAS* (1916), 250–1.

77 D. Johnson, *Adwalton Moor, 1643: The Battle that Changed a War* (Pickering, 2003).

78 Newman, *The Old Service*, p. 262.

79 Beinecke Rare Book and Manuscript Library, Yale University, Osborn shelves b233, fo. 38.

80 BL, Harleian MS 165, fo. 118.

81 WYRO, Calderdale: Brearcliffe MS, MISC: 182; H. P. Kendall, 'The civil war as affecting Halifax and the surrounding towns', *THAS* (1910), 26–7; Hanson, 'Three civil war notes', 253.

82 Boyle (ed.), *Memoirs of Master John Shawe*, p. 165.

83 BL, Egerton MS 2647, fo. 371; E. Hope (ed.), *A puritan parish clerk: a commentary on current events made in the registers of S. Mary's church, Beverley, by Nicholas Pearson, parish clerk 1636–1653* (Beverley, no date), p. 7.

84 *Lowndes MS*, HMC, 7th report, appendix (London, 1879), p. 559; HRO, BRS/7/6, BRS/7/9, BRS/7/16; A. C. Wood, *Nottinghamshire in the Civil War* (Oxford, 1937), p. 56.

85 YML, CWT, 44–06–18, *Hull's managing of the kingdom's cause* (London, 1644), p. 17.

86 *The parliamentary or constitutional history of England*, vol. 12, p. 423; Rushworth, *Historical collections*, part 3, vol. 2, p. 282; P. Gaunt, *Oliver Cromwell* (Oxford, 1996), p. 228.

87 Turner (ed.), *The autobiography of Captain John Hodgson*, p. 25; WYRO, Calderdale, Brearcliffe MS, MISC 182; Kendall, 'The civil war as affecting Halifax', 36; TNA, SP 23/177/183.

88 Rushworth, *Historical collections*, part 3, vol. 2, p. 302; BL, E252(19), *A perfect diurnall of some passages in parliament*, 29 January–5 February (London, 1644), p. 223; BL, E252(21), *A perfect diurnall of some passages in parliament*, 12–19 February (London, 1644), p. 235.

89 Firth (ed.), *The life of Cavendish*, p. 199; D. Farr, *John Lambert, Parliamentary Soldier and Cromwellian Major-General* (Woodbridge, 2003), pp. 34–6.

90 YML, CWT, 44–04–19, *A letter sent from the right honourable, the Lord Fairfax, to the Committee of Both Kingdoms: concerning the great victory, lately obtained (by Gods blessing) at Selby in York-shire* (London, 1644), pp. 3–5; *The parliamentary or constitutional history of England*, vol. 13, pp. 172–3; P. R. Newman, 'The defeat of John Belasyse: civil war in Yorkshire, January–April 1644', *YAJ*, 52 (1980), 123.

91 P. Wenham, *The Siege of York, 1644* (York, 2nd edn, 1994), passim; BL, E54(9), *The kingdomes weekly intelligencer*, 2–9 July (London, 1644), p. 500; Bod., MS Fairfax 36, fo. 13r.

92 BL, E2(1), *A continuation of true intelligence from the English and Scottish forces in the north for the service of King and Parliament*, 13 July (London, 1644), p. 6; BL, E2(14), *A more exact relation of the late Battell neer York, by Leon Watson*, 17 July (London, 1644), p. 7; Bod., MS Fairfax 36, fos. 12v–13r.

93 YML, Add. MS 258; BL, E54(19), *A full relation of the late victory obtained through Gods providence by the forces under the command of Generall Lesley, the Lord Fairfax, and the Earl of Manchester*, 11 July (London, 1644), pp. 6–7.

94 P. R. Newman, *Marston Moor* (Chichester, 1981), p. 68; D. Scott, *Politics and War in the Three Stuart Kingdoms, 1637–49* (Basingstoke, 2004), p. 84.

95 BL, E254(28), *Perfect occurrences of parliament*, 30 August–6 September (London, 1644).

Chapter 3

'The brutish general' and the year of victories

This chapter explores Sir Thomas Fairfax's significance in the formation of the New Model Army and in ending the first civil war. His promotion to command the New Model was the most important event in his life and therefore demands close attention (Figure 3). Although the events surrounding his appointment have been intensely studied, few historians have considered the affair from his personal perspective. Cromwell is usually represented as the creator of the New Model Army, pushing Fairfax's role to the periphery. A range of academic opinion upholds that Cromwell was effectively commander 'in all but name', rendering Fairfax naive, overpromoted and politically irrelevant.[1] Popular historians too have claimed that Fairfax 'had no outstanding abilities as a general', and was appointed 'for reasons quite unconnected with his own merits', depicting a simplistic Fairfax whose 'politics were inoffensive', a person 'well liked and trusted on all sides'.[2] A closer investigation of how and why Fairfax was appointed commander-in-chief challenges such views. It fell to Fairfax, not Cromwell, to structure the new army, appoint its officers and overcome political hostility in Parliament before taking the field. Fairfax was better equipped than Cromwell to do this. His concept of honour that stressed humility and shrank from personal advancement helped undermine hostility to his appointment. Yet his lack of ambition should not be interpreted as evidence that he was divorced from Westminster politics. Challenging the usual dismissals of his political relevance, this chapter will argue that his appointment and conduct as general both impacted upon high politics. A reassessment of Fairfax is so essential because the tendency towards a hindsight-driven, Cromwell-centric history has overlooked Fairfax's importance in the birth of the New Model and his personal role in directing the military campaign that defeated the King.

His Excellencie the Lord Fairfax: Generall of
the forces raised by the Parliament
In English, His Integrity hath broken the wilde Ass.

Figure 3 Sir Thomas Fairfax as commander of the New Model Army

I

The background to the New Model Army's creation is too well known to warrant lengthy repetition, but a brief overview is necessary to provide context for reappraising Fairfax's role. After Marston moor, the most committed parliamentarians became increasingly frustrated at their generals' failure to capitalise upon their military advantages. Once the armies of Essex, Manchester and Waller failed to defeat Charles at Newbury on 27 October 1644, there was a growing realisation that a national army was required with a unified command that would overcome regional interests and rivalries to prosecute a sustained war effort. Cromwell believed that several parliamentarian commanders, especially Manchester, had been deliberately sluggish, preferring a negotiated settlement over outright victory. A notoriously venomous exchange followed between Cromwell and Manchester, in which Cromwell argued that if Parliament failed to deliver victory soon the people would tire of the war. Manchester, supported by Parliament's generalissimo, the earl of Essex, felt that Cromwell's championing of sectarian officers and advocating decisive victory over the King was tantamount to treason. Convalescing from his wound in York, Sir Thomas Fairfax had not been directly involved in these disputes, although he was not politically disconnected from them.

Who first proposed Fairfax as general remains uncertain. One possibility is Philip, fourth baron Wharton, who was in regular correspondence with Lord Fairfax at the time. On 5 February 1645 he wrote to Ferdinando that 'both houses have resolved to robbe the north of a good friend of itts and yours'.[3] David Scott and John Adamson believe that Fairfax was proposed as general by 'one of the Saye-St John grandees', with whom Wharton was politically identified, and have suggested Algernon Percy, earl of Northumberland, 'who played a leading role in new-modelling and was a long-time friend of the Fairfax family'. Both Northumberland and Wharton had been prominent in the anti-Essex faction at Westminster, and Adamson has claimed that the Fairfaxes were loyal protectors of the Percy interest in Yorkshire, restraining their troops from spoiling Northumberland's estates.[4]

The Self-Denying Ordinance, first proposed in the House of Commons by Zouch Tate on 9 December 1644, was presented as a bipartisan measure that intended to bar MPs and peers from holding army commissions in order to generate a more professional command. However, its first effect was to remove Essex and Manchester as generals, and the ordinance's proponents well knew that Sir Thomas Fairfax was the foremost eligible commander remaining. Mark Kishlansky has argued that this legislation, rather than the formation of the New Model Army that followed, was the real moment of innovation. The ordinance passed that day in a surprise that affected many; 'a very unexpected vote', John Lambert informed Sir Thomas Fairfax in York.[5]

Objections to the ordinance in the House of Lords were circumvented when the Commons denied sustenance to the old field armies of Essex, Manchester and Waller, thereby forcing their soldiers to re-enlist in the new army. John Adamson has argued that the parliamentary work behind the military reforms that winter was accomplished not by Cromwell, as is so often claimed, but by a 'pro-Fairfax caucus' and 'anti-Essexian' group within the Committee of Both Kingdoms, including Northumberland, Saye, Wharton, Vane and St John. These were leading statesmen of national importance, the latter of whom had married Anne Fairfax's sister, Catherine Vere.[6]

Sir Thomas was commissioned as commander-in-chief of the New Model Army on 21 January 1645. The traditional view, that he owed his appointment to his political apathy, was advanced by Conrad Russell's contention that Fairfax, 'then as later, had no identifiable line on any of the political questions which divided the parliamentarians'. Similarly, Mark Kishlansky argued that Fairfax's uncontroversial promotion 'had a soothing effect' upon the rift opened up by Cromwell's attack on Manchester. This seems unlikely as Cromwell was a highly visible teller for the pro-Fairfax vote in the Commons. Russell and Kishlansky downplayed the Fairfaxes' connections with Westminster, doing little to integrate local and national politics. Both mistakenly believed Sir Thomas rather than Ferdinando was general of the northern army, reflecting a lack of engagement with northern parliamentarianism.[7] Admittedly, Sir Thomas was not noted for his politics in 1644 and he was uninvolved in the acrimony between the southern commanders, but this did not make him an apolitical choice. Several royalists suspected that Sir Thomas 'their new high flying hawk of the North' was implicated in Cromwell's attack on Manchester.[8] The Fairfaxes were known to be among Parliament's most aggressive military commanders. Although he had been absent from London, northern officers in the capital continually kept him and Ferdinando informed of events.[9]

John Adamson initiated a challenge to the view that Fairfax's appointment was apolitical, describing it as a victory for 'the Saye-Northumberland' interest at Westminster, rather than a triumph of consensus decision-making. There is much truth in this, but his view of a peerage-dominated Westminster politics tends to downplay Fairfax's personal significance. He argued that Fairfax, 'apparently lacking in either interest or acumen for politics', was appointed because he 'seemed an able and malleable choice', whose 'mediocrity in politics commended him to the Saye-Northumberland interest at Westminster no less than his distinction in the field'.[10] Ian Gentles has extended Adamson's argument but presents Fairfax in a less passive light, arguing that he was identified as 'a man of known radical connections, who was regarded with suspicion by many'. Gentles described Fairfax as the 'anti-Essex nominee', who was 'imposed as the war party's choice for commander-in-chief' by a Commons' vote of 101 to 69.[11]

Table 1 *The Fairfax interest in the House of Commons, 1640–8*

Name	Constituency	Dates	Notes
Sir William Allanson, alderman	York	1640–8	
John Alured, esq*	Hedon	1640–8	Colonel under Ferdinando
John Anlaby	Scarborough	1647–8	Captain under Ferdinando
Henry Arthington, esq	Pontefract	1646–8	Son-in-law to Ferdinando
Sir John Bourchier, knt*	Ripon	1647–8	Cousin to Mauleverer
Sir Matthew Boynton, bart	Scarborough	1645–7	Son married Saye's daughter
Thomas Chaloner, esq*	Richmond	1645–8	Brother to James Chaloner
James Chaloner, esq	Aldborough	1648	Married Ursula Fairfax
Sir William Constable, bart*	Knaresborough	1642–8	Brother-in-law to Ferdinando
Henry Darley	Northallerton	1640–8	
Ferdinando, baron Fairfax	Yorkshire	1640–8	
Thomas Hoyle, alderman	York	1640–8	
Francis Lascelles, esq	Thirsk	1645–8	Colonel under Ferdinando
Sir Thomas Mauleverer, bart*	Boroughbridge	1640–8	Colonel under Ferdinando
Peregrine Pelham, alderman*	Hull	1640–8	Enemy to Sir John Hotham
Sir William Strickland, bart	Hedon	1640–8	
Thomas Stockdale, esq	Knaresborough	1645–8	War secretary to Ferdinando
Francis Thorpe, esq	Richmond	1645–8	
John Wastell, esq	Northallerton	1640–8	Colonel under Ferdinando
William White, esq	Pontefract	1645–8	Colonel under Ferdinando
Sir Thomas Widdrington, knt	Berwick	1640–8	Son-in-law to Ferdinando

* Denotes signatory of death warrant of Charles I, January 1649

Sources: Oxford DNB; W. W. Bean, *The parliamentary representation of the six northern counties of England* (Hull, 1890); G. E. Cokayne (ed.), *Complete Baronetage* (Gloucester, 1983); A. Gooder, *The Parliamentary Representation of the County of York, 1258–1832, vol. 2* (YASRS, 96, 1937); R. L. Greaves and R. Zaller (eds), *A Biographical Dictionary of British Radicals in the Seventeenth Century* (3 vols, Brighton, 1982); A. J. Hopper, 'A directory of parliamentarian allegiance in Yorkshire during the civil wars', *YAJ*, 73 (2001), 85–122; M. F. Keeler, *The Long Parliament, 1640–1641: A Biographical Study of Its Members* (Philadelphia, 1954); J. R. MacCormack, *Revolutionary Politics in the Long Parliament* (Cambridge, Massachusetts, 1973); D. Underdown, 'Party management in the recruiter elections, 1645–1648', *EHR*, 83 (1968).

Conversely, there has always been suspicion that political historians have neglected the excellent military reasons for Fairfax's appointment. While Austin Woolrych agreed that Fairfax 'had no political leanings', he placed less emphasis upon political considerations, asserting that Fairfax was appointed primarily on his military merits.[12] There is a good case for this but it risks accepting the retrospective polemic of Fairfax's chaplain, Joshua Sprigge, who claimed that Fairfax was appointed 'upon no other grounds than the observation of his valour'. Writing in 1647, Sprigge sought to downplay the political nature of Fairfax's appointment to minimise the army's increasing unpopularity.[13]

These are all tenable views, but they risk deflating the importance of the Fairfax family by 1645, and denying them a political standpoint. Against all odds, the Fairfaxes' leadership had played an important part in defeating the northern royalists. Ferdinando's generalship had produced more success with drastically fewer resources than Essex, Manchester and Waller. This success mattered a great deal because to contemporaries, the northern theatre of war was not the sideshow it has become for many historians. Far from the Fairfaxes being Northumberland's grateful or submissive clients, by 1645 they had constructed a formidable political network of their own, with an influence stretching from its West Riding base northwards to the Scottish border.[14] By 1647 Ferdinando Fairfax had the largest personal following in the House of Commons of any MP, with twenty members among his family, former officers and associates (Table 1). There is a danger in overstating the Fairfaxes' control over these MPs, many of whom considered themselves as family and friends rather than clients. Several, including Ferdinando's son-in-law, the well connected Sir Thomas Widdrington, had become important figures in their own right. Among the most active MPs, Widdrington was counsellor at law to Northumberland and chaired the Commons' standing committees for northern affairs. Rather than being national political figures at Westminster, the Fairfaxes' political leadership was restricted to northern England. When Ferdinando's commission was supplanted by the Northern Association in 1645, David Scott has argued that this body 'was dominated by the Fairfax interest and again tended to articulate the concerns of Yorkshire and the counties to the north'.[15] From 1645 Ferdinando utilised his son's influence as general to place 'recruiter' MPs and increase the family's connections at Westminster.[16] Although attempts to win seats in southern England miscarried, Fairfax's influence helped return nine recruiter MPs in Yorkshire between 1645 and 1647, establishing an important regional political force broadly sympathetic to the Independents and the New Model Army.

II

Depictions of Fairfax's appointment as apolitical have become orthodox because of the historical preoccupation with the quarrel between Cromwell and Manchester. There has also been an important failure to connect northern and Westminster politics. Although prior to 1645 Sir Thomas Fairfax was hardly a figure of national importance, he nevertheless became one when the northern politics in which he was involved began to feature on the national stage. At the heart of this politics was the enmity between the Fairfaxes and the Hothams, the repercussions of which were keenly felt at Westminster contemporaneously with the Self-Denying Ordinance. Although the Fairfaxes approved of removing Essex and Manchester, their prime concern was in trying Sir John Hotham and his son for attempting to betray Hull to the royalists. Cromwell's quarrel with Manchester and the Hothams' trials were intimately linked, but the connections between them have been neglected. The Hothams were tried by court martial at the Guildhall, London, with Sir William Waller in the chair, beginning on 30 November 1644. The affair was intensely political and little doubt remained over the Fairfaxes' position at the time, even if historians have largely ignored it since. Those that supported the Fairfaxes' concerns for retribution against the Hothams became advocates of new modelling the army. Those that urged clemency opposed the new army and Fairfax as its commander.

So rather than being apolitical, the Fairfaxes became the allies of Lord Saye, Oliver St John, Oliver Cromwell and the anti-Essex interest. This made such sense because the Hothams were still strongly favoured at Westminster among Essex's supporters, often headed in the Commons by Sir Philip Stapleton, a son-in-law of Sir John Hotham and commander of Essex's lifeguard.[17] Essex had shielded the Hothams from Lord Fairfax's authority in 1642–3, and Essex's supporters shared the Hothams' fear of 'the popularity' and desire for a negotiated treaty. The Fairfaxes' supporters were anxious that Essex would delay the trials by not appointing a president of the council of war. Essex desired his own colonels to try John Hotham, encouraging fears in the Commons that he would engineer an acquittal.[18]

The fate of the Hothams became a major test of the political strength of the Fairfaxes and their allies. Although both Ferdinando and Sir Thomas were absent in Yorkshire, they still fielded thirty witnesses for the prosecution.[19] The Hothams were accused of corresponding with the enemy, endeavouring to betray Hull and denying Fairfax weapons and ammunition, thereby endangering his soldiers' lives on Adwalton moor. The enmity between the Fairfax and Hotham interests grew bitter, personal and violent. In June 1644 John Hotham's former father-in-law, Sir John Wray, launched a Commons' motion that Hotham should either stand trial or be released. Shortly before, three of

Wray's family assaulted one of Fairfax's officers, a Mr Boynton, in New Palace yard.[20] Boynton had recently endorsed Cromwell's complaints in Parliament against John Hotham's friend, Lord Willoughby of Parham. Willoughby had to be formally cleared of complicity with the Hothams, as it transpired he had been incriminatingly named in John Hotham's letters to Newcastle.[21]

The Wrays' violence may also have been in revenge for the Boynton family's prominence in Sir John Hotham's arrest. The Wrays' victim was most probably one of Sir Matthew Boynton's two sons, Francis or Matthew, both of whom were colonels under Lord Fairfax and leading prosecution witnesses at Sir John's trial.[22] Francis Boynton had married a daughter of Saye, the peer who soon became instrumental in ensuring Sir Thomas Fairfax's appointment as general. Sir Matthew Boynton, hailed by the royalist press as 'a declared Anabaptist', had been involved in the Saybrook project with Fairfax's uncle, Sir William Constable, both of whom attended the English church at Arnhem in 1640. The Fairfaxes' determination to eliminate the Hothams naturally identified them with the anti-Essex interest with whom they already had familial ties and connections.[23]

Essex's protégés Sir Philip Stapleton and Lionel Copley were prominent in defending Sir John Hotham in December 1644. Sir John's masterly defence accused the Fairfaxes of failing to aid him against the Queen and claimed that their advisers, chiefly Thomas Stockdale and John Alured, had hatched a conspiracy against him. Sir John complained his officers had been imprisoned for 'halfe a yeare to try if miserie would ripen a confession'. Despite his efforts, on 30 December 1644 the House of Commons voted for Sir John's execution by ninety-four votes to forty-six. Predictably, Oliver Cromwell was teller for the anti-Hotham vote, with Sir Philip Stapleton opposing him. The following day Sir John was being led towards the scaffold on Tower Hill when a reprieve from the House of Lords dramatically halted proceedings. On 1 January the Commons passed a motion that no postponement could be granted without the approval of both houses. John Hotham was executed that day, and Sir John the day after, despite a further Commons' motion to spare him.[24]

The beheading of the Hothams was accomplished against strong opposition, and it bolstered the Fairfaxes' position locally and nationally. The Fairfaxes' political links to Essex's enemies were solidified right at the very time when Essex's replacement was being discussed. Essex and some of his key supporters clearly distrusted Fairfax, embittered that his rise had been at their expense. Matters were only smoothed over by Fairfax's tact, forbearance and humility. So, in contrast to the usual hurried explanations, Fairfax's appointment as general was not apolitical but highly divisive, and unwelcome for many. His political position was so evident that it was stained in the blood of his predecessor's friends and supporters. His military reputation was such that he was not appointed as second choice because Cromwell's candidature was not yet politically acceptable. When Fairfax entered London to accept command of the New Model Army on 18 February 1645, two notorious sectarians were at his side to herald his arrival on the national stage: his uncle, Sir William Constable, and Sir John Hotham's arch-enemy, Colonel John Alured. Small wonder that James Chaloner warned Lord Fairfax of his son's maligners, observing that Sir Thomas's arrival in London was 'as little pleasing to some here as to them at Oxford'.[25]

Once Fairfax was appointed general, Essex and Manchester's faction courted the Scots hoping they would provide a military counterweight to the New Model Army. This was a dangerous political strategy as it risked alienating northern MPs and solidifying parliamentary support for the Fairfaxes. Anti-Scots feeling increased among Yorkshire's parliamentarians from 1644 to 1646 because the Scots army, largely quartered in the north, absorbed all the revenue from the sequestered property in the region. On 7 November 1644 the Fairfaxes had complained about the Scots cavalry being wintered in Yorkshire, arguing the county was too overburdened even to support its own troops. Some £220,000, originally allocated to the northern army's arrears, was granted to the Scots, leaving Ferdinando's army with a mere £20,000. Most of the Yorkshire assessment also went to the Scots. The northern officers went unpaid while Parliament voted the Scots £400,000 at the end of the first civil war. Unsurprisingly the animosity of Ferdinando's officers towards the Scots was sharpened by this grievance; they had recruited and equipped forces for Parliament out of their own pockets only for their estates to suffer under royalist and then Scottish occupation. After Marston moor the failure of the Scots to intervene more decisively against the royalists encouraged the belief that they were deliberately prolonging their stay in England to live off free quarter and parliamentary subsidies. This anti-Scots politics was another way in which the northern interest, headed in the Commons by Lord Fairfax and Sir Thomas Widdrington, became identified with Northumberland, Wharton, the parliamentary Independents and the New Model Army. David Scott has even argued that the northern counties became 'the parliamentary Independents' principal regional power base'.[26]

III

By 1645 the Fairfaxes were integrated into the political network of Independents at Westminster through their enmity with the Hothams and their anti-Scots politics. This section will demonstrate how internecine conflict within the parliamentarian coalition persisted after Fairfax's appointment as general. The next political struggle erupted over Fairfax's choice of officers. On 18 February 1645, Widdrington informed Ferdinando that Sir Thomas had met the Speaker and had gone 'to wayte upon my Lord Generall'. Kishlansky has hypothesised that Fairfax heeded Essex's advice to choose whole regiments wherever possible and preserve existing command structures. Yet Fairfax clashed with Essex again, insisting on officers the earl found objectionable and embroiling himself in political controversy over the new army's structure. On 1 March 1645 the House of Commons heard that speculation over which MPs supported or opposed Essex extended to lists passed among prisoners in the Compter.[27]

Kishlansky has downplayed this struggle, stressing evidence of continuity and consensus. He emphasised the lack of novelty in the New Model at the time of its inception, rightly pointing out that it was a merger of Parliament's three southern armies and maintained by Parliament's pre-existing administrative committees. He even claimed it was 'the last great achievement of consensus decision-making' by the Long Parliament. However, his view that the formation of the New Model was 'a rather drab affair' strains credibility. In 1994 Ian Gentles suggested this historical revisionism was overblown. Arguing for the very points Kishlansky sought to discredit, Gentles reasserted that the New Model's establishment 'was attended by intense political conflict', that it was 'a fundamental turning-point' in the war and 'a great alteration of the war strategy of the Long Parliament'.[28]

Gentles examined Fairfax's proposed list of officers and an article that published this list with the House of Lords' annotations, replacements and alterations.[29] Despite Kishlansky's contention that Fairfax was ignorant of the personnel that composed the southern armies, Fairfax knew his business and produced his list of officers within ten days of arriving in London. One novel aspect of the new army was the relative youth of its commanders. Fairfax was only just thirty-three in 1645 whereas Essex was fifty-four, Waller forty-six and Manchester forty-three. Many of Fairfax's colonels were also relatively young: Ireton was thirty-four, Fleetwood twenty-seven, Hammond and Ingoldsby twenty-four, Harley twenty-one and Montagu only twenty. The Commons debated and raised objections against eight of Fairfax's nominations. Right from the outset Fairfax was prepared to disobey Parliament. When the Commons voted to remove his nomination of Captain William Bough, he ignored their order, retained Bough on his list, and the House relented two days later. He wrote a personal letter to the House which overwhelmed their objections to Major Thomas Harrison's appointment. He also circumvented Parliament by granting colonelcies to Nathaniel Rich and Henry Ireton.[30]

Securing the House of Lords' concurrence to Fairfax's list proved more difficult. On 4 March, Widdrington observed that there were as many who plotted to crush Fairfax's new army 'in the budd' as there were others who wanted to bring it to perfection. On 11 March he complained that Fairfax's list was disapproved of by the Lords 'with a recommendation of other persons in there places'. The London trader Thomas Juxon noted that the Lords opposed

Fairfax's army, 'knowing that the war will neither be carried on to their, nor the king's interests by this'. Juxon felt their tampering with Fairfax's list showed 'how little they regard the good of the nation, their peerage being their great idol'. The clause in Fairfax's commission obliging him to protect the King's person had been removed, angering many of Essex's faction further. Essex, Stapleton and Holles headed opposition to Fairfax's list in alliance with the Scots. Juxon thought this was not out of affection for the Scots, 'but in revenge and despite to the other party'.[31]

Although the Lords quickly approved the officers for six of Fairfax's regiments on 6 March, they spent the next four days subjecting the other three-quarters of Fairfax's list to what Gentles calls 'microscopic scrutiny'. They objected to 56 of his remaining 148 officers. Their opposition had a broader focus than hostility to Fairfax; many of their objections were directed at officers who had testified against Manchester during his quarrel with Cromwell. Essex, Manchester and the other peers knew a great deal about the views of the men they sought to promote or exclude: 'Known religious Independents, win-the-war radicals and enemies of Manchester, or men who would in future show their radical colours, were to be replaced by Scots, friends and clients of the earl of Essex and future political Presbyterians.' Only two of the fifty-six cases flouted this pattern.[32]

The Scots commissioners complained at their exclusion from selecting the new army's officers, so Fairfax responded by not commissioning Scotsmen. He offended the House of Lords by replacing the Scottish officers of Lawrence Crawford's regiment with his own nominees headed by Isaac Ewer. He had not forgiven Crawford's costly indiscipline at the siege of York, for which he later claimed Crawford should have stood trial.[33] The Lords also tried to replace Colonel Thomas Rainborough with Colonel William Ogleby, a Scots 'protégé of Essex'. Essex had formerly tried to appoint Ogleby as sergeant-major-general in the north in November 1642, when the wily Ferdinando tactfully responded that although the Scots officers had joined him, 'we are so straitened that we can have no money to pay them'. Ferdinando appointed John Gifford instead, so by 1645 Essex had twice been outmanoeuvred by the Fairfaxes in frustrating Ogleby's appointment.[34]

Eventually, Fairfax's supporters foiled the Lords' objections by persuading the City magistrates to make their £80,000 loan to establish the army conditional upon there being no altering of Fairfax's list. The list was finally passed in the Lords on 18 March, only when the House allowed Saye to use the proxy of the earl of Mulgrave, Fairfax's grandfather. When Essex tried the same ploy with his half-brother the earl of Clanricarde's proxy, he was disqualified due to Clanricarde's catholicism. Fairfax's list was forced through against the votes of the earls of Essex, Manchester, Denbigh, Bolingbroke, Rutland, Stamford, and the lords Bruce, Maynard, Berkeley and Grey.[35] Nevertheless Holles and

Stapleton's attempt to exempt Essex from the Self-Denying Ordinance was only defeated by 100 votes to 93. Subsequently a revised Self-Denying Ordinance was passed that allowed peers and MPs to seek reappointment to office, so Essex's return to command was a continual threat for Fairfax. The noble generals Essex, Manchester, Stamford and Denbigh 'bitterly recorded their dissents' to Fairfax's list in the House of Lords. Removed from their military posts, Essex, Manchester, Robartes and Stapleton became freer to exert influence within the Committee of Both Kingdoms, and it was feared that acting in concert with the Scots, they might use this committee to sabotage the military reforms by starving Fairfax of funding. With this in mind, Lord Savile informed George, Lord Digby early in 1645 'if yow can but beate or disgrace Fairfaxe his Independent armie, Essex and the Scots will be greater than ever, which I assure yow they look for certainlie; and ... will not only revive but improve the former designe, and doe the King's business the safest, speediest and noblest way'. Until his death in September 1646, Essex would conspire for his restoration as general in Fairfax's place.[36]

After the resignations of Essex and Manchester, Juxon noted that many soldiers refused to continue serving, 'and this not only in scorn to Sir Thomas but to ruin the army and make us intreat their help again' so that Essex would be recalled to command.[37] The attitudes harboured by some of Essex's supporters are revealed by the acerbic remarks of Sir Samuel Luke, governor of Newport Pagnell. Soon after Fairfax's appointment he wished the new army 'as good success as they have formerly had under our old general'. Given the disastrous surrender of Essex's army in Cornwall on 2 September 1644 this was not much of an endorsement. In June Luke scorned Fairfax's men as drunkards and when Fairfax unsurprisingly refused to dine with him, he turned on Fairfax's major-general, Philip Skippon, blaming him for having 'dealt so unworthily' with Essex in Cornwall. Luke assured himself 'I am confident the Lord will reward them in due time for all their works of darkness.'[38] With friends such as these, the construction of the New Model was no easy matter.

The royalists were dismissive of Fairfax and Skippon's achievement of putting the New Model into the field and the King's confidence remained high. In May 1645 Charles wrote to his queen that Fairfax was the 'rebels new brutish general'. By this he probably meant Fairfax's low social status when compared to Essex. The King had usually preferred negotiating with Essex rather than Parliament; he understood how to deal with the ambitions of an overmighty nobleman far more than how to deal with the self-denial and humility that governed Fairfax's deportment.[39] It is also conceivable that 'brutish' was referring to Fairfax's uncompromising military reputation and his association with non-gentry and sectarian officers. Perhaps memories of Heworth moor lingered in the royal mind. The King and his lifeguards may even have believed that Fairfax had boxed General Browne's ears or that the pair had 'cudgell'd one another', such was their perception of disunity among the boorish rebel command prior to Naseby.[40]

The Committee of Both Kingdoms has been heavily criticised for retaining direction of the New Model's strategy from April to June 1645. With Essex, Manchester and Waller assiduously attending, this committee deprived Fairfax of full command and split the New Model into three parts, sending 2500 horse to assist Leven's Scots and 4000 men to relieve Taunton. Essex, Manchester and Waller exercised their habitual caution, fearing that Fairfax was hot-headed enough to lose the war in a single day. Malcolm Wanklyn has recently defended their strategy, arguing that the committee performed their groundwork well by insuring that Fairfax's army would outnumber the royalists at Naseby.[41] Yet Wanklyn may have overestimated parliamentarian solidarity. Even once Sir Thomas Fairfax was installed as general, Essex's faction still endeavoured political revenge. In April 1645 Sir Philip Stapleton's bid to associate the six northern counties was probably an attempt to restrain Lord Fairfax's political power in the north. In May, Stapleton argued in Parliament that Sir Thomas Fairfax's main force should be tied into the siege of Oxford. There was plentiful speculation that Essex and Manchester's continued ability to influence strategy through the Committee of Both Kingdoms was prejudicial to military success. In June, Stapleton attacked Hotham's old enemy, Peregrine Pelham, MP for Hull, for having said that Essex and Manchester 'were unfit to manage ye affaires of ye Warr & yt it could not prosper as long as they were trusted'.[42] As a result of these ongoing political battles, Fairfax was only granted freedom from the committee's direction after the royalists had captured and sacked Leicester with shocking brutality.[43]

IV

This final section examines how Fairfax's initial conduct as general and his management of the army impacted upon national politics. The success of Fairfax and Skippon in restructuring the army and placating the soldiers' discontent in spring 1645 was critical for the parliamentary cause. Their new establishment could not embrace all serving officers under Essex, Manchester and Waller. Many officers, sergeants and corporals accepted a reduction to the ranks largely due to the tact and persuasive skills of Fairfax, Skippon and those chosen by them. On 8 April, when Skippon reorganised his regiment at Windsor, one cashiered officer complained that 'he had rather parted with his wife then his company'.[44] Improvements in military discipline have long been regarded critical to the New Model's success, and this was personally associated with Fairfax himself. Fairfax's stance as a stern disciplinarian was facilitated by the New Model's more regular pay. In 1644 Fairfax had punished his wagonmaster for taking bribes, requiring him to stand in Maxfield market in Cheshire 'on a tubb with a paper on his breste declaringe his offence three market daies'.[45] In November 1645 the *Moderate intelligencer* reported Fairfax having a soldier's tongue bored through with a hot iron for swearing. During its first campaign the New Model earned a reputation among civilians for being comparatively well disciplined and this accelerated the King's defeat as the inhabitants of royalist-held regions became increasingly unco-operative with demands of cavalier commanders. Unlike Essex before him, Fairfax was deeply conscious of sparing civilian populations from contact with the military, a concern especially evidenced in his restrictions of the New Model's movement prior to Naseby.[46]

A detailed account of the Naseby campaign is unnecessary here as there is an excellent recent study by Glenn Foard, but Fairfax's battlefield role stands in need of revision. Naseby is the victory for which Cromwell is most remembered and credited, yet Ian Gentles has argued that if one thing was evident at the battle 'it was the central role of Sir Thomas Fairfax'. He claims that while Clarendon, Abbott, Gardiner, Firth, Woolrych and Young concentrated on Cromwell's significance in the battle, 'the eye witness accounts place much more emphasis on Fairfax's role'.[47] Fairfax ignored the House of Lords' refusal to allow him to appoint Cromwell as lieutenant-general of horse, and on the eve of battle Fairfax was on horseback personally scouting enemy positions and testing his sentries until dawn. He knew from his scout John Tarrant that the King was without Sir George Goring's cavalry.[48] Rather than stationing himself in one place, he rode from regiment to regiment during the battle giving orders, and then leading Cromwell's cavalry reserves to break the exposed royalist infantry. Despite being personally engaged in this close quarter fighting, he held back from the initial attack, reformed the New Model's line of battle and judged the optimum moment to personally lead the co-ordinated final charge that swept the royalists from the field.[49] Most of the newsbooks describing the battle highlighted Fairfax's personal courage in inspiring his men to victory. Such descriptions were conventional, but some suggested that Fairfax had transcended the limits of human spirit: 'Sir, had you seen him, and how his spirit was raised, it would have made an impression in you never to be obliterated.' The writer praised God, Fairfax, Skippon and Cromwell for the victory, in that order.[50] Another newsbook described how Fairfax led the second charge after the rout of the royalist left wing: 'The valour that Sir Thomas Fairfax manifested just upon the charge, was a great incouragement to the Souldiers: his Spirit was so raised, that it was admired by all men.'[51] Another newsbook remarked upon Fairfax's 'alacrity of spirit', and that he 'promised by his countenance Victory'. It added that 'before the fight his former lookes were like a dead man, to what he had when he went to ingage', and he 'had a spirit heightened above the ordinary Spirit of man, he was to and againe in the Front, carrying Orders, bringing on Divisions in midst of

Dangers, with gallant bravery, and received not the least wound; though he ingaged bareheaded, and routed the enemy'.[52]

It is often forgotten that Fairfax sent two accounts of the battle to Parliament. The first was sent by a boy on 16 June, and the second to Speaker Lenthall. The latter praised the steadfastness of his commanders, in particular the wounded Skippon, Ireton and Butler, and it also showed that Fairfax, like Cromwell, was not too meek to remind Parliament of its duty, desiring that 'the honour of this great never to be forgotten mercy, may be given to God in an extraordinary day of thanksgiveing; And that it may be improved to the good of his Church, and this kingdome'.[53] After Naseby, Fairfax marched the New Model swiftly into the west to deal with Goring's royalist army. Sir Thomas informed his father that the victory at Langport on 10 July had prevented Goring from being reinforced by royalists from south Wales and the Cornish under Sir Richard Grenville, 'so as we cannot esteeme this mercy less all things considered then that of Naseby fight'.[54] Fairfax once again sent a letter to the Speaker to relate the victory to Parliament, significantly entrusting Major Thomas Harrison, the noted religious radical, with its delivery.[55]

From July 1645, Fairfax was presented with a fresh challenge by the West Country clubmen movement. Unlike other parliamentary generals, Fairfax was well suited to dealing with them. Having led the Bradford and Halifax clubmen in 1643, he possessed the skills required for successful negotiation with armed popular movements. Although the Devon and Somerset clubmen of 1645 were less explicitly anti-royalist than their West Riding counterparts of 1642, many clubmen from north-east Somerset rallied to Fairfax's banner during the siege of Bristol in September 1645.[56] Another clubmen uprising in north Devon demonstrated their allegiance by crying out 'a Fairfax a Fairfax' and disarming royalist troops that fell within their power.[57] David Scott has praised Fairfax's 'careful handling of the clubmen', and 'ability to subdue, and in some cases harness, the considerable military strength of the clubmen'. Ian Gentles agrees that this was a 'diplomatic and military triumph' for Fairfax.[58] Fairfax's ability to channel the clubmen's popular politics in a parliamentarian direction certainly hastened the royalist defeat.

After Langport, Fairfax had the confidence to dictate army strategy personally. Overruling his council's decision, he turned the army back to besiege Bristol. The rank and file were mustered on 3 September and Fairfax asked them if they wanted to storm the city. Their affirmative response rebuked the doubters on his council and underlined his personal standing with the rank and file.[59] On 4 September Fairfax summoned Rupert to surrender the city. His chosen words provide a revealing glimpse into his political thinking at the time: 'the King in Supream Acts concerning the whole State, is not to be advised by men of whom the Law takes no notice, but by His Parliament, the great Councell of the Kingdom'. As two of Fairfax's uncles had been killed fighting for Rupert's mother in the Palatinate,[60] Fairfax's admonishing of Rupert had a gritty, personal edge: 'And let all *England* judge, whether the burning of its Towns, ruining of its Cities, and destroying its people, be a good requital from a person of your family, which hath had the Prayers, Tears, Purses, and Blood of its Parliament and people.'[61] When Bristol surrendered soon after, Fairfax confided to his father that 'it would be happy for the Kingdom' if Rupert left England.[62]

Mark Stoyle has credited Fairfax with averting a bloodbath in Cornwall, despite calls for vengeance on the Cornish for their brutal treatment of Essex's army in September 1644. After the fall of Dartmouth and battle of Torrington, Fairfax gave Cornish royalist soldiers two shillings each to return home. News spread of Fairfax's lenience and his troops' discipline. Thomas Juxon noted how 'Sir Thomas and his army conquered not only by the sword [but also by] love, especially that county [Cornwall] who were thought irreconcilable.' On 8 September 1645 Fairfax wrote to Cornwall's high sheriff, addressing the Cornish as if they were 'semi-autonomous players in the conflict', offering them the chance to claim their allegiance had been forced by unscrupulous cavaliers. This tactful approach bore political fruit when on 5 March 1646 the Cornish gentry surrendered at Millbrook isolating the royalist general, Lord Hopton, who was forced to surrender ten days later.[63]

V

Parliament's victory in the first civil war cannot be ascribed to any one individual, and an overemphasis on Fairfax's role would prove as questionable as a preoccupation with Cromwell. Fairfax's generalship was so successful partly because he was the beneficiary of the administrative improvements brought by his forces enjoying better finance and a unified command. Fairfax's achievements in instilling greater discipline in his men and in advancing less damaging relations with civilian populations were only possible once his men were enjoying more regular pay and provision. Fairfax's temperament was well suited to negotiating the political minefield brought by his appointment as general. It is worth pausing to consider what might have happened if his wound at Helmsley had proved mortal. The formation of the New Model Army would certainly have been more problematic without him, especially as there appears to have been so little discussion of rival candidates.

In 1645 Fairfax grew in confidence to become a significant political operator, especially with regard to military affairs. Supported by the Independents and his father's interest in the Commons, and the Saye-Northumberland group in the Lords, he furthered his family's political alignments forged by their demolition of the Hothams and conduct of the northern war. Fairfax's energetic leadership style and his good working relationships with subordinates undoubtedly created a more effective army command. Admittedly, his task was aided by royalist strategic mistakes prior to Naseby and Langport, and by the King's undermining of Rupert from August 1645. Yet by not dispersing his army into winter quarters as his predecessors had, Fairfax allowed the royalists little time to recover. When the King was unable to provide the strong leadership to forestall the collapse of his cause, Fairfax, unlike his predecessors, possessed the finances, resources and above all the will to finish the matter.[64]

NOTES

1   C. Hill, *God's Englishman: Oliver Cromwell and the English Revolution* (London, 1970), p. 72; S. E. Prall (ed.), *The Puritan Revolution: A Documentary History* (London, 1968), p. 310; J. Morrill, 'Introduction', in J. Morrill (ed.), *Oliver Cromwell and the English Revolution* (Harlow, 1990), p. 13.

2   Ashley wrongly depicted the Fairfaxes as 'an old Scottish family' and that Sir Thomas was in his early twenties when he took command in 1645: J. Ridley, *The Roundheads* (London, 1976), p. 128; M. Ashley, *Cromwell's Generals* (London, 1954), pp. 14–16.

3   BL, Add. MS 18979, fo. 173.

4   D. Scott, *Politics and War in the Three Stuart Kingdoms, 1637–49* (Basingstoke, 2004), p. 88; J. Adamson, 'The baronial context of the English civil war', *TRHS*, 5th series, 40 (1990), 116.

5   M. Kishlansky, 'The case of the army truly stated: the creation of the New Model Army', *Past and Present*, 81 (1978), 58; BL, Sloane MS 1519, fo. 37.

6   J. Adamson, 'The triumph of oligarchy: the management of war and Committee of Both Kingdoms, 1644–1645', in J. Peacey and C. Kyle (eds), *Parliament at Work: Parliamentary Committees, Political Power and Public Access in Early Modern England* (Woodbridge, 2002), pp. 122–5; Markham, p. 15.

7   C. Russell, *The Crisis of Parliaments: English History, 1509–1660* (Oxford, 1971), p. 358; Kishlansky, 'The case of the army truly stated', 63.

8   M. A. Gibb, *The Lord General: A Life of Thomas Fairfax* (London, 1938), p. 89.

9   BL, Add. MS 18979, fos. 149, 174, 178, 182, 184; BL, Sloane MS 1519, fo. 37.

10 Adamson, 'The baronial context', 116.

11 I. Gentles, *The New Model Army in England, Ireland and Scotland, 1645–1653* (Oxford, 1992), pp. 17–19, 23; I. Gentles, 'The choosing of officers for the New Model Army', *Historical Research*, 67 (1994), 266.

12 A. Woolrych, *Britain in Revolution, 1625–1660* (Oxford, 2002), pp. 304–5.

13 J. Sprigge, *Anglia rediviva* (London, 1647), p. 8.

14 In September 1646, Ferdinando stood against Northumberland for the lord lieutenant of Yorkshire: BL, Add. MS 10114, fo. 19r.

15 D. Underdown, *Pride's Purge: Politics in the Puritan Revolution* (Oxford, 1971), p. 48; D. Scott, 'Sir Thomas Widdrington', *Oxford DNB*; D. Scott, 'Motives for king-killing', in J. Peacey (ed.), *The Regicides and the Execution of Charles I* (Basingstoke, 2001), p. 139.

16 BL, Add. MS 21506, fo. 41.

17 J. R. MacCormack, *Revolutionary Politics in the Long Parliament* (Cambridge, Massachusetts, 1973), p. 5; A. J. Hopper, 'Sir Philip Stapleton', *Oxford DNB*; Clarendon, *State papers collected by Edward, earl of Clarendon* (Oxford, 1773), vol. 2, p. 184.

18 BL, Add. MS 31116, fo. 83r.

19 A. M. W. Stirling, *The Hothams: Being the Chronicles of the Hothams of Scorborough and South Dalton from their hitherto unpublished family papers* (London, 1918), vol. 1, p. 89.

20 BL, Add. MS 31116, fos. 114r, 142r–v, 171r; *Cowper MS*, HMC, 12th report, appendix, part 2 (London, 1888), vol. 2, p. 342; *JHC*, vol. 3, p. 387.

21 *Ibid.*, fo. 235r; *Portland MS*, HMC, 29, 13th report, appendix, part 1 (London, 1891), vol. 1, supplement, pp. 702, 704; *Lowndes MS*, HMC, 7th report, appendix (London, 1879), p. 564.

22 Other prosecution witnesses in Sir John Hotham's trial included Colonel John Lambert, Captain John Lawson, Captain Lawrence Moyer, John Saltmarsh, John Bernard and Maccabeus Hollis: BL, E59(2), *A true relation of the discovery of a most desperate and dangerous plot, for the delivering up, and surprising of the townes of Hull and Beverley*, 4 July (London, 1643), pp. 5–6; BL, E21(2), *Mercurius civicus*, 28 November–5 December (London, 1644), p. 736.

23 J. T. Cliffe, *The Yorkshire Gentry from the Reformation to the Civil War* (London, 1969), pp. 274, 306, 308; J. T. Cliffe, *Puritans in Conflict: The Puritan Gentry During and After the Civil Wars* (London, 1988), p. 104; B. English, *The Great Landowners of East Yorkshire, 1530–1910* (Hemel Hempstead, 1990), p. 253n; P. W. Thomas (ed.), *The English Revolution III, Newsbooks I, Oxford Royalist* (London, 1971), vol. 1, p. 351.

24 HULA, Hotham MS, DDHO/1/34–5; BL, Add. MS 31116, fos. 182r–183v; J. Rushworth, *Historical collections* (London, 1721), vol. 5, pp. 745–50; D. Scott, 'Sir John Hotham', *Oxford DNB*; Hopper, 'Sir Philip Stapleton'.

25 BL, E258(27), *A perfect diurnall of some passages in Parliament*, 17–24 February (London, 1645), p. 649; R. Bell (ed.), *The Fairfax correspondence: memorials of the civil war* (London, 1849), vol. 1, p. 162.

26 P. Edwards, 'Logistics and supply', in J. Kenyon and J. Ohlmeyer (eds), *The Civil Wars: A Military History of England, Scotland and Ireland, 1638–1660* (Oxford, 2002), p. 263; *CSP dom. 1644–5* (London, 1890), p. 104; D. Scott, 'The "northern gentlemen", the parliamentary Independents, and Anglo-Scottish relations in the Long Parliament', *Historical Journal*, 42:2 (1999), 355–7.

27 Gentles, 'The choosing of officers', 266; BL, Add. MS 18979, fo. 178; Kishlansky, 'The case of the army truly stated', 65; BL, Add. MS 31116, fo. 196v.

28 Kishlansky, 'The case of the army truly stated', 57–9, 68; M. Kishlansky, *The Rise of the New Model Army* (Cambridge, 1979), chapter 2; Gentles, 'The choosing of officers', 264, 265n, 285.

29 Gentles, 'The choosing of officers', 265n; R. K. G. Temple, 'The original officer list of the New Model Army', *Historical Research*, 59 (1986), 50–77.

30 Kishlansky, 'The case of the army truly stated', 65; Gentles, 'The choosing of officers', 266n, 267.

31 BL, Add. MS 18979, fos. 182, 184; K. Lindley and D. Scott (eds), *The Journal of Thomas Juxon 1644–1647* (Camden Society, 5th series, 13, 1999), pp. 74–6.

32 Gentles, 'The choosing of officers', 269, 272, 279.

33 Bod., MS Fairfax 36, fo. 12v; Gentles, 'The choosing of officers', 270.

34 Gentles, 'The choosing of officers', 272; TNA, SP 28/262/iii/271; SP 28/262/iv/380–1; SP 28/262/iv/389; BL, Add. MS 18979, fo. 130r; BL, Add. MS 31116, fo. 33v.

35 Gentles, 'The choosing of officers', 282–3; Kishlansky, 'The case of the army truly stated', 69n.

36 Gentles, 'The choosing of officers', 265, 283–4; Adamson, 'The triumph of oligarchy', p. 122; Scott, *Politics and War*, pp. 92, 96, 126.

37 Lindley and Scott (eds), *The Journal of Thomas Juxon*, p. 79.

38 H. G. Tibbut (ed.), *The Letter Books of Sir Samuel Luke, 1644–1645* (Publications of the Bedfordshire Historical Records Society, 42, 1963), p. 324.

39 YML, XX1.F.25(7), *The king's cabinet opened* (London, 1645); Adamson, 'The baronial context', 111.

40 C. V. Wedgwood, *The King's War, 1641–1647* (Manchester, 1958), p. 422; G. Foard, *Naseby, The Decisive Campaign* (Barnsley, 2004), p. 132.

41 M. Wanklyn and F. Jones, *A Military History of the English Civil War, 1642–1646: Strategy and Tactics* (Harlow, 2005), pp. 231, 238–40.

42 BL, Add. MS 31116, fos. 203v, 215r; Clarendon, *State papers*, vol. 2, p. 184; BL, E256(45), *A perfect diurnall of some passages in Parliament*, 2–9 December (London, 1644), p. 561.

43 Woolrych, *Britain in Revolution*, pp. 312–13; Foard, *Naseby*, p. 94; Tibbut (ed.), *The Letter Books of Sir Samuel Luke*, pp. 554–5.

44 BL, Harleian MS 252, fo. 331r–v.

45 TNA, SP 19/128/123.

46 BL, E309(25), *The moderate intelligencer*, 13–20 November (London, 1645), p. 204; Foard, *Naseby*, p. 175.

47 I. Gentles, 'The Civil Wars in England', in Kenyon and Ohlmeyer (eds), *The Civil Wars*, p. 124; Gentles, *New Model Army*, pp. 59–60, 460.

48 Bod., MS Tanner 59, fo. 750.

49 Woolrych, *Britain in Revolution*, pp. 314–18; Foard, *Naseby*, pp. 270, 275, 281.

50 BL, E288(22), *A true relation of a victory obtained over the Kings forces by the army of Sir Thomas Fairfax: being fought between Harborough, and Nasiby*, 16 June (London, 1645).

51 BL, E288(25), *A relation of the victory obtained by Sir Thomas Fairfax, generall of the Parliaments forces, over the enemies forces, neer Harborough, on Saturday, June, 14*, 16 June (London, 1645), p. 4.

52 BL, E288(38), *A more particular and exact relation of the victory obtained by the Parliaments forces under the command of Sir Thomas Fairfax*, 19 June (London, 1645), p. 2.

53 BL, E288(27), *Three letters from the right honourable Sir Thomas Fairfax, Lieut. Gen. Cromwell and the committee residing in the army*, 17 June (London, 1645), pp. 1–2.

54 BL, Add. MS 18979, fo. 204.

55 BL, Add. MS 31116, fos. 220v–221r.

56 D. Underdown, *Somerset in the Civil War and Interregnum* (Newton Abbot, 1973), pp. 106,

113; A. Hopper, 'The clubmen of the West Riding of Yorkshire during the first civil war: "Bradford club-law" ', *Northern History*, 36:1 (2000), 70–1.

57 BL, E262(29), *Perfect occurrences of Parliament*, 18–25 July (London, 1645).

58 Scott, *Politics and War*, p. 97; Gentles, *New Model Army*, p. 66.

59 Woolrych, *Britain in Revolution*, p. 322; Gentles, *New Model Army*, pp. 71–3

60 Rupert saved Denton from a sacking after having seen Fairfax's uncles' portraits on 29 June 1644: Markham, p. 151.

61 Bristol Record Office, 41084/6: *A true relation of the storming Bristoll and the taking the town, castle, forts, ordnance, ammunition and arms, by Sir Thomas Fairfax's army*, 11 September (London, 1645), pp. 4–5, 14.

62 Bristol Record Office, 8029(9).

63 Lindley and Scott (eds), *The Journal of Thomas Juxon*, p. 110; Bod., MS Tanner 59, fo. 745; M. Stoyle, *West Britons: Cornish Identities and the Early Modern British State* (Exeter, 2002), pp. 76, 84, 142, 154; M. Stoyle, *Soldiers and Strangers: An Ethnic History of the English Civil Wars* (New Haven, 2005), pp. 184–91.

64 Wanklyn and Jones, *Military History*, p. 259; R. P. Cust, *Charles I: A Political Life* (London, 2005), p. 408.

Chapter 4

———◆———

Parliament, the army
and the second civil war

This chapter discusses the period from the end of the first civil war to the violent conclusion of the second. It shows how Fairfax's politics were transformed by Parliament's treatment of his army and the increased assertiveness of his soldiers. When Fairfax's control over the army slipped in summer 1647, instead of resigning as a more temperamental commander might have, Fairfax recovered his authority by re-engaging with popular politics and championing the rights of his men. His subsequent role directing the army's occupation of London and the impeachment of his old enemies among the eleven 'incendiary' MPs collapses the view that he was 'clean of politics'. Fairfax's low profile in the *Heads of Proposals* negotiations with the King and in the Putney debates with the agitators and Levellers, suggests that his ill health, never a problem on the battlefield, became an issue when faced with difficult political problems. His saving London from the Kent and Essex rebels needs to be rated alongside Cromwell's victory at Preston for a more rounded understanding of the second civil war. Finally, his conduct at Colchester will be discussed to suggest that the second war hardened not just his soldiers' politics, but also his own.

I

Far from bringing relief, victory in 1646 brought greater strain upon Fairfax. Rather than granting his army a legal indemnity and their arrears of pay, a powerful interest within Parliament viewed Fairfax's army as a political obstacle to settlement. Constructed around the army's old enemies among the earl of Essex's group, it was led in the Commons by Denzil Holles and Sir Philip Stapleton. Supported by many Presbyterians at Westminster and in the City, Holles and Stapleton courted the Scots Covenanters and the provincial forces under Major-General Edward Massey and Colonel-General Sydenham

Poyntz, hoping thereby to construct a military counterweight to Fairfax upon which they could rely to impose their terms of settlement by force.

Under these circumstances, Fairfax slowly emerged as a political guardian of his army's interests. His first concerns were to neutralise rival sources of military power in England. Even before the war was over, Fairfax turned on Massey's western brigade, complaining to Speaker Lenthall on 13 June 1646 that their indiscipline alienated Somerset's civilians. Fairfax demanded their disbandment, complaining they had affronted his honour by breaching Worcester's surrender articles.[1] On 17 October the House of Lords attempted to delay the brigade's disbandment, but Fairfax defied them, claiming on 26 October that it had been accomplished before their order arrived. This infuriated many in the Lords and heralded Fairfax's post-war political device of protesting full obedience to Parliament while achieving contrary objectives.[2]

During 1646 the earl of Essex sought to have himself reinstated as general in Fairfax's place so that he might force the House of Commons to come to terms with the King. Therefore Essex's death on 14 September 1646 was a major relief to Fairfax. Thomas Juxon believed God had taken Essex's life to foil 'great mischief', for 'had he lived but a week longer, the Lords had voted him generalissimo and Sir Thomas laid aside for his good service'. Fairfax and Cromwell were notable absentees from the earl's funeral on 22 October.[3] With his political enemies reeling from Essex's demise, Fairfax returned to London on 13 November 1646. A hero's welcome from both Houses awaited him at his residence on Queen Street. The military and political successes of the last eighteen months heightened Fairfax's belief that God had taken special interest in his life. Lenthall celebrated the army's victories remarking that as the Romans added the epithet Caesar to victorious generals, the English would henceforth add 'Fairfax' to theirs.[4]

Fairfax's pleasure was short-lived as support for his army soon crumbled. He recognised he needed a stronger political voice to protect the army's concerns and stood for election to the House of Commons as MP for Cirencester in January 1647. His plans were thwarted when the election was prevented. One newsbook claimed that although Fairfax had been fairly returned, the sheriff had refused to acquiesce, alleging that a faction in the House of Commons would support him.[5] Such a faction would have included Holles and Stapleton, whose alliance with the Scots and English Presbyterians was finally bearing fruit. As long as the Scots army lingered in the north, the Independents profited from anti-Scots sentiment, but once the Scots returned to Scotland in January 1647 the Independents lost their ascendancy at Westminster.[6] Holles and the Presbyterians took political advantage from post-war frustration and directed it at Fairfax's army, depicting them as a crippling burden upon civilians and an obstacle to settlement. In February their Commons' motion to replace Fairfax as general with the Presbyterian Colonel Richard Graves was defeated by only 159 to 147 votes.[7]

The parliamentary Presbyterians called for a drastic reduction of Fairfax's army, and the dispatching into Ireland of much of what remained. They planned to fracture army unity by offering to pay those who enlisted for Ireland but to punish those who spoke against it. Legislation followed ordering the dismantling of the New Model. All foot were to be disbanded or dispersed into garrisons. The field army was to be reduced to 5400 horse and 1000 dragoons, while a further 4200 horse and dragoons were to enlist for Ireland.[8] A propaganda campaign spearheaded by Thomas Edwards's *Gangraena* depicted the soldiers as sectaries, oppressors and dangerous social subversives.[9] While in London, Cromwell warned Fairfax of the prevalence of such views on 11 March: 'There want not, in all places, men who have so much malice against the Army as besots them ... Never were the spirits of men more embittered than now.'[10] Despite Fairfax's protestations of obedience to Parliament, Holles and his supporters perceived him as their enemy; William Strode declared in March 1647: 'Sir Thomas Fairfax will be deceived, for part of his army will join with us,' adding ominously: 'We will destroy them all.'[11]

Parliament's first indication of the army's co-ordinated opposition came when three MPs visited headquarters to organise the army for Ireland on 21 March. Fairfax summoned a large council of war which raised the army's concerns over pay and indemnity with them. It also transpired that the army's grievances had been distilled into a single petition to Fairfax. Although this petition restricted itself to military grievances and was not presented to Parliament, on 29 March Holles secured parliamentary approval for a 'declaration of dislike' against it, branding the army enemies of the state and threatening legal action against them as disturbers of the peace. This attack on the army's honour proved counterproductive, rendering the soldiers even less ready to accept disbandment.[12]

Fairfax's first instinct was for conciliation. On 30 March he informed Lenthall that, despite the petition, his men would still obey Parliament, but that he was obliged to listen to his officers' fears concerning the troubles soldiers would face once disbanded.[13] When very few officers enlisted for Ireland, Fairfax was criticised in Parliament for failing to strongly support the service. He answered that he had not used the word 'require' in his orders because it was 'his constant course to use the word "desire" to his officers'. Deliberately contrasting his style of command with Parliament's peremptory orders, he added that 'hee doubted not but' his way 'would find a ready obedience'.[14] On 15 April 1647 parliamentary commissioners visited Fairfax again, requiring him to punish all who obstructed the Irish service, but Fairfax countered that he would find none guilty before proof was made.[15]

Having failed to reconcile his army with Parliament, on 21 April Fairfax travelled to London for medical treatment. In his absence the confrontation gathered momentum. Holles procured a majority vote in Parliament that the army should be disbanded with six weeks' pay. This amounted to only £70,000, a tiny fraction of their arrears. Many in Parliament assumed that by denying them maintenance, army morale would plummet and the soldiers would desert. Instead, this vote marginalised those army officers that still advocated full obedience to Parliament. Fifty-seven of them left the army by the end of May, leaving the militants in control.[16]

During Fairfax's absence an army press was established at Oxford, resistance to disbandment organised and several regiments elected agents known as 'agitators' to represent their grievances. On 16 May these agitators met with sympathetic officers in the newly constituted 'General Council of the Army', in Saffron Walden church. Colonel John Lambert communicated to Fairfax this meeting's details, assuring him that he had moderated their demands.[17] Many in the army hoped Fairfax would champion their case, so the agitators circulated rumours of how Fairfax was abused in London by the army's enemies who questioned the credibility of his illness: 'there was never a Generall did like him, hee is now in Towne and courts Ladies, and itt is a shame for him that he should now be in Towne and his Armie in a distemper'.[18]

Despite his illness, Parliament ordered Fairfax back to the army to restore order and Fairfax confided to his father on 18 May: 'I think in a few days to go down to it (god willing) I shall expect to have great difficulties put upon me but I trust the Lord will bring me out of them.' He then let slip his exasperation with Parliament, remarking: 'nothing wil be acceptable that comes from the army'.[19] Fairfax returned to a very different army at Saffron Walden on 20 May and found he could do little to stifle its political activism. Having interrupted his medical treatment too soon, he fell very ill. He ordered the agitators to stop meeting and on 29 May he sought Skippon's advice on disbandment. The two men probably resolved to continue as mediators, but they were circumvented when the council of war at Bury St Edmunds passed a remonstrance against disbandment. The soldiers rightly feared that if Parliament was prepared to treat them this poorly while they remained in arms, the omens for their treatment once disbanded were not good.[20]

Outside the army, the soldiers' political activism appeared subversive and dangerous. Several of Fairfax's friends urged him to resign in protest against his men's actions. On 28 May 1647, William White, MP for Pontefract, urged Fairfax that 'Your excellencie I confesse hath a most difficult game to play ... I cannot see that your stay in the Army in any unquiet distemper (upon this occasion) can be for your safetie.' Another northern officer agreed, arguing that if a settlement was agreed while Fairfax sided with the agitators it would 'robb the kingdome' of his future service.[21]

Parliament compelled Fairfax to choose between obeying their commands or maintaining his authority. Siding with his soldiers, he still represented himself as a restraining force upon them, remarking to Lenthall on 30 May: 'I am forced to yield to some things out of order to keepe the Army from disorders or worse inconveniences to the Kingdome.' Fairfax added that his council of war was now unanimous, and pleaded that 'there may be ways of love and composure thought upon' to reconcile army and Parliament.[22] The following day, Fairfax maintained this conciliatory stance to the Derby House Committee, writing: 'I humbly desire I may not be thought to neglect your orders (considering the temper of the Army and my desires to prevent greater inconveniences).'[23] Until June 1647, Fairfax's natural instincts were to comply with Parliament and bring the army under control. If the parliamentary Presbyterians had not slighted him and his army's honour so persistently, disbandment might have proved possible. Instead, Fairfax proved a stronger advocate of his army's rights and interests than is often appreciated.

II

In May 1647, with Holles and the Presbyterians dominating Parliament, the King came very close to being received in London. A settlement was underway with the Scots and the army's future looked bleak.[24] The army required desperate measures for self-preservation but regained the initiative in June due to three principal factors: their refusal to disband, their seizure of the King and their winning over of Fairfax. The latter's importance is reflected by the surprise in the Commons when they heard Fairfax's report on 2 June that the army would not disband. It is underlined further by the soldiers' joy when Fairfax denied himself a night's sleep to personally visit and address each regiment at Kentford Heath on 4 June.[25]

On 1 June 1000 troopers commanded by a newly elected agitator, Cornet George Joyce, arrived at Holdenby House in Northamptonshire, where the King was held by other parliamentary forces under Colonel Richard Graves. How far Joyce's actions were approved by the army command has long been controversial, but two recent key accounts agree that on 31 May Cromwell covertly approved Joyce's planned securing of the King at Holdenby, but not Charles's removal.[26] The agitators feared that Graves plotted to convey Charles to London to make peace with Holles and the Presbyterians, who were conspiring to invite a Scottish force south to crush Fairfax's army. Graves fled but his officers threatened Joyce they would return with force. Fearful of bloodshed, Joyce and his fellow agitators exceeded their instructions and removed the King from Holdenby on 4 June. Charles consented but Joyce showed no written orders for this spontaneous decision. He later denied ever claiming to have had Fairfax's orders.[27]

The seizure of the King was so politically embarrassing because Joyce's commission placed him close to Fairfax. Although there has been confusion over whether he was a cornet in Fairfax's horse regiment, or a cornet in his lifeguard,[28] either of these posts made him personally known to Fairfax in a capacity that may have included functioning as Fairfax's messenger and man of affairs with Westminster politicians.[29] Under normal circumstances Joyce would have been third in command of up to ninety troopers, so his 1000-strong force at Holdenby suggests either an alternative command structure controlled by agitators had emerged, or that Joyce was known to be acting on behalf of senior officers. The latter is more likely. While actually at Holdenby, Joyce wrote, probably to Cromwell: 'lett us knowe what wee should doe. Wee are resolved to obey noe orders but the Generall's.'[30]

Although he was incapacitated by sickness over seventy miles away at Bury, Fairfax knew of events at Holdenby and he explained the arrival of Joyce's troops to Lenthall on 4 June:

> This day I received advertisement from Holdenby that the soldiers of that partee formerly assigned to attend the Commissioners there, together with some others belonging to the Army (of whose number or qualitie I have had no Account, nor how they came thither) have of themselves undertaken by placing other & stronger Guards about the Kinge than formerlie, to secure his Majesty from being secretlie convayed away ... I understand, That Col: Grevis is thereupon secretlie slipt away and therefore I have immediately ordered Col: Whalley his Regiment to march upp thither, and himself (in the Roome of Col: Grevis) to attend the Commissioners and take the charge of the Guards.[31]

Fairfax was probably aware of orders to secure the King on 1 June, but was genuinely surprised by Joyce's spontaneous initiative to remove Charles on 4 June. If the King's removal had been planned a destination would have been decided. Instead Charles himself chose to be conducted to Newmarket.[32] When Fairfax learnt that Joyce had exceeded his orders, he sent Colonel Whalley with two horse regiments to return Charles to Holdenby, but was surprised by the King's refusal to do so.[33]

On 7 June Fairfax protested his innocence to Lenthall: 'I can clearly profess (as in the presence of God) for myself, and dare be confident of the same for the officers about me, and the body of the Army, that the remove of his Majesty from Holdenby was without any design, knowledge, or privity thereof on our part.'[34] That day Fairfax's conciliatory efforts were shunned by the parliamentary commissioners. Having consulted them concerning the King, he complained they 'were pleased wholly to refuse giving of any Advice or Opinion at all in the Business'.[35] Too busy to write to his father, John Rushworth vindicated the army to Ferdinando, arguing that if Holles and Stapleton had maintained custody of Charles the Scots would soon have invaded to crush the New Model.[36]

Once he overcame the shock of how far the army had slipped beyond his control, Fairfax saw the benefits of Joyce's action. On 3 June the Commons rescinded the 'Declaration of dislike' and on 5 June they finally granted the army's indemnity. Fairfax's letter to Parliament of 6 June approving of the King's removal was published within two days.[37] Fairfax then arranged an army rendezvous on Triploe Heath on 10 June for the parliamentary commissioners to communicate these conciliatory gestures, but the concessions came too late, the soldiers rightly suspecting they were prompted by fear rather than goodwill. The commissioners were allegedly booed off the field. Fairfax, Cromwell and other senior officers now decisively seized the initiative. They warned the corporation of London that the army was approaching and co-ordinated the soldiers' political demands.[38] First among these was revenge.

On Naseby's second anniversary, a written impeachment was prepared against Denzil Holles, Sir Philip Stapleton and nine other 'incendiary members' involved in political attacks on the army. It was delivered in Fairfax's name two days later on 16 June. Fairfax's distrust of Holles and Stapleton stretched back to his clash with the Hothams, and both had acted as tellers for the votes against his appointment as general.[39] Now Fairfax accused them of secret correspondence with royalists to plot a Scots invasion, in order 'to bring in the King upon their own tearmes' and 'to destroy the Army and their friends'. The eleven members also stood accused of having countenanced 'rude persons' to threaten and assault MPs outside Westminster.[40] By advocating the purging of corrupt MPs from Parliament, this document marked Fairfax's full conversion to the army's cause.[41] A further army declaration was published on 14 June, penned by Ireton, but probably under pressure from agitators, which included the famous statement that they were 'not a mere mercenary army'.[42] The army began to usurp political power and by failing to resign, Fairfax endorsed them. When penning his 'Short memorials' after the Restoration Fairfax recognised this as the moment when the army became a revolutionary force, maintaining untruthfully that 'from ye time they declared their usurped Authority at Triplo Heath, I never gave my free consent to anything they did'.[43]

Consternation that Fairfax had supported his soldiers persisted through the summer; on 27 June it was reported that Parliament feared Fairfax 'as although he shows submission to the Houses, and writes with protests of obedience and respect, his action belies it'.[44] Outrage at his conduct prompted comparisons of his men to Jack Cade and the Munster Anabaptists, along with a vituperative sermon in the House of Commons by the Presbyterian Mr Ward[45] on 3 July: 'If the wheeles turnes thus I knowe not whether Jesus Christ or Sir Thomas Fairfax bee the better driver.'[46]

Fairfax's handling of the Northern Association's mutiny against their commander, Colonel-General Sydenham Poyntz, also reveals greater collusion with popular politics and the army's agitators than he later admitted. The northern regiments elected their own agitators by June 1647, many of whom resolved to support Fairfax's army. This upset plans to use these forces in conjunction with the Scots against the New Model. Poyntz informed Fairfax that Parliament had ordered him to arrest any soldiers that came to his army from the south, but on 29 June Fairfax warned Poyntz not to do so.[47] Fairfax stipulated that should any arrive they were to be countenanced and protected.[48] He even gave the northern agitators explicit support, addressing them as 'the same with the Army more imediately under my command ... which I am the more engaged to doe because I cannot forget the former labours and hardshipps which you under my command have soe willingly undergone ... and that upon as small and inconsiderable satisfaction as any forces in this Kingdome'.[49] The northern agitators responded to this personal touch by wearing blue and white – Fairfax's colours – in their hats.[50]

Recently returned from the continent, Poyntz was the professional soldier who succeeded Lord Fairfax as commander–in-chief of Parliament's northern army after the Self-Denying Ordinance. He could not match Fairfax's popularity with the soldiery; the Yorkshire forces that had never mutinied under the Fairfaxes, did so almost immediately under his command.[51] Poyntz's closeness to Holles and the New Model's enemies clashed with the Fairfax interest in the north and Poyntz became particularly frustrated when his soldiers wished to petition their old cavalry commander, remarking: 'I would faine know why they should make their grievances knowne to Sir Thomas more than they have done formerly. And why to Sir Thomas? They all knowing these forces are a distinct Army and not under the command of Sir Thomas.'[52] In June 1647 Poyntz angered his men further by executing two soldiers without calling a council of war. Subsequently five agitators arrived from Pontefract and forced their way into Poyntz's council in York. They presented an engagement from many troops and companies to stand with the southern army. Although they were dismissed, most of the officers subsequently signed their engagement.[53]

On 8 July the northern agitators arrested Poyntz and slighting his honour, they 'led him bootless through the streets of York' before carrying him off to Pontefract. Their first charge against Poyntz was that he had scorned Fairfax and rendered his 'authority contemptible'. Accusing Poyntz of calling the New Model Army mutineers, they claimed that he had published printed papers on posts in market places across the north which related that Fairfax's army had taken the King by force and that Charles had struck Fairfax. They conveyed Poyntz under guard to Fairfax's headquarters at Reading and requested a new commander.[54] Fairfax connived in the northern mutiny and used it to propose to Lenthall that all land forces in England and Wales should be under his command.[55] Parliament acquiesced on 17 July and although Fairfax released Poyntz, he replaced him with John Lambert. Poyntz's captors were then paid £30 by Fairfax's headquarters.[56] Once again Fairfax championed popular parliamentarianism in the north to the alarm of erstwhile allies. The mutiny

The Pourtraicture of his Excellency Sr: Thomas
Farfax Generall of all the English forces for
the Seruice of ye two houses of Parliament.

Figure 4 Sir Thomas Fairfax in 1648, engraving by William Faithorne

against Poyntz rekindled Sir Henry Cholmley's fears of subversive plebeian soldiers, and he urged Lenthall to a speedy settlement 'for otherwise (I fear) clubs and clouted shoes will in the end be too hard for them both'. The phrase 'clubs and clouted shoon' was among John Lilburne's favourites, and was politically explicit, having occurred in the Norfolk commotions of 1549 and Shakespeare's *Henry VI*.[57] Cholmley's fears of 'the popularity' led him to obstruct Fairfax's orders in 1648 and gloat at Thomas Rainborough's death.[58]

III

We now turn to Fairfax's role in army politics from the seizure of the King to the outbreak of second civil war (Figure 4). Once Charles was in the army's custody, speculation grew that Fairfax and the generals would conduct secret negotiations with him. Fairfax waited on Charles at Sir John Cutts's house near Cambridge on 7 June 1647 and later recalled that Charles had mistaken the army's kindnesses for weakness: 'He said to me, Sr, I have as great an Interest in ye Army as you. By wch I plainly saw ye broken Reed he leaned on.'[59] Fairfax had previously met the King near Nottingham in February 1647 during Charles's southward journey from Newcastle to Holdenby, on which occasion Fairfax dismounted, kissed the King's hand and conversed with him for some time.[60] Charles was again surprised by Fairfax's cordiality and several private interviews followed also involving Cromwell and Ireton. Charles naturally distrusted Fairfax and Cromwell because they had not asked for rewards or favours, but on 8 July Fairfax was obliged to deny rumours that the commanders had secretly treated with the King. Fairfax defended his decision to permit Charles to see his children, stressing that allowing it 'might gain more upon His Majesty than denying it'. Fairfax allowed the duke of Richmond and two royal chaplains access to Charles in order to rebut 'those common Prejudices suggested against us, as if we were utter Enemies to Monarchy, and all Civill Order or Government'.[61]

Although Sir Thomas was not involved in drafting the *Heads of Proposals*, he indicated to his father on 18 July that his hopes rested on maintaining dialogue between the moderates within the army and the army's friends in Parliament: 'many turbulent spirits are yitt in the citty & army but I hope their fury shall not prevaile ... I trust by Gods providence we shall discern what is good & not be led along with the multitude.'[62] These hopes were dashed the next day when the eleven MPs returned to deny Fairfax's charges against them in the House of Commons and a counter-revolution against the army gathered pace in London.[63] On 26 July a crowd of citizens, apprentices and reformadoes invaded the House of Commons demanding Charles's restoration. Spurred on by the return of the eleven members, the City prepared to resist the New Model, organising trained bands and new units under Waller, Massey, Browne and Poyntz. During the furore, eight peers and fifty-seven members fled to the army. On 27 July Rushworth condemned these tumults to Lord Fairfax, describing how crowds abused the army's friends 'by pulling them by ye eares & noses & so leading them upp & downe saying these are the Independents'. He called the rioters 'Apprentices' and the 'rude multitude', asserting that it was 'believed that the 11 members underhand set this business on foot'. On 29 July Fairfax warned Parliament that he held them responsible for not fulfilling their undertakings, and that he knew the recent tumults had been encouraged by the City's Presbyterian common council.[64] On 6 August at Kensington Fairfax met the army-friendly MPs headed by Speaker Lenthall and the earl of Manchester who had recently fled Westminster. Fairfax then led his soldiers into the City and armed resistance to the army collapsed. These MPs were restored to Parliament and all business passed at Westminster since 26 July was voided. Fairfax was appointed Constable of the Tower and a chair was set for him in the Commons. He only sat after 'much Importunity', and Lenthall gave him the thanks of the House. Every soldier wore a laurel in his hat and Charles was forced into more negotiations based upon the *Heads of Proposals*. Fairfax had sealed his army's political victory over its enemies in Parliament, and he utilised new powers of patronage, demanding the return of Gilbert Mabbott as Licenser of the Press and the appointment of Robert Tichborne as deputy at the Tower.[65]

That autumn Fairfax turned to bridling the agitators' political activism and defending his officers from charges of underhand dealings with the King. The infiltration of Leveller ideas into the army was limited by the reluctance of Leveller leaders, fearful of Fairfax's popularity, to criticise him personally. When John Lilburne urged the soldiers 'not to trust your great officers at the Generalls quarters', it was because, Lilburne claimed, they had 'most unjustly stolne the power both from your honest Generall, and your too flexible Adjutators'.[66] Fairfax sought to re-establish a regular command structure and vetoed proposals to promote Joyce and other radicals in September 1647.[67] He was absent from most of the important debates at Putney owing to renewed illness but he returned to the chair on 5 November, apparently presiding in silence. Like the King, he was conscious of an occasional impediment in his speech.[68] Chairman again on 8 November, he threw his support behind Cromwell, intimidating the radicals and ordering the agitators to return to their regiments. He was immediately obeyed, suggesting that his political authority in the army at this stage remained intact. He had been a marginal figure at Putney but he was decisive during the mutiny at Corkbush field near Ware on 15 November. He wisely contained disruption by dividing the army into three separate meetings. Understanding the blend of reassurance and threats required to defuse such occasions, he undermined the mutineers' position by incorporating many of their desires into his own remonstrance and threatening to resign if this was not adopted and unity restored.[69] Fairfax pledged that he would champion their professional grievances and join them in advocating regular and equitable elections, implying his consent to an extended franchise. He restored discipline by utilising his charisma in personal confrontations with the regiments. Only one soldier was executed, which by contemporary military standards was extremely lenient. With renewed conflict likely, an effective and unified army was Fairfax's prime concern. When Fairfax pruned the army's size that winter he selectively reduced more from regiments perceived as mutiny risks.[70] This included his own lifeguard which mutinied on 23 February 1648 and two of its representatives, William Clarke and Francis Thirkill, were imprisoned at Whitehall. This must have been galling for Fairfax as Thirkill was from Colton, near his Nun Appleton estate, and had ridden with him since 1642. Nevertheless, the lifeguard was disbanded and thereafter Fairfax was guarded by ordinary troopers.[71]

On 9 January 1648 Fairfax and his council of war endorsed the Commons' vote that no further addresses would be made to the King, agreeing that a settlement could be imposed without royal consent. Fairfax revisited the north, attending his father's funeral on 15 March. The next day the Commons confirmed his succession to his father's offices of *Custos Rotulorum* and keeper of Pontefract castle.[72] The funeral allowed Fairfax to reacquaint himself with his family, former officers and clergymen, several of whom had grown alarmed by Thomas Edwards's accounts of his soldiers' excesses in his book *Gangraena*. Many West Riding ministers signed the *Vindiciae veritatis*, a protestation against sectarians published in London in April 1648. The signatories included ministers particularly close to the Fairfaxes such as Elkanah Wales, Joshua Witton, Robert Todd and Nathaniel Rathband. Although they had strongly supported Fairfax in 1643 many now turned against his army, perceiving it as a dangerous hotbed of extremists.[73]

IV

We now turn to reappraising Fairfax's role in the second civil war. By May 1648 a Scots invasion was expected and parliamentary troops in Wales declared for the King, forcing Fairfax to split the army, sending detachments under Cromwell and Lambert into Wales and the north respectively. Fairfax led the remaining 4000 men against the most serious immediate threat: a royalist insurrection in Kent of 11,000 men. More experienced at directing urban-based engagements than Cromwell, his aggressive strategy was to protect London by storming those Kent towns hosting the insurgents. On 1 June 1648 Fairfax, in great pain from gout, stormed Maidstone, exposing himself to great danger. Despite premature reports in London of his defeat and death, Fairfax's troops pacified Kent in less than two weeks. Then Fairfax conducted a lightning pursuit of the royalist fugitives who crossed into Essex to join other insurgents there. From 11 to 12 June Fairfax's small army pursued them from Gravesend via Tilbury to Colchester.[74]

Emulating his tactics at Maidstone, Fairfax launched a furious assault on Colchester, but his men were bloodily repulsed on 13 June, and a gruelling ten-week siege followed.[75] Fairfax ordered ten forts built, connecting them with massive earthworks to completely surround the town. His uncompromising approach was to starve insurgents and citizens alike into submission, although his own troops suffered too in the atrocious wet weather. During the siege, Fairfax's anti-royalism hardened; when the Prince of Wales wrote to him requesting mercy for captured royalist commanders in Wales, Fairfax replied that although their fates would be decided by Parliament, he hoped 'thatt all obstacles of a just & firme peace may be removed'.[76] In Fairfax's view, royalist parole breakers and parliamentarians that had changed sides, such as Poyer and Laugharne, forfeited their honour by betraying his notions of public duty, service and trust.

On 22 August 1648, Fairfax refused the earl of Norwich's request to allow starving non-combatants to leave Colchester. The royalist commanders perceived a new viciousness in their foes and complained that royalist prisoners had been 'rudly stript and wounded', desiring from Fairfax 'to know how you will proceed for the future'.[77] Among them, Sir Charles Lucas was particularly worried. He had surrendered at Stow-on-the-Wold in March 1646 and been released on parole. Lucas was instrumental in repelling the assault on 13 June and he grew perturbed by Fairfax's refusal to treat with him thereafter. Sensing his predicament, Lucas led desperate sallies, and offered Fairfax excuses for his breach of parole.[78] William Osborne, who was among Fairfax's army, wrote that the royalist commanders fortified their soldiers with wine and tobacco to persuade them to make one final sally, but their men refused, saying they would not lay down their lives so that their commanders might escape. Fairfax's strategy encouraged royalist soldiers to turn on their commanders and this was reflected in his terms for surrender. Rank and file soldiers were granted quarter, but senior officers were forced to surrender to Fairfax's mercy, which hitherto had a reputation for lenience. Osborne recalled that when the royalist commissioners negotiated the surrender, Fairfax's soldiers 'could not without much difficulty & slashing be kept from falling upon ym, soe greedy they were of new cloathes, and of ye spoyles of their enemyes'. On 27 August Fairfax appointed Ireton, Whalley and Rainsborough as commissioners to negotiate the surrender, and a short delay followed over 'the meaning of the submitting to Mercy'.[79]

Soon after entering Colchester on 28 August, Fairfax's council of war sentenced Sir Charles Lucas and Sir George Lisle to death. Lucas had spent two months rehearsing his arguments for this moment and vainly disputed his sentence with Ireton. Fairfax may have believed Lucas had prevented an earlier surrender by claiming to the royalist soldiers that Fairfax had offered the royalist leaders favourable terms if they would abandon their men. Lucas was no doubt perturbed when Fairfax's soldiers started chanting for the deaths of his friends 'ye souldiery much crying out for Goring, Capell, & Hastings'. Osborne's account suggests that Fairfax's soldiers were irritated by his refusal to allow plunder, and that the executions were required to appease them. Ian Gentles has shown that the case against Lucas was strengthened when two soldiers testified that at Stinchcombe, Gloucestershire, Lucas had ordered the execution of over twenty prisoners. Although Fairfax acted within martial law, these executions were unprecedented and clearly motivated by vengeance. The royalists were so shocked because before Colchester few had expected such severity from him.[80]

Fairfax informed the earl of Manchester on 29 August that he had ordered the executions 'for some satisfaction to Militarie Justice, and in parte of avenge for the innocent bloud they have caused to be spilt, & the trouble, damage, and mischief they have brought upon the Towne, this Country & the Kingdome'.[81] Five months later, similar arguments and language were employed to sentence Charles I. The war, and Fairfax with it, had taken a new course. Parliament interpreted the second civil war as a treasonous act against a settled state meriting justice against traitors.[82] Although Fairfax was well aware that most royalists would never forgive him, even his 'Short memorials' made no apology for these executions. On 18 August 1660 Fairfax 'stammered out a few unintelligible words' in the House of Commons defending his decision, to little avail. On 7 June 1661 an ostentatious funeral of Lucas and Lisle processed through Colchester and a commemorative stone there recalled how they were 'in cold blood barbarously murdered', by the 'command of Sir Thomas Fairfax'. This was a very public stain on his honour but Fairfax's 'Short memorials' defensively maintained that: 'Sr Charles Lucas & Sr George Lysle being meer Soldiers of Fortune, & falling into our hands by ye chance of war, execution was done upon ym. And in this Distribution of Justice I did nothing but according to my Commission, & ye Trust Reposed in me.'[83] Here Fairfax stretched the term 'soldier of fortune' beyond its limits and clearly intended it as an insult. Fairfax was accused of a vendetta against Lucas for having routed him at Marston moor, and of dishonourably endeavouring to divide royalist officers and soldiers by offering common soldiers separate terms for surrender.[84] Accusing him of having broken a promise of mercy, the royalist press depicted Fairfax as 'the scorne of true Gallantry', suggesting he had degenerated from his family's honour. Within days of the executions eight pamphlets appeared condemning this 'most barbarous unsoldierly murder'. Edmund Verney called it 'an act so horrid and barbarous', while Clarendon overcame his dislike of Lucas to condemn it as murder.[85] Lucas's sister, Margaret, later duchess of Newcastle, declared her brother had been 'most inhumanely murdered and shot to death'.[86] Fairfax was even criticised by parliamentarians who claimed that he had usurped Parliament's powers to deal with the vanquished.[87] The historian P. R. Newman showed his distaste for Fairfax, describing it as an 'exemplary bloodletting', and citing royalist allegations that the corpses of Lucas's female relatives were disinterred from the family chapel at nearby St John's during the siege: 'Some of those Godly soldiers chose to adorn their hats with bones and hanks of hair.'[88] The priorities of much royalist historiography are revealed by the continued fascination with Lucas and Lisle in contrast to the relative silence over the maltreatment of plebeian royalists. Many of these men were pillaged as they were delivered to prisons or servitude in Barbados, while stragglers were allegedly 'pistolled in the highways' by their guards.[89]

There is no evidence that Fairfax pleaded for Lucas and Lisle, but several stories that he opposed their execution surfaced in royalist polemic. They portrayed Fairfax's inclination to mercy as being overruled by Ireton, Rainborough and Whalley, probably as these officers made more believable villains in royalist propaganda.[90] Clarendon agreed that the executions were 'generally imputed to Ireton, who swayed the general, and was upon all occasions of an unmerciful and bloody nature'.[91] These misrepresentations inclined John Wilson to believe that Fairfax had 'allowed his better judgement' to be overridden by Ireton and his council of war. The fiction that Fairfax was inclined to spare them is furthered by the caption of a miniature engraving of Thomas among the Fairfax manuscripts, that claimed, even more erroneously, that Parliament 'basely caused' them 'to be put to death, refusing to ratify the treaty of lord Fairfax'.[92] This refashioning took place because Fairfax's retribution at Colchester was later widely construed as uncharacteristic. Not even Cromwell had been so arbitrary in victory, consigning the fate of the Welsh mutineers Colonel John Poyer, Colonel Rice Powell and Major-General Rowland Laugharne along with the duke of Hamilton and the Scots commanders captured in 1648 to Parliament's verdict rather than his soldiers' muskets. Hamilton and Poyer were executed only after they had been tried by Parliament, dying in March and April 1649 respectively.[93]

Despite his slowness to take the political initiative, Fairfax remained a highly significant individual from 1646 to 1648. His support for his soldiers and participation in the army's politics lent his army a corporate unity and strength of purpose that could have scarcely been replicated under another commander. The scale and venom of the parliamentary Presbyterians' attack upon his personal integrity and the honour of his men transformed him, however reluctantly, into a revolutionary figure. Unashamed of his army's interference in politics, writing to his father on 18 July 1647 he referred to the army's negotiations as 'Our treaty'.[94] Divisions within the parliamentary ranks had led Fairfax to place his trust in his 'social inferiors' before, during

1643, and by acknowledging the agitators and using force against Parliament, Fairfax did so again in 1647. His stern response to the second civil war, rooted in what he perceived as the royalists' abuse of the lenient terms offered in 1646, raised the prospect of him acting with further severity against those who had defied God's providence.

NOTES

1 Bod., MS Tanner 59, fos. 330, 444.

2 BL, Add. MS 10114, fos. 17r, 21v; Bod., MS Tanner 59, fo. 573; I. Gentles, *The New Model Army in England, Ireland and Scotland, 1645–1653* (Oxford, 1992), p. 144.

3 K. Lindley and D. Scott (eds), *The Journal of Thomas Juxon, 1644–1647* (Camden Society, 5th series, 13, 1999), p. 138; BL, E360(1), *The true mannor and forme of the proceeeding to the funerall of the right honourable Robert, earle of Essex and Ewe*, 31 November (London, 1646).

4 J. Rushworth, *Historical collections* (London, 1721), part 4, vol. 1, pp. 388–9.

5 S. Kelsey, 'Constructing the council of state', *Parliamentary History*, 22:3 (2003), 225n.

6 D. Scott, ' "The northern gentlemen", the parliamentary Independents, and Anglo-Scottish relations in the Long Parliament', *Historical Journal*, 42:2 (1999), 374.

7 Gentles, *New Model Army*, p. 148.

8 A. Woolrych, *Britain in Revolution: 1625–1660* (Oxford, 2002), p. 351.

9 A. Hughes, *Gangraena and the Struggle for the English Revolution* (Oxford, 2004), passim.

10 T. Carlyle (ed.), *Oliver Cromwell's letters and speeches with elucidations* (London, 3rd edn, 1849), vol. 1, p. 217.

11 D. Underdown, *Pride's Purge: Politics in the Puritan Revolution* (Oxford, 1971), p. 79.

12 Gentles, *New Model Army*, p. 152; Woolrych, *Britain in Revolution*, p. 354.

13 Rushworth, *Historical collections*, part 4, vol. 1, p. 445.

14 C. H. Firth (ed.), *The Clarke papers, vol. 1* (Camden Society, new series, 41, 1891), pp. 10, 12.

15 *Ibid.*, p. 6.

16 Gentles, *New Model Army*, pp. 159, 168.

17 Firth (ed.), *Clarke papers, vol. 1*, pp. 80–2.

18 *Ibid.*, p. 85.

19 BL, Add. MS 18979, fo. 234.

20 Firth (ed.), *Clarke papers, vol. 1*, pp. xiv, xxi, 102, 106–7, 113.

21 *Ibid.*, pp. 103, 122.

22 Bod., MS Tanner 58, fo. 118.

23 Firth (ed.), *Clarke papers, vol. 1*, p. 116.

24 R. Cust, *Charles I: A Political Life* (Harlow, 2005), p. 430.

25 Firth (ed.), *Clarke papers, vol. 1*, p. 117; A. Woolrych, *Soldiers and Statesmen: The General Council of the Army and its Debates, 1647–1648* (Oxford, 1987), p. 117.

26 Gentles, *New Model Army*, p. 169; D. Scott, *Politics and War in the Three Stuart Kingdoms, 1637–1649* (Basingstoke, 2004), p. 147.

27 Rushworth, *Historical collections*, part 4, vol. 1, pp. 513–17.

28 Firth (ed.), *Clarke papers, vol. 1*, p. xxiv, 77n; J. Holstun, *Ehud's Dagger: Class Struggle in the English Revolution* (London, 2000), p. 3; Gentles, *New Model Army*, p. 169.

29 I am grateful to John Adamson for raising this point.

30 Firth (ed.), *Clarke papers, vol. 1*, pp. 118–19; BL, Add. MS 31116, fo. 312v.

31 Bod., MS Tanner 58, fo. 136.

32 Firth (ed.), *Clarke papers, vol. 1*, p. xxix; Rushworth, *Historical collections*, part 4, vol. 1, pp. 513–17.

33 Firth (ed.), *Clarke papers, vol. 1*, p. 122.

34 *Ibid.*, p. xxvii.

35 Rushworth, *Historical collections*, part 4, vol. 1, p. 550.

36 BL, Add. MS 18979, fo. 238.

37 BL, Add. MS 31116, fos. 311v, 312r; BL, E391(7), *A letter from his excellency Sir Thomas Fairfax, 8 June* (London, 1647).

38 Woolrych, *Soldiers and Statesmen*, pp. 123–6.

39 Woolrych, *Britain in Revolution*, p. 304.

40 YML, CWT: FAI 1644–9(11), *A particular charge of impeachment in the name of his excellency Sir Thomas Fairfax and the army under his command, against Denzil Holles esquire, Sir Philip Stapleton, Sir William Lewis, Sir John Clotworthy, Sir William Waller, Sir John Maynard, Knights, Major Generall Massie, John Glynne, esquire, Recorder of London, Walter Long esquire, Col. Edward Harley and Anthony Nicoll, esquire, members of the honourable House of Commons* (London, 1647), pp. 6–8.

41 Rushworth, *Historical collections*, part 4, vol. 1, pp. 564–70.

42 Holstun, *Ehud's Dagger*, p. 211; Woolrych, *Soldiers and Statesmen*, p. 126.

43 Bod., MS Fairfax 36, fo. 4v.

44 A. B. Hinds (ed.), *Calendar of State Papers Venetian, 1647–1652* (London, 1927), p. 2.

45 This was most probably the minister Nathaniel Ward, who had returned from New England to deliver a fervent anti-army sermon at Parliament's monthly fast on 30 June 1647: Hughes, *Gangraena*, pp. 325, 391; *JHC*, vol. 5, p. 204; K. Grudzien Baston, 'Nathaniel Ward (1578–1652)', *Oxford DNB*.

46 Holstun, *Ehud's Dagger*, p. 213; Firth (ed.), *Clarke papers, vol. 1*, p. 150.

47 BL, Add. MS 18979, fo. 242; Firth (ed.), *Clarke papers, vol. 1*, p. 146n; Gentles, *New Model Army*, p. 167.

48 BL, Add. MS 18979, fo. 244.

49 Firth (ed.), *Clarke papers, vol. 1*, p. 146.

50 J. Morrill, 'Mutiny and discontent in English provincial armies, 1645–1647', *Past and Present*, 56 (1972), 70.

51 *Portland MS*, HMC, 29, 13th report, appendix, part 1 (London, 1891), vol. 1, p. 240.

52 Firth (ed.), *Clarke papers, vol. 1*, p. 144.

53 BL, Add. MS 18979, fo. 244.

54 Holstun, *Ehud's Dagger*, p. 210; Firth (ed.), *Clarke papers, vol. 1*, pp. 163, 168–9.

55 Gentles, *New Model Army*, p. 180.

56 Rushworth, *Historical collections*, part 4, vol. 1, p. 626; Gentles, *New Model Army*, p. 173.

57 H. Cary (ed.), *Memorials of the great civil war in England from 1646 to 1652* (London, 1842), vol. 1, p. 293; C. Hill, *The World Turned Upside Down* (London, 1980), pp. 116–17.

58 *Leyborne Popham MS*, ed. S. C. Lomas, HMC, 51 (London, 1899), pp. 6, 8; W. R. D. Jones, *Thomas Rainborowe (c.1610–1648): Civil War Seaman, Siegemaster and Radical* (Woodbridge, 2005), pp. 116–18, 123–5.

59 Bod., MS Fairfax 36, fo. 3v.

60 Carlyle (ed.), *Oliver Cromwell's letters and speeches*, vol. 1, p. 215.

61 Rushworth, *Historical collections*, part 4, vol. 1, pp. 610–11.

62 BL, Add. MS 18979, fo. 247.

63 Rushworth, *Historical collections*, part 4, vol. 1, pp. 626–7.

64 Woolrych, *Britain in Revolution*, p. 377; BL, Add. MS 29747, fos. 15–16; Rushworth, *Historical collections*, part 4, vol. 1, p. 647.

65 Rushworth, *Historical collections*, part 4, vol. 2, p. 756; L. Daxon, 'The politics of Sir Thomas Fairfax reassessed', *History*, 90:4 (2005), 496.

66 Woolrych, *Soldiers and Statesmen*, p. 192.

67 I. Gentles, 'Thomas, third baron Fairfax', *Oxford DNB*.

68 Firth (ed.), *Clarke papers, vol. 1*, pp. 226, 440; J. Sprigge, *Anglia rediviva* (London, 1647), p. 323.

69 Gentles, *New Model Army*, pp. 219, 224.

70 Woolrych, *Britain in Revolution*, pp. 395–8; Gentles, *New Model Army*, p. 233.

71 J. M. Heumann, 'Fairfax and the lifeguard's colors', *Albion*, 26:3 (1994), 443–60; TNA, E121/1/7, n57; E121/5/7, n2; TNA, SP 28/3a/246; TNA, SP 28/195.

72 Rushworth, *Historical collections*, part 4, vol. 2, p. 1030.

73 B. Dale, 'Ministers of the parish churches of the West Riding during the puritan revolution', *Bradford Antiquary*, new series, 1 (1900), 431–41.

74 W. Bray (ed.), *Diary and correspondence of John Evelyn, F.R.S.* (London, 1859), vol. 3, p. 28; Scott, *Politics and War*, p. 174; Gentles, *New Model Army*, pp. 248–53.

75 P. Jones, *The Siege of Colchester, 1648* (Stroud, 2003), p. 53.

76 BL, Egerton MS 2618, fo. 27; BL, Add. MS 19399, fo. 60; Bod., MS Tanner 57, fo. 201.

77 C. H. Firth, *Cromwell's Army* (London, 1962), p. 179; R. Ashton, *Counter–Revolution: The Second Civil War and its Origins, 1646–8* (New Haven, 1994), p. 474; BL, Sloane MS 1519, fo. 74.

78 B. Donagan, 'Sir Charles Lucas', *Oxford DNB*; BL, Add. MS 15858, fo. 66.

79 BL, Harleian MS 7001, fo. 189r; Bod., MS Tanner 57, fo. 247.

80 Donagan, 'Sir Charles Lucas'; BL, Add. MS 15858, fo. 255; BL, Harleian MS 7001, fo. 189v; Gentles, 'Thomas, third baron Fairfax'.

81 Bod., MS Tanner 57, fo. 252.

82 B. Donagan, 'Atrocity, war crime, and treason in the English civil war', *American Historical Review*, 99 (1994), 1158–62; Woolrych, *Britain in Revolution*, p. 419; Ashton, *Counter–Revolution*, p. 438.

83 B. D. Henning (ed.), *The House of Commons, 1660–1690* (London, 1983), vol. 2, p. 293; Donagan, 'Sir Charles Lucas'; Bod., MS Fairfax 36, fo. 4r–v.

84 BL, E462(8), *Mercurius pragmaticus*, 29 August–5 September (London, 1648); B. Donagan, 'The web of honour: soldiers, Christians, and gentlemen in the English civil war', *Historical Journal*, 44:2 (2001), 376, 379n, 381, 383; Donagan, 'Sir Charles Lucas'.

85 C. Carlton, *Going to the Wars: The Experience of the British Civil Wars, 1638–1651* (London, 1994), p. 328; Clarendon, *History of the rebellion and civil wars in England*, ed. W. Dunn Macray (Oxford, 1888), vol. 4, pp. 387–9; J. H. Round, 'The case of Lucas and Lisle', *TRHS*, new series, 8 (1894), 157–80.

86 C. H. Firth (ed.), *The Life of William Cavendish, Duke of Newcastle by Margaret, Duchess of Newcastle* (London, 1906), p. 49.

87 B. Donagan, 'The army, the state and the soldier in the English civil war', in M. Mendle (ed.), *The Putney Debates of 1647: The Army, the Levellers and the English State* (Cambridge, 2001), p. 99.

88 P. R. Newman, *The Old Service: Royalist Regimental Colonels and the Civil War, 1642–1646* (Manchester, 1993), pp. 183, 224; *Beaufort MS*, HMC, 12th report, part 9 (London, 1891), p. 28.

89 Carlton, *Going to the Wars*, pp. 327–8.

90 BL, E466(11), *Mercurius pragmaticus*, 3–10 October (London, 1648); University of Cambridge Library, Wing 491:33, *The famous tragedie of King Charles I basely butchered* (London, 1649), pp. 24–5.

91 Clarendon, *History of the rebellion and civil wars in England*, ed. Dunn Macray, vol. 4, p. 389.

92 Bod., MS Fairfax 30, fo. 9; J. Wilson, *Fairfax* (New York, 1985), p. 139.

93 R. Ashton, 'John Poyer (d.1649)', *Oxford DNB* (Oxford, 2004); Ashton, *Counter–Revolution*, p. 338.

94 R. Bell (ed.), *The Fairfax correspondence: memorials of the civil war* (London, 1849), vol. 1, p. 371.

Chapter 5

Fairfax and the King killers

The army's infamous purge of Parliament and seizure of political power have traditionally been viewed as having made the King's trial and execution unstoppable. At best, Fairfax has been portrayed as an ineffectual passenger in these events, pulled along by revolutionary elements in his army. At worst, he has been depicted as the northern halfwit tricked or coerced over the King's death by a wily and omnipotent Cromwell. These interpretations endured due to recriminations from both royalists and republicans that Fairfax neither prevented nor endorsed the regicide. If Fairfax had strongly supported the purge, trial and execution, he might have become the most powerful man in England. Had he opposed them a renewal of civil war would have been likely.[1] He never fully explained his role in these events, and the picture he crafted in his 'Short memorial' of a powerless general eclipsed by unnamed agitators and Levellers has satisfied nobody. Untangling his involvement is fraught with difficulty as the army increasingly acted in his name regardless of his approval. Fairfax's refusal to commit himself forcefully either way reveals the dilemma at the core of the English revolution: how could a settlement be achieved with Charles I without endangering those who had rebelled against him? It also shows how effective the King was at undermining the moderates and strengthening the militants among his enemies. The usual approaches of condemnation or exoneration must be eschewed to judge how far Fairfax colluded in the events surrounding the regicide. A more balanced and complex perspective needs to be established, one that is less shaped by royalist or Cromwellian perspectives.

This at last may prove possible because recent work from Sean Kelsey, John Adamson and others has persuasively reinterpreted events surrounding the King's trial and execution. They have argued that, even after Pride's purge, the army leaders were reluctant to try the King and for most of December sought alternatives. Five weeks of indecision followed the purge before the decision for a trial was taken. Once the trial was underway, Kelsey has argued that many commissioners sought an alternative sentence other than death, and that the court repeatedly tried to accommodate the King.[2] If such uncertainty persisted over the King's fate, then Fairfax's behaviour during these weeks, and his melancholy thereafter, become much more explicable.

I

Fairfax was radicalised by his experiences in the second civil war. The King had defied providence in seeking to reverse God's judgements upon the battle-fields of the first civil war. Fairfax had tarnished his customary moderation in dealing with his defeated foes, but how far his hardened attitude would shape his response to a settlement remained uncertain. Despite the army council's vote of no further addresses the previous November, initially he seems to have supported Parliament's renewed negotiations with the King at Newport on the Isle of Wight. In September 1648 when Edmund Ludlow warned Fairfax that Parliament's commissioners at Newport sought a royal restoration and the destruction of his army, Fairfax allegedly made the vague, non-committal response that he would act in the public interest. Ludlow sensed Fairfax was irresolute, and approached Henry Ireton to exert influence upon him. Ludlow then claimed he procured Ireton's agreement that the army should intervene to prevent the treaty's accomplishment.[3] If this is true it marks recognition among senior officers that Fairfax would not seize the political initiative for them.

While Ireton and Ludlow were in favour of trying the King, the rest of Fairfax's council were divided. At first Fairfax persuaded a majority to go along with Parliament's proceedings and around the end of September Ireton disagreed with him and attempted to resign. On 10 October *Mercurius pragmaticus* confidently reported that Fairfax would support the forthcoming treaty and that Ireton had retired from headquarters in protest.[4] Advised by a core of moderates that included Captain John Gladman, Dr William Staines and Henry Whalley, judge advocate of the army, during October Fairfax continued to oppose forceful political intervention by the army. As in 1647 his first concern was maintaining order in an army denied pay. Many soldiers felt that Parliament were forcing them upon free quarter to turn the people against them, but Fairfax still hoped that Parliament might reach a just settlement with the King that would calm his soldiers and facilitate honourable disbandment. Although David Underdown remarked that Fairfax was 'maddeningly indecisive', and 'psychologically incapable of acting decisively' in politics, Fairfax was hardly alone in his uncertainty that autumn. Cromwell chose to stay in the north rather than prematurely commit himself.[5] Both men, like many others, waited for God to show them the way.

In autumn 1648 over thirty petitions from army regiments and garrisons bombarded Fairfax with condemnations of Parliament's negotiations at Newport and demands for justice against 'capital delinquents'. At first Fairfax tried to suppress these petitions, hoping that efforts to satisfy the soldiers' material grievances would mitigate their anger against the King.[6] On 7 November, Fairfax firmly opposed Ireton's calls to try the King during a council of officers at St Albans, but Charles undermined Fairfax's efforts by refusing to call off Ormond's military activities in Ireland. On 11 November the council considered Ireton's draft of the army remonstrance, which had distilled the autumn's petitions for justice into a demand to try the King. Fairfax opposed it, arguing that it would entail overthrowing Parliament. Fairfax carried all but six of the council's votes with him and his stand might have borne fruit if Charles had not been so confrontational.[7] On 16 November, the council of officers finally approved the army remonstrance, which proposed a new constitution framed by the 'Agreement of the People', and called for 'capitall punishment upon the principall Author and some prime instruments of our late warres'. Although it remained ambiguous, this implied the trial and execution of the King. John Rushworth signed Fairfax's approval on 18 November. Although one informant claimed that Fairfax had 'absolutely refused to concur', Fairfax sent Colonel Isaac Ewer to present the remonstrance to the House of Commons on 20 November, adding a personal letter informing Speaker Lenthall that his council's decision was unanimous. Then he 'most humbly and earnestly' entreated that the remonstrance might be heard. The Commons undermined Fairfax by postponing its consideration for a week.[8] On 29 November Fairfax again requested Lenthall to urge Parliament to consider the remonstrance, warning that 'through fault of such helps as we might have had from you; We are attending and improving the providence of God, for the gaining of such ends as we have proposed in our foresaid Remonstrance'. Upon hearing this threatening tone, some MPs moved that Fairfax's commission be terminated, others that the army retreat forty miles away from London.[9]

Responding to Parliament's ignoring of the army remonstrance, Fairfax made a point of sending Ewer to take charge of Charles on the Isle of Wight and arrest Colonel Robert Hammond for disobeying Fairfax's orders. He ignored instructions from the Commons to countermand this order.[10] On 30 November Lieutenant-Colonel Cobbett supervised the King's removal from Carisbrooke to Hurst castle, for which *Mercurius pragmaticus* accused Fairfax of attempting regicide by stifling 'him up with *Fogs* and *Mists*, as a more plausible way of *murther*, than by *Pistoll* or *Poyson*'.[11] Parliament still ignored the army remonstrance, but rightly fearful that the army would march on London, Lenthall wrote to Fairfax on 30 November informing him that Parliament were preparing £40,000 for the army, but had commanded that they should not enter London.[12]

Considering Parliament's maltreatment of his army, Fairfax's ability to maintain discipline in London was remarkable. On 1 December his orders addressed every regiment, 'proclaimed by sound of Trumpet, or beat of Drum'. Plundering or unlawful violence would be punished with death. Soldiers giving abusive language to the citizens were to suffer court martial. No officers were to leave their posts without written leave.[13] On 2 December Fairfax led them over Hounslow heath to London. Aggravated by his incapacity to conciliate his army and Parliament, there was substance to royalist claims that his public deportment was proud and aloof. When Fairfax arrived at his new headquarters in Whitehall, 'as if he meant to King it', a parliamentary delegation waited upon him bareheaded, and Lord Grey of Groby, playing the role of servant, held Fairfax's stirrup as he alighted. The Venetian ambassador at Munster reported that the 'affairs of England grow ever worse for the king. The military control everything. Fairfax has great pretensions.'[14]

Fairfax defended his army's occupation of London, writing to Lenthall on 3 December 1648. He claimed he had sent Sir Hardress Waller to inform Parliament that Lenthall's letter of 30 November had not reached him until it was too late to reverse his orders. Angered that Waller had been denied entry to the House of Commons, Fairfax again urged Parliament to consider the army remonstrance 'for the Reason and Righteousness that is in them, and as they are for the publique Interest, a sound peace, and the safety of the nation'.[15] Despite Fairfax having initially opposed the remonstrance, he had now urged Parliament personally and forcefully to consider it on at least three occasions.

Although by now it was principally Ireton that was directing army strategy, Fairfax's later claim that he was not forewarned of Pride's purge is highly dubious. His 'Short memorial' maintained that the purge was so secret that 'I had not ye least Intimation of it till it was Done', and that he had been 'upon Especiall business' with several MPs 'wn yt horrible Attempt was made by Coll: Pride'. Clarendon accepted that Fairfax had known nothing of the purge, but lodged as he was in Whitehall, such ignorance was unlikely. The army council would have been discussing which MPs to remove for days; Grey of Groby had attended headquarters on 23 November, possibly with this question in mind. Fairfax's uncle, Sir William Constable, was among the committee of six that finalised the details. Tellingly, Fairfax named none as responsible for giving the orders, only 'Agitating Council', and he failed to explain why he did not reverse the purge once it was brought to his knowledge.[16] Uneasy as he was about it, allowing Parliament to negotiate away his army's victories of 1648 was no alternative. When on 5 December six MPs informed Fairfax that the Commons had voted to proceed with further negotiations, he replied that many in Parliament had forfeited and betrayed their trust. He dismissed them with advice to comply with the army remonstrance. According to Ludlow, Ireton informed Fairfax of the planned purge that evening.[17]

On 6 December MPs found that the approaches to Parliament were guarded by two of Fairfax's regiments. At the top of the Parliament house stairs stood Colonel Thomas Pride. Assisted by Grey of Groby, derisively known as the 'grinning dwarf', Pride denied entry to MPs that had supported the treaty. Forty-one of these were imprisoned in a Palace-yard basement known as 'Hell' and confined there, wanting beds 'and other necessaries'. It was some time before Fairfax dispersed them under guard to several inns in the Strand. Perturbed as they were, Fairfax and Skippon stood by their men, Skippon defusing a potential military clash by prevailing upon the London trained bands to return home.[18] Onlookers assumed the soldiers had acted on Fairfax's orders and, later that day, Fairfax 'stonewalled' a committee of MPs who came to protest.[19] Subsequently, the House of Commons made several requests to Fairfax to explain in writing why their members had been arrested. Confused, embarrassed and wary of implicating himself so explicitly, he declined.[20] This evasion persisted on 20 December when a delegation of sixteen secluded MPs waited on Fairfax. They were kept waiting by Ireton for three hours and then dismissed, being told the general was 'indisposed'. On 29 December, Fairfax desired the parliamentary committee concerning the secluded MPs not to 'trouble themselves to send any more to him concerning this business'.[21]

Cromwell had been absent during the purge. On 28 November Fairfax had written to him from Windsor ordering his attendance there 'with all convenient speed'. As his foremost deputy, Fairfax expected Cromwell to act as his enforcer and to support him in restraining the army's more extreme elements. Although his arrival might have been expected from 2 December, Cromwell did not arrive until the evening after the purge.[22] One royalist tract expressed a widespread suspicion, mocking the convenience of his absence: 'and when all was done, in came Nol. Cromwell to Towne at night, as if he (poore man) had no hand in the Busines'.[23]

On 7 December the army's demands were published in Fairfax's name and signed by his secretary John Rushworth. They required that Denzil Holles, Edward Massey, Richard Browne and Lionel Copley should stand trial and they reprimanded Parliament for negotiating with the King in contravention of the vote of no addresses the previous January.[24] To consolidate Fairfax's hold over the army's discipline, his soldiers seized treasuries at Goldsmiths' Hall, Weavers' Hall and the Guildhall.[25] Underdown has noted that Fairfax enjoyed bullying the City into paying his men's arrears; he 'sarcastically assured the citizens, the continued quartering of the Army would "facilitate your work" in collecting the money'.[26] On 8 December Fairfax informed the Lord Mayor that the treasuries were seized because of the City's delays and denials in paying the army's arrears. Pointing out that many English counties had endured free quarter because of the City's tardiness, Fairfax offered to withdraw the army and restore the treasuries as soon as the City settled its arrears. To help avoid trouble Fairfax had quartered men in 'void houses, Inns and the like, without trouble to private families', ordering that aldermen supervise collections of bedding for his soldiers.[27]

II

The vengeful mood of the soldiery in autumn 1648 was particularly prevalent among the northern regiments. Cromwell's secretary, Robert Spavin, wrote to William Clarke on 2 November 1648: 'I verily think God will break that great idol the Parliament, and that old job-trot form of government of King, Lords and Commons.'[28] Fighting had not concluded in Yorkshire. Under Major-General John Lambert, many of Fairfax's first soldiers were still besieging Pontefract castle. They declared their support for Fairfax's army in a council of war on 5 December. Only Colonel Bright and Captain Westby dissented and a declaration supporting the army remonstrance was published a week later. It declared all MPs voting for the Treaty of Newport had betrayed their trust. The northern officers looked to Fairfax, declaring that God 'hath raised in you such a Spirit of discerning wisdom and Justice'. God's providence would show Fairfax the way and 'honour you with being the happy Instrument of Redemption and Deliverance to a poor dying Kingdom'. On 13 December Lambert's secretary, Thomas Margetts, wrote to William Clarke to dispel doubts over Lambert's agreement with the army's proceedings. Lambert sent a covering letter explaining that the northern officers had formed a weekly council to maintain 'mutual correspondency between the Forces, that there may be a joint acting in this publique service'.[29] During 1648 many northerners viewed the King as responsible for the renewed Scots occupation that had brought more hardship, and as David Scott has argued 'provoked a powerful xenophobic and patriotic reaction which helped transform the post war quest for settlement into revolution'. Scott has argued that the many northern commissioners for the King's trial suggest a regional grievance against Charles I, and was probably intended 'to bolster the wavering Lord General with as many members of his circle as possible'. His uncle, Sir William Constable, his brother-in-law, Sir Thomas Widdrington, his cousin, James Chaloner, his old colonels, John Lambert, Francis Lascelles and Robert Overton, were all named commissioners, along with the Yorkshire MPs Sir William Allanson, John Anlaby, Sir John Bourchier and Sir Thomas Mauleverer. Constable also joined Fairfax on the committee of MPs, Levellers and officers responsible for drawing up the revised 'Agreement of the People' in December 1648.[30] Ultimately six Yorkshiremen became regicides.[31] On 22 January 1649, Fairfax received another letter from the northern officers at Pontefract, approving the King's trial and the secluding of corrupt MPs.[32]

On 14 December 1648 Fairfax chaired a long debate of the army council at

Whitehall. The council was supposed to be debating the 'Agreement of the People', and it was attended by Lilburne and other Levellers, but Fairfax rarely permitted them to speak, while allowing Ireton to orate freely. John Evelyn claimed he went to Whitehall to watch, and recalled how the council were 'young, raw and ill spoken men' who used uncivil terms and could scarcely agree on one point.[33] When it became clear the council would not endorse the Agreement without substantial alterations, Lilburne withdrew to write a bitter account of proceedings. It was addressed to Fairfax and published on 29 December. He argued that the proposed alterations, 'tedious disputes and contests' had rendered the Agreement of no value.[34] Fairfax was in favour of some religious toleration, but not of destroying tithes and reforming the franchise, probably feeling that changing the nature of government would lead to anarchy. Lilburne demanded that Fairfax should 'instantly reduce your Councel into a certain method of orderly proceeding', to implement an unmodified 'Agreement of the People'. Fairfax, disdaining Lilburne's confrontational presumption in ordering him how to run his own council, did not personally respond. However, a startling pamphlet appeared on 7 January, signed by Rushworth in Fairfax's name. It offered annual or biennial parliaments, the supremacy of the House of Commons, and electoral reform to render the Commons 'an equal representative of the whole People electing'. It also stipulated that future English monarchs would be elective and stripped of their negative voice, with the general settlement established by an 'Agreement of the People'. These pledges exceeded Fairfax's preferences, and if he consented to this pamphlet, it was a reflection of how far the army leaders courted radical support.[35]

Fairfax was deliberately absent from the council on 15 December, not desiring to be present when it was decided to move the King from Hurst to Windsor 'in order to the bringing of him Speedily to justice'. An order signed in Fairfax's name that day authorised Colonel Thomas Harrison to supersede Cobbett and to guard the King's passage with horse and dragoons.[36] Fairfax may have selected Harrison to unnerve the King into behaving more reasonably; Charles was evidently shocked by Harrison's arrival, confiding to Thomas Herbert: 'do not you know that this is the Man who intended to assassinate me?' Harrison had earned notoriety on 11 November 1647 by calling for the punishment of the King, as 'that man of blood'.[37] The shadowy royalist informant John Lawrans wrote to the exiled Secretary Nicholas on 18 December that several secluded MPs predicted that the army leaders were not intent on executing the King, but hoped to keep him in close imprisonment to 'worke him by terror (if they can) to renounce ye Regall dignity, & to confirme their agreemt'.[38]

The notion that the army grandees were trying to frighten rather than eliminate the King became prevalent among contemporaries. To further this reading of events, Jason Peacey has exposed the considerable overlap between the manuscript newsletters by John Lawrans with the printed reports in Marchamont Nedham's *Mercurius pragmaticus*. Both anticipated that the army leaders threatened a trial in order to extort concessions from the King and string along support from the Levellers. Both considered that army control of Charles was an indispensable asset in preserving the army's political dominance and furthering their desire to crush the Presbyterian and Scottish interest. There may be much truth in this speculation, because Nedham was among the best informed newsbook editors, adept at acquiring information from inside Westminster, and understanding of the grandees' purposes.[39] These scare tactics extended to the construction of a scaffold to greet the King's arrival at Windsor.[40] Fairfax ordered Charles's new custodian, Colonel Matthew Thomlinson, to intensify security. Much to the King's annoyance guards were posted in his room day and night, while it was rumoured none was permitted into his presence without authorisation from Fairfax.[41]

In December Cromwell and Fairfax remained united in their endeavours to save the King's life, while outwardly supporting their men's petitions for justice. Rumours persisted that the King would be kept in prison for the army leaders to appeal to in their differences with Parliament, and one royalist informant predicted: 'You shall heare ere long yt there wilbe a cooling by degrees in the present prosecution of his Ma:.'[42] This became apparent on 19 December when the earl of Denbigh attended Fairfax to discuss visiting Charles at Windsor with a final offer. The army leaders and the Derby House Committee feared that a recent naval treaty between the Irish confederates and the Dutch republic would enable Ormond to land a royalist army in England. Denbigh's offer to the King constituted part of the grandees' diplomacy by intimidation: if Charles would call off Ormond and abandon his negative voice, then preparations for his trial would end and negotiations resume.[43] Fairfax probably instructed Cromwell to answer criticisms of this strategy in the army council. On 21 December Cromwell argued that executing the King would merely render the exiled Prince of Wales more dangerous.[44] On 25 December Cromwell propounded that 'there was no policy in taking away his life' and the council voted by six to one that if Charles accepted Denbigh's terms he should be spared.[45] Fairfax's hopes were shattered later that day when Charles refused even to receive Denbigh. News of this decisively swung Fairfax's council against the King and such formalities of state that Charles enjoyed at Windsor were dispensed with.[46] Making it even more difficult for Fairfax to counter momentum for a trial, Charles turned the grandees' threat on its head, publishing a tract that warned if his trial proceeded Ormond and the Prince of Wales would invade England and commence a third civil war to rescue him.[47] The council of officers voted to proceed with the trial on 27 December. Once again Charles had overestimated his importance and the grandees had not grasped that if they threatened him he would respond in kind. Their attempt to intimidate Charles into concessions failed; Whitelocke reported on 2 January that 'the King was cheerfull, & tooke no notice of any proceedings agt him, as to his tryall, & sayth he doubts not butt within 6 months to see peace in England, & in case of not restoring, to be righted from Ireland, Denmarke & other places'. Another report from Windsor described that Charles was 'exceeding high in his expressions, and very bitter against divers of the Army', predicting they would 'divide among themselves, and be destroyed'. By undermining the more moderate commanders and threatening the army, Charles separated Fairfax from Cromwell, but doing so only brought his execution closer.[48]

III

Until January 1649 it had been Ireton, not Cromwell, who led calls for the King's trial and execution. Fairfax may have interpreted Cromwell's support for the trial from 27 December as purely tactical, particularly if Cromwell had made private pledges to Fairfax to maintain the King's life. Even once the decision was taken to try Charles, it remained unclear whether execution was certain. So Fairfax attended to the maintenance of order and the supply of his army's needs. By early January the soldiers were becoming restive. Quartered in uncomfortable empty houses, they were suspicious that their officers were enriching themselves and fearful that their generals would make peace with the King. Fairfax responded by tending to the army's administration, tightening security, and on 9 January issuing a proclamation to expel all royalists ten miles from the City.[49]

Fairfax grew increasingly uncomfortable, but he clung to command to preserve his post from the hands of a more dangerous occupant. He could hardly remain a moderating force within the army if he resigned. Sean Kelsey has asserted that Fairfax may have favoured the Commons' vote of 5 December advocating further talks with Charles. He endeavoured to release some of the purged MPs and protected Presbyterian ministers from harassment by the army. Even William Prynne, still in custody on 3 January, proclaimed he was sorry that Fairfax had been 'dishonoured, abused, misled by rash ill advised officers', who had supposedly forced the general into uncharacteristic acts to his 'best friends amazemt'.[50] During December and January Fairfax endured vitriolic criticism of his army's proceedings from several godly ministers. Some of this was of a personal nature, and deeply wounding as these ministers included several of his former chaplains.[51] Characteristically, he responded not by taking offence, but by increasing his endeavours to mend the shattered parliamentarian coalition. He invited 'some of the most ridged' Presbyterian clergy to his house on 11 January to debate their differences with his officers.

He persuaded some leading Presbyterian divines, including Edmund Calamy, to accept the King's trial and conviction, providing execution was avoided. On 13 January Fairfax returned to chair the army's council for the first time since 16 December, but his recent efforts to negotiate with the Presbyterians were met with a reproof from Captain George Joyce who declared to the assembly that 'a spirit of feare' was upon Fairfax because he had been 'studying to please men'.[52]

Despite Fairfax's withdrawal from sitting as a commissioner, during the trial he 'was much distracted in his mind, and changed purposes often every day'.[53] This reflected the conflicting courses of action daily pressed upon him from all quarters. His uncertainty was little different from many other political actors. His brother-in-law, Sir Thomas Widdrington, condemned the trial and lamented 'he knew not wither to goe to be out of the way'.[54] On the eve of the trial, Colonel Barkstead reportedly said that 'he knew not what would be ye issue, but he knew their next councells might overthrow their former resolucons'. Right until the court's opening session Fairfax harboured doubts over Cromwell and Ireton's commitment to executing the King, and he was correct.[55]

Three recent articles by Sean Kelsey support this contention, that a capital sentence against Charles was not a foregone conclusion, even once the trial was underway. Debate and division between the commissioners persisted, creating an unpredictable and volatile atmosphere. The army officers were divided over what charges the King should face. Fairfax led the faction that favoured limiting them to the King's sins since 1642 and a vague charge of betraying subjects' liberties. Limiting the charges increased the likelihood of acquittal, encouraged the King to blame 'evil counsellors' and held better prospect for preserving more of the ancient constitution. The charges were contested for ten days before they were finally settled on 19 January. Even then most of the commissioners remained reluctant to impose a capital sentence and were urged in official sermons from Hugh Peter and Joshua Sprigge on 21 January to seek alternatives. Still hoping to persuade Charles to continue as a monarch stripped of power, they differed over the details and purpose behind such a course. Even on 27 January when sentence was to be delivered the King was given a further opportunity to plead and a large minority of judges sought to comply with his request to address Parliament. Astoundingly the court offered Charles between nine and twelve opportunities to plead, but he fatally misinterpreted this as a sign of his continued indispensability.[56] This interpretation of the trial does much to explain Fairfax's eleventh-hour uncertainty over whether the King really would be executed and his estrangement from Cromwell thereafter. Kelsey's argument also casts Fairfax's passivity in a more incriminating light than if we accept that the King's fate was sealed at an earlier stage.

Fairfax withdrew from the trial commissioners' initial meeting on 8 January, but this did not conclude his involvement. He remained a key figure during the trial because both the trial commissioners and those pleading for the King's life were desperate for him to join them. Even Charles himself, while venting his hatred of the army, was careful to cast 'a favourable construction upon the Lord Generall'.[57] As we shall see in Chapter 10, Fairfax's wife twice interrupted the court's business with hostile remarks that undermined proceedings. Her voice was personally known to several of the commissioners. Her words embarrassed both the commissioners and her husband, and rendered Fairfax's task of restraining those in the High Court still more difficult. As Fairfax's opposition grew widely known, he became the channel through which Dutch, French and Scottish negotiators blended threats with their pleas for the King's life.[58] On 4 January 1649 the French ambassador presented him with a letter from the Queen, but Fairfax merely passed it on to the House of Commons, who laid it aside unopened. She wrote to Fairfax again on 6 January requesting permission to join her husband.[59] Again, he never read the letter, but he did advise caution, postponement and a consideration of alternatives to regicide and republic, probably reviving the army council's speculation that the King's youngest son, the duke of Gloucester, might succeed as a limited monarch.[60] On the evening of 23 January, Fairfax was 'bayted with fresh dogs' all night to rejoin the commissioners in Westminster Hall, but he refused. On 26 January, John Lawrans's newsletter added tantalisingly that sentence had been postponed because Fairfax had recently done something to displease the judges.[61] On 28 January, Fairfax received the Dutch ambassadors who desired his aid in delivering pleas for the King's life to Parliament. On 29 January, he urged his council of war to postpone the sentence and on 30 January attended Whitehall to do so again.[62] It is difficult to conceive how he could have done more without resort to arms.

Few, including Fairfax, of those who were directly responsible for the King's execution actually witnessed it. Fairfax was attending a prayer meeting at Whitehall when the blow was struck. Contemporaries and historians have recognised that Fairfax was the only man with the power to stop the trial and execution. Most consider his failure to oblige was rooted in his own inability, because as David Scott suggests 'he lacked the political acumen to challenge Cromwell and Ireton'.[63] Yet there were many strong reasons why Fairfax was reluctant to act with force to save the King. Charles's actions had isolated Fairfax from his subordinates in the army, and aside from Skippon there were few senior officers upon whom Fairfax could rely to support a halt to proceedings. Fairfax's nature was to strive for unity among his comrades, not division. Like Cromwell, he understood that any eleventh-hour royal reprieve risked an army mutiny and renewed civil war, from which only the royalists could profit.[64]

Unsurprisingly, Fairfax's 'Short memorials' fall silent in describing his conduct in January 1649. They stress he laboured to save the King's life, but provide no details of how. Brian Fairfax maintained that when Fairfax was approached on 29 January to attempt a royal rescue he replied that he was 'ready to venture his own life, but not the lives of others', knowing that no newly raised force could prevail against his army.[65] Fairfax probably felt that if he allowed Charles to provoke further conflict against his army then providence would turn against God's people. His repeated efforts at conciliation had been in vain, and forced upon him a realisation that fighting for a settlement with such an intransigent King was no longer worthwhile. The King had repeatedly reminded parliamentary negotiators from as early as 1646 that he was willing to face martyrdom. In this deadly game of brinkmanship, both sides raised the stakes until the alternatives were regicide or renewed civil war. Therefore Fairfax may even have accepted that because Charles refused to call off Ormond's army, it had become more risky to keep him alive than to kill him.[66]

The notion that God would punish them if they failed to execute the King motivated many of the regicides into acting, but by the 1660s this explanation was no longer advisable or credible.[67] Therefore Fairfax's 'Short memorial' did not detail the events and considerations that brought about the King's death. Instead Fairfax concentrated on demonstrating his reaction to the regicide, drawing from royalist language and imagery to express his sorrow: 'My Afflicted & Troubled mind for it, & my earnest endeavors to prevent it, will, I hope, sufficiently Testify my Abhorrance of ye Fact.'[68] He mixed penitence with a desire to exonerate himself. The regicide had so traumatised him that self-doubt clawed at his self-representation ever thereafter: what could he have done differently, what if he had intervened? His cousin Brian Fairfax maintained that, later in life, Fairfax 'never mentioned it but with Tears in his Eyes'. In his retirement Fairfax wrote a poem, entitled 'On the Fatal day, Jan 30: 1648', in which his laments for the King's death constituted an outlet for his sorrow and guilt. His only consolation was expressed by clinging to his belief in God's providence:

> Oh Lett that Day from time be blotted quitt
> And lett beleefe of't in next age be waved
> In deepest silence th'Act concealed might
> Soe that the King-doms-Credit might be saved
> But if the Power devine permited this,
> His Will's the Law & ours must acquiesce.[69]

These arguments have made no impact upon the weight of historical condemnations of the regicide. Graham Edwards has recently referred to them as 'pusillanimous vapourings', while Lord Braybrooke remarked 'these wretched verses have obviously no merit' claiming that they were not even Fairfax's own, but rather a poor translation of Statius that had earlier been used to describe the massacre of St Bartholomew. Fairfax was an intense bibliophile so this may well be true, but the sentiments had retained some power as the verses were again utilised by William Pitt to condemn the murder of Louis XVI in 1793.[70]

NOTES

1 D. Underdown, *Pride's Purge: Politics in the Puritan Revolution* (Oxford, 1971), pp. 189–94.

2 J. Adamson, 'The frighted junto: perceptions of Ireland, and the last attempts at settlement with Charles I', in J. Peacey (ed.), *The Regicides and the Execution of Charles I* (Basingstoke, 2001), pp. 36–70; S. Kelsey, 'The trial of Charles I', *EHR*, 118:477 (2003), 583–616; S. Kelsey, 'The death of Charles I', *Historical Journal*, 45:4 (2002), 727–54.

3 C. H. Firth (ed.), *The memoirs of Edmund Ludlow* (Oxford, 1894), vol. 1, pp. 203–4.

4 BL, E466(11), *Mercurius pragmaticus*, 3–10 October (London, 1648).

5 I. Gentles, *The New Model Army in England, Ireland and Scotland, 1645–1653* (Oxford, 1992), p. 268; Bod., MS Tanner 57, fo. 332; Underdown, *Pride's Purge*, pp. 115–16, 176–7, 193.

6 Underdown, *Pride's Purge*, p. 191; Gentles, *New Model Army*, p. 268.

7 Underdown, *Pride's Purge*, pp. 117–18; C. H. Firth (ed.), *The Clarke papers, vol. 2* (Camden Society, new series, 54, 1894), p. 147n.

8 BL, E473(11), *A remonstrance of his excellency Thomas, lord Fairfax, lord generall of the Parliament's forces. And of the generall councell of officers held at St Albans, the 16 of November* (London, 1648); Underdown, *Pride's Purge*, p. 191; *JHC*, vol. 6, p. 81.

9 Bod., MS Tanner 57, fo. 442; BL, E475(8), *The moderate*, 28 November–5 December (London, 1648), p. 185.

10 Bod., MS Tanner 57, fo. 417; Firth (ed.), *Clarke papers, vol. 2*, p. 59; J. Rushworth, *Historical collections* (London, 1721), part 4, vol. 2, p. 1340.

11 BL, E476(2), *Mercurius pragmaticus*, 5–12 December (London, 1648).

12 BL, E475(18), *The declaration of Major-Generall Brown concerning the Lord Fairfax and the army*, 6 December (London, 1648), p. 2.

13 BL, E475(9), *Three proclamations by his excellency the lord general Fairfax* (London, 1648), pp. 3, 4.

14 BL, E476(2), *Mercurius pragmaticus*, 5–12 December (London, 1648); BL, E475(22), *Mercurius elencticus*, 29 November–6 December (London, 1648), pp. 523–4; A. B. Hinds (ed.), *Calendar of State Papers Venetian, 1647–1652* (London, 1927), p. 84.

15 Bod., MS Tanner 57, fo. 452.

16 Bod., MS Fairfax 36, fo. 4r; Clarendon, *History of the rebellion and civil wars in England*, ed. W. Dunn Macray (Oxford, 1888), vol. 4, p. 467; Gentles, *New Model Army*, pp. 278–82.

17 BL, E475(29), *The staffe set at the Parliaments owne doore*, 8 December (London, 1648), p. 3; BL, E476(2), *Mercurius pragmaticus*, 5–12 December (London, 1648); Firth (ed.), *The memoirs of Edmund Ludlow*, vol. 1, p. 210.

18 BL, E476(2), *Mercurius pragmaticus*; C. V. Wedgwood, *The Trial of Charles I* (London, 1964), pp. 46–7; *JHC*, vol. 6, p. 93.

19 Underdown, *Pride's Purge*, pp. 141, 146.

20 G. Dyfnallt Owen (ed.), *De L'Isle and Dudley MS, vol. 6, 1626–98*, HMC, 77 (London, 1966), p. 576; Gentles, *New Model Army*, p. 297.

21 Bod., MS Clarendon 34, fo. 12r; Rushworth, *Historical collections*, part 4, vol. 2, p. 1369.

22 Underdown, *Pride's Purge*, p. 149.

23 BL, E476(2), *Mercurius pragmaticus*.

24 BL, E475(25), *The humble proposals and desires of his excellency the Lord Fairfax and of the general council of officers in order to a speedy prosecution of justice and the settlement formerly propounded by them*, 7 December (London, 1648), pp. 3, 5, 6.

25 BL, E475(36), *The demands and desires of his excellency the lord general Fairfax and his general councell of officers* (London, 1648), p. 1.

26 Underdown, *Pride's Purge*, p. 156.

27 BL, E475(39), *A letter from the lord mayor, aldermen, and common council of the city of London in answer to a letter from the l. general* (London, 1648); BL, E475(40), *A declaration of his excellency the lord general Fairfax concerning the supply of bedding required from the city of London* (London, 1648), p. 6.

28 S. C. Lomas (ed.), *Leyborne Popham MS*, HMC, 51 (London, 1899), p. 8.

29 WYRO, Wakefield, C469/1; Firth (ed.), *Clarke papers*, vol. 2, p. 70; BL, E477(10), *The declaration of the officers belonging to the brigade of Colonel John Lambert*, 12 December (London, 1648), pp. 4–8.

30 D. Scott, 'Motives for king-killing', in Peacey (ed.), *The Regicides*, pp. 140, 143, 148; BL, E537(20), *Mercurius pragmaticus*, 26 December–9 January (London, 1649), p. 7.

31 See Table 1 and W. L. F. Nuttall, 'The Yorkshire commissioners appointed for the trial of King Charles the first', *YAJ*, 43 (1971), 147–57.

32 BL, Add. MS 37344, fo. 247v.

33 Firth (ed.), *Clarke papers*, vol. 2, pp. xix, 73–132; W. Bray (ed.), *Diary and correspondence of John Evelyn, F.R.S* (London, 1859), vol. 3, pp. 33–4.

34 BL, E536(22), *A plea for common right and freedom to his excellency the lord general Fairfax*, 29 December (London, 1648), pp. 3–5.

35 Wedgwood, *The Trial of Charles I*, pp. 82–3; BL, E536(24), *A new-years gift: presented by Tho. Lord Fairfax and the general-council of officers*, 7 January (London, 1649), pp. 5–8.

36 Firth (ed.), *Clarke papers*, vol. 2, pp. 132–3, 147n.

37 T. Herbert, *Memoirs of the last two years of the reign of King Charles I* (London, 1813), pp. 134, 142; C. H. Firth (ed.), *The Clarke papers*, vol. 1 (Camden Society, new series, 41, 1891), p. lxxv.

38 Bod., MS Clarendon 34, fo. 12r.

39 J. Peacey, 'Marchamont Nedham and the Lawrans letters', *Bodleian Library Record*, 17:1 (2000), 24–35; S. Kelsey, 'Politics and procedure in the trial of Charles I', *Law and History Review*, 22:1 (2004).

40 Bod., MS Clarendon 34, fo. 19r.

41 Firth (ed.), *Clarke papers, vol. 2*, p. 145; Bod., MS Clarendon 34, fo. 18r.

42 Bod., MS Clarendon 34, fo. 13r.

43 Adamson, 'The frighted junto', pp. 37, 43.

44 Peacey, 'Marchamont Nedham and the Lawrans letters', 28.

45 Firth (ed.), *Clarke papers, vol. 2*, p. xxx; BL, E536(27), *Mercurius melancholicus*, 25 December–1 January (London, 1648), p. 7; J. Morrill and P. Baker, 'Oliver Cromwell, the regicide and the sons of Zeruiah', in Peacey (ed.), *The Regicides*, p. 30.

46 Kelsey, 'Politics and procedure in the trial of Charles I'.

47 BL, E536(13), *His majesties last proposals to the officers of the armie*, 28 December (London, 1648), pp. 1–2.

48 BL, Add. MS 37344, fo. 241v; BL, E536(25), *His majesties declaration concerning the charge of the army*, 7 January (London, 1649), pp. 2–3.

49 BL, Add. MS 37344, fo. 243v; Underdown, *Pride's Purge*, p. 191; Rushworth, *Historical collections*, part 4, vol. 2, p. 1387.

50 S. Kelsey, 'Constructing the council of state', *Parliamentary History*, 22:3 (2003), 226; BL, Egerton MS 2618, fo. 31.

51 BL, E537(20), *Mercurius pragmaticus*, 26 December–9 January (London, 1649); BL, E536(16), *Mr William Sedgwicks letter to his excellency Thomas lord Fairfax* (London, 1649); BL, E540(13), *Certain weighty considerations ... by Joshua Sprigge* (London, 1648).

52 BL, E538(15), *The moderate*, 9–16 January (London, 1649); Firth (ed.), *Clarke papers, vol. 2*, p. 182.

53 G. Burnet, *History of his own time* (Oxford, 2nd edn, 1833), vol. 1, p. 85.

54 BL, Add. MS 37344, fo. 239v.

55 Bod., MS Clarendon 34, fo. 72v; Underdown, *Pride's Purge*, p. 193.

56 Kelsey, 'Politics and procedure in the trial of Charles I'; Kelsey, 'The death of Charles I', 745–8; Kelsey, 'The trial of Charles I', 585, 592, 611, 615. Gentles speculates that Fairfax appointed these preachers: Gentles, *New Model Army*, p. 306; R. Cust, *Charles I: A Political Life* (Harlow, 2005), p. 457.

57 BL, E536(25), *His majesties declaration concerning the charge of the army*, p. 3.

58 Kelsey, 'Constructing the council of state', 226–7.

59 BL, E537(13), *His majesties declaration and speech* (London, 1649), p. 3; Bod., MS Tanner 57, fo. 493.

60 BL, E537(9), *The Queens majesties letter to the Parliament of England*, 5 January (London, 1649), p. 5; BL, E537(20), *Mercurius pragmaticus*.

61 Bod., MS Clarendon 34, fos. 86r, 88r.

62 BL, E541(4), *The moderate intelligencer*, 25 January–1 February (London, 1649), p. 1169; BL, E541(5), *The kingdomes faithfull scout*, 26 January–2 February (London, 1649), p. 3.

63 D. Scott, *Politics and War in the Three Stuart Kingdoms, 1637–49* (Basingstoke, 2004), pp. 194–5.

64 Kelsey, 'The trial of Charles I', 612.

65 B. Fairfax, *A catalogue of the curious pictures of George Villiers, duke of Buckingham, in which is included the valuable collection of Sir Peter Paul Rubens with the life of George Villiers, duke of Buckingham, the celebrated poet written by Brian Fairfax, esq* (London, 1758), p. 32.

66 Cust, *Charles I*, pp. 421, 461.

67 Scott, 'Motives for king-killing', pp. 140, 143, 148.

68 Bod., MS Fairfax 36, fo. 4r.

69 B. Fairfax (ed.), *Short memorials of Thomas, lord Fairfax* (London, 1699), p. 6; Bod., MS Fairfax 40, fo. 600.

70 G. Edwards, *The Last Days of Charles I* (Stroud, 1999), p. 185; H. B. Wheatley (ed.), *The diary of Sir Samuel Pepys, with Lord Braybrooke's notes* (London, 1897), vol. 1, pp. 5–6n; L. Namier and J. Brooke (eds), *The House of Commons, 1754–1790* (London, 1964), vol. 2, p. 16.

Chapter 6

Republic and Restoration

This chapter traces Fairfax's political significance from the regicide to his own death in 1671. There is insufficient space to provide a comprehensive account of this twenty-two-year period, so I have focused in particular on the critical moments of his brief but important role as republican commander–in–chief, his resignation in 1650 and his political re-emergence in 1659. Although Fairfax abstained from royalist conspiracy during the 1650s, his subsequent importance in the Restoration invited rumours to the contrary. Finally, I will discuss how Fairfax's response to the demise of the 'good old cause' during the 1660s, that of secluded disillusion, provides a dark contrast to the joviality popularly held to characterise Restoration political culture.

I

Fairfax is usually held to have withdrawn from politics after the regicide, but this was not the case. Instead, he took his place assertively at the centre of the new regime. As Sean Kelsey has observed, his nomination to the republic's Council of State was a matter of controversy, forced through despite attempts to prevent soldiers sitting and thereby constituting 'an important moment in the orientation of the fledgling kingless commonwealth'. On 14 February 1649, Fairfax was the ninth nominee to this new executive body behind the peers, high court judges and John Bradshaw. Unlike the other two soldiers nominated, Cromwell and Skippon, Fairfax was still not an MP. He had stood for Cirencester in January 1647, but had encountered riotous local opposition, and a high sheriff who would not allow the poll to be taken.[1] Although the 'relevant paperwork had gone missing in mysterious circumstances', Fairfax was officially returned to the Rump on 17 February 1649. He appears never to have taken his seat.[2]

Nevertheless, Fairfax's return as MP and member of the Council of State bolstered his position against potential challengers such as Lord Grey of Groby, who had been discussed as an alternative lord general in early 1649. Kelsey has also argued that although Fairfax strengthened the interest of his aristocratic friends the earls of Mulgrave, Northumberland and Pembroke, 'he was as much of a "revolutionary" as any other' because he engaged fully in the political struggle to shape the new republic. Fairfax's personal influence remained strong in the Rump, with seven of his kinsmen sitting as MPs.[3] By remaining at his post and maintaining his political connections he hoped to moderate the revolution's direction. He indicated his continued willingness to serve the Parliament, but initially would not subscribe to the Engagement to be true to the Commonwealth. The new regime was concerned to secure his endorsement, permitting him to draft his own Engagement, one that omitted approval of past acts.[4] On 28 January 1650 the Council of State urged him to publish his own subscription, as by his example 'the malignants much encourage themselves, and animate others to desist from taking it'.[5] When he finally acquiesced he was mocked by John Crouch for doing so just as his appointment to the Council of State was reconfirmed: 'Pray Ring the Bells, my Lord *Fairfax* has taken the Engagement ... which hath given the *Junto* such content, that they have ordered a *Letter* of thankes to be sent to his Foole-ship.'[6]

In the regicide's aftermath Fairfax's principal task was restoring discipline to the army, a difficult prospect with Leveller activism and threatened mutinies. On 26 February 1649 John Lilburne presented the Rump with *England's new chains discovered*, a tract that criticised the generals, accusing the Rump of abandoning the *Agreement of the People* and descending into tyranny. When eight troopers petitioned Fairfax on 1 March in support of *England's new chains discovered*, they were court-martialled and five were cashiered. In retaliation another pamphlet appeared on 21 March entitled *The hunting of the foxes from Newmarket and Triploe heaths to Whitehall by five small beagles (late of the army)*. Probably penned by Richard Overton, this constituted a rancorous attack on the generals, accusing them of ambition, hypocrisy and betraying the soldiers' interests.[7] The Leveller leaders tended to be wary of Fairfax's popularity with the soldiers, and rather than attacking him directly, targeted Cromwell and Ireton as more believably devious villains for their propaganda. Brailsford once contended that 'no one criticised Fairfax', 'the soldier incarnate, round whose name blazed a legend of invincible courage'.[8] He was right that Fairfax was less criticised by discontented radicals, but Fairfax did not escape entirely.

One venomous attack upon Fairfax came from Captain William Bray. Bray was among Robert Lilburne's mutinous soldiers on Corkbush field in 1647 and he returned to notoriety in March 1649. He defended the five troopers Fairfax had expelled and appealed to the Rump with a printed petition entitled 'for the peoples sake against Thomas Lord Fairfax'. Referring to Fairfax as his 'profest enemye', Bray accused Fairfax of favouritism, bribery and an 'evill spirit of unrighteousness' likened to Ahab. His petition was judged scandalous, 'tending to stir up sedition in the people and mutiny in the army', and the Rump ordered his imprisonment at Windsor.[9]

In late April 1649, a troop of Colonel Edward Whalley's regiment mutinied in London. This time fifteen troopers were court-martialled and six were sentenced to death. After they made humiliating submissions, Cromwell was inclined to pardon them, but Fairfax insisted on one exemplary punishment to restore discipline, and Robert Lockyer was chosen. John Lilburne and Richard Overton accused Fairfax and Cromwell of 'treason and murder' for suppressing this mutiny. They sent Fairfax intimidating letters warning a popular rising would follow if Lockyer was executed.[10] Contemptuous of such threats, Fairfax had Lockyer shot in St Paul's churchyard on 27 April. Fairfax had needed to demonstrate that matters of army discipline would not be dictated by civilian political prisoners, but in doing so provided the Levellers with their first martyr and funeral since Rainborough's death the previous autumn. Lockyer's funeral was attended by 4000 people, including several hundred soldiers, and the affair increased rather than defused unruliness within the army the following month.[11]

On 1 May 1649 the four Leveller leaders imprisoned in the Tower published the last version of the *Agreement of the People* in an attempt to strip the generals of their soldiers' support. Mutinies followed in the horse regiments of Thomas Harrison, Henry Ireton and Adrian Scroop. That May up to 2500 men became actively engaged in mutiny. In order to suppress the mutineers, Fairfax mustered 4000 loyal troops in Hyde Park. The speed and resolution that characterised Fairfax's leadership during the civil wars were the hallmarks of his last operation as general. By riding forty-five miles on 14 May, Fairfax's force surprised the main body of mutineers at Burford at around midnight. Entering from both ends of the main street, there was minimal resistance with a handful of casualties. Despite the mutiny's large size, only three mutineers were executed, shot in Burford churchyard. Ian Gentles has provided the best account of the army mutinies elsewhere, but Fairfax and Cromwell's contrasting roles within this episode will be discussed further in Chapter 11.[12]

After Burford, Fairfax and Cromwell were entertained at All Souls, feasted at Magdalen and granted honorary doctorates of law by Oxford University. Returning towards London on 26 May Fairfax found twelve Diggers labouring upon the common on St George's Hill in Surrey. Several of Fairfax's officers questioned one among them, Gerard Winstanley. When Fairfax 'made a short speech by way of admonition to them', Winstanley returned sober answers that impressed him.[13] The Diggers were already known to Fairfax because on 16 April the Council of State ordered him to disperse them. Fairfax disobeyed, merely sending Captain John Gladman to gather intelligence. Gladman reported that the business was unworthy of notice, and that the Council had been abused with false information.[14] Fairfax met Winstanley and his colleague William Everard at Whitehall on 20 April 1649, and even promised them protection.[15] On 9 June Winstanley thanked Fairfax in a letter that 'we did receive mildness and moderation from you'. Considering the Diggers had undermined the manorial system, declared themselves against private property and sparked newsbook reports that the poor would rise on Newmarket, Hampstead and Hounslow heaths, Fairfax's lenience towards them was remarkable.[16] Considering that Fairfax may have been acquiring local interests in northern Surrey, his mildness was still more extraordinary.[17] It was not until 28 November 1649 that soldiers acted against the Diggers, compelling them to appeal to Fairfax to 'continue your former kindness' towards them.[18]

Soon after Fairfax's return to London, on 7 June 1649 a great feast costing £3600 was given at Grocers' Hall in his honour, and a day of solemn thanksgiving was ordered by a City magistracy relieved at the Levellers' defeat.[19] Sat between Speaker Lenthall and the earl of Pembroke, Fairfax was presented with a basin and ewer of gold worth £1000.[20] John Evelyn scoffed that Fairfax 'upon one of the late king's horses, went modestly through the streets to Christ Church'.[21]

II

If Fairfax's appointment to command the New Model in 1645 was the most important moment in his life, then his decision to resign five years later was his next most important moment. Historians have been divided over whether his resignation was prompted by genuine scruples over invading Scotland, a general dissatisfaction with Parliament going back to Pride's purge, or a realisation that invading Scotland precluded all chances of restoring a Stuart to the throne. With Cromwell's stage-managed victorious return from Ireland in May 1650, rumours circulated about who would lead the army against the Scots. Fairfax's dissatisfaction with the regicide was common knowledge and his portrayal as a guilt-ridden ghost in the royalist press fuelled speculation. During early 1650 his attendance on the Council of State dropped until only one member attended less frequently (Table 2). By June, satirical polemicists depicted him as on the brink of resignation:

> *The* Regicides *stinke at the stake,*
> *cause* Fairfax *went to Church,*
> Cromwell *must his Commission take,*
> *Least* Tom *gives them the lurch.*[22]

In June *Mercurius elencticus* reported the preparations against Charles II's forces in Scotland: 'as yet they are not resolved upon the point who shall goe,

Table 2 *Fairfax's attendance on the Council of State, 1649–50*

Month	Attendances
February 1649	6
March 1649	15
April 1649	6
May 1649	4
June 1649	8
July 1649	8
August 1649	4
September 1649	4
October 1649	1
November 1649	2
December 1649	11
January 1650	7
February 1650	1
March 1650	0
April 1650	6
May 1650	8
June 1650	3

Sources: CSP dom. 1649– 50, pp. lxxiv–lxxv; CSP dom. 1650, pp. x–xli.

Black Tom, or Nose-almighty'. *The man in the moon* mocked Fairfax once again as Cromwell's fool:

> *And art return'd* (Great Noll) *againe,*
> *and left* Ireland *behind?*
> *Nay then I see god* Nose *must reign,*
> *and* Tom-asse *come behinde.*
>
> *What* mischief *now have wee in hand?*
> *what* change *shall we next have?*
> *If* Tom *gives* Cromwell *his command*
> *he is more Fool then Knave.*[23]

On 6 June 1650 Fairfax welcomed Cromwell's return from Ireland on Hounslow heath amid ceremonial pomp attended by MPs, Councillors of State and detachments from the army. Soon after, Cromwell visited Fairfax at his house in Queen Street, which encouraged the official press to rebut the rumours in the underground satires; *Mercurius politicus* reported that 'many remarkable expressions of mutuall love and courtesie' passed between Fairfax and Crom-well, 'sufficient to check the false Tongues and wishes of the enemies of the Nation'.[24]

With the Scots intending to invade England in support of Charles II, Fairfax was confirmed as army commander by the Rump on 14 June, with additional powers to grant new commissions.[25] Later that month Charles II arrived in Scotland and took the Solemn League and Covenant, making a military clash certain. However, Fairfax doubted the legitimacy of the Rump's plan for an English invasion of Scotland as a pre-emptive strike. On 25 June the Rump appointed a committee to persuade him to comply that included Oliver Cromwell, John Lambert, Thomas Harrison, Oliver St John and Bulstrode Whitelocke. Meeting Fairfax in Whitehall, the conference began with Crom-well leading them in prayer. The remarkable debate that followed was reported by Whitelocke in his memorials.[26] Fairfax began by declaring 'I thinke I need not make to you or to any that know me, any protestation of the continuance of my duty & affection to the Parlemt.' He then argued that the projected invasion was unjustified as England was still bound to Scotland by the Covenant, and the Scots had not yet given sufficient cause for them to invade. Conceding that the Committee's arguments were strong, he admitted that war was probable, but only consented to fight a defensive war, reminding Harrison: 'Human probabilities are not sufficient grounds to make war uppon a neighbor nation, especially our brethren of Scotland, to whom we are ingaged in a Solemne League & Covenant.' Cromwell fought hard to persuade Fairfax to remain, even resorting to emotional blackmail: 'I hope your Lp will never give so great an advantage to the publique ennemy, nor so much dishearten your friends as to thinke of laying down your Comn.'[27] For all the depictions of Fairfax in the popular press as weak-willed and fickle, on this occasion he was immov-able, perhaps suggesting that Scotland was an excuse rather than a reason for his resignation. Fairfax had no love for the Scots. They had despoiled York-shire several times and, after the battle of Preston, Fairfax ordered Cromwell to punish them by invading Scotland and occupying Edinburgh.[28] Yet in 1650 Fairfax's guilt over the regicide widened the political gulf between him and his lieutenants. He may even have worried that his persistent ill health was punishment from God for failing to prevent the King's death. To invade Scot-land would deepen this sin, threatening the young King and ending any possi-bility of an accommodation with the Stuarts. With his wife pressing him to disassociate himself from the republic, the proposed invasion of Scotland at last provided him with a pretext to tender his long-postponed resignation.

His retirement was not received well by his former soldiers in Yorkshire, and the news was met with a troubled blend of disbelief, speculation and confusion. On 5 July Colonel Hugh Bethell circulated happy rumours that Fairfax had not resigned. Cornet John Baynes lamented that it was 'very ill received here by most, I wish it may prove to his honor & advantage, for my part nothing has troubled me so much alonge as this of his'. Colonel Thomas Rokeby concurred that 'I am very sorry for this business of my Ld Generall I could earnestly wish he might be ingaged if possible.' Captain William Siddall agreed that his resignation was 'estranged by most men'.[29] Lucy Hutchinson later reflected that his resignation was so timed that 'it could not have been done more spitefully and ruinously to the whole Parliament interest'.[30] As shall be seen in Chapter 10, Lady Fairfax shouldered much of the blame among contemporaries for the episode. Exiled royalists overestimated the harm caused by Fairfax's resignation, eagerly reporting that 'Fairfax is said to be under restraint', and that several troops and companies had refused the march into Scotland.[31]

The transfer of Fairfax's command to Cromwell proceeded smoothly enough. To save the regime's face, Fairfax announced his retirement was owing to 'debilities both in body and mind, occasioned by former actions and businesses'.[32] The official press denied any hint of political disagreement between Fairfax and the republic; when one officially printed sermon that summer was found to contain comments critical of Fairfax, the work was ceremoniously burnt in public.[33] Fairfax departed well paid for his service. His pay as lord general was for 1909 days from 3 April 1645 to 26 June 1650. At £10 per day this totalled £19,090, of which only £160 remained due. For part of these arrears he was given the manor of Helmsley and York House in the Strand which had been confiscated from the Villiers family. This compared most favourably with his father, who was owed a total of over £13,480 for his arrears from 1642 to 1645, of which he had received less than £2070 by August 1646.[34] Fairfax's resignation was so important because it damaged the republic's attempts to conciliate mainstream puritans. Even in 1654 John Milton feared that Fairfax's resignation fuelled speculation of an estrangement between Fairfax and Cromwell, remarking in praise of Fairfax that 'nothing could have torn you away from the service of the State unless you had seen what a Saviour of Liberty, what a firm and faithful support and bulwark of the English Commonwealth, you were leaving in your successor'.[35]

III

The 1650s would prove a much quieter decade for Fairfax but he did not immediately retire to Yorkshire. Ludlow recalled Fairfax was at Hampton Court with other MPs in September 1650 when news of the victory at Dunbar arrived, which he 'seemed much to rejoice at'.[36] Fairfax remained active in Yorkshire's political life, named as a justice of the peace in all three ridings, where around twenty fellow justices had been officers under him in the northern army.[37] His uncle, Charles Fairfax of Menston, aided the foundation of a radical chapel at

Bramhope, in Otley parish, in 1649, and by 1654 was presiding over secular marriages at Menston Hall.[38] On 3 June 1651 the Council of State thanked Fairfax for providing his coach and horses for two doctors to visit an ailing Cromwell in Scotland. That summer, Fairfax briefly re-engaged in military affairs after the Scots army invaded England. On 12 August with the Scots already in Lancashire, the Council of State begged Fairfax to defend Hull from the invaders. Now satisfied that he would be engaged in a defensive war, Fairfax finally engaged himself in support of the republic, raising the local militia to defend Yorkshire, and riding with Cromwell around Doncaster and Rotherham. This public show of support enabled Cromwell to stress his old commander's assistance.[39]

The Rump were quick to reward Fairfax for his continued support, appointing him Lord of the Isle of Man on 15 October 1651 to succeed the recently executed royalist earl of Derby. Fairfax was empowered to collect the late earl's rents and administer religious reformation on the island. Fairfax spent much of the following year in Surrey and appointed his cousin James Chaloner a commissioner alongside Robert Dyneley and Joshua Witton to settle Manx affairs.[40] Chaloner was a Rump MP and had married Ursula, sister to Sir William Fairfax. During the early 1650s Chaloner acted as Fairfax's political correspondent and man of business in London. Twenty-one of Fairfax's letters to Chaloner survive from 1651 to 1659, furnishing us with glimpses of his retirement's concerns. Spending much of the 1650s at Denton, Nun Appleton or York, Fairfax discussed with Chaloner his plans to build a new house on Bishophill in York, with the aid of the architect Edward Carter.[41] Maintaining an interest in political events, he frequently requested news from London. When Parliament granted him the duke of Buckingham's estates, he protested that he was 'unfit every way to undertake such a business neither have I any desire to purchase great things'.[42] Most of his letters informed Chaloner of his continuous illness; he complained attacks of the gout and stone 'hath been so extreame as I have not been able to ride 3 miles this six month'. In 1652 he was prescribed asses' milk for his continued infirmities.[43]

In January and February 1653 the Council of State corresponded with Fairfax over the Isle of Man and Fairfax travelled to London that March. Royalists gossiped that Fairfax had visited Cromwell, but that Cromwell had refused to see him. They also speculated that some of the Rumpers sought to reinstate him as general, believing he would be more compliant than Cromwell. On 13 April Sir William Brereton and Sir Arthur Hesilrige were appointed to confer with Fairfax in person over Manx affairs, but if they had secretly sought his return to command they were disappointed.[44] When Cromwell dissolved the Rump on 20 April, Fairfax was possibly still in London, and his relations with Cromwell had not deteriorated completely as Fairfax was invited to sit in the Nominated Assembly. Much to Cromwell's frustration, Fairfax refused, offering the republic another destructive snub.[45] In August 1654 Fairfax was elected MP for the West Riding in the first Protectorate Parliament but again refused to take his seat. Fairfax intervened in local politics concerning the corporation of Leeds at Christmas in 1656, siding with the town oligarchy and charter against Adam Baynes's coalition of reformers.[46]

Royalist conspirators hoped to draw Fairfax into conspiracy and John Thurloe's spies frequently reported Fairfax was in correspondence with Charles Stuart. Unsubstantiated rumours about Fairfax's dalliance with royalism began in 1650, with a reported royal offer to Fairfax of the earldom of Essex and £10,000 per annum. There were even rumours of a proposed match between Fairfax's daughter and the duke of Gloucester. Despite much speculation, Fairfax's involvement in royalist conspiracy remains unproven; much of the surviving evidence is at third or fourth hand. Circumspect in his dealings, he was careful to avoid direct contact with royalists.[47]

While refraining from conspiracy, it nevertheless remained sensible for him to befriend a man close to the King as insurance against future regime change, a man whose estates he would be held to account for in the eventuality of a restoration. This opportunity came in 1657, when George Villiers, duke of Buckingham, returned to England. Buckingham's interest in Fairfax's daughter Mary had been rumoured since 1653. Fairfax believed he was distantly related to Buckingham through the earls of Rutland, and had been safeguarding part of the young duke's estate. Lady Mary Vere and Robert Harley helped with the marriage arrangements. Some of the Protector's councillors remained suspicious of Buckingham's royalism, and viewed the marriage as 'a Presbyterian plot'.[48] The couple married in Bolton Percy church on 15 September 1657,[49] Dugdale commenting that the wedding was presided over by Mr Vere Harcourt, 'a great Presbyterian, who assured my Lady Fairfax that he saw God in the Duke's face'.[50] While some exiled royalists raised their hopes that Fairfax would turn royalist, others regarded Buckingham as a renegade for having married Fairfax's daughter.[51]

On 9 October 1657 the Council of State ordered Buckingham's arrest after he defied their ban on entering London. They ordered his imprisonment on Jersey, provoking impassioned pleas for his release from Lord and Lady Fairfax who now visited the Cromwells more than they had done in years. On 5 December Cromwell presented written arguments on Buckingham's behalf, but his council would not acquiesce and the duke was not released until April 1658.[52] Brian Fairfax later rather unfairly blamed Cromwell for Buckingham's imprisonment, writing he 'would have brought him to Tower–hill had he lived a moment longer'.[53] During this time Fairfax fell under increasing suspicion of involvement in royalist conspiracy. On 25 December 1657 one royalist correspondent claimed Fairfax had said 'since the dissolving of the [Long] parliament, which was broke up wrongfully, there was nothing but shifting and a kind of confusion; and that he knew not but he might chuse by his old commission as generall to appeare in armes on behalf of the people of these nations'.[54] On 8 January 1658 Percy Church informed Sir Edward Nicholas: 'Some think Lord Fairfax will be questioned about the last plot, when Sir John Wagstaffe was in the west.'[55]

In spring 1658 Lord and Lady Fairfax resided in London with their daughter and the newly released Buckingham. Within weeks, Buckingham was arrested again and Fairfax went to Cromwell to arrange his release. According to Brian Fairfax who claimed to be present, an ill-tempered quarrel ensued and Fairfax stormed out.[56] Buckingham was imprisoned in the Tower on 24 August 1658, and scarcely a week later Cromwell was dead. Fairfax heard this news very promptly, suggesting he had remained in London. On 4 September he wrote to James Chaloner:

> Yesterday and this day hath seen great changes on the one the Lord Protector died on the other his son the Lord Richard proclaimed Prot but all things so quiet as if neither were happened. The Lord look upon this nation that when we are weake he may be our strength til he hath perfected Peace & Truth amongst us. I shall be glad to hear of your health and that the place agrees with you. My wife is extreemly ill of a continual violent paire the Lord fitt us for our troubles.[57]

Having refused to serve in the parliaments of 1653, 1654 and 1656, at the first opportunity after Cromwell's death, Fairfax terminated his political retirement and returned to the House of Commons as knight of the shire for Yorkshire in Richard Cromwell's Protectorate Parliament. Taking his seat on 3 February 1659, he petitioned successfully for Buckingham's release, with Sir Arthur Hesilrige, Sir Henry Vane and Sir Anthony Ashley Cooper making speeches in Fairfax's favour. Otherwise Fairfax spoke little, but he expressed himself against military rule, sided with the republican opposition and sat next to Sir Arthur Hesilrige. He won support for declaring that the militia should remain 'out of our hands to any single person, but that it be intrusted where it may be serviceable to itself and to the people'.[58] Buckingham was freed on 21 February 1659 but Fairfax was still required to provide £20,000 bail.[59]

When the Rump reassembled on 7 May 1659 Fairfax was soon after returned to the Council of State. The new government courted his goodwill and his name headed the Yorkshire militia commission. He had co-operated with the republicans during Richard Cromwell's Parliament, but he now remained aloof. He did not object to the new regime, neither did he serve it, only contacting his fellow councillors to secure Buckingham's exemption from their Act against Delinquents.[60]

IV

Fairfax briefly returned to prominence in the prelude to the Restoration, when his reputation helped ensure the return of Charles II without a significant military engagement.[61] By October 1659 Fairfax was weary of the breakdown in government and abuses of the soldiery, and was heartened when General George Monck, commander of the republic's army in Scotland, declared himself for an end to military interference in politics. Fairfax sent two emissaries who arrived in Edinburgh on 7 November to investigate Monck's intentions.[62] Monck's deputy, Major-General Thomas Morgan, who had served under Fairfax in 1643, also visited Nun Appleton before returning to Monck's headquarters. Thereafter Fairfax employed Edward Bowles, his 'chaplain, counsellor and agitator', to conduct secret negotiations with Monck.[63] Amidst the constitutional chaos of December 1659, Fairfax hoped that Monck would restore the Long Parliament as it had been before Pride's purge, as a means to negotiate restoration of a limited monarchy. Satisfied that Monck would join his calls for a 'free' Parliament, on 20 December 1659 Fairfax sent his cousin, Brian Fairfax, from Nun Appleton in the guise of a 'young country clown' to deliver the verbal message to Monck that Fairfax would take up arms on 1 January 1660. Fending off an attack from a moss-trooper, Brian reached Monck at Coldstream near midnight on 25 December, later writing an account of his adventure entitled *Iter boreale*.[64] Fairfax's plan was to prevent John Lambert's army in northern England from hindering Monck's passage south. The next day, Colonel Robert Lilburne, Lambert's governor of York, sent a troop to arrest Fairfax and Buckingham at Nun Appleton. Forewarned, Fairfax escaped that night through Selby into marshland beyond Castleton ferry. Lilburne believed Fairfax had abandoned his plans and fled into Lancashire, but instead Fairfax began mustering cavalry. At Knaresborough on 30 December he met 300 of his former officers and Yorkshire gentry including Sir Francis Boynton, Sir Henry Cholmley, Colonel Hugh Bethel, Major George Smithson and Captain Thomas Strangeways. That night he heard from an officer of Lambert's Irish brigade of horse that they were ready to defect and the next day they joined him on Marston moor. The duke of Buckingham withdrew after objections were raised against his presence, and with his numbers swelled to 1800, Fairfax marched on York.[65]

Fairfax appeared in force before Micklegate bar on New Year's Day, sending a letter explaining his conduct to Speaker Lenthall.[66] Within the city, Sir Philip Monckton spread word to the citizens to gather at the Minster when the bells rang. Once inside they loudly cried out 'a Fairfax, a free Parliament' to suggest they were there in greater numbers. Colonel Lilburne cunningly offered to admit Fairfax's men if they would swear an engagement against government by 'a King or any Single Person whatsoever', thus splitting Fairfax's supporters. Frustrated, Fairfax tore it up before its promoters' faces. After a confrontation on the fields between York and Poppleton that threatened to turn violent, Fairfax finally permitted those who swore this engagement to enter York while he remained outside. Many did so and some of Lilburne's own soldiers joined them, seizing a church in the city and crying 'a Fairfax'.[67] On 2 January 1660 Lilburne ended his opposition to Fairfax entering York and when Monck's cavalry crossed the Tweed that day none of Lambert's army opposed him. Monck had been cautious and deliberate in timing his march. Despite having been in readiness for weeks, he began his campaign to coincide exactly with Fairfax's Yorkshire rising, having sent his infantry across the Tweed on 1 January, just as Fairfax's force appeared before York.[68]

Monck rode into York on 11 January. He paused there for five days, hearing Bowles preach in York Minster and dining with Fairfax in York and at Nun Appleton. Dr Price, one of Monck's chaplains, maintained that Bowles had urged Fairfax to openly declare for the King, but Fairfax had stalled, Price finding 'him a little perplexed in his thoughts'.[69] The common council which had invited Fairfax to 'liberate the city' connived at occupation by Fairfax's armed supporters. On 10 February Fairfax presented to the corporation a petition to Monck, which demanded free elections or a return of the members secluded by Pride's purge. It was signed by many families of old parliamentarian gentry, and the common council and aldermen of York followed suit.[70]

The Restoration would hardly have remained impossible without Fairfax, despite the self-regarding claims of Buckingham,[71] Horatio, baron Townshend[72] and Sir Philip Monckton[73] that they had urged him to action. Nevertheless, as Austin Woolrych has pointed out, Fairfax's role was critical. Only he could have headed the parliamentarian gentry's rising against army rule without provoking Lambert's men into active defiance. By barring all former royalists from joining his forces, Fairfax minimised premature divisions among his supporters. His reputation legitimised the rising, identifying it with 'an earlier, broader, and as it now seemed a more honourable phase of the revolution'.[74] Yorkshire played a critical role in 1642 and again in 1660. Once Fairfax cleared Monck's path, he modestly stepped aside, as described by Thomas Gower on 19 January:

> My Lord Fairfax hath laid down his arms, and with them an opportunity, in some men's opinion, to make himself great, and the nation quiet by a free Parliament; it is most certain he might have done what he list; Lambert's army disbanded and melted only by the fame of his rising ... General Monk made a halt till he heard what his proceedings were, and we are assured London had their eye principally upon him; and though all this and more was fully represented, yet he chose rather to sit down contented with the thanks of the House, than to make use of these great opportunities. Some ascribe it to dullness, others that an order of Parliament hath more power upon him then all reason; some to farther design yet ripe, some to one thing, some to another.[75]

Gower was premature in believing that Fairfax would melt into obscurity quite so swiftly. On 3 March Fairfax was appointed to the new Council of State and later that month was elected to the Convention Parliament for Yorkshire. By April royalists grew fearful that Fairfax had joined the earl of Manchester and his Presbyterian allies in calling for the King's return to be made conditional upon their terms.[76] Their concerns were certainly possible as earlier on 21 January Monck claimed that Fairfax had assured him 'hee would joyne with mee to the opposeing of Charles Stuart's family'.[77] Although Fairfax would no doubt have preferred some safeguards in place against excessive royal power, he was powerless to act otherwise. Whatever short-lived spirit of reconciliation existed, it mobilised strongly to Charles II's advantage. On 16 April 1660 Sir John Hotham's grandson appealed to Fairfax's uncle, Charles Fairfax, the military governor of Hull, to end the enmity between their families, so that they might go 'hand in hand' in the 'common cause', meaning thereby the King's restoration.[78] Fairfax co-operated with another old enemy, Denzil Holles, in heading the commission to the Hague from 18 to 26 May 1660 to invite the King's return. He was accompanied by Brian Fairfax and Edward Bowles. Fairfax secured a royal pardon under the Great Seal for his past conduct, and the horse upon which Charles II rode to his coronation was named 'Nun Appleton', a foal of the mare Fairfax rode at Naseby. This gift from Fairfax was intended to remind Charles of what he owed his father's conqueror and it symbolised Fairfax's hopes for healing, settlement and a broad, inclusive government.[79]

These hopes were soon dashed. Given that the Act of Indemnity exempted twenty non-regicides from pardon, it was fortunate for Fairfax that his role in the Restoration was so conspicuous. In 1660 his uncle Sir William Constable's body was exhumed from Westminster Abbey and 'flung on a dung heap'. In August 1662 the Act of Uniformity deprived another uncle, Henry Fairfax, of his living at Bolton Percy.[80] Struggling against the tide of resurgent royalism, and after much hesitation, Fairfax stood as knight of the shire in the Yorkshire election of 1661. A correspondent of Bishop Cosin noted that a son of Lord Darcy and Sir John Goodricke of Ribston stood against Fairfax, who was now derided as the 'black Presbiter'. Royalists hoped that 'the Honest party indeavours unanimously against the L[or]d Fairefax', would 'much discountenance the Presbiters pride'. By 2 April Cosin's tenants voted in strength for Darcy and Goodricke, 'who without dispute Baffled Fairfax'.[81] Having been battered by Bradford clubs in 1642, Goodricke now sought to vanquish his civil war demons, denouncing the local people as 'the beast with many heads', and moving Parliament to prevent all comprehension of dissenters.[82] We know little of Fairfax's reaction to his defeat or the removal of other family members from office, such as Sir Thomas Widdrington, who was ousted as MP for York in 1661 by the politics of popular royalism.[83]

V

It seems likely that Fairfax responded to these defeats with his usual stoic forbearance, embracing the twin consolations of religion and retirement. He maintained his faith in difficult circumstances during the 1660s. He filled two pocket books with detailed sermon notes that suggest a persistent, meticulous concern for learning about God's purposes.[84] Despite his illnesses and infirmity, he attended many sermons, travelling from Nun Appleton up to Otley to do so. Typical of the man, he heard both Presbyterian and Independent preachers. The clergyman that featured most frequently in his notes was the Congregationalist Thomas Smallwood. Smallwood had been chaplain of Fairfax's first regiment of horse from January 1643, and was famed for feats of physical strength and his remarkable memory for sermons. He had attended Christopher Marshall's Independent church at Woodkirk with James Nayler.[85] In July 1660 Smallwood was suspected of involvement in the alleged Sowerby plot against Charles II and was ejected from Batley vicarage for preaching in Halifax, that 'the whore of Babylon is rising and setting up!'[86] In July 1662 he lectured the godly on the sufferings of Job 'in the worst of times', reminding them that 'ye p[eo]pl[e] of God are p[eo]pl[e] of ye lowest of men as to this world their inheritance is not here'. Continuing to preach illegally, he was indicted at the York Assizes in 1664.[87] Smallwood reminded Fairfax that God would 'separate ye enemies of ye church from ye godly', and would 'complete ye deliverance of ye church from Babylon'. In language still reverberating with millenarianism, he orated that 'the signes of ye day are upon us', and that 'when we heare a noyse of trumpets & drums we know there is an Army cuming'. If Fairfax was seeking to conform to the restored Anglican church, Smallwood was exactly the man to avoid. Instead Fairfax stood by his old chaplain and tasted the harassment inflicted upon other dissenters when he was presented for non-communicating in 1663.[88]

Fairfax also noted six sermons made by a Mr Wales, probably the Presbyterian Elkanah Wales, minister at Pudsey. Fairfax 'had a singular esteem' for Mr Wales, attracted by his reputation as being 'especially remarkable for his Humility and self Denyall'. With his motto 'less than the least of all saints', Wales was offered several lucrative livings by Ferdinando Fairfax in the 1640s. He took a leading role in organising the West Riding clergy's *Vindiciae veritatis* petition against sectarians in 1648, but now it was he who was 'branded a shismatick & disaffected to the Governm[en]t'. In 1659 his 'Mount Ebal Levelled: or the Curse removed' was dedicated to Fairfax. Wales was ejected from Pudsey in 1663, his house occupied and belongings thrown into the street.[89]

Fairfax also heard a sermon from Dr Winter, probably the Samuel Winter who had been provost of Trinity College, Dublin, during the 1650s. Winter's former 'very awakening & piercing' ministry at Cottingham near Hull had 'greatly affrighted' his congregation, and he won further notoriety for his pulpit deliberations on the fate of Ahaz and Saul upon the arrival of Charles I in York in March 1642.[90] Fairfax noted two sermons from Mr Denison, probably the Timothy Denison, minister of Normanton who had signed the *Vindiciae veritatis* of 1648. Denison preached on the dangers of Romish idolatry, the futility of carnal and worldly matters, and in an echo of Bowles's funeral sermon for Ferdinando Fairfax, the reforms of King Hezekiah of Judah.[91] The examples of just these four ministers illustrate that Fairfax's inclination to downplay doctrinal distinctions between the Presbyterian and mainstream Independent godly was not a political device of the 1640s but rather a cherished conviction that persisted to his death.

He also heard sermons from Mr Waterhouse, Mr Crosley, Mr Sharpe, Mr Nesse, Mr Charnocke, Mr Banes, Mr Crosland and Dr Harrison. Some of these were combination lectures in what appears to have been an attempt to preserve the tradition of the pre-war West Riding exercises in spite of the Restoration church settlement. Denison's sermon continued to stress the dangers of idolatry and faults of papists, while Nesse's preaching on Moses and the hard times for the Israelites was especially suited to a godly audience struggling with the restrictions of nonconformity in the 1660s.

No doubt pleased that the interregnum's turmoil was over, Fairfax nevertheless feared the consequences of the perceived irreligion that followed. In another set of his sermon notes, he reflected on Matthew 3:10: 'Nothing makes judgments come sooner on a people then to slight the gospel when it is amongst them ... We must fear it is our case in England, doe we see how his lesser judgements threatens us & shall we not looke about us?'[92] A sermon from his chaplain, Richard Stretton, on Romans 8:37, warned that 'the beloved of Christ hath many enemies', but preached of 'the triumphs over those difficultys saints meete with in ther way to heaven'. Stretton urged his listeners to disentangle themselves from 'the things of this world', hoping to please his master with a figurative example reminiscent of Rupert at Naseby: 'itt is pitty to loose the victory for the baggage'.[93]

Popular memory of Fairfax became dangerous with the failure of the northern risings of 1663. These ill-co-ordinated conspiracies of former parliamentarian soldiers and ejected ministers scarcely mustered one hundred men between their appointed risings on 12 October 1663. The high sheriff and deputy lieutenants knew those responsible and a thorough investigation rounded up hundreds of suspects, giving royalists ample opportunity to settle old scores. One rebel testified under interrogation that 'My Lord Fairfax was much desired among the Plotters'. One of Fairfax's servants was approached to draw him into the conspiracy. Fairfax used ill health as an excuse not to attend Buckingham's efforts to suppress the risings. In vain he attempted to soften the government's retribution, declaring 'these distempers will soon blow over'. He urged Buckingham to recommend mercy for the captured rebels, pleading 'not to let them be destroyed and ruined by some men's private passions, under colour of doing public service'. Yet sixteen plotters, among them former officers and troopers under Fairfax in the perilous days of 1643, were hanged, drawn and quartered within sight of his Bishophill mansion in York in January 1664.[94] The whole affair was a lesson in his political irrelevance. Soon after, he disapproved of the looming Dutch war, but conceded 'this is above my spheare'.[95]

Brian Fairfax left recollections of his cousin's last years. From 1664 Fairfax was confined to his wheelchair by gout and the stone, 'wherein he sate like an old Roman, his manly countenance striking Awe and Reverence into all that beheld him, and yet mixt with so much modesty, and meekness, as no figure of a mortal man ever represented more'. Most of his time was spent in religious duties and reading. His decline hastened after the death of his wife in 1665. He died after a short fever at Nun Appleton on 11 November 1671. His will left his estates to his daughter during her lifetime, but on her death they were to revert to his cousin, Henry Fairfax, who succeeded him as fourth baron. His executors were his brother-in-law, Henry Arthington, his nephew, Thomas Hutton, and his cousin, Henry Fairfax, while the supervisors of his will were Gilbert Holles, earl of Clare[96] and Horatio, baron Townshend.[97] The last morning of his life he called for a Bible. Saying that his eyes were growing dim, he read the forty-second Psalm and then expired.[98]

NOTES

1 D. Underdown, 'Party management in the recruiter elections, 1645–1648', *EHR*, 83 (1968), 245–6; BL, E371(5), *Perfect occurrences*, 8–15 January (London, 1647), p. 13.

2 S. Kelsey, 'Constructing the council of state', *Parliamentary History*, 22:3 (2003), 225–7; B. Worden, *The Rump Parliament, 1648–1653* (Cambridge, 1974), pp. 28, 74.

3 Kelsey, 'Constructing the council of state', 225, 228–9; Worden, *The Rump*, pp. 28, 187.

4 I. Gentles, *The New Model Army in England, Ireland and Scotland, 1645–1653* (Oxford, 1992), p. 314.

5 *CSP dom. 1649–50*, p. 495.

6 G. Dyfnallt Owen (ed.), *De L'Isle and Dudley MS, vol. 6, 1626–98*, HMC, 77 (London, 1966), pp. 468, 472; BL, E594(9), *The man in the moon*, 20–27 February (London, 1650), pp. 348–9.

7 A. Woolrych, *Britain in Revolution, 1625–1660* (Oxford, 2002), p. 443.

8 H. N. Brailsford, *The Levellers and the English Revolution* (London, 1961), p. 292.

9 BL, Egerton MS 1048, fos. 93–7; BL, E548(2), *The moderate*, 13–20 March (London, 1649), p. 8.

10 I. Gentles, 'The agreements of the people and their political contexts, 1647–1649', in

M. Mendle (ed.), *The Putney Debates of 1647: The Army, the Levellers and the English State* (Cambridge, 2001), p. 172.

11 Gentles, *New Model Army*, p. 329; Woolrych, *Britain in Revolution*, p. 445; A. Woolrych, *Soldiers and Statesmen: The General Council of the Army and its Debates, 1647–1648* (Oxford, 1987), p. 342.

12 Gentles, *New Model Army*, pp. 329–49.

13 BL, E530(24), *The speeches of the Lord Generall Fairfax and the officers of the armie to the diggers at St Georges Hill in Surry, and the diggers several answers and replies thereunto*, 31 May (London, 1649), p. 40.

14 C. H. Firth (ed.), *The Clarke papers, vol. 2* (Camden Society, new series, 54, 1894), pp. 210–12.

15 BL, E529(21), *Perfect occurrences*, 20–27 April (London, 1649), pp. 987–8; BL, E551(11), *The declaration and standard of the levellers of England*, 23 April (London, 1649), pp. 1–3; BL, E552(2), *The perfect weekly account*, 18–25 April (London, 1649), pp. 454–5.

16 W. Oldys and T. Park (eds), *The Harleian Miscellany, vol. 8* (London, 1811), p. 586; BL, E529(20), *The impartiall intelligencer*, 18–25 April (London, 1649), p. 60.

17 D. Hirst and S. Zwicker, 'High summer at Nun Appleton, 1651: Andrew Marvell and Lord Fairfax's occasions', *Historical Journal*, 36:2 (1993), 258n.

18 BL, Egerton MS 2618, fo. 38; Firth (ed.), *Clarke papers, vol. 2*, p. 216.

19 BL, E530(34), *A perfect summary of an exact dyarie of some passages in Parliament*, 10 June (London, 1649), p. 165; BL, E559(5), *A modest narrative of intelligence fitted for the republique of England & Ireland*, 2–9 June (London, 1649).

20 Dyfnallt Owen (ed.), *De L'Isle and Dudley MS*, p. 588.

21 W. Bray (ed.), *Diary and correspondence of John Evelyn, F.R.S.* (London, 1859), vol. 3, p. 55.

22 BL, E602(2), *The man in the moon*, 8–23 May (London, 1650), frontispiece.

23 BL, E602(21), *Mercurius elencticus*, 27 May–3 June (London, 1650); BL, E602(24), *The man in the moon*, 29 May–5 June (London, 1650), frontispiece.

24 P. W. Thomas (ed.), *The English Revolution III, Newsbooks 5, Volume 1, Mercurius Politicus* (London, 1971), pp. 17–18.

25 BL, Egerton MS 1048, fo. 113.

26 BL, Add. MS 37345, fos. 81r–84r.

27 *Ibid.*, fos. 82v–83v.

28 J. Morrill, 'Introduction', in J. Morrill (ed.), *Oliver Cromwell and the English Revolution* (Harlow, 1990), p. 7.

29 East Riding of Yorkshire Record Office, Beverley, DDRI 43/8; BL, Add. MS 21419, fos. 184, 189, 194.

30 L. Hutchinson, *Memoirs of the Life of Colonel Hutchinson*, ed. N. H. Keeble (London, 1995), pp. 240–1.

31 *CSP dom. 1650*, pp. 234, 273.

32 S. R. Gardiner, *History of the commonwealth and protectorate, 1649–60* (London, 1894), vol. 1, pp. 290–2.

33 J. Peacey, *Politicians and Pamphleteers: Propaganda During the English Civil Wars and Interregnum* (Aldershot, 2004), p. 297.

34 Bod., MS Fairfax 32, fo. 173; TNA, SP 23/3/214; B. Fairfax, *A catalogue of the curious pictures of George Villiers, duke of Buckingham, in which is included the valuable collection of Sir Peter Paul Rubens with the life of George Villiers, duke of Buckingham, the celebrated poet written by Brian Fairfax, esq* (London, 1758), p. 28.

35 D. Masson, *The life of John Milton* (7 vols, London, 1877), vol. 4, pp. 601–2.

36 C. H. Firth (ed.), *The memoirs of Edmund Ludlow* (Oxford, 1894), vol. 1, p. 254.

37 G. C. F. Forster, 'County government in Yorkshire during the interregnum', *Northern History*, 12 (1976), 102–3.

38 A. Woolrych, 'The civil wars, 1640–9', in B. Worden (ed.), *Stuart England* (Oxford, 1986), pp. 114–15; H. Speight, *Upper Wharfedale* (London, 1900), p. 55.

39 B. Dale, 'Cromwell in Yorkshire', *Bradford Antiquary*, new series, 1 (1900), 427; *CSP dom. 1651*, pp. 235–6, 323–4; Hirst and Zwicker, 'High summer at Nun Appleton', 254–5.

40 Hirst and Zwicker, 'High summer at Nun Appleton', 249; Markham, p. 364; B. Dale, 'Bramhope Chapel', *Bradford Antiquary*, new series, 1 (1900), 326; BL, Add. MS 71448, fos. 23r, 25r.

41 This house was completed by the 1660s and became known as Buckingham House or the Duke's Hall, after Fairfax's son-in-law. Illustrated on Samuel Buck's *South prospect of the city of York*, it boasted twenty-nine hearths, the largest number of any home in the city, rendering the Fairfaxes among York's largest employers: G. Webb, 'Fairfax homes: York, Bishophill', *The Fairfax Society*, 18 (2004), 12–14.

42 BL, Add. MS 71448, fos. 3r–9r, 32r.

43 *Ibid.*, 7r, 11r, 17r, 27r, 29r, 34r, 36r, 38r.

44 BL, Add. MS 71448, fo. 13r; A. Woolrych, *Commonwealth to Protectorate* (Oxford, 1982), p. 69; *CSP dom. 1652–3*, pp. 82, 126, 141, 276.

45 Woolrych, *Commonwealth to Protectorate*, pp. 138–9.

46 B. D. Henning (ed.), *The House of Commons 1660–1690* (London, 1983), vol. 2, p. 292; D. Hirst, 'The fracturing of the Cromwellian alliance: Leeds and Adam Baynes', *EHR*, 108 (1993), 887.

47 T. Birch (ed.), *A collection of the state papers of John Thurloe, esq* (London, 1742), vol. 3, p. 312, vol. 4, p. 169, vol. 5, p. 319, vol. 6, pp. 616–17, 706, 809; G. F. Warner (ed.), *The Nicholas papers, vol. 2* (Camden Society, new series, 50, 1892), pp. 218–22, 232; G. F. Warner (ed.), *The Nicholas papers, vol. 3* (Camden Society, new series, 57, 1897), pp. 54, 68, 259.

48 Birch (ed.), *Thurloe papers*, vol. 6, pp. 616–17.

49 Brian Fairfax remembered the date as 7 September but Bolton Percy parish registers specify 15 September: Fairfax, *Life of Buckingham*, p. 31; Markham, p. 372.

50 D. Underdown, *Royalist Conspiracy in England* (New Haven, 1960), pp. 39, 118–22, 224; *Sutherland MS*, HMC, 5th report, appendix (London, 1876), p. 177.

51 R. Hutton, *The Restoration: A Political and Religious History of England and Wales, 1658–1667* (Oxford, 1985), p. 252; *CSP dom. 1657–8*, p. 122.

52 C. H. Firth, *The Last Years of the Protectorate* (London, 1909), vol. 2, p. 57; *CSP dom. 1657–8*, pp. 124, 196; C. H. Firth (ed.), *The Clarke papers, vol. 3* (Camden Society, new series, 61, 1899), pp. 123, 129; Birch (ed.), *Thurloe papers*, vol. 6, pp. 616–17.

53 Fairfax, *Life of Buckingham*, p. 31.

54 Birch (ed.), *Thurloe papers*, vol. 6, p. 706.

55 *CSP dom. 1657–8*, p. 259.

56 Fairfax, *Life of Buckingham*, p. 31.

57 BL, Add. MS 71448, fo. 36r.

58 T. Burton, *Diary of Thomas Burton, esq*, ed. J. T. Rutt (London, 1828), vol. 3, pp. 56, 273.

59 *Ibid.*, p. 370.

60 R. E. Mayers, *1659: The Crisis of the Commonwealth* (Royal Historical Society, Studies in History, new series, 2004), pp. 33, 34n, 108.

61 The magisterial account of this episode remains A. Woolrych, 'Yorkshire and the Restoration', *YAJ*, 39 (1958).

62 F. M. S. McDonald, 'The timing of General George Monck's march into England, 1 January 1660', *EHR*, 105:415 (1990), 375.

63 Woolrych, 'Yorkshire and the Restoration', 487; Burton, *Diary of Thomas Burton*, ed. Rutt, vol. 3, p. 292n.

64 A. J. Hopper, 'Brian Fairfax', *Oxford DNB*; R. Bell (ed.), *The Fairfax correspondence: memorials of the civil war* (London, 1849), vol. 2, pp. 151–74.

65 *Sutherland MS*, HMC, 5th report, appendix, pp. 193–4; BL, E1013(9), *A letter from a captain of the army to an honourable member of Parliament*, 9 January (London, 1660), pp. 4–5.

66 BL, E1013(5), *A letter sent from the Lord Fairfax, &c. Dated at Popleton, January 1. 1659*, 7 January (London, 1660).

67 Woolrych, 'Yorkshire and the Restoration', 496–7.

68 McDonald, 'The timing of Monck's march', 375–6.

69 Woolrych, 'Yorkshire and the Restoration', 498–9; Burton, *Diary of Thomas Burton*, ed. Rutt, vol. 3, p. 292n.

70 D. Scott, 'Politics and government in York, 1640–1662', in R. C. Richardson (ed.), *Town and Countryside in the English Revolution* (Manchester, 1992), p. 60.

71 BL, Add. MS 18979, fos. 285–7.

72 Clarendon, *History of the rebellion and civil wars in England*, ed. W. Dunn Macray (Oxford, 1888), vol. 6, p. 165; J. Rosenheim, *The Townshends of Raynham* (Middletown, Connecticut, 1989), chapter 1.

73 A. J. Hopper, 'Sir Philip Monckton', *Oxford DNB*.

74 Woolrych, 'Yorkshire and the Restoration', 483, 487, 505.

75 *Sutherland MS*, HMC, 5th report, appendix, p. 194.

76 I. Gentles, 'Thomas, third Lord Fairfax', *Oxford DNB*.

77 C. H. Firth (ed.), *The Clarke papers, vol. 4* (Camden Society, new series, 62, 1901), p. 251.

78 BL, Stowe MS 744, fo. 40.

79 Markham, p. 384; Woolrych, 'Yorkshire and the Restoration', 486, 491, 496, 507; P. Withington, 'Views from the bridge: revolution and restoration in seventeenth-century York', *Past and Present*, 170 (2001), 141.

80 Woolrych, *Britain in Revolution*, p. 782; B. English, *The Great Landowners of East York-*

shire, 1530–1910 (Hemel Hempstead, 1990), p. 135; W. Smith (ed.), *Old Yorkshire* (London, 1881), vol. 2, p. 218.

81 Durham University Library, Mickleton-Spearman MS 46/139, 46/151, 46/165.

82 B. D. Henning (ed.), *The House of Commons, 1660–1690* (London, 1983), vol. 1, p. 468, vol. 2, p. 412; BL, E88(23), *The rider of the white horse and his army* (London, 1643).

83 Scott, 'Politics and government in York', p. 62.

84 My thanks to Dr Jason Peacey for kindly communicating his discovery of this source: Folger Shakespeare Library, Washington DC, V.a.14–15, unfol., sermon notes of Thomas, 3rd baron Fairfax, c.1661–7.

85 R. Thoresby, *Ducatus Leodiensis* (London, 1715), p. 612; B. Dale, 'Ministers of parish churches and chapels round about Bradford during the Puritan revolution', *Bradford Antiquary*, 2 (1905), 364–6.

86 J. H. Turner, *Nonconformity in Idle* (Bradford, 1876), p. 19; A. Laurence, *Parliamentary Army Chaplains, 1642–1651* (Woodbridge, 1990), p. 174.

87 BL, Add. MS 45674, fos. 212–15; J. Raine (ed.), *Depositions from the castle of York, relating to offences committed in the northern counties in the seventeenth century* (Surtees Society, 40, 1861), p. 83n.

88 Folger Shakespeare Library, Washington DC, V.a.14, unfol.; H. Aveling, *Northern Catholics: The Catholic Recusants of the North Riding of Yorkshire, 1558–1790* (London, 1966), p. 305.

89 BL, Birch MS 4460, fos. 17, 35–40; B. Dale, 'Ministers of the parish churches of the West Riding during the puritan revolution', *Bradford Antiquary*, 1 (1900), 433; Dale, 'Ministers of parish churches and chapels round about Bradford', 367–71; BL, E444(5), *Vindiciae veritatis or an unanimous attestation to Gods blessed truth revealed in his word* (London, 1648), p. 11.

90 BL, Birch MS 4460, fo. 34; W. J. Sheils, 'Provincial preaching on the eve of the civil war: some West Riding sermons', in A. J. Fletcher and P. Roberts (eds), *Religion, Culture and Society in Early Modern Britain: Essays in Honour of Patrick Collinson* (Cambridge, 1994), p. 291; T. Barnard, 'Samuel Winter (1603–1666)', *Oxford DNB* (Oxford, 2004).

91 Folger Shakespeare Library, Washington DC, V.a.14, unfol.; BL, E444(5), *Vindiciae veritatis*, p. 12.

92 BL, Add. MS 4929, fos. 87–90.

93 *Ibid.*, fos. 7–10.

94 BL, Add. MS 33770, fo. 35; A. Hopper, 'The Farnley wood plot and the memory of the civil wars in Yorkshire', *Historical Journal*, 45:2 (2002), 296.

95 Beinecke Rare Book and Manuscript Library, Yale University, Osborn files, folder 17645.

96 The mother of Gilbert Holles was Elizabeth Vere, sister of Anne Fairfax, while Gilbert was also a nephew of Denzil Holles: G. E. Cokayne, *Complete Peerage* (London, 1913), vol. 3, pp. 248–9.

97 Borthwick Institute of Historical Research, University of York, Fairfax's will: 52/145, proved 8 December 1671. The will is transcribed in Markham, pp. 440–6.

98 BL, Egerton MS 2146, fo. 38r.

Part II

Fairfax and the political culture
of seventeenth-century England

Chapter 7

The Fairfaxes and the causes of the civil war

In September 1642 when Sir William Savile attempted to raise the trained bands in Halifax for the King, it was reported that the people 'refused, crying with loud acclamation *a Fairfax, a Fairfax*, they would live and die with *a Fairfax*'. The people then 'turned him out of the Towne, and not a man would obey him'.[1] These reports highlighted the developing relationship between the Fairfax name and the cloth towns of Yorkshire's West Riding, especially Bradford, Leeds and Halifax. As Sir Thomas Fairfax rode into Leeds in January 1643, again the townsmen reportedly cried 'a Fairfaxe, a Fairfaxe' to demonstrate their support.[2] Among them stood Matthew Stable of the Headrow who had recently baptised his son Ferdinando and was soon to enlist as a parliamentarian trooper.[3] This personal identification between the Fairfaxes and people of the clothing towns is the focus of this chapter. A study of the nature of popular parliamentarian politics in this region, in conjunction with an examination of the Fairfaxes' talents for popular leadership, will illuminate wider themes about the causes of war and shaping of allegiance. It also provides useful comparisons with the work of Ann Hughes and John Walter on popular parliamentarian politics in Warwickshire and East Anglia.[4]

By 1642 Bradford, Leeds and Halifax were so linked to the Fairfaxes that their parliamentarian allegiance was considered a formality. Royalists believed that the 'communalty' of Leeds was 'wholly' at Lord Fairfax's command, while the terms 'insurrection', 'multitude' and 'Roundheads' were increasingly used by them to describe the clothing towns.[5] A reassessment of the outbreak of war from the perspective of these towns needs to employ a 'history from below' analysis to the problem of allegiance, an approach that has grown in recent years alongside wider historiographical concerns to broaden the scope of political history. As neither the Fairfaxes nor their leading allies had sufficient estates to raise an army from their tenants, John Adamson's contention that the outbreak of war was dominated by baronial faction cannot be applied to the Yorkshire parliamentary forces.[6] Indeed, more generally, John Walter has recently questioned accepting the notion that mobilisation of support was primarily rooted 'in the territorial influence of the county gentry'.[7] How and from where the Fairfaxes drew their popular support is critical to explaining the outbreak and outcome of the war. John Morrill has argued that this process of allegiance formation 'in the inns and secluded manor houses of rural England' was more significant than events on the battlefield.[8] In the past twenty years, through the work of David Underdown, Ann Hughes and Mark Stoyle, it has become increasingly accepted that many ordinary English people chose their allegiance for themselves.[9] The outbreak of war in Yorkshire provides an opportunity to explore ways in which such a 'post-revisionist' approach to its causes might be developed from a local context. An important focus of this historiography has been the discourse between the gentry and the people, how each courted the other's support, and the explicit recognition that this was often a two-way process.[10]

I

Popular politics in the West Riding's clothing districts was shaped by two key factors: the socio-economic structure of the cloth trade and the religious culture of godly reform. The cloth trade had generated communities that were highly populous and particularly vulnerable in times of dearth. Yorkshire justices reported in 1618 that all the West Riding's clothing districts required corn and malt from more fertile arable land in the East Riding, Lincolnshire, Notting-hamshire and Norfolk 'as anciently hath been used'.[11] In 1638 the West Riding clothing districts were described as 'partly barren land, and replenished with clothiers that have spread themselves all over the country, as well in closes and parcels of waste ground as in towns'. The poor, upland, Pennine soils were insufficient to maintain such populations, and a petition to the Court of Exchequer that year complained that the terrain was 'so mountainous and rough, soe barren and unfruitful, as it will not suffice to yield victuals for the third part of the inhabitants'.[12]

The clothing districts were largely contained in a quadrilateral running from Leeds to Otley through to Rochdale and then Wakefield, although they featured in Pennine regions further south and west. Patterns of settlement tended to be scattered with many clothiers maintaining smallholdings. The urban–rural divide was blurred while Leeds 'merged almost imperceptibly into its huge rural hinterland'. Halifax contained over twenty townships, Brad-ford eleven. Morley wapentake comprised the parishes of Halifax, Bradford, Batley, Birstall, Calverley and Dewsbury, and contained 5302 households in the hearth tax returns of the 1660s.[13] By 1638, about 22,000 people were employed in the cloth industry in Bradford, Bingley, Halifax and Keighley. These populations had a high concentration of medium-sized landholders and tradesmen, a group accustomed to taking political action, and politically labelled in the 1640s as 'the middling sort'. In places they may have approached 20 per cent of the inhabitants.[14]

The cloth trade had been seriously depressed since 1640 before it neared collapse in spring 1642. Communities enduring this depression were ill placed to fulfil royal demands for billeting soldiers during the bishops' wars. In March 1641, Thomas Stockdale complained of the soldiers' abuses 'under which burden this part of Yorkshire now groanes and cannot longe subsist without ruine'. When the Yorkshire gentry petitioned Parliament against forced billeting, arguing that the plight of the manufacturing trade 'may prove to bee of a dangerous Consequence', Sir Thomas and Sir William Fairfax were among the leading petitioners.[15] A petition to the King was organised by the clothiers of Leeds and Halifax in April 1642. It complained of 'various illegal pressures and impositions', from 'Officers under pretence of power and commission issued out from your Majesty'. It added that 'divers of the meaner sort' had been 'utterly disabled to manage their Trades, their stockes being exhausted by those crafty Inventions'. The clothiers blamed Charles for 'secession from your great Court', claiming this had put thousands out of work, as 'Merchants fearing what evill event may ensue upon these distractions', would no longer purchase cloth. Charles I's suspicion of popular conspiracy prejudiced him against such petitions and he dismissed their complaints as grounded upon 'false reports, and relations'.[16] Sir Thomas Fairfax's Heworth moor petition again stressed the misery of the cloth manufacturers. It claimed the trade was obstructed by the King's arrival in York and that thousands were 'at the Point of utter Undoing'. Charles dismissed the petition as seditious, believing it was organised in London, 'solicited by a few mean inconsiderable Persons'. He claimed the number and quality of its supporters was not 'so considerable as is pretended', and that it was avowed by no man but Sir Thomas Fairfax himself.[17]

By the outbreak of war the identification of the Fairfaxes with the cloth trade was conspicuous. The trade collapsed in July 1642 when the siege of Hull blocked access to the port through which most Yorkshire cloth was exported.[18] By September royalist troops in the vale of York disrupted food supplies reaching the clothing districts. Many clothiers such as Samuel Priestley of Goodgreave joined the Fairfaxes' army because they were unemployed.[19] The necessity of staving off subsistence crisis generated substantial recruitment for the Fairfaxes but came at the cost of dictating their strategy. In May 1643 Lord Fairfax warned Speaker Lenthall that the cloth towns were at breaking point:

> Leeds, Bradford and Halifax, being a mountainous barren Country, the people now begin to be sensible of want, their last year provisions being spent, and the enemies Garrisons stopping all provisions of Corn and Flesh, and other necessaries that

were wont to come from the more fruitfull Countries to them, their trade utterly taken away, their poor grow innumerable, and great scarcity of means to relieve them.[20]

II

The godly religious culture of the cloth towns employed a 'Providentialist politics' to explain this socio-economic crisis as punishment from God for having permitted the sinful and idolatrous policies of Charles I.[21] From the 1590s, the ministries of Alexander Cooke at Leeds and John Favour at Halifax brought a powerful if belated reformation to the area by reinvigorating its chapelries and establishing 'exercises' of godly lectures at Leeds and Halifax. Favour was connected to the Fairfaxes through his friendship with Toby Matthew, the Jacobean Archbishop of York. William and Sarah Sheils have suggested these developments were partly rooted in a revival of the region's enthusiastic pre-Reformation lay piety. By 1642 around eighty Yorkshire benefices were under the control of godly lay patrons, many of whom permitted worship to be supplemented with Psalm singing, discussion and repetition of sermons. Such exercises, attended by clergy and laity, were established in Bingley, Bradford, Halifax, Leeds, Sheffield and Wakefield.[22]

During the 1630s, Richard Neile, Archbishop of York, employed commissioners to investigate churches suspected of dissenting from the King's religious policies, and 70 of the 100 churches they visited were parishes later known for parliamentarian recruitment, either adjacent to Hull or in the West Riding's clothing districts.[23] Despite Neile's attentions, the sheer size of many Pennine parishes, especially Halifax, enabled Presbyterian practices to be established in moorland chapelries distant from the parish church. Flouting Charles I's religious ideology, the curates of these chapelries depended upon voluntary contributions from the congregations that elected them.[24] Ronald Marchant has noted that during the 1630s there was increasing 'abandonment of the Book of Common Prayer at all or most of these chapels, and in Birstall church itself'. In Batley parish, the matter had become so notorious that Morley chapel was ordered closed in 1638,[25] while in July 1642, Batley's vicar preached a sermon in favour of armed parliamentarianism.[26]

On 29 September 1633, Robert More, rector of Guiseley, pandered to the Fairfaxes' self-fashioning as protectors of the godly, writing to Thomas, first baron Fairfax of 'my long experience of your godlie & Christian care of the peaceable & happie estate of gods Church'. He sought aid against the 'sudden conceits' of the archbishop's commissioners at Bradford, who had restricted sermons and seized the town's minister, ordering him to appear before the court of High Commission.[27] Bradford again clashed with Neile in 1637 when Neile flouted local custom by imposing his own candidate as schoolmaster, summoning objectors before High Commission. By 1642, Bradford's puritans sought revenge, maintaining that Edward Hudson, the new under–minister appointed by Neile, had violated the Protestation by using the sign of the cross in baptisms. Lord Fairfax was absent at Westminster but Thomas Stockdale informed him that Bradford's churchwardens had kept Hudson out of the pulpit 'and will suffer him neither to preach nor pray, but put others to officiate in his place'. Bradford's royalist vicar, Francis Corker, later described the town as 'very full and populous, soe verry factious and seditiory'.[28] Corker's linking of sedition to populous places soon became commonplace in royalist explanations for the war, especially in Yorkshire.

Most of the curates of Halifax's chapelries were identified as defaulters during Archbishop Neile's visitations in 1633 and 1635, and the parish was a 'notorious black spot for disobedience to the Church courts'. Nonconformist doctrine extending to antinomianism was preached at Todmorden and Rochdale.[29] Despite the cloth trade's downturn, Halifax's chapelries maintained ten preachers by voluntary contributions. In March 1642, nobody in Halifax or Rochdale refused the Protestation. The royalist vicar of Halifax, Dr Richard Marsh, was imprisoned soon after the outbreak of war, and his estate revenue was paid directly to the Fairfaxes' troops. A tradition of hiring ministers was established and in 1645 Henry Roote founded an Independent church at Sowerby.[30]

Between Leeds and Wakefield lay Woodkirk, another parish with nonconforming traditions. Their minister during the 1630s refused to read set prayers or wear a surplice and eight parishioners were charged with refusing to receive Communion kneeling and 'vilifying the Book of Common Prayer'. The royalists ejected Woodkirk's minister and the parishioners later petitioned Parliament for the parish's 'great losses by the enemye in these warres'. In January 1643, James Nayler and his kinsmen rode from Woodkirk to join Sir Thomas Fairfax, and in 1648 Christopher Marshall established a church there which John Lambert called 'a very sweet society of an Independent church'.[31]

The Fairfaxes' stance as protectors of godly clergy provided them with several ministers to act as intermediaries in mobilising congregations for war. William Dewsbury joined Fairfax's army after he heard Robert Todd preach 'Meroz Cursed' at St John's church in Leeds. Todd had co-ordinated opposition at Heworth moor and his inflammatory rendition of 'Meroz Cursed', first preached by Stephen Marshall, was notorious for stimulating parliamentarian recruitment, earning Marshall the title of 'the great incendiary of this unhappy war'.[32] Other ministers even engaged in combat. David Ellison, a master at Otley grammar school, was probably in Bradford during the club-law, while Andrew Latham, curate of Coley, urged his congregation to smite the royalists attacking Bradford. In January 1643 Jonathan Scholefield, curate of Croston, led a storming division at Leeds, while Thomas Crompton served in Sir William

Fairfax's regiment and wrote an account of the fight.[33] Royalists recognised the vital roles played by these clergy in rallying parliamentarian volunteers, and the earl of Newcastle argued they did 'prostitute the Ordinance of God to the rebellious designs of ambitious men'. He warned Lord Fairfax that any ministers found in arms would not be treated as clergymen.[34]

The Irish rebellion unravelled the religious disobedience of the Fairfaxes' neighbours into open rebellion, transforming the perceived motives behind the persecution of puritans during the 1630s into a terrifying new prospect. When Sir Phelim O'Neill produced a commission that claimed he had the King's permission for the rising, this had a frightening plausibility because Charles had negotiated with the Irish nobility the previous summer. When the Irish lords Dillon and Taafe joined Charles at York, royal advisers urged their dismissal to rebut allegations of collusion with the Irish rebels. The West Riding towns were concerned that once the rebels captured Dublin, they were 'resolved for Lankeyshire and have barks ready to waft over twenty thousand men'.[35] A new bitterness developed towards English catholics, and Thomas Stockdale remarked: 'I have heard some propound to have them all put to the sword, which methinks is a Councell better becoming a Turke then a Christian.' Instead Stockdale stressed that enforcing the laws against recusants would eventually achieve 'their Reformation, or at least, in tyme wearie them out'. He suggested the national catholic population be calculated by using the subsidy rolls.[36] He sought to win the Fairfaxes political advantage from the crisis, informing Ferdinando on 12 February 1642 that he had recently examined a suspected recusant for having said 'that there were 2 pieces of ordinance mounted on the top of Plumpton Tower towards Knarsbrough; and that, if Henry Benson should be taken ... there would be many a fatherless baarne made in Knarsbrough'. The Plumptons were a local recusant family, who had supported Benson's endeavours to prevent the election of Ferdinando's brother-in-law, Sir William Constable, as MP for Knaresborough. Although Stockdale disdained the matter as a 'foolish bragg of a drunken knave in an alehouse', he understood the power of rumour upon the people, suggesting that Ferdinando might make political use of the episode.[37] The day before, Sir Edward Rodes informed Ferdinando of another scare at Sheffield, where Kellam Homer, armour dresser to the earl of Arundel, had allegedly said 'that before May day they should have such a peal rung in Sheffield as had not been heard these hundred years'. In response local inhabitants demanded urgent action to disarm recusants and secure county magazines.[38]

These local panics were inspired by news of the Irish rebellion, which dominated the West Riding's pulpits. Sermons in Otley sponsored by the Fairfaxes in summer 1642, warned the congregation that if they failed to act English protestants would be 'deprived of public assemblies, bibles taken, children murdered and wives ravished'. Gory pamphlets lamenting the fate of Ireland's protestants abounded in York by March 1642, and fast days were linked to Irish events to bolster support for Parliament.[39] The memoirs of three members of the clothing districts' 'middling sort' strongly suggest that such considerations shaped popular politics; all three used the Irish rebellion to legitimise their parliamentarian allegiance. Joining Fairfax's army at Bradford in December 1642 as an ensign, John Hodgson recalled 'that noise of the dreadful massacre in Ireland startled many, and constrained them to whet their swords, and to prepare such instruments as they possibly could to defend themselves'. Jonathan Priestley wrote that his brother Samuel joined the Fairfaxes because he feared the Irish rebellion was about to be enacted in England.[40] Finally, Joseph Lister bewailed the murderous cruelty of the Irish, linking them to a royalist conspiracy to inflict the same upon England's godly.[41] Lister remembered the panic when Elkanah Wales's sermon at Pudsey was interrupted by exclamations that the Irish had landed: 'The congregation was all in confusion, some ran out, others wept, others fell to talking to their friends ... But O what a sad and sorrowful going home had we that evening, for we must needs go to Bradford, and knew not but Incarnate Devils and Death would be there before us, and meet us there.'[42] Although Lister was writing retrospectively, and after 1688, his virulent anti-royalism and belief in Charles I's popish plot had in no way mellowed:

> King Charles the first, then upon the throne, to say nothing of his own wicked disposition, did by the constant solicitation of the bloody Queen together with the swarms of Jesuits and evil affected Councellors, Bishops, and men of great estate, place, and trust, all put their heads together to destroy Christ's interest in the nation, and betray their trust every way to the utter ruin and overthrow of Religion, and to cut off the lives of all the Protestants, and so have enslaved this land to Rome, the mother of harlots; whose kingdom is established by blood.[43]

The violence of this popular parliamentarianism lends support to Robin Clifton's emphasis that 'fear of papists supplied the basis of the popular political vocabulary'.[44] Clarendon noted how the 'imputation raised by the parliament upon the King, of an intention to bring in, or ... of conniving at and tolerating, Popery, did make a deep impression upon the people generally'. He believed the rebels represented Newcastle's forces as the 'Queen's Army' or the 'Catholic Army', 'thereby to expose her Majesty the more to the rude Malice of the People, and the Army to their prejudice; perswading them ... that it consisted of none but profess'd Papists, who intended nothing but the extirpation of the Protestants'. Bulstrode Whitelocke also reflected that the Yorkshire minister John Saltmarsh had recommended to 'cherish the war under the notion of Popery, as the surest means to engage the people'.[45] Clarendon and Saltmarsh were correct in assuming that joining parliamentary armies through fear of catholics rather than for preserving liberties and property appealed to those with little liberty or property to protect. With anti-catholicism inculcated in the people by the Book of Martyrs and Gunpowder Treason Day celebrations, and with local catholic personalities often likely to be their social 'superiors', a civil war appeared to offer them the possibility of bringing them down.

In September 1642, Charles rescinded his earlier declaration barring catholics from his army.[46] As catholic gentry began to raise men, the 'popish plot' warned of in the sermons at Otley appeared to be taking shape. Newcastle's forces became the largest royalist army and its officer class was heavily catholic. This army's historian, P. R. Newman, referred to the north as 'the heartland of Catholic Royalism', questioning the misplaced attempts of Keith Lindley and John Morrill to stress catholic neutrality. Newman traced 97 out of 266 northern army officers as catholic, and showed how over 40 per cent of royalist colonels in the north were catholic.[47] The catholic presence in Newcastle's army sparked a remarkable propaganda battle between Newcastle and Lord Fairfax that witnessed both leaders attempting to shape popular allegiance. Both employed the device of the duologue to set up and then demolish the other's arguments. Intending to bridge the gap between literate and oral culture, this approach foreshadowed the printed bids for popular support during the Exclusion crisis.[48] When Newcastle bravely published a declaration defending his commissioning of catholics, Fairfax claimed arming recusants was illegal and that Newcastle's arguments contained 'more in them of the Jesuit than of the States-man or Lawyer'.[49] In 1642 fear of catholics, cavaliers and plunderers merged in the popular mentality, worsened by the belief of some royalist commanders, such as George Goring, in the use of terror and plunder to enforce obedience.[50] Parliamentarian clergy such as John Shaw, vicar of Rotherham, thundered out against 'the Egyptian darkness of popery', while William Styles, vicar of Hull, claimed the royalists intended to revive the Marian persecution. A declaration from Halifax in 1643 suspected Charles of having written to the Pope offering to return England to Rome.[51] Captain Goodricke considered Sir Hugh Cholmley had deserted Parliament to join with 'the popish parties friends', while another of Fairfax's officers declared that he served the King more 'than the Queen and all her Papists in her Army doe'.[52]

Parliamentary propaganda transplanted the atrocities of Irish rebels on to the northern royalists. Newsbooks explicitly linked the two groups in reporting violence, rape and murder. Nehemiah Wallington kept his account of the 'most savage cruelties of Bradford and Leeds' alongside an account of the 'cruelties in Ireland'.[53] Stories of cavalier bestial excess, rooted in the 'Black Legend' of English depictions of Spain since 1588, were used to demonise Englishmen as 'wolves, dragons, and other malicious beasts', bent on rape, infanticide and cannibalism.[54] Cavaliers came to be known as 'rutters' for their supposed sexual excess and Sir John Hotham even supported a proposal to geld priests and Jesuits.[55] The language of anti-catholic propaganda was explicitly employed by the Fairfaxes and the London press, to mobilise popular opinion in 1642 and maintain it thereafter. Without the Irish rebellion and the reputation of Newcastle's 'popish' army, it is difficult to envisage them being successful in either.

III

From about fifty years prior to the outbreak of civil war, anti-catholicism had been a feature of an assertive popular politics in the West Riding clothing districts. Sir John Savile of Howley had encouraged and utilised this popular prejudice to facilitate his election as knight of the shire in 1597, defeating candidates supported by most of the county gentry. His success was based upon support from godly ministers, lesser gentry and freeholders from the clothing districts, an electoral alliance that foreshadowed the Fairfaxes' wartime support. Yorkshire had several contested elections during the 1620s. With a large freeholder electorate, no leading county family and a powerful clothier interest in the West Riding towns close to York, turnouts ran into thousands. During the 1620s Sir John Savile appealed for re-election directly to the clothing districts' freeholders. Utilising rumours of popish plots, he forged a reputation for anti-catholicism that was indulged by the influential ministers Alexander Cooke and John Favour. The Fairfaxes witnessed Sir Thomas Wentworth, later earl of Strafford, become deeply troubled by Savile's identification with popular politics. Seeking to challenge Savile in the county elections, Wentworth warned Savile of the advantage 'meane fellowes' would take from quarrels among the county elite. In 1620 Wentworth warned how a victory for Savile would 'imbolden' the commons, portraying Savile as 'bent on stirring up the lower orders to defy the gentry'.[56] Although Savile lost the election he attracted strong support, and loud cries of 'A Savyle!', unsettled his opponents. In the county election of 1625 Wentworth warned his running mate, the future first baron Fairfax, against Sir John Savile's supporters, writing that: 'it should be handsomely infused into the gentry how much it concerns them to maintain their own act', in case 'Sir John be able to carry it against you and me' and 'all the gentlemen too besides'. Fears that Savile was courting electors who lacked the freehold voting qualification alarmed the gentry. When Savile's supporters thronged York castle yard, one of Wentworth's allies described it as more like a 'rebellion than an election', while Fairfax warned 'at the day of the election shouts, not reasons, must be heard'. By the 1629 by-election, Sir John Savile's reputation was tarnished by his connections at court, so a group of clothier freeholders took the initiative. They approached Sir Henry Savile to stand and secured his return. The popular politics behind Savile's support in the 1620s reflected an assertive electorate that considered broad issues and was not merely concerned with local affairs.[57]

By 1642 Sir John Savile was dead and the Fairfax family had displaced him as champion of the West Riding's freeholders and clothiers. They had learned to emulate his identification with the people as patron of the local cloth industry. In 1626, Savile had written to the burgesses of Leeds 'to give you an accompte upon what termes things now stand in Parliamente', relating to them his efforts on behalf of the cloth trade. The Fairfaxes adopted similar measures, supervising Protestation returns, presenting petitions on behalf of the clothiers and meeting them at Leeds in September 1642. Their patronage of godly ministers, their clash with Archbishop Neile and Lord Fairfax's voicing of the county's grievances over paying for the bishops' wars all engaged with this popular politics. When Lord Fairfax was returned to the Long Parliament as knight of the shire, he witnessed the development of such techniques, observing how effectively the parliamentary opposition utilised the thirst for news and print to physically mobilise London crowds against royal policies. Aided by printed propaganda from London, the Fairfaxes' identification with the people was able to surpass Savile's and mobilise the clothing districts for war. Richard Cust has argued that by 1642 literate yeomen and freeholders were clearly capable of discussing national politics 'with considerable sophistication' owing to the impact of news, and that they did so in a more forthright way than the gentry, leaving out the 'consensual phraseology and polite restraint' stressed by revisionist historians.[58] By 1642 this consumption of news unleashed excited passions among the north's godly; Oliver Heywood recalled how Thomas Crompton 'and severall more excellent men did pray all night in a parlour at Ralph Whittels, as I remember upon occasion K. Charles I demanding the five members of the house of commons, such a night of prayers, teares, groans as I was never present at in all my life'.[59]

From August 1642, printed declarations urged the people 'to defend themselves from Rapine and Force', claiming that the royalists intended to 'disarm the middle sort of people, who are the body of the Kingdome'.[60] The King's disarming of Yorkshire's trained bands appeared to confirm these allegations and was among the principal immediate causes why the Fairfaxes raised forces. Much of this printed material reached the clothing districts. In Halifax, John Hodgson recalled how 'papers flew up and down in every place'. The impact of print upon popular politics helped drive Sir Marmaduke Langdale into the King's camp; exhibiting a royalist disdain for print and popularity, he lamented 'the Parliament is far too nimble for the King in printing; the common people believe the first story which takes impression in their minds, and it cannot be beaten out'.[61] In contrast, parliamentarian tracts talked not of bludgeoning the people into obedience but rather encouraged their sense of self-worth and protestant identity.[62]

Writing retrospectively, Clarendon generalised that the Fairfaxes drew all their support from below the county gentry, noting that: 'besides the Lord

Fairfax, there were in truth few of good Reputation and Fortune, who run that way'.[63] In contrast, Thomas Stockdale celebrated the Fairfaxes' popular support, boasting that the West Riding clothing districts were 'the most constant part of the kingdom'.[64] Many years later Joseph Lister recalled how 'Bradford was deeply engaged', remarking that 'the generality of the town and parish, and the towns about, stood up for the Parliament'. The royalist Sir Henry Slingsby admitted: 'Strange fortune we have had at this Town ... we never attempt'd any thing upon it but receiv'd an affront.'[65] In explaining such patterns of popular allegiance, Ann Hughes has suggested that wherever support for Parliament was strong among the middling and poorer sorts, the gentry, fearful for preserving social order, 'were more inclined to an authoritarian politics'.[66] This was largely the case in Yorkshire, where royalist gentry outnumbered their parliamentarian counterparts by two to one, and in the West Riding their dominance was still more pronounced. There were more royalist gentry families in the West Riding than in the rest of Yorkshire combined, and there were more royalist colonels from the West Riding than any other English or Welsh county. In the clothing districts themselves, the royalist gentry heavily outnumbered their parliamentarian counterparts.[67] Here gentry influence was not the foremost determinant of popular allegiance. On the contrary, as Hughes has suggested for Warwickshire, it was attitudes towards the people that dictated gentry allegiance. John Hotham's disdain for the common people clearly pushed him in a royalist direction when he complained that 'one Captain White had been imployed against him who was latelie but a yeoman'. The royalist Sir John Brooks feared that such non-gentry rebels would escape retribution in the event of a negotiated peace, so he drew up a list of traitors that included yeomen and woollen drapers.[68]

After the Bradford club-law, the gentry's nightmares about the unruly clothing districts appeared to be taking shape. As clubmen threatened royalist estates, landowners such as Richard Richardson of North Bierley demanded what the royalist garrison in Leeds was going to do about it.[69] John Hotham sought to exploit these widespread fears when he wrote to Newcastle on 9 January 1643:

> My Lord there is one thing more, which I feare much that if the honorable endeavours of such powerfull men as yourselfe doe not take place for a happy peace the necessitious people of the whole Kingdome will p[re]sently rise in mighty numbers & whosoever they p[re]tend for att first, within a while they will sett up for themselves to the utter ruine of all the Nobility and Gentry of the Kingdome. I speake not this merely at random, the West part of this County affords mighty numbers of them wch I am very confident you will see necessitated and urged to rise in farr greater bodys that thrice the Armies that are already gathered here. My Lord necessity teaches subsistence, and if this unruly rout have once cast the Rider, itt will run like wildfire in the Example through all the Counties of England.[70]

Hotham's words paraphrased Charles I's answer to the Nineteen Proposi-
tions, which alleged that the common people would 'set up for themselves
... destroy all rights, properties, all distinctions of families and merit'.[71] His
language linked these deep-rooted fears explicitly with the West Riding. In
1643 a royalist press in York published a tract describing German Anabaptist
uprisings, using strikingly similar terms. It depicted the Anabaptists 'overthrowing all in their way like a sudden inundation; for when the bankes of
authority are once broken down, nothing can stop the popular fury, till they
lose themselves in their confusion'.[72] Such language reflected the conventional
literature warning of the terrible dangers of popular rebellion to the property,
estates and lives of the gentry.[73]

Zealous parliamentarians worried that such concerns would strip their
cause of its elite leadership. Among them was the writer of *Plaine English*,
a tract published in January 1643, soon after the Bradford club-law. David
Wootton has argued that this was Edward Bowles, a minister soon high in the
Fairfaxes' favour. The tract warned against a premature peace and reminded
readers that under an accommodation, prelates would regain power, delinquents go unpunished and no godly ministry would be established to drive out
scandalous clergy. It undermined official parliamentary declarations that the
quarrel was against 'evil counsellors', declaring that Charles had acted of his
own volition. It proposed forming an association pledged to fight on to maintain religion 'in case the Parliament should unhappily miscarry'. The writer
claimed that too many parliamentarian officers were fearful of the people, and
that he had heard some of them say:

> they doubt the people aim at some *infandum*, something too big for their mouthes
> though not for their hearts, which they are so horribly afraid of being serviceable to,
> that they many times doubt whether themselves should doe their own duty, because
> they suspect other men forget theirs. Not considering that this is the way to beget a
> counter–jealousie which may undoe all, but the Parliament first.[74]

Plaine English praised the popular risings at Bradford and Manchester and
elevated the common people: 'Sure you are not so contemptible a thing as
some would make you; your right is much, and your power no lesse, if you
would know the one and use the other.'[75] This tract marked the end of unques-
tioning respect for Charles I. Its proposed association drew on the Elizabethan
precedent of 1584 designed to prevent the succession of Mary Stuart. It also
reflected Thomas Stockdale's advice for an association based on the Protestation.[76] *Plaine English* raised prospects of peace imposed by a popular political
coalition without the consent of King or Parliament. Wootton has pointed out
that an orthodox parliamentarian tract soon attacked *Plaine English* for the
same reasons as Henry Ireton attacked the Levellers at Putney, while Richard
Baxter implied that the tract heralded the removal of the clause in Fairfax's

commission that obliged him to protect the King's person.[77]

Like the vicar of Bradford, Clarendon exhibited a royalist distrust of towns and populous areas in his description of Yorkshire parliamentarianism. He remarked that the West Riding cloth districts were 'so notoriously disaffected, especially in matters relating to the Church, that they wanted only conductors to carry them into rebellion'. He even suggested that the people of Halifax, Leeds and Bradford 'naturally maligned the gentry'.[78] After the Restoration, the duke of Newcastle provided Charles II with similar remarks shaped by his experience of defeat at Leeds and Hull: 'The truth Is that Everye Corporation Is a pettye free state agaynste monarkeye, and they have don[e] your Ma[jes]tie more mischeefe In these late disorders with their Lecterors then anye thinge Else hath don ... For your Ma[jes]tie knows by towe woefull Experience Thatt these Lectorors have preachte your Ma[jes]tie out off your Kingdomes.'[79] Both Newcastle and Clarendon downplayed the Fairfaxes' gentry support and magnified their reliance upon an urban popular politics mobilised by renegade ministers to provide an explanation well suited to noble preconceptions of popular disorder.

IV

The connections between popular politics and parliamentary allegiance have been examined at length by Brian Manning, Ann Hughes and John Walter. Manning focused on popular parliamentarianism within the West Riding's disproportionately high middling sort population in order to support his theory of class division in seventeenth-century England.[80] However, relying upon print, propaganda and biased retrospective commentators as evidence for a national class struggle risked taking the likes of Clarendon, Hotham and Newcastle at face value. The aggressive nature of popular parliamentarian politics drove the Fairfaxes on, even occasionally dictating their strategy, but there is no evidence it sought to overthrow their leadership. Mutiny, agitators and disorder within West Riding parliamentarian forces surfaced only after the Fairfaxes relinquished their commands. Manning also neglected the deeper regional contexts, flattening out contrasts within the West Riding and neglecting the strength of royalism and recusancy around Ripon, Nidderdale and Skipton. A thorough explanation of this region's inclination to popular royalism awaits its historian, but it is possible that old-fashioned paternalism, good neighbourhood and traditional festivities persisted there after they had been expunged from the clothing districts. Newman's work on the northern royalist officer corps was not concerned with popular allegiance and his remark that 'the Fairfaxes were Parliamentarianism in Yorkshire' suggests disdain for the topic.[81]

The Fairfaxes' interaction with popular politics can be closely compared with Ann Hughes's study of Lord Brooke and Warwickshire. Brooke faced a similar problem to the Fairfaxes in attempting to mobilise support in a county where most gentry were royalist or neutral. Both Lord Fairfax and Lord Brooke depended heavily upon lesser gentry advisers such as Thomas Stockdale and William Purefoy. Royalist strength among Warwickshire's gentry was rendered irrelevant by the more powerful non-gentry support Brooke mobilised among north Warwickshire's towns and 'middling sort'. Clarendon described urban parliamentarianism in Birmingham in very similar language to that in Leeds, Bradford and Halifax. Like the Fairfaxes, Brooke's support 'was not based on seigneurial ties but on ideological appeal'. Brooke became a skilled popular leader who utilised music, feasts, pamphlets and church bells to rally support. He addressed volunteers with respect, even allowing them to elect their own officers. By his deliberate adoption of 'a militant, popular campaign', Brooke enhanced feelings of self-worth among sub-gentry groups, thereby limiting his gentry support further.[82] His reputation extended into the West Riding; the inn at Adwalton was called 'the Lord Brook's' and was much frequented by parliamentarian soldiers.[83] Yet there is little evidence that the Fairfaxes emulated Brooke's recruitment methods, relying more upon their ministers and captains to instigate enlistment. In 1642 the Fairfaxes appeared less prepared and less committed to war than Brooke, while Brooke enjoyed advantages over them in his links with London and his fortified bases at Warwick and Coventry. However, unlike in Warwickshire where popular parliamentarianism faded in Brooke's absence, in Yorkshire's clothing districts popular parliamentarianism was more resilient, persisting through 1643 and 1644 in the Fairfaxes' absence.

Another region that exhibited anti-royalist insurgency comparable to the West Riding was the clothing district around the Stour valley in Essex and Suffolk. Here the attacks on noble and gentry houses by roving crowds in August 1642 have often been represented as the English revolution's foremost example of class conflict. Both the West Riding and this region suffered the high levels of volatile poverty linked to the cloth trade. Both regions featured godly ministers, electoral disputes and virulent anti-catholicism. Where such economic and political crises combined, John Walter has argued not for naked class conflict, but for 'an active citizenry mobilised by the politics of anti-popery and popular parliamentarianism'. The class nature of the violence was limited because the crowds' targets were catholics or Laudians, upon whom it was felt Parliament had legitimised attacks. The crowds believed they were performing what their backward local gentry should have already organised. Walter uncovered plentiful evidence that the 'middling sort' were actively involved in these riots. The local godly magnate, the earl of Warwick, controlled many Essex benefices, encouraging supporters among a network of 'honest radicals' and 'well affected that existed below, but connected with, the level of their better recorded gentry counterparts'. Warwick avoided imperious tones and wrote to

Colchester's corporation as 'Gentlemen and my very good friends'. Through such intermediaries, Warwick also mobilised mass support in a parliamentarian direction. Like the Fairfaxes, Warwick was sensitive to the feelings of sub-gentry groups, acknowledging the 'middling sort' and their view of themselves as 'the better sort'.[84]

The politics of godly reform took hold in the West Riding a great deal later than they did in the Stour valley which had been among England's first localities to embrace the protestant reformation. The other main contrast between popular insurgency in the West Riding and Essex is that initially Bradford's insurgents were defending their homes from plunder rather than launching pre-emptive strikes against catholic or royalist estates. War was upon them before they struck, but as with popular parliamentarianism in Essex and Warwickshire, the club-law's wave of violent pillaging was selective and limited to the estates of perceived 'enemies of the people'.[85] Walter's study concurred with John Morrill's earlier point that the cloth industry's presence was a more important explanatory factor in popular parliamentarianism than Underdown's broader wood-pasture cultural hypothesis synthesised in *Revel, Riot and Rebellion*.[86] Historians generally recognise that there was a link between cloth manufacture, radical religion and rebellion, that it was a tradition not confined to the British civil wars and a phenomenon recognised by contemporaries. Royalists plundered convoys of cloth regularly, and in Gloucestershire, Andrew Warmington has found that clothiers were often presumed to be rebels by royalist officers. Mark Stoyle has uncovered similar fears of 'the popularity' in the depressed clothing districts of north Devon, and in September 1645 Devon's cloth manufacturers cried out 'a Fairfax, a Fairfax' to demonstrate their allegiance just as those of Halifax and Leeds had done three years earlier.[87]

The popular politics behind Fairfax's West Riding support in 1643 sought neither to raise up 'the middling sort', nor to radically redistribute land and wealth. Yet those who engaged in this urban-based popular politics showed they could organise and mobilise effectively without leadership from county gentry.[88] They rebelled because many of them faced a subsistence crisis and because their trusted local officeholders, parochial gentry, churchwardens and ministers, were prepared to lead them. Convinced that their livelihoods, property and religion were in danger, they exhibited the same 'politics of popular parliamentarianism' as John Walter has investigated in Essex and Suffolk. This politics was so receptive to parliamentarian propaganda that John Hodgson believed the 'middling sort', a term itself invented by parliamentarians to distance their supporters from the godless multitude, had been the salvation of the kingdom, and was so disdainful of Scotland because he felt the Scottish gentry 'have such influence over the commonalty, that they can lead them what way they please'.[89]

Revisionist views that downplay divisions in early Stuart culture flounder once attention is focused beyond Westminster. The importance of popular activism in Yorkshire's parliamentarian army and the views expressed in *Plaine English* provide a reminder that a concentration on high politics risks underplaying the significance of ordinary people during the civil wars. An emergence of popular political awareness on both sides was a direct cause of civil war, and understandings of high politics need to be constructed within this context of broader political culture.[90] The assumption that landowners raised regiments from their tenants does not always hold. The Fairfaxes did not. Sir Clements Markham and C. V. Wedgwood both claimed – without citing evidence – that the Fairfaxes exerted strong feudal influences in mustering their tenantry.[91] When one of Fairfax's first officers, Christopher Copley of Wadworth, recruited his cavalry troop, sixty-one of his ninety-two troopers were from the West Riding, and most of these were from the clothing districts, thirty miles from Copley's seat. Only one was from Wadworth.[92] Major royalist landowners such as the marquess of Hertford, the earl of Bath and Sir William Savile all failed to enforce the commission of array in towns located in the midst of their family estates.[93]

It should be emphasised that popular support for the Fairfaxes was strongest in a specific region of Yorkshire which assumed an importance beyond its size. Without it, the rise of Sir Thomas Fairfax and Parliament's war effort in the north would not have been possible. The mobilisation of support was a two-way process, with military leaders and the people seeking to influence and manipulate each other, often through a network of local officeholders, ministers and lesser gentry. While most of the gentry feared popular politics, they were not all completely withdrawn from it; Lord Brooke, the earl of Warwick and the Fairfaxes all proved adept at riding tides of popular support. They succeeded not just by manipulating their followers with propaganda but by encouraging intermediaries to organise mass support for them. While some royalist commanders were contemptuous of civilian participation in the war effort, the Fairfaxes embraced and relied upon it, harnessing rather than destroying local interests and co-operating with urban elites in Leeds, Bradford, Halifax and Hull.[94] Clarendon remarked that the Fairfaxes were ruled by two or three individuals of 'inferior quality', who were 'more conversant with the people'. One such was clearly Thomas Stockdale, who had frequently urged Lord Fairfax to engage with popular politics, and had thereby earned the scorn of the Hothams.[95] David Scott has argued that 'the common people, even the more assertive elements among the "middling sort", generally sought legitimation for their wartime undertakings by enlisting the approval or leadership of the gentry', framing their attempts to enlist gentry support in a language of deference: 'We will live and die with a Fairfax!'[96] Scott makes a convincing point; a salient feature of popular politics in the West Riding was to court the

Fairfaxes' support by exalting their name. Yet because the first year of civil war in Yorkshire was so perilous for the parliamentarians, on occasions, such as at Bradford, Halifax and in Calderdale, popular parliamentarianism organised itself to fight on, doing without the Fairfaxes, the county gentry and customary languages of deference.

NOTES

1 BL, E119(24), *Special passages*, 27 September–4 October (London, 1642), p. 57; BL, E116(9), *The last true newes from Yorke, Nottingham, Coventry and Warwicke*, 24 August–4 September (London, 1642).

2 BL, E86(40), *The kingdoms weekly intelligencer*, 24–31 January (London, 1643), p. 39.

3 G. D. Lumb (ed.), *The registers of the parish church of Leeds from 1639 to 1667* (Publications of the Thoresby Society, 7, 1897), p. 27; BL, Add. MS 21427, fo. 9.

4 A. Hughes, *Politics, Society and Civil War in Warwickshire, 1620–60* (Cambridge, 1987); J. Walter, *Understanding Popular Violence in the English Revolution: The Colchester Plunderers* (Cambridge, 1999).

5 BL, E116(32), *A private letter, from an eminent cavalier, to his highly honoured friend in London*, 10 September (London, 1642), p. 4.

6 J. S. A. Adamson, 'The baronial context of the English civil war', *TRHS*, 5th series, 40 (1990), 93–120.

7 Walter, *Understanding Popular Violence*, p. 113.

8 J. Morrill, *Revolt in the Provinces: The People of England and the Tragedies of War, 1634–1648* (London, 2nd edn, 1999), p. 74.

9 D. Underdown, *Revel, Riot and Rebellion: Popular Politics and Culture in England* (Oxford, 1985); Hughes, *Warwickshire*; M. Stoyle, *Loyalty and Locality: Popular Allegiance in Devon during the English Civil War* (Exeter, 1994).

10 D. Scott, 'The wars of the three kingdoms, 1642–1649', in B. Coward (ed.), *A Companion to Stuart Britain* (Oxford, 2003), p. 317; Morrill, *Revolt in the Provinces*, p. 187.

11 BL, Add. MS 34727, fo. 29.

12 *CSP dom. 1637–8*, p. 433; W. Page (ed.), *The Victoria County History of Yorkshire* (London, 1912), vol. 2, p. 415.

13 C. Cross, *Urban Magistrates and Ministers: Religion in Hull and Leeds from the Reformation to the Civil War* (University of York, Borthwick Paper, 67, 1985), p. 2; J. D. Purdy, *Yorkshire Hearth Tax Returns* (Studies in regional and local history, 7, University of Hull, 1991), p. 123.

14 H. Heaton, *The Yorkshire Woollen and Worsted Industries* (Oxford, 2nd edn, 1965), pp. 183, 197; R. Bennett, 'Enforcing the law in revolutionary England: Yorkshire, 1640–1660' (Ph.D. thesis, University of London, 1988), p. 37.

15 A. Fletcher, *The Outbreak of the English Civil War* (London, 1981), p. 223; BL, Add. MS 18979, fos. 69r–70v; HULA, Hotham MS, DDHO/2/8.

16 BL, E144(6), *To the Kings most excellent majestie: The humble petition of the clothiers, inhabiting in the parish of Leeds, vicaridge of Hallifax and other parts adjoining, in the county of*

Yorke. Presented unto his majestie at Yorke the 14 of April (London, 1642).

17 *The parliamentary or constitutional history of England, being a faithful account of all the most remarkable transactions in parliament from the earliest times to the restoration of King Charles II, by several hands* (London, 1753), vol. 11, p. 246.

18 G. Rimmer, 'The evolution of Leeds up to 1700', in *Thoresby Miscellany* (Publications of the Thoresby Society, 50, 1967), p. 117.

19 J. Priestley, 'Some memoirs concerning the family of Priestleys', in C. Jackson (ed.), *Yorkshire diaries and autobiographies of the seventeenth and eighteenth centuries* (Surtees Society, 77, 1883), p. 26.

20 *The parliamentary or constitutional history of England*, vol. 12, p. 272; E. Peacock, 'On some civil war documents relating to Yorkshire', *YAJ*, 1 (1870), 102.

21 Walter, *Understanding Popular Violence*, pp. 326–7.

22 W. and S. Sheils, 'Textiles and reform: Halifax and its hinterland', in P. Collinson and J. Craig (eds), *The Reformation in English Towns, 1500–1640* (Basingstoke, 1998), pp. 130–43; J. T. Cliffe, *The Yorkshire Gentry from the Reformation to the Civil War* (London, 1969), pp. 264, 268; D. Lamburn, 'Politics and religion in early modern Beverley', in Collinson and Craig (eds), *The Reformation in English Towns*, p. 69.

23 A. Foster, 'Church policies of the 1630s', in R. P. Cust and A. Hughes (eds), *Conflict in Early Stuart England: Studies in Religion and Politics 1603–1642* (London, 1989), p. 204.

24 J. Addy, 'The uncontrollable and ungovernable parish of Halifax in the seventeenth century', *THAS*, new series, 1 (1993), 37.

25 R. A. Marchant, *The Puritans and the Church Courts in the Diocese of York, 1560–1642* (London, 1960), p. 110; D. N. R. Lester, *The History of Batley Grammar School* (Batley, 1962), p. 24.

26 W. J. Sheils, 'Provincial preaching on the eve of the civil war: some West Riding sermons', in A. Fletcher and P. Roberts (eds), *Religion, Culture and Society in Early Modern Britain: Essays in Honour of Patrick Collinson* (Cambridge, 1994), p. 310.

27 BL, Add. MS 20778, fo. 4.

28 BL, Add. MS 34274, fo. 94; *House of Lords MS*, HMC, 4th report, part 1, report and appendix (London, 1874), p. 46; A. Holroyd (ed.), *Collectanea Bradfordiana: a collection of papers on the history of Bradford and the neighbourhood* (Saltaire, 1873), p. 157.

29 Marchant, *Puritans and Church Courts*, p. 113; R. A. Marchant, *The Church under the Law: Justice, Administration and Discipline in the Diocese of York, 1560–1640* (Cambridge, 1969), p. 207; M. and F. Heywood and B. Jennings, *A History of Todmorden* (Otley, 1996), pp. 40–2.

30 T. W. Hanson, 'Halifax parish church, 1640–1660, part 1', *THAS* (1915), 45, 54; *JHL*, vol. 5, p. 666; C. T. Clay, 'The Protestation of 1641: Halifax signatories', *THAS* (1919), 107; WYRO, Calderdale, Brearcliffe MS, MISC: 182.

31 J. Newton, 'Puritanism in the diocese of York, 1603–1640' (Ph.D. thesis, University of London, 1956), pp. 32–3; J. Rushworth, *Historical collections* (London, 1721), part 3, vol. 2, p. 140; TNA, SP 23/133/219–20; TNA, E121/5/6; TNA, SP 28/250/part ii/ 205–11; J. Gregory, 'Annals of an old Yorkshire village', *Bradford Antiquary*, new series, 2 (1905), 474; B. Dale, 'James Nayler, the mad Quaker', *Bradford Antiquary*, new series, 2 (1905), 166, 179.

32 E. Smith, *The life of William Dewsbury* (London, 1836), pp. 28–9; Sheils, 'Provincial preaching', p. 301.

33 F. Cobley and L. Padgett, *Chronicles of the Free Grammar School of Prince Henry at Otley* (Otley, 1923), p. 77; Sheils, 'Provincial preaching', pp. 295, 298, 304, 309; W. Robertshaw (ed.), 'Ministers and churchwardens named in the Bradford cathedral registers of the seventeenth-century', *Bradford Antiquary*, new series, 8 (1962), 292; H. Speight, *Upper Wharfedale* (London, 1900), p. 68; J. H. Turner (ed.), *The autobiography of Captain John Hodgson of Coley Hall, near Halifax* (Brighouse, 1882), pp. 22–3; Hanson, 'Halifax parish church, 1640–1660, part 1', 51; A. Laurence, *Parliamentary Army Chaplains, 1642–1651* (Woodbridge, 1990), p. 118; BL, E88(19), *A true and plenary relation of the great defeat given by my Lord Fairfax forces unto my lord of Newcastles forces in Yorkshire*, 6 February (London, 1643).

34 Rushworth, *Historical collections*, part 3, vol. 2, p. 136.

35 K. Lindley, 'The impact of the 1641 rebellion upon England and Wales, 1641–1645', *Irish Historical Studies*, 18 (1973), 154–5, 163–4, 167.

36 BL, Add. MS 18979, fos. 90r–91v.

37 *Ibid.*, fos. 117–18.

38 *House of Lords MS*, HMC, 5th report, appendix (London, 1876), p. 7; *JHC*, vol. 2, p. 431; *JHL*, vol. 4, p. 583.

39 Sheils, 'Provincial preaching', pp. 301–4.

40 Turner (ed.), *Autobiography of Captain John Hodgson*, p. 22; Priestley, 'Some memoirs concerning the family of Priestleys', 26.

41 T. Wright (ed.), *The autobiography of Joseph Lister of Bradford in Yorkshire* (London, 1842), pp. 5–6.

42 *Ibid.*, pp. 7–8.

43 *Ibid.*, p. 10.

44 R. Clifton, 'Popular fear of catholics during the English revolution, 1640–1660', *Past and Present*, 52 (1971), 24, 45, 55.

45 Clarendon, *The history of the rebellion and civil wars in England* (Oxford, 1717), vol. 2, part 1, p. 143; B. Whitelocke, *Memorials of English affairs* (London, 1682), p. 68.

46 *The parliamentary or constitutional history of England*, vol. 11, p. 372; G. Trease, *Portrait of a Cavalier: William Cavendish, First Duke of Newcastle* (London, 1979), p. 95.

47 K. Lindley, 'The part played by the Catholics', in B. Manning (ed.), *Politics, Religion and the English Civil War* (London, 1973), pp. 126–76; Morrill, *Revolt in the Provinces*, p. 74; P. R. Newman, *The Old Service: Royalist Regimental Colonels and the Civil War, 1642–1646* (Manchester, 1993), pp. 214, 241–2, 266.

48 T. Harris, ' "Venerating the honesty of a tinker": the King's friends and the battle for the allegiance of the common people in Restoration England', in T. Harris (ed.), *The Politics of the Excluded, c. 1500–1850* (Basingstoke, 2001), p. 208.

49 YML, Old Library, XXI.f.30(23), *A declaration made by the earl of Newcastle* (York, 1642), p. 13; YML, Old Library, XXI.f.30(8), *A declaration of the right honourable the earl of Newcastle* (York, 1643), pp. 4–5; Rushworth, *Historical collections*, part 3, vol. 2, p. 140.

50 BL, E244(24), *A perfect diurnall of the passages in Parliament*, 19–26 December (London,

1642); Morrill, *Revolt in the Provinces*, p. 117.

51 J. Shaw, 'The life of master John Shaw', in C. Jackson (ed.), *Yorkshire diaries and autobi-ographies of the seventeenth and eighteenth centuries* (Surtees Society, 65, 1877), appendix, p. 363; D. H. Atkinson, *Ralph Thoresby, the topographer: his town and times* (Leeds, 1885), vol. 1, p. 23; J. Tickell, *History of the town and county of Kingston-upon-Hull* (Hull, 1790), p. 454; WYRO, Calderdale, FW:14/1.

52 YML, CWT, 43–07–12, *Two letters, the one being intercepted by the parliament's forces which was sent from Sir Hugh Cholmley to Captain Gotherick* (London, 1643), p. 3; Worcester College, Oxford, Wing 2251A, *The Pindar of Wakefield* (London, 1643), p. 3.

53 J. Raymond (ed.), *Making the News: An Anthology of the Newsbooks of Revolutionary England, 1641–1660* (Moreton-in-Marsh, 1993), p. 130; YML, CWT, 43–02–04, *A declara-tion of the lords and commons assembled in parliament for the vindication of Ferdinando, lord Fairfax* (London, 1643), pp. 5–6; P. S. Seaver, *Wallington's World: A Puritan Artisan in Seventeenth-Century London* (Stanford, 1985), p. 168.

54 W. S. Maltby, *The Black Legend in England: The Development of Anti-Spanish Sentiment, 1558–1660* (Durham, North Carolina, 1971), pp. 17, 48, 54, 78.

55 C. Russell, *The Fall of the British Monarchies, 1637–1642* (Oxford, 1991), p. 340.

56 J. P. Cooper (ed.), *Wentworth Papers, 1597–1628* (Camden Society, 4th series, 12, 1973), p. 218; R. Cust, 'Wentworth's "change of sides" in the 1620s', in J. F. Merritt (ed.), *The Political World of Thomas Wentworth, Earl of Strafford, 1621–1641* (Cambridge, 1996), p. 67.

57 R. P. Cust, 'Politics and the electorate in the 1620s', in Cust and Hughes (eds), *Conflict in Early Stuart England*, pp. 145–51; P. Salt, 'Sir Thomas Wentworth and the parliamen-tary representation of Yorkshire, 1614–1628', *Northern History*, 16 (1980), 136–8, 143.

58 Salt, 'Sir Thomas Wentworth and the parliamentary representation of Yorkshire', 137–9; R. Cust, 'News and politics in early seventeenth-century England', *Past and Present*, 112 (1986), 89.

59 J. Horsfall Turner (ed.), *The autobiography and diaries of Rev. Oliver Heywood, 1630–1702* (Brighouse, 1882), vol. 1, p. 83.

60 BL, E114(7), *A declaration of the lords and commons assembled in parliament*, 24 August (London, 1642), pp. 4–5; BL, E129(26), *Two declarations of the lords and commons assem-bled in parliament*, 10 December (London, 1642).

61 Turner (ed.), *Autobiography of Captain John Hodgson*, p. 21; F. H. Sunderland, *Marmaduke, Lord Langdale* (London, 1926), p. 66.

62 BL, E121(34), *Weekly intelligence from severall parts of this kingdome, received from very good hands*, 11 October (London, 1642), p. 8; BL, E121(45), *A true & exact relation of the several passages at the siege of Manchester*, 12 October (London, 1642), pp. 8–9.

63 Clarendon, *The history of the rebellion and civil wars in England*, vol. 2, part 1, p. 138.

64 *Portland MS*, HMC, 13th report, appendix, part 1 (London, 1891), vol. 1, supplement, p. 718.

65 Wright (ed.), *Autobiography of Joseph Lister*, p. 14; D. Parsons (ed.), *The diary of Sir Henry Slingsby of Scriven, bart.* (London, 1836), p. 103.

66 A. Hughes, *The Causes of the English Civil War* (Basingstoke, 2nd edn, 1998), p. 140.

67 Cliffe, *Yorkshire Gentry*, pp. 338–40; Newman, *Old Service*, pp. 250–1.

68 BL, Harleian MS 164, fo. 234; Worcester College, Oxford, aaI.15, *A declaration of the commons assembled in Parliament, upon two letters sent by Sir John Brooks*, 10 May (London, 1643).

69 TNA, SP 28/249; TNA, SP 19/17/157.

70 HULA, DDHO/1/18.

71 B. Coward, 'The experience of the gentry, 1640–1660', in R. C. Richardson (ed.), *Town and Countryside in the English Revolution* (Manchester, 1992), p. 202.

72 YML, CWT, 43–00–00, *A short history of the anabaptists of high and low Germany. The second edition, augmented with the passage of Anabaptisme into England* (York, 1643), pp. 7–8.

73 *Portland MS*, HMC, 29, 13th report, appendix, part 1, vol. 1. p. 99.

74 BL, E84(42), *Plaine English: or, a discourse concerning the accommodation, the armie, the association. Si populus vult decipi, decipiatur. Printed (unlesse men be the more carefull, and God the more mercifull) the last of liberty*, 12 January (London, 1643), pp. 5, 11, 17–18, 22, 28.

75 *Ibid.*, pp. 25–6.

76 BL, Add. MS 18979, fos. 78r–79v.

77 D. Wootton, 'From rebellion to revolution: the crisis of the winter of 1642–1643 and the origins of civil war radicalism', *EHR*, 105 (1990), 655, 664n; R. Baxter, *The Autobiography of Richard Baxter*, ed. N. H. Keeble (London, 1974), p. 47.

78 Clarendon, *History of the rebellion and civil wars in England*, ed. W. Dunn Macray (Oxford, 1888), vol. 2, p. 285; Clarendon, *The history of the rebellion and civil wars in England*, vol. 2, part 1, p. 141.

79 Walter, *Understanding Popular Violence*, p. 71.

80 B. Manning, *The English People and the English Revolution*, (London, 2nd edn, 1991), pp. 298–305.

81 Newman, *Old Service*, p. 264.

82 Hughes, *Warwickshire*, pp. 149–56.

83 *The original memoirs written during the great civil war being the life of Sir Henry Slingsby and memoirs of Captain John Hodgson with notes*, ed. W. Scott (Edinburgh, 1806), p. 170; A. Eyre, 'A dyurnall or catalogue of all my accions', in C. Jackson (ed.), *Yorkshire diaries and autobiographies of the seventeenth and eighteenth centuries* (Surtees Society, 65, 1877), p. 82.

84 Walter, *Understanding Popular Violence*, pp. 112–13, 150, 287.

85 Hughes, *Warwickshire*, p. 156.

86 Walter, *Understanding Popular Violence*, pp. 339–40; J. Morrill, 'The ecology of allegiance in the English revolution', *JBS*, 26 (1987), 462.

87 D. Underdown, 'The problem of popular allegiance in the English civil war', *TRHS*, 5th series, 31 (1981), 84–5; BL, Add. MS 31116, fo. 34r; A. R. Warmington, *Civil War, Interregnum and Restoration in Gloucestershire, 1640–1672* (Royal Historical Society, studies in history, new series, 1997), p. 49; Stoyle, *Loyalty and Locality*, pp. 15–16, 33, 38–40, 50, 117.

88 C. Holmes, 'The county community in Stuart historiography', *JBS*, 19:2 (1980), 72.

89 *The original memoirs written during the great civil war*, ed. Scott, p. 124.

90 T. Cogswell, 'Underground verse and the transformation of early Stuart political culture', in S. D. Amussen and M. Kishlansky (eds), *Political Culture and Cultural Politics in Early Modern England: Essays Presented to David Underdown* (Manchester, 1995), pp. 293–4.

91 Markham, p. 51; C. V. Wedgwood, *The King's War, 1641–1647* (Manchester, 1958), p. 196.

92 Worcester College, Oxford, Clarke MS 4/2.

93 D. Underdown, *Somerset in the Civil War and Interregnum* (Newton Abbot, 1973), p. 31; Stoyle, *Loyalty and Locality*, p. 143; BL, E116(9), *The last true newes from Yorke, Nottingham, Coventry and Warwicke*.

94 A. Hughes, 'The king, the parliament and the localities during the English civil war', *JBS*, 24:2 (1985), 241, 253.

95 Clarendon, *History of the rebellion and civil wars in England*, ed. Dunn Macray, vol. 2, p. 287; *Portland MS*, HMC, 13th report, appendix, part 1, vol. 1, p. 84.

96 Scott, 'The wars of the three kingdoms, 1642–1649', p. 317.

Chapter 8

Religion and honour

Sir Thomas Fairfax believed that serving God and acquiring honour should never be contradictory activities. His religious preferences and sense of honour were closely intertwined and mutually reinforcing. The twin goals of the protestant cause in Europe and further reformation in England shaped a Fairfax family identity that fused a martial sense of honour with a blend of Calvinism, humanism and classical republicanism. Many of the ideas that constituted Sir Thomas Fairfax's religion and honour were similar to and inherited from his father, grandfather and wider family. For that reason this chapter focuses more widely than on just Sir Thomas himself, discussing his beliefs and deportment within the context of his close male family. Despite Sir Thomas being brought up under his grandfather's influence, there seems to be more similarity than divergence between Ferdinando and Sir Thomas's professed ideas about religion and honour. The cornerstone of this, shared by Sir Thomas and his father, was a Calvinist upbringing that encouraged them to humble themselves before God. For Sir Thomas, a striving for humility became inseparable from his elect status. His concept of honour cherished his lineage because it had brought him towards serving God and the common-wealth, but his belief that God had taken a special interest in his life inclined him towards notions of public service and civic virtue.

I

Sir Thomas was born into a family that was deeply protestant, and becoming more so. In the 1590s, his grandfather, the future first baron Fairfax, fought against the Spanish in the Low Countries and Normandy. The first baron's brother Sir Charles Fairfax was killed by the Spanish at the siege of Ostend in 1604, while two of the first baron's sons, John and William, were also killed by the Spanish in the Palatinate in 1621. In his grief, the old lord discussed ideas on how best to weaken Spanish power in an essay entitled 'The highway to Heidelberg'. In it he argued that Europe's wars were not caused by religious divisions but by the tyranny and pride of the king of Spain. He penned an open letter to the kings, princes and states of Europe, hoping to galvanise them into action against Spain, revealing what became a family concern to serve God above worldly sovereigns. He stressed the responsibilities rather than the rights of rulers, and warned them 'you know well that God hath not placed you in thrones of Majesty for your own glories but for his whom you serve'. He warned princes that God was 'incomparablie more transcendent over you then you are over your subjects'; God would call rulers to account and 'demand of you how you have discharged your stewardships'. He later advised his son Henry: 'If it be honor to serve a kinge it is more to serve the king of kings.'[1]

He bestowed upon his eldest son a godly upbringing; Ferdinando Fairfax's younger years were 'given to the study of Arts and Sciences, that must make him useful and serviceable to his Countrey, and not to Dogs, Hawkes &c'. In 1614, he wrote 'my greatest care ... hath been and still is, to breed my son a scholar'.[2] By the 1630s Ferdinando was among the most active justices in the West Riding, his regular service from 1637 to 1642 was punctuated only by his attendance at Westminster. This tireless industry widened the Fairfaxes' network, and in 1637 his father complimented Ferdinando for 'your paines in those businesses'.[3] Ferdinando's nephew, Brian Fairfax, later recalled that when Ferdinando had time free from serving on the commission of peace and reconciling disagreements he proved to be a fine poet and mathematician.[4] The Fairfaxes considered learning an indispensable part of the godly magistrate, and Ferdinando was involved in attempts to found a university at both Manchester and York, sponsoring a petition to Parliament despite the opposition of most MPs who proved jealous guardians of the status of Oxford and Cambridge.[5] Ferdinando was an enthusiastic book collector, acquiring many from the libraries of Sir John Hotham, viscount Saye and Sele, and Archbishop Neile. Andrew Cambers, the expert on Ferdinando's library, has argued that he emulated Thomas Bodley in protestant library building. After the capture of York in 1644, Ferdinando ordered the city corporation to pay for a keeper of the Minster Library to safeguard the protestant literary heritage established there by Archbishop Matthew. He then donated 443 volumes to York Minster Library between 1644 and 1648 in an attempt to develop the city's reputation for godliness and lay the foundations for a university library. Of these books, 347 have been classed by Cambers as related to godly culture, but there were also Arminian and Roman catholic volumes among them, reflecting Ferdinando's realisation of the academic need for a variety of Christian theology. Cambers has interpreted Ferdinando's library as 'a marker both of his godly culture and ideas about the virtues, if not of republicanism, then of accountable monarchy'.[6]

Love of antiquarian pursuits in the seventeenth century was often more prevalent among Roman catholics and religious conservatives, whose nostalgia could manifest itself as an anti-puritan force stressing more traditional concepts of honour.[7] Yet the Fairfaxes and several of their associates were also prominent antiquaries. Ralph Thoresby, author of *Ducatus Leodiensis*, was a dissenter and the son of one of Ferdinando's captains. In 1650, Ferdinando's brother Charles Fairfax of Menston directed 'my old friend Mr Knight', one of the heralds, to paint his regiment's colours. He later compiled the 'Analecta Fairfaxiana', which contained detailed pedigrees of the Fairfax family, with anagrams, epigrams and elegies in Latin concerning different family members. After the siege of York, he searched through the rubble of St Mary's Tower with a family friend, the antiquarian Roger Dodsworth, recovering several ancient relics and documents.[8] Dodsworth collaborated with William Dugdale on the 'Monasticon Anglicanum', and was granted a pension of £50 per year by Sir Thomas Fairfax, who ultimately donated Dodsworth's manuscripts to the Bodleian Library. Sir Thomas's brother-in-law Sir Thomas Widdrington compiled an antiquarian collection concerning the city of York entitled *Analecta Eboracensia*.[9] So when Sir Thomas Fairfax arrived in Oxford with Cromwell on 17 May 1649 to receive their degrees 'rigged up in the scarlet gowns and caps of doctors of civil law', it was important for his family's scholarly reputation to prove himself more than a mere soldier. He recommended Edward Reynolds, Joseph Caryl and Thomas Goodwin for three new lectureships in scripture.[10]

Despite Ferdinando's uneasy relationship with his father, discussed in Chapter 1, he embraced his father's religious outlook so much that by the 1630s Ferdinando was increasingly recognised as leader of the West Riding's godly. Ferdinando informed his father on 5 February 1629 that 'the danger by the growth of Arminianism and countenancing of the professors' amounted 'to an insensible subversion of the religion now established'. He believed this was 'now the great business, and indeed the greatest that can concern this kingdom'. Local ministers looked to the Fairfaxes for support against the Caroline church authorities.[11] Samuel Winter, Richard Clarkson and David Ellison were among the godly ministers who enjoyed the Fairfaxes' confidence who were prosecuted by ecclesiastical courts during the 1630s. As lord of Otley manor, the influence of Richard Neile, Archbishop of York, intruded on to the Fairfaxes' estates. Neile's resentment of the appointment of preaching ministers by local laymen led him into conflict with the Fairfax family. The Fairfaxes felt particularly aggrieved as their friend Archbishop Matthew had previously allowed them this practice. Neile's attempt to select the headmaster at Otley grammar school upset Ferdinando who was the leading school governor.[12]

Thomas Stockdale's letter to Ferdinando on 5 March 1641 revealed how closely religion and politics were entwined for the Fairfaxes and their associates. He wrote that the Triennial Act would promote 'the purity of the Gospell' as well as guard against times when princes 'have governed not by law; but according to their own fancies, or their flattering favourites malevolent affections'.[13] The reported atrocities committed by the Irish rebels affected the Fairfaxes so deeply that, by summer 1642, Ferdinando was sponsoring lectures at Otley that prepared the congregation for armed resistance to the crown. These sermons were delivered by a younger generation of puritan clerics in trouble with diocesan authorities, such as Richard Clarkson, David Ellison and John Cooper. They discussed Saul's fate as a warning to kings who displeased God, and William Sheils has argued that a volume of these sermon notes was prepared for a member of Fairfax's household, probably to articulate and legitimate their choice of a parliamentarian allegiance.[14]

Ferdinando had been present at Westminster throughout much of 1641, but only glimpses of his religious politics that year survive. One such came in March 1641 when he wrote to his brother Henry: 'the next will be my Lord of Canterbury's trial, and with that, Episcopacy and Church-government (I hope not the liturgy, which many shoot at)'.[15] This comment suggests there were limits to his zeal for further reformation and that at that stage he may have been only mildly Presbyterian in his sympathies. Yet in 1642, Ferdinando deepened the rift with his more religiously conservative allies, the Hothams. He promoted John Alured to a colonelcy, despite Alured's sectarianism and public opposition to the Hothams. He allowed the godly minister John Shaw, ejected from Hull by Sir John Hotham, to preach to his army at Selby. Shaw fashioned an image of Fairfax's outnumbered men as 'the people of God' who had been 'scorned and nicknamed a long time for Waldenses, Hussites, Lollards, Lutherans, Hugenots, Precisians, Puritans (or all in one), Round-heads'.[16] In doing so he was distancing the Fairfaxes and their men from the Caroline church, and presenting a Jacobean orthodoxy that viewed medieval heretical sects as precursors of protestantism, spurned by the medieval Romish 'false church of Antichrist'.[17] After Ferdinando's death, another puritan minister celebrated him as 'our Patient Huzzite', remarking that Fairfax, the 'Self-Conqueror', had mastered his passion, stoically accepting defeats as well as victories as the will of God. By 1644 Lord Fairfax's religious credentials were so trusted by Parliament that they empowered him to appoint ministers to Yorkshire's vacant benefices.[18]

Sir Thomas's religious views were similar to his father and grandfather. The first sentence of one of his own translations of a prayer addressed God as 'comforter of the elect'.[19] He later translated the whole Psalter. During the civil wars he protected the godly as his father had done in the 1630s. In June 1645, Sir Thomas insisted on the release of his officers Captains Hobson and Beaumont who had been arrested for lay preaching and he demanded the cashiering of Sir Samuel Luke's officers who had maltreated them. By 1645 it appears that Fairfax had adopted a similar attitude to Cromwell in not discriminating against tender protestant consciences in his commissioning of officers.[20] In 1647 Joshua Sprigge remarked of Fairfax that: 'In the midst of our Troubles in Religion, he was thus farre in Peace, that he could beare the different opinions in their unity to the publick, seeing the Work goe on as well as if all had been of one mind.'[21] This might have been Sprigge attempting to downplay the corrosive effects of religious disunity in the army, but Richard Stretton, Fairfax's Presbyterian chaplain during the 1660s, agreed with him:

> He never placed Religion in being for or against the circumstances, and ritual of worship. He was never so bigoted, to any Party or Faction as to place Religion in being of such a way, or such a Party. And though his acquaintance and converse did afford him most instances of serious piety in one set of men (whom he loved and honoured for it) yet he never did it with excluding of others, that in some things were of different persuasions and practices ... He ever loved and honoured them whatsoever their persuasions were about lesser things that did look after and labour to perform the essentials of Religion and that did exemplify Christianity most in the course of their conversations.[22]

Stretton believed Fairfax disliked religious controversy over trifling matters, feeling that it opened the way for atheism and profanity. He added that Fairfax 'equally disliked factious spirits that would keep no order but disturb the peace of Church and state, and those that would rigorously impose upon their brethren and exclude them from their Communion that were not satisfied in conscience in some lesser things'.[23] Even in the 1660s Fairfax still advocated tempering compulsion with toleration, a troublesome balancing act that had vexed all interregnum regimes.

Fairfax's religion is resistant to denominational labels and categories. He patronised ministers from a broad range of godly opinion while his tolerant attitude encouraged both Presbyterians and Independents to believe they had his support. Much of his religion was reflected in the reforms he ordered on the Isle of Man after the Rump granted him lordship of the island in 1651. Charged by the Council of State to enforce laws against drunkenness, swearing, adultery and profanation of the Sabbath, he endeavoured the further reformation of the island. He commanded the removal of all ministers 'as through gross ignorance or intolerable debauchery were judged unfit for such a service'. Stretton recalled that he then established a preaching ministry: 'And he took care to send over such pious men of competent parts and allowed them considerable stipends to the number of 16 (as I remember I have heard him say) and to one whom he designed as a superintendent or overseer (the true office of a Bishop) he allowed a treble advantage.' Stretton added that Fairfax established a grammar school and library along with scholarships for young Manxmen to study at Oxford and Cambridge to become ministers.[24] In 1658 he sent a small library to the island to foster learning, in the care of his cousin the governor,

James Chaloner.[25] Although Chaloner had written a book about the island dedicated to him, Fairfax failed to understand the island's religious customs and clumsily sought to resolve disagreements by applying the practices of the West Riding godly.[26] He failed to appreciate that a godly reformation based on scripture would be difficult for English ministers to accomplish in an island where the majority language was Manx. Stretton insinuated that the failure of these measures was deliberately kept from him for fear of breaking his heart.

Stretton reflected that Fairfax saw religion's surest defence as 'a learned, painful, faithful ministry', and that he 'would often say this was the best and surest way to keep out Popery, more than making or executing any severe and rigorous laws against them, which he never delighted in'.[27] However, he was not above interfering in the affairs of the catholic branch of his family, and wrote to Ferdinando in March 1642 that he intended to bind their cousin Lady Fairfax of Gilling for £3000 that her son, William, third viscount Fairfax, would 'be not conveyed beyond seas', but delivered to viscount Saye and Sele who arranged for a godly education at Felsted school.[28] While Sir Thomas often displayed lenience to vanquished catholic foes and showed scepticism of rumoured catholic plots, he nevertheless patronised clergy such as Joshua Witton whose thanksgiving sermon for Marston moor dehumanised catholic royalists as:

> men of cruelty, men of bloud, men as yet not satiated with the bloud of the Saints, many of them forraign and savage beasts, in the shapes of men; others of them bloudy, obstinate and malicious Papists, who are glad to see the day they are loosed out of their Collers, to worry such as have for many years kept them in by the power of good Lawes.[29]

J. T. Cliffe has observed that: 'To the extreme Puritan the parliamentary cause was a religious crusade or it was nothing.' In some measure, this applied to the Fairfaxes too. For all his attempted moderation, Sir Thomas Fairfax was fighting a religious war, and his cousin Sir William Fairfax expressed this in stark terms in a letter to his wife: 'For Thomas's part and mine, we rest neither night nor day, nor will willingly till we have done God some good service against His and our enemies.'[30]

II

Closely linked to the Fairfaxes' godly religion was their concept of honour that stressed public duty, civic virtue, restraint and, above all, modesty. This last value was not an innate quality among the English gentry. Linda Pollock has even argued that it had to be taught, but Ferdinando and Thomas Fairfax were masters of it. Ferdinando reflected that his commission as general in 1642 was 'of great honour and trust, far above my Ambition or Merit'.[31] John Shaw praised Ferdinando's humility, while Bulstrode Whitelocke, who liked to think he was related to the Fairfaxes, contrasted their modesty with the Hothams' pride.[32] Like his father before him in 1642, Thomas considered declining his commission as commanding general in 1645, thinking himself unworthy. He later reflected: 'Myself was nominated, though most unfit, & so far from desiring of it, yt had not so Great an Authority commanded obedience ... I should have hid my selfe to have avoided so Great a Charge.' The fate of the earl of Strafford, the last overambitious Yorkshireman popularly nicknamed 'Black Tom', was notorious; Fairfax endeavoured to banish pride from his deportment, and in political affairs his usual instinct was to bow to the will of Parliament.[33] On 18 February 1645 his entry into London was reported as being 'in a private manner, desiring to avoid all ostentation'. The next day he appeared before the House of Commons. Despite being hailed by Speaker Lenthall as 'the new Agamemnon', he answered modestly and refused the chair set for him.[34] His humility was a refreshing departure from the practice of his predecessor, the earl of Essex. On 3 April, the cavalcade accompanying his arrival among the regiments at Windsor was very small. Joshua Sprigge remarked that he 'went in a private manner, purposely avoiding that pomp, which usually accompanies a General into the field', while Rushworth reflected: 'Better to come in, then goe out in Triumph.' Sprigge's assertion that Fairfax accepted his command 'with much modesty' was no understatement.[35] To some extent, Sir Thomas's comparatively low status required it; although the Fairfaxes were among the foremost Yorkshire gentry, they clearly did not share the social eminence of the earl of Essex.

Austin Woolrych has contrasted Fairfax's style with the 'almost vice-regal pomp' that Essex assumed as lord general. Reminiscent of a scene in *Henry V*, the night before Naseby Fairfax rewarded a sentinel for challenging him when he forgot the watchword. Wearing no helmet to facilitate recognition, he killed a royalist ensign personally. When a trooper was reprimanded for claiming this deed, Fairfax responded: 'I have honour enough, let him take that to himself.' Ralph Josselin detected similar self-abasement when he dined with Fairfax in March 1647, remarking that Fairfax was 'a man thankefull for respects, and yet casts away honour from himself'.[36]

Fairfax believed this humility was desired by God but was clearly aware that his self-fashioning as the lowly, humble and pious general was immensely attractive politically. Virginia Black has asserted that Edward Bower's portrait of Sir Thomas in the Cromwell Museum, Huntingdon, 'permits a glimpse of the autocrat which he usually concealed both from himself and everyone else by a conscious striving for modesty to which he attached great importance'. Charles I distrusted Fairfax in 1647 because he had not asked for reward or favour. Charles II misunderstood him in the 1650s, offering him the earldom of Essex, £10,000 per annum in land and whatever office he chose. His allegiance could not be bought with promise of worldly reward and several royalist attempts during the interregnum to engage him in conspiracy failed.[37]

In December 1647, this humility was tested when his chaplain, John Salt-marsh, refused to remove his hat before Fairfax at Windsor saying: 'That he had not command from God to honour him now at all: That he had honoured him so much, that he offended in doting upon his person.' Not removing one's hat was a notorious act of social insubordination. Few of Fairfax's standing would let it pass unpunished, and Saltmarsh's act became notorious, provoking intense debate (Figure 5).[38] Again, in April 1649, the Digger leaders Everard and Winstanley refused to remove their hats before Fairfax at White-hall. Nevertheless Fairfax enjoyed 'a series of amicable conversations' with Winstanley. Remarkably, he attempted to provide them with protection and (as seen in Chapter 6) even seems to have expressed sympathy for them.[39] Fairfax's desire to humble himself before God restrained him; his refusal to act against them despite their failure to show him deference was remarkable for a time when many of the gentry still responded with physical violence towards plebeian insults to their honour.

Writing to justify Fairfax's retirement, Andrew Marvell declared humility to be 'the lowliest but the highest of all Christian qualifications', and that it was exemplified in Fairfax. During the 1660s, Fairfax's chaplain, Richard Stretton, preached to him that a consequence of the victory of the saints was 'the more they overcome the more humble they are'.[40] Among Fairfax's schol-arly endeavours, Andrew Cambers has observed that he adapted the text of the French Jesuit Jean Puget de la Serre's *Douces pensées de la mort* for a protestant readership.[41] Attracted by its condemnation of pride and praise of modesty, Fairfax wrote 'ther is nothing more great in this world then a hart that dispises greatnes'. He even echoed his grandfather's warning to princes in 'The highway to Heidelberg': 'If ye Crownes & septers be so sweete during life yit in death they are fearful for thou must render account of thy sturdship.'[42] Both Fairfax and his grandfather's discourse on monarchies as 'stewardships' stressed notions of service over divinity. Around this time Fairfax wrote several deliberations and reflections upon Biblical passages and the Psalms that high-light his continued belief that humility was inseparable from godliness:

> The doctrine is that gratious persons hath lowe thoughts of themselves. Abraham he accounted himself dust ... David compared himself to a flea & a worme. Patient Job though God speake favourably of him yet saith he I am vile ... see how low thoughts these holy persons had of themselves. The reason is because they see their own nothingness ... for I know nothing of my selfe saith Paul but he that judges me is the Lord ... humble thoughts of ourselves comes of high thoughts of God.[43]

This studied humility persisted beyond death: his will stipulated that his burial was to be conducted 'in such a manner as may be convenient and decent

VVonderfull
PREDICTIONS
DECLARED

In a MESSAGE, as from the LORD,
To his Excellency

Sʀ. THOMAS FAIRFAX

and the Councell of His Army.

By JOHN SALTMARSH Preacher of the Gospell.

His severall speeches, and the manner of his Death.

December 29. 1647.

THis Narrative concerning Mr. Saltmarsh hath been sent to the Army; and there per-
used, corrected, and made perfect, to be printed and published for the Kingdomes satisfaction.   Imprimatur, Gilbert Mabbot.

Printed at *London* by *Robert Ibbitson*, in Smithfield, neer the
Queenes-head Tavern, 1648.

Figure 5 Title page of one of the several tracts that reported John Saltmarsh's notorious
insolence to Fairfax at Windsor in December 1647

rather than pompous'. This was strikingly similar to Ferdinando's will which had directed: 'I give my body to be buried without much pomp or ceremony in what place it shall please God to call me out of this sinfull world.'[44] The godly's concern that elaborate funerals promoted idolatry neatly complemented Fairfax's concerns for modesty. His uncle Sir William Constable instructed that his funeral should be 'without ostentation', while Thomas Stockdale set aside only £10 for his funeral.[45] Ferdinando was buried at Bolton Percy in March 1648 with 300 mourners 'entertained with Wine and cakes' at his brother's house, and 'each a black Riband was given'.[46] A simple service and a sermon followed concerning the burial of King Hezekiah, the great reformer of the church of Judah. Ferdinando's Latin funeral transcription stated that he was 'a sanctuary to the religious, a patron to the learned, and himself was the very standard of humanity and good breeding'. The funeral sermon given by Edward Bowles specifically linked Ferdinando's scholarship with his 'sobriety and temperance', and the virtues of his 'modesty and courtesy in speech and behaviour'.[47] These virtues were then linked to the parliamentarian cause and the promise of further reformation in the north. Although the funeral became expensive, no heralds were present and most of the mourners were either family or officers from Ferdinando's old army in what became a nakedly partisan and Yorkshire affair. There were no effigies, only simple wall tablets commemorating Ferdinando and Thomas.[48] In the 1980s it took a fundraising appeal to repair the collapsed roof of the dilapidated chapel in which Thomas was buried.

III

Inextricably bound with the Fairfaxes' religion was their idea of honour. This not only influenced their allegiance but also governed their self-fashioning and public deportment. The early seventeenth century was a time of intense status consciousness among the English gentry as notions of what constituted a gentleman's worth and honour were increasingly debated. Studies of gentry honour in the seventeenth century have come some distance since J. G. Marston's simplistic assertion that honour biased the gentry towards a royalist allegiance. Subsequently, Mervyn James stressed a shift from a 'lineage' to a 'civil' society reflected in changing concepts of honour, but this view has been criticised as too inflexible and schematic. Richard Cust, among others, has argued for 'the simultaneous existence of a variety of concepts, or discourses, of honour in early modern England'. Cust outlined two coexisting notions of honour among the English gentry. One stressed godliness, Christian humanism, education, virtue, service, restraint, sobriety and magistracy. The other stressed blood, pedigree, lineage, loyalty, outward display, nostalgia, hunting, hospitality and was more prone to violence. Although these notions were not necessarily mutually exclusive and could be blended or appropriated for different purposes, puritan gentry such as the Fairfaxes tended to favour the former, while royalist gentry often drew more from the latter. In an article more narrowly focused on military honour, Barbara Donagan has rightly argued that mutually recognised notions of honour were a source of stability in that they 'ameliorated relations between enemies', but when differing concepts of honour clashed, such occasions fuelled discord and questioned old certainties about the meaning of honour.[49]

Sir Thomas's concept of honour did draw upon pride in his lineage and love of antiquities, but it was more rooted in godliness, service and humility. He felt that blood and pedigree were insufficient guarantors of honour without service and virtue. His chaplain, Richard Stretton, recalled: 'He was much delighted to speak of the worthy actions of virtuous men in former times and did often bewail the degeneracy of persons of noble rank and ancient family from the virtues of their ancestors.'[50] The Fairfaxes' destructive clash with the Hothams illustrates how religious and political differences were strongly articulated in changing conceptions of honour. Sir Thomas Fairfax's professed notions of service and modesty were clearly at odds with the Hothams' lengthy expostulations on their family's status and honour. John Hotham told the earl of Newcastle that 'I have neither hopes nor fears that can remove me from what befitts a Gentleman,' and indicated his concern that Newcastle's envoy would treat him 'in such a way as is fitt for Gentlemen that value their honor above anything, for he is a knave that desires to outlive itt'.[51] Sir Thomas Fairfax preferred to allow his actions, military service and faith in providence to supersede such discussion. His Calvinist belief that he was among the elect endowed him with an inner strength and deep resolve on the battlefield that went beyond desire for glory and recognition.

The origins of Ferdinando and Thomas's notions of honour, like that of many puritan gentry of the time, were drawn from a blend of Calvinism, humanism and classical republicanism. The way to honour was held to be through public service informed by years of study and wisdom. This mode of thinking was shaped by the classical writers known as the Stoics, such as Plutarch, Seneca and Cicero. They emphasised the importance of virtue in defining a man's nobility, influencing many English humanists into discarding lineage and wealth as the leading determinants of honour. The truly honourable public man could disregard his personal and private interests in serving the commonwealth and public good. Erasmian notions of moderation and resistance to extremes had grown strong among the Calvinist gentry. Richard Cust has shown that the Cheshire MP Sir Richard Grosvenor was particularly attracted to this construction of honour, and that it consistently won him recognition and popular support. Like the Fairfaxes, Grosvenor placed great emphasis on learning, remarking that it was 'the best ornament that can beautify a gentleman'. Similarly, his public maintenance of preaching ministers was echoed by the Fairfaxes, as were his wariness of Arminianism and his encouragement of freeholders to take a more active role in politics.[52]

During the 1660s, Sir Thomas Fairfax noted a sermon by his chaplain, Richard Stretton, based on Proverbs 19: 'the discretion of a man defereth his anger & tis his glory to pass by an offence ... As God corrects his children with moderation soe doth thou moderate thy passions of anger & revenge.' Sir Richard Grosvenor had offered similar stoical advice to his son in 1628, calling pride 'the tynder of the worst dispositions', and adding 'a gentle answer pacifieth wrath, as Solomon saith, when furious words, threats & tanting recriminations doe no good att all'.[53] Both Grosvenor and the first baron Fairfax were concerned that their offspring should be able to master their passions. During the first bishops' war, the first baron warned Thomas to: 'avoide private quarrels as much as you canne, and shewe your valour upon the Comon Enemey, the first will but shew your pride and bringe you hatred the second give you honor and reputacon. I write this because amonghst soe many as you shall converse with you shall meete with men of variouse hewmors.'[54] The first baron Fairfax knew from experience how the English gentry could adapt their notions of honour to suit their circumstances. In 1625 he had partnered Sir Thomas Wentworth, later earl of Strafford, in standing for election as knights of the shire. He had doubtless been attracted by Wentworth's appropriation of stoic virtues: the theme of honesty, rhetoric of service and Wentworth's self-representation as the protector of the public and country interest. However, the Fairfaxes soon witnessed how maintaining the restraint and forbearance of such stoicism proved exceedingly difficult for Wentworth's choleric character.[55]

The Hothams of Scorborough, Fairfax's estranged allies in the civil war, shared some of Wentworth's characteristics. They expressed how their notions of duty and service had overcome their concern for self-preservation in denying their sovereign access to Hull, but, like Wentworth, they found modesty and restraint hard to sustain. Whitelocke deliberately contrasted Sir John Hotham with Ferdinando: 'Hotham was so high and morose as the other was meek and courteous.' Unlike the Fairfaxes, the Hothams were no godly reformers. They chose to stress blood, pedigree and lineage in their ideas about honour far more than the Fairfaxes did. Their capacious kinship network, largely the result of their virile loins and ill-fated wives, related them to all the East Riding's leading parliamentary gentry.[56] Such continuity of lineage was held to prove a family's virtue, as longer, purer pedigrees concentrated levels of noble blood. The Hothams boasted an unbroken lineage of direct succession from father to son stretching back to the twelfth century, so it was hardly surprising that their concept of honour stressed their pedigree.[57] In part because of this, they were notoriously sensitive to perceived slights. On the scaffold Sir John admitted that for 'rash words, anger and such things, no man has been more guilty'.[58] Wentworth considered Sir John was 'extreme sensible of honour, and discourtesies perhaps a little overmuch', while in 1642 John Hampden sent placatory letters reassuring Hotham that his honesty 'shall never be questioned by mee upon slight grounds'.[59]

In 1642 the Hothams felt their honour was affronted by parliamentary orders for them to obey Lord Fairfax's commands. Holders of an established Yorkshire baronetcy, they considered their status equal or superior to Fairfax's Scottish barony. In February 1643 an anonymous draft letter among their papers concerning John Hotham and Lord Fairfax lamented of the 'unhappy difference twixt men soe equally worth'.[60] Only a family particularly aggressive about its status would acclaim an esquire the equal of a baron. In October 1642 John Hotham protested 'it is a strange command they should assume over Captaine Hotham, that oweth them no such obedience'. Sir John even warned the Fairfaxes to 'give not law to those from whom you ought to receive'.[61] The Hothams were dismayed by an order from the earls of Northumberland, Warwick and Holland for John Hotham to take commands from Lord Fairfax.[62] They successfully lobbied the earl of Essex, probably through Sir John's son-in-law, Sir Philip Stapleton, to have this reversed. Essex bestowed the governorship of Cawood castle upon John Hotham, and granted Sir John permission to overrule Fairfax with regard to Hull's garrison forces.[63]

This confusion in command enabled further prickliness from the Hothams in defence of their autonomy. The Fairfaxes were not above provocative acts towards the Hothams, and Sir Thomas complained of John Hotham's 'peevish humour' in disobeying Lord Fairfax's orders. By January 1643 *Mercurius aulicus* knew that 'there hath been a great falling out' between the two families.[64] Sir John Hotham complained to Parliament of Ferdinando's secretary at war, Thomas Stockdale, 'who I thought usurped more authoritie than either his estate or understanding in warre could challenge', while John Hotham grumbled that 'our Secretary Stockdale thinks he knows all as he directs all to our General'. Stockdale had a history of clashing with Sir John Hotham who in turn objected to Stockdale's religious radicalism.[65] After the Hothams' arrest, the Fairfaxes knew how to add insult to injury: they appointed Stockdale to inventory the Hothams' confiscated possessions. Lord Fairfax requisitioned Sir John's library, and in a calculated affront, the Hothams' rich apparel was sold to Fairfax's officers in lieu of their weekly allowance.[66]

This last act was laden with symbolism. They were divesting the Hothams of their identity, and demonstrating that for the Fairfaxes, notions of service were more important than rank or status. Allowing their officers, some of whom were only on the fringes of gentry status, to dress themselves in the attire of a baronet, demonstrated a flagrant disregard of the apparel laws. The Fairfaxes were displaying what Patrick Collinson has called 'downward deference', where gentry befriended and advanced their social 'inferiors' in constructing networks of loyalty and allegiance. Clarendon hinted at this when he claimed that the Fairfaxes were ruled by two or three individuals of 'inferior quality', who were 'more conversant with the people'.[67]

The Hothams' concept of honour was much less accommodating to sub-gentry groups. John Hotham's letter of protest to Speaker Lenthall of 27 June 1643 complained that Cromwell had employed Captain White against him, 'who was latelie but a yeoman'. He claimed Cromwell's non-gentry officers had abused the honour of Hotham's troops, arguing 'that the valour of these men [i.e. Cromwell's] had onlie yet appeared in their defacing of churches'.[68] This language of injured honour grew increasingly royalist in tone, and he warned Colonel Rossiter: 'You shall see in a short time there will never be a gentleman but will be gone to the King.'[69] Hotham then confided to the earl of Newcastle: 'I never expected better from the popularity; for none of these ever reward their best citizens with anything but death or banishment.'[70]

I have dealt with the defection of the Hothams and Sir Hugh Cholmley in greater detail elsewhere, but by 1643 their notions of injured honour were undermining their parliamentary allegiance.[71] Their defections were prompted by fears for their personal safety, influenced by their uneasiness with the social and religious radicalism that the war in general, and the Fairfaxes in particular, appeared to be unleashing. Newcastle hoped to exploit such fears by declaring in February 1643 how 'the Badges and Monuments of ancient Gentry in Windows, and Pedigrees have been by them defaced; Old Evidences, the Records of private Families, the Pledges of Possessions, the boundaries of mens Properties have been by them burned, torn in pieces, and the Seals trampled under their Feet'. Grounded in reality, such propaganda found a ready audience. Unruly parliamentarian forces might murder surrendering royalist officers, as at Bradford, or deface gentry monuments, as at Ripon.[72] A letter among the Hotham papers reflected these nightmares, fearing 'the wounds of dissension made wider, and strangers brought in by degrees among us to possess our Inheritances'. The Hothams' sense of honour militated them towards royalism after they had chosen a parliamentarian allegiance. The key factor in their ruin was that they were among the most status-obsessed of gentry families in a status-obsessed age. Unlike the Fairfaxes, their idea of honour was unable to adapt itself to the horrors of popular risings, yeomen captains and sectarian officers. They also lacked the Fairfaxes' veneer of restraint. Sir John Hotham's idea of working alongside the municipal dignitaries of Hull was a public humiliation of the mayor.[73] John Hotham was even rumoured to have vowed to decapitate the Archbishop of York, while Sir Hugh Cholmley emulated his violent father by assaulting a trained bandsman for insolence in 1639.[74]

IV

The temperaments of military commanders are often best revealed by their reactions to defeat. Internecine violence, drunkenness and mutual recrimination were common responses among royalist commanders in 1645–6. Newcastle and Eythin famously abandoned the struggle after Marston moor, choosing exile rather than mockery at court. Sir John Belasyse and Sir Richard Willys clashed at Newark in 1645, and Sir George Goring's drunkenness that year reached such proportions he was relieved of command. Barbara Donagan has noted that duels and quarrelling were 'more visible and damaging among royalists' where they assumed a 'dangerous and distinctive role in royalist culture'. Robert Ashton agreed that royalists 'showed a propensity to pick quarrels' with their comrades at 'real or imagined slights', even in 1648. However, David Bates has pointed out that there were no known cases of duels between royalist officers in the north, and that the fiery royalist officer 'was a staple of Parliamentarian propaganda' that 'still influences Royalist historiography'. Quarrels were most often settled by superior officers or councils of war as royalist officers bridled their passion with military duty. Nevertheless, Bates concedes that while duelling was rare, 'opinionated assertiveness and quickness to take offence appear more characteristic of Royalist interpersonal relations than humility and tact'.[75]

In contrast, the Fairfaxes showed more restraint than violence in reaction to their defeat at Adwalton moor. They channelled their frustration not into drinking and quarrelling, but into a legal inquiry, instituting a committee to interrogate those suspected of treachery.[76] Ferdinando Fairfax was the model of stoic fortitude in response to defeats and personal losses. In September 1644, he lamented 'the mortal wounds of my dear nephew Sir William Fairfax'. Although his second son, Charles, had just been mortally wounded at Marston moor, and Sir Thomas remained dangerously ill, having been shot at Helmsley, Ferdinando still wrote 'blessed be God, the victory obtained over our enemies doth abate my sorrow for any particular friends'.[77] Here Ferdinando indicated that although he had endured suffering and grief, they would not overwhelm him. Expressions of this sort were highly esteemed and enhanced the Fairfaxes' growing reputation.

Ferdinando again showed restraint in response to the earl of Newcastle's challenge in February 1643 to settle the northern war in a trial by battle. Newcastle taunted Fairfax that such an affair would be 'conformable to the Examples of our Heroic Ancestors, who used not to spend their time in scratching one another out of holes, but in pitched fields determined their doubts'. Newcastle's rhetoric of honour betrayed his strategic frustrations: Newcastle knew his army would enjoy great advantage in open battle and Ferdinando shrewdly declined the offer. Articulating his refusal in his own language of honour, John Adamson has shown how Ferdinando quoted from Ben Jonson's *The New Inn* in his response to Newcastle, who had been the playwright's old friend and patron. Disregarding romantic chivalry and arguing that the sufferings of the country could not be determined in one day, Ferdinando remarked that he would not follow 'the rules of Amadis de gaule, or the Knight of the Sun'. This divergence in notions of honour is underlined by Gerald Aylmer's observation that most condemnation of duels came from puritans, and most of the declining of challenges came from parliamentarians.[78]

Another episode that hints at the Fairfaxes' forbearance was when Ferdinando and Thomas were slandered by the royalist commissioner of array, Solomon Swale, who was charged with saying: 'Sir Tho: Fairfax was dead and gone to the devil, and my lord would presently follow him, for how should it be otherwise for he had raised Armes against the King.' Swale wrote to Lord Fairfax denying the speeches, 'w[hi]ch I abhor to think on, much less to have spoken of your Lordship and your honourable Sonn'.[79] After Marston moor the fortunes of war had dictated that Swale humble himself before the Fairfaxes, but with Swale already in deep legal trouble there was no need for them to issue martial challenges. Swale's letter blamed the allegations on 'a known felon', but nevertheless praised Fairfax's 'always noble thoughts', echoing strongly the language of formal submission performed by those convicted in the Court of Chivalry during the 1630s.

Both Ferdinando and Sir Thomas self-consciously strove to become living embodiments of the Erasmian emphasis on moderation and temperance. They demonstrated their stoical virtues by keeping an unpaid army in the field from 1642 to 1644, rising above their dismay at Parliament failing their men. Firstly Hotham's forces and then the Scots Covenanters were paid in preference to their army, but unlike Cholmley and Hotham, they were less inclined to interpret setbacks in receiving pay and supply as personal slights to their honour.[80] Their recovery from defeat contrasts with the petulance and resignation of a number of vanquished royalist commanders, and was rooted in their notions of service and duty, not to an individual, but to a public or commonwealth.[81] Ferdinando and Sir Thomas's professed reluctance to accept their commissions as generals in 1642 and 1645 went beyond natural modesty. Both men understood that a deportment of humility and moderation did much to neutralise opposition towards them. Their demeanour was part of a recognised stoic humanist tradition of forbearance, well highlighted by a remark from Archbishop Grindal, that 'those men that sue for bishoprics do in that declare themselves unmeet for the room'.[82]

In commanding the New Model, Sir Thomas Fairfax displayed extraordinary composure over Parliament's persistent refusal to settle the pay and indemnity of his soldiers. Parliament slighted his honour in March 1647, declaring his soldiers to be 'enemies of the state', and the following month voted his army should receive only £70,000 of their £1,000,000 of pay arrears. In May they insulted him further, suggesting that all his men supported John Lilburne.[83] Parliament denigrated Fairfax's honour repeatedly by not adhering to the articles of surrender he granted royalists.[84] Fairfax reinvented the frustrations of these years in his 'Short memorials', claiming he wished to resign in protest at the rising power of the agitators, but his inclination to resign rather grew from the contempt many MPs had shown him and his soldiers. John Rushworth wrote to Ferdinando on 18 May 1647 'were I as the General, I would scorn to hold my command an hour longer; but truly his patience is great'.[85] When Fairfax finally did resign in 1650, he maintained he had stoically declined 'yt height of power & other Advantages', instead 'ever valueing Loyalty & Conscience before this perishing Felicity'.[86] Fairfax's stoic sense of honour and self-fashioning as the honest public man emulated Cicero, who was often described as 'pater patriae', meaning the 'father of the commonwealth'.[87] It was clearly a discourse that was widely recognised, because in conscious emulation, several of the army and county petitions of December 1648 and January 1649 that urged Fairfax to reject the Newport treaty negotiations hailed him as 'pater patriae'.[88] Fairfax's religion and concept of honour were mutually supporting. Firmly grounded in his family and background, they shaped a sense of duty that kept him at his post in circumstances that few other English gentry would have suffered with such patience.

NOTES

1 BL, Add. MS 28326, fo. 10v; Bod., MS Fairfax 34, fos. 7, 32.

2 BL, E433(13), *A perfect narrative of the late proceedings of the parliament of Scotland, in relation to the affaires of England. Also the manner of the funerall of the right honourable Ferdinando Lord Fairfax with the chief heads of his lordships funerall-sermon, preached by Mr. Bowles. 15 March instant*, 22 March (London, 1648); F. Heal and C. Holmes, *The Gentry in England and Wales, 1500–1700* (Basingstoke, 1994), p. 268.

3 J. Lister (ed.), *West Riding Sessions Records: Orders 1611–1642, Indictments 1637–1642* (YASRS, 53, 1915), passim; Bod., MS Fairfax 31, fo. 106.

4 BL, Egerton MS 2146, fo. 34r.

5 The Fairfaxes were involved in attempts to start a university at Manchester in April 1641 and a later attempt at York aimed at countering a perceived rise in popery in the north: Bod., MS Fairfax 32, fos. 5, 157.

6 A. Cambers, 'Print, manuscript and godly cultures in the north of England, c.1600–1650' (Ph.D. thesis, University of York, 2003), pp. 247–70.

7 R. Cust, 'Catholicism, antiquarianism and gentry honour: the writings of Sir Thomas Shirley', *Midland History*, 23 (1998), 60–3.

8 I. Gentles, 'The iconography of revolution', in I. Gentles, J. Morrill and B. Worden (eds), *Soldiers, Writers and Statesmen of the English Revolution: Essays Presented to Austin Woolrych* (Cambridge, 1998), p. 95; A. J. Hopper, 'Charles Fairfax', *Oxford DNB*.

9   G. Parry, 'Roger Dodsworth', *Oxford DNB*; C. Caine (ed.), *Analecta Eboracensia: some remaynes of the ancient city of York* (London, 1897).

10   S. Kelsey, *Inventing a Republic: The Political Culture of the English Commonwealth, 1649–1653* (Stanford, 1997), pp. 69–70.

11   G. W. Johnson (ed.), *The Fairfax correspondence: memoirs of the reign of Charles I* (London, 1848), vol. 1, pp. 155–6, 335–6.

12   R. A. Marchant, *The Puritans and Church Courts in the Diocese of York, 1560–1642* (London, 1960), pp. 112–13, 239, 245, 293; W. J. Sheils, 'Provincial preaching on the eve of the civil war: some West Riding sermons', in A. J. Fletcher and P. Roberts (eds), *Religion, Culture and Society in Early Modern Britain: Essays in Honour of Patrick Collinson* (Cambridge, 1994), pp. 291, 295–6, 298–9.

13   BL, Add. MS 18979, fos. 69r–70v.

14   Sheils, 'Provincial preaching', pp. 294, 298.

15   Johnson (ed.), *The Fairfax correspondence*, vol. 2, p. 180.

16   J. Shaw, 'The life of master John Shaw', in C. Jackson (ed.), *Yorkshire diaries and autobiographies in the seventeenth and eighteenth centuries* (Surtees Society, 65, 1877), appendix, 369; *JHC*, vol. 2, p. 40; HULA, Hotham MS, DDHO/1/34; Bod., MS Fairfax 36, fo. 7v.

17   A. Milton, 'The church of England, Rome and the true church: the demise of a Jacobean consensus', in K. Fincham (ed.), *The Early Stuart Church, 1603–1642* (Basingstoke, 1993), p. 191; A. Friesen, 'Medieval heretics or forerunners of the Reformation: the protestant rewriting of the history of medieval heresy', in A. Ferreiro (ed.), *The Devil, Heresy and Witchcraft in the Middle Ages* (Brill, 1998), pp. 165–89.

18   BL, Add. MS 11743, fo. 20r; C. H. Firth and R. S. Rait (eds), *Acts and Ordinances of the Interregnum, 1642–1660* (London, 1911), vol. 1, pp. 391–2.

19   Bod., MS Fairfax 31, fo. 141.

20   C. Hill, *A Turbulent, Seditious, and Factious People: John Bunyan and his Church* (Oxford, 1988), p. 51.

21   J. Sprigge, *Anglia rediviva* (London, 1647), p. 322.

22   Bod., MS Fairfax 33, fos. 25r–27r.

23   *Ibid.*, fo. 27r.

24   *Ibid.*, fo. 24r–v; *CSP dom. 1652–3*, p. 141.

25   BL, Add. MS 71448, fos. 34r–40r.

26   *Ibid.*, fo. 38r; D. Scott, 'James Chaloner', *Oxford DNB*.

27   Bod., MS Fairfax 33, fo. 23r.

28   Bod., MS Fairfax 32, fo. 30; H. Aveling, *Northern Catholics: The Catholic Recusants of the North Riding of Yorkshire, 1558–1790* (London, 1966), p. 283; G. Webb, *Fairfax of York: The Life and History of a Noble Family* (York, 2001), p. 49.

29   YML, CWT, 44–07–18, *A sermon preached at Kingston-upon-Hull upon the day of thanksgiving after the battell, and that marvailous victory at Hessam Moore neare Yorke. By J.W. B.D* (London, 1644), p. 9.

30   J. T. Cliffe, *The Yorkshire Gentry from the Reformation to the Civil War* (London, 1969), p. 347; C. R. Markham, *The life of Robert Fairfax of Steeton, 1666–1725* (London, 1885), p. 14.

31 Heal and Holmes, *The Gentry in England and Wales*, p. 250; *JHL*, vol. 5, p. 494.

32 Shaw, 'The life of master John Shaw', 367–9; B. Whitelocke, *Memorials of English affairs* (Oxford, 1853), vol. 1. p. 206.

33 Bod., MS Fairfax 36, fo. 1v; T. Kilburn and A. Milton, 'The public context of the trial and execution of Strafford', in J. F. Merritt (ed.), *The Political World of Thomas Wentworth, Earl of Strafford, 1621–1641* (Cambridge, 1996), p. 251.

34 BL, E258(27), *A perfect diurnall of some Passages in Parliament*, 17–24 February (London, 1645), pp. 649–50.

35 BL, Harleian MS 252, fo. 33r; Sprigge, *Anglia rediviva*, pp. 9, 322.

36 G. Foard, *Naseby: The Decisive Campaign* (Barnsley, 2004), pp. 182, 272; A. Woolrych, *Britain in Revolution, 1625–1660* (Oxford, 2002), p. 280; A. Macfarlane (ed.), *The Diary of Ralph Josselin, 1616–1683* (Oxford, 1991), pp. 89–90.

37 V. Black, 'In search of Black Tom Fairfax', *York Historian*, 3 (1980), 24; Woolrych, *Britain in Revolution*, pp. 374, 482, 620.

38 YML, CWT, FAI 1644–9(13), *Wonderfull predictions declared in a message, as from the Lord, to his Excellency Sr. Thomas Fairfax and the councell of his army. By John Saltmarsh, Preacher of the Gospell, 29 December 1647* (London, 1648), p. 4; C. Hill, *The World Turned Upside Down: Radical Ideas During the English Revolution* (London, 1980), p. 113; C. H. Firth (ed.), *Clarke papers, vol. 2* (Camden Society, new series, 54, 1894), p. 249.

39 BL, E530(24), *The speeches of the Lord Generall Fairfax and the officers of the armie to the diggers at St Georges Hill in Surry, and the diggers several answers and replies thereunto*, 31 May (London, 1649); D. Hirst, *England in Conflict, 1603–1660: Kingdom, Community, Commonwealth* (London, 1999), p. 263.

40 Hill, *A Turbulent, Seditious, and Factious People*, p. 279; A. Marvell, *The Works of Andrew Marvell*, ed. A. Crozier (Ware, 1995), pp. 5–6; BL, Add. MS 4929, fo. 8.

41 The work had been translated into English by Henry Hawkins in 1632: Cambers, 'Manuscript and godly cultures in the north of England', p. 289.

42 Fitzwilliam Museum, Cambridge, CFM 13, Thomas, 3rd baron Fairfax 'The thoughts of eternity', fos. 4v, 18r.

43 BL, Add. MS 4929, fos. 158–9.

44 Markham, p. 440; J. W. Clay (ed.), *Abstracts of Yorkshire wills* (YASRS, 9, 1890), p. 5.

45 Clay (ed.), *Abstracts of Yorkshire wills*, p. 82; Cliffe, *The Yorkshire Gentry*, p. 279.

46 BL, E433(13), *A perfect narrative of the late proceedings of the parliament of Scotland*.

47 H. Speight, *Lower Wharfedale* (London, 1902), p. 129; BL, Add. MS 51054, fo. 57v.

48 My thanks to Michael Webb for this reference: Bod., MS Top Yorks C14, fos. 246v–247r.

49 J. G. Marston, 'Gentry honour and royalism in early Stuart England', *JBS*, 13 (1973), 43; M. James, 'English politics and the concept of honour, 1485–1642', *Past and Present*, supplement, 3 (1978), 85, 92; R. Cust, 'Honour and politics in early Stuart England: the case of Beaumont v. Hastings', *Past and Present*, 149 (1995), 60; B. Donagan, 'The web of honour: soldiers, Christians, and gentlemen in the English civil war', *Historical Journal*, 44:2 (2001), 365.

50 Bod., MS Fairfax 33, fo. 33r.

51 HULA, Hotham MS, DDHO/1/29.

52 R. Cust, 'The "Public Man" in late Tudor and early Stuart England', in P. Lake and S. Pincus (eds), *The Politics of the Public Sphere in Early Modern England* (Manchester, 2007); R. Cust (ed.), *The Papers of Sir Richard Grosvenor, 1st Bart, 1585–1645* (The Record Society of Lancashire and Cheshire, 134, 1996), pp. xv, xix, xxv.

53 BL, Add. MS 4929, fo. 26; Cust (ed.), *Grosvenor Papers*, p. 36.

54 Bod., MS Fairfax 31, fo. 137.

55 R. Cust, 'Wentworth's "change of sides" in the 1620s', in J. F. Merritt (ed.), *The Political World of Thomas Wentworth, Earl of Strafford, 1621–1641* (Cambridge, 1996), pp. 72, 77, 80.

56 Whitelocke, *Memorials of English affairs*, vol. 1, 206; Clarendon, *The history of the rebellion and civil wars in England* (Oxford, 1717), vol. 2, part 2, p. 621; D. Parsons (ed.), *The diary of Sir Henry Slingsby of Scriven, bart* (London, 1836), p. 92; W. Dugdale, *The visitation of the county of Yorke* (Surtees Society, 36, 1859), p. 386.

57 Cust, 'Catholicism, antiquarianism and gentry honour', 49; A. M. W. Stirling, *The Hothams: Being the Chronicles of the Hothams of Scorborough and South Dalton from their hitherto unpublished family papers* (London, 1918), vol. 1, p. 21.

58 J. Morrill, *The Nature of the English Revolution* (London, 1993), p. 184; Heal and Holmes, *The Gentry in England and Wales*, p. 171; Stirling, *The Hothams*, vol. 1, pp. 96–7.

59 P. Saltmarshe, *History and Chartulary of the Hothams of Scorborough in the East Riding of Yorkshire, 1100–1700* (York, 1914), p. 112; HULA, Hotham MS, DDHO/1/8.

60 HULA, Hotham MS, DDHO/1/60.

61 BL, E119(29), *Fourteen articles of peace propounded to the king and parliament by the gentry and commonalty of the county of York*, 4 October (London, 1642); YML, CWT, 1642–3(2), *Reasons why Sir John Hotham, trusted by the parliament, cannot in honour agree to the treaty of pacification made by some gentlemen of York-shire at Rothwell*, 29 September (London, 1642), pp. 2, 8.

62 BL, Add. MS 18979, fo. 127r.

63 Saltmarshe, *History and Chartulary of the Hothams*; BL, Add. MS, 18979, fo. 131r–v; BL, Add. MS 34195, fo. 35.

64 R. Bell (ed.), *The Fairfax correspondence: memorials of the civil war* (London, 1849), vol. 1, p. 36; P. W. Thomas (ed.), *The English Revolution III. Newsbooks I. Oxford Royalist* (London, 1971), vol. 1, p. 28.

65 Saltmarshe, *History and Chartulary of the Hothams*, p. 142; B. N. Reckitt, *Charles the First and Hull, 1639–1645* (London, 1952), appendix 2, p. 121; *Portland MS*, HMC, 29, 13th report, appendix, part 1, vol. 1, pp. 83–4; BL, Add. MS 18979, fo. 65v; Cliffe, *The Yorkshire Gentry*, p. 328.

66 HRO, BRS/7/74, BRS/7/77.

67 P. Collinson, 'De Republica Anglorum: or, history with the politics put back', in P. Collinson, *Elizabethan Essays* (London, 1994), p. 22; Clarendon, *History of the rebellion and civil wars in England*, ed. W. Dunn Macray (Oxford, 1888), vol. 2, p. 287.

68 BL, Harleian MS 164, fo. 234.

69 J. Rushworth, *Historical collections* (London, 1721), vol. 5, p. 746.

70 Stirling, *The Hothams*, vol. 1, p. 81.

71 A. J. Hopper, ' "Fitted for desperation": honour and treachery in Parliament's Yorkshire command, 1642–1643', *History*, 86:2 (2001), 138–54.

72 Rushworth, *Historical collections*, part 3, vol. 2, p. 137; B. Donagan, 'Codes and conduct in the English civil war', *Past and Present*, 118 (1988), 82; E. Hailstone (ed.), *Portraits of Yorkshire worthies* (London, 1869), vol. 1, p. lxviii; Cliffe, *The Yorkshire Gentry*, p. 338.

73 BL, E107(32), *Exceeding good newes from Beverley, Yorke, Hull, and Newcastle*, 20 July (London, 1642), p. 3.

74 J. Hackett, *Scrinia reserata: a memorial offered to the great deservings of John Williams D.D.* (London, 1692), p. 186; HULA, Cholmley MS, DDCY/17/4, fos. 6, 8; Cholmley, *The memoirs of Sir Hugh Cholmley*, pp. 12, 36,

75 B. Donagan, 'Did ministers matter? War and religion in England, 1642–1649', *JBS*, 33 (1994), 137; R. Ashton, *Counter–Revolution: The Second Civil War and its Origins, 1646–8* (New Haven, 1994), p. 202; D. Bates, 'The honour culture of royalist officers in the north during the first civil war, 1642–1646', (M.Phil. thesis, University of Birmingham, 2002), pp. 56–8, 72.

76 HRO, BRS/7/13, BRS/7/19, BRS/7/48, BRS/7/52, BRS/7/53.

77 *CSP dom. 1644*, p. 529.

78 J. Adamson, 'Chivalry and political culture in Caroline England', in K. Sharpe and P. Lake (eds), *Culture and Politics in Early Stuart England* (London, 1994), pp. 183–5; BL, E91(28), *The answer of Ferdinando lord Fairfax to a declaration of William earle of Newcastle*, 3 March (London, 1643), p. 8; G. E. Aylmer, 'Collective mentalities in mid-seventeenth-century England: I. The puritan outlook', *TRHS*, 5th series, 36 (1986), 15.

79 TNA, SP 23/172/281; Bod., MS Fairfax 34, fo. 40.

80 BL, Add. MS 31116, fo. 27v; BL, E252(29), *A perfect diurnall of some passages in parliament*, 15–22 April (London, 1644); *Portland MS*, HMC, 29, 13th report, appendix, part 1, vol. 1, p. 102; BL, E95(9), *A true and exact relation of all the proceedings of Sir Hugh Cholmley's revolt*, 7 April (London, 1643), p. 4.

81 A. Hughes, 'The king, the parliament and the localities during the English civil war', *JBS*, 24:2 (1985), 259–60.

82 P. Collinson, 'Sir Nicholas Bacon and the Elizabethan via media', in P. Collinson, *Godly People: Essays on English Protestantism and Puritanism* (London, 1983), p. 144.

83 D. Scott, *Politics and War in the Three Stuart Kingdoms, 1637–49* (Basingstoke, 2004), p. 145.

84 Kelsey, *Inventing a Republic*, p. 131.

85 Bell (ed.), *The Fairfax correspondence*, vol. 1, p. 344.

86 Bod., MS Fairfax 36, fos. 2r, 4v–5r.

87 Cust, 'The "Public Man" in late Tudor and early Stuart England'.

88 BL, E538(15), *The moderate*, 9–16 January (London, 1649), p. 252.

Chapter 9

'The rider of the white horse':
image and reputation

It has recently been highlighted that the gentry of seventeenth-century England were displaying growing concerns for their self-representation and public image.[1] Therefore the question of how Fairfax shaped his own political identity, or how far it was constructed and maintained for him by others, raises an important issue. The civil wars amplified such concerns further as the role of image, reputation and the cult of personality among commanders on both sides, facilitated by an explosion of print, assumed enormous proportions. Such was the self-consciousness of the royalist marquis of Montrose, that Gilbert Burnet felt he 'had taken upon him the port of a hero too much, and lived as in a romance; for his whole manner was stately to affectation'. Lucy Hutchinson suggested that Sir John Gell, a parliamentary commander in Derbyshire, 'kept the diurnall makers in pension' to magnify his role and importance.[2] Like Montrose and Gell, from 1642 Fairfax appreciated that he was 'on stage', in the view of a news-hungry mass public. Indeed, the first two 'celebrities' produced at the outbreak of war were Yorkshiremen: Sir John Hotham for refusing the King entry to Hull, and Sir Francis Wortley for drawing his sword in a public gesture against Hotham's treason. The ensuing paper war provoked both into justifying themselves in print and their names became polemical slogans. John Turbervill wrote on 23 June 1642: 'All men that are now for the Parliament, are no more termed Roundheads, but Hothamites, from Sir John Hotham; and all those that are for the King, are called Wortheleshites, from Sir George [sic] Wortheley.'[3] It would not be long before the northern parliamentarians were referred to as 'Fairfaxian'. While his political enemies mocked Fairfax for false modesty and a lack of intellect, Fairfax's self-fashioning as the lowly, humble general remained immensely attractive to the godly, and he knew it. This chapter traces representations of Fairfax in the world of print, and considers how his image was reported and shaped by his contemporaries.

I

Sir Thomas Fairfax first began to be noticed in London during his winter campaign of 1642–3, upon which Thomas May elucidated: 'no season of the yeare, nor stormes of winter, could quench the rage of this Civil Fire'. Newsbook sellers and a London public short of good news needed stories of heroes that winter.[4] They found one in the capture of Leeds on 23 January 1643. This was Parliament's most spectacular victory of the war thus far, for which one tract implied Fairfax was 'the Rider of the White Horse'.[5] This image drew upon the well-known Biblical passage from Revelation 19:11: 'And I saw heaven opened, and behold a white horse; and he that sat upon him was called Faithful and True, and in righteousness he doth judge and make war.' The Rider was understood as a symbol of Christ's conquering power, with apocalyptic and millenarian overtones. Immediately, it enshrined Fairfax in the propaganda of those who viewed the conflict in religious terms. For the godly the religious reputation of their leaders was of paramount importance. For example, later that year parliamentary troops in Wallingford had heard that the earl of Essex was John the Baptist, while one preacher told Fairfax's army at Selby that Ferdinando was 'our Joshua of the North'. In November 1644 Ferdinando was again hailed as 'Just Joshua, ye mirrour of our age'.[6] This rhetoric of godliness was easily turned to the purposes of parliamentary propaganda. Ideally, parliamentary commanders were supposed to act for the joint benefit of sovereign and subject, and to hold no ambitions of personal advancement. One northern officer describing Lord Fairfax's leadership praised 'the guide Lourd Fairfaxe, whea loves God, Religion, the King, and his Countries guid in his saule, and has nea ends of his awne, God knawes'.[7]

The millenarian imagery of 'the Rider of the White Horse' was deliberately revived after the capture of Wakefield on 20 May 1643 by Francis Cheynell's sermon to the House of Commons. He orated: 'And I saw the Beast and the Kings of the earth, and their armies gathered together to make war against him that sate on the Horse, and against his army. And the Beast was taken, and with him the false Prophet.'[8] This degraded the royalists as enemies of God, but was high exaltation for Fairfax and his men. It nurtured Fairfax's conviction that, owing to his elect status, he had been chosen as God's instrument of war. Ever fearful of the withdrawal of God's pleasure, Fairfax attributed Wakefield 'more to the effects of God's divine power than humaine force'.[9]

Like the duke of Monmouth in 1685, the Fairfaxes had waged a war based on popular support drawn from cloth-manufacturing towns, from whence they had raised an ill-equipped, unpaid army, short of cavalry and ammunition. Unlike Monmouth, the Fairfaxes had shown little dismay at their lack of gentry support, and were prepared to trust their neighbours among the 'middling sort' at a time when most of their peers agreed with Lord Conway's remark: 'There is no trust to be put in the common people; they have neither constancy nor gratitude.'[10] Their slim base of gentry support had forced them to trust the people, so much so that over a quarter of their West Riding officers ranked at captain or above were from non-gentry backgrounds.[11] The London press celebrated this reliance upon popular allegiance by repeatedly linking the Fairfax name with the clubmen movement in the cloth towns in 1643. As seen in Chapter 2, Bradford became a national symbol of popular defiance of the royalists. Propagandists like John Vicars devoted more words to it than the battle of Edgehill, and when Devon clubmen defeated royalists at Modbury, Vicars hailed them as 'imitating their brave Bradfordian brethren in the North'.[12] London polemicists urged all England to 'rise and execute Bradford Club Law upon the Cavaliers', calculating that 31,000 clubmen could be raised in southern England to supplement Parliament's field armies and render them numerically unstoppable. Unrealistic expectations extended to the belief that clubmen forces would deliver victory for Parliament.[13] During 1643 Sir Thomas Fairfax continued to deploy clubmen in support of his soldiers, relying on men such as William Critchlaw, who 'was not a souldier, yet when he heard of a fight nigh at hand, or a town to be taken by the Parliaments army he used to take his musket, and run to the army to be the formost in any hazardous expedition'.[14]

Newsbooks seeking to rally popular parliamentarianism shrank from recognising the fluid nature of these forces, placing ever higher and unsustainable expectations on the Fairfaxes, using the family name to inspire hope in desperate circumstances. Yorkshire was sufficiently distant from London to preserve some mystery and allure; one tract reporting Fairfax's victory at Wakefield in 1643 purported to be written by one of Fairfax's infantry subalterns, and was published entirely in Newcastle dialect, 'not altering it from his native tone, more like Chaucer's English, then ours here'.[15] John Vicars praised 'the renowned Manchesterians and the noble Fairfaxians' in Lancashire and Yorkshire, who were 'a handful of men', against the 'nefarious potent enemies of the gospel and growth of the Protestant religion', more numerous there 'than in any other part else'.[16] Likewise, Josiah Ricraft dismissed the north as 'a malevolent Countrey the greatest part being Papists and Athiests'.[17]

Londoners looked to the Fairfaxes to protect them from this threatening northern darkness embodied by Newcastle's 'popish' army. Sir Thomas Fairfax was hailed as 'that couragious undaunted Gentleman', in a newsbook of April 1643, and Sir Edward Nicholas introduced him in a letter to Prince Rupert that month as 'the man most beloved and relyed upon by ye Rebells in ye North'.[18] In May Sir Thomas's fame spread further when Lord Fairfax's letter describing the victory at Wakefield was read in all London's churches, prompting a public thanksgiving.[19] Such events impacted upon the popular imagination; a week later, Nehemiah Wallington dreamt on 4 June that Lord Fairfax came to his house: 'if he were in my shope what coming & lookeing there would be on him. Saying This is the Lord Fairefaxe. this is he that wone so many great battils and so what honour it would be to mee to have such a person at mine House.'[20] This suggests the Fairfaxes were becoming national figures in the eyes of a news-hungry public. After their capture of Wakefield the London press declared Fairfax's men had learnt 'to walk by Faith and not by Sight'. Such exaltation, combined with the fast days and thanksgivings, enhanced expectations of the Fairfaxes beyond what their army could deliver. The earl of Newcastle reflected wisely on the problems such adulation posed for generals in a letter to Rupert on 7 August 1643:

> Noe Creature is more overjoyed to heer of your victories then my selfe, nor doth more harteley Congratulat them to you but I must tell you trewly as they are to bigg for any bodye else, so they Appeer to Litle for you, your Name is growne so Triumphant, & the Worldes Expectation to Looke for more frome you then man can doe, butt that is their falter Sir & not yours.[21]

Newcastle's remarks were pertinent for the Fairfaxes too. The family had been represented as godly heroes so often in London that when news of their defeat came on 5 July 1643 its impact was seismic. The House of Commons panicked and urged the Lords 'in great Consternation' to send a committee to Scotland to solicit aid.[22] On 15 July Wallington lamented that the north had been 'over rune with those cruel enemies of God'.[23] This collapse of public confidence in the Fairfaxes' supposed invincibility critically widened the war by accelerating the Scots' entry into the conflict.

For the royalists, this was a long-awaited opportunity to show that parliamentarian polemic about Fairfax's reputation had been hot air. *Mercurius aulicus* scoffed at the Fairfaxes' clubmen 'whereof we hear such notable Romances in the London Newesbooks'. 'Romances' implied fictional stories, that were 'written to satisfy the imagination of women', and therefore wholly illegitimate. *Aulicus* smugly reflected that 'the so much celebrated Club-men' were now 'strangely shrunke up and now unable to relieve his Lordship'.[24] The predictable social derogation followed in a comparison with the moorlanders of north Staffordshire, who had also risen against the King without gentry leadership: 'for the Moorlanders and the Club-men are Brethren well basted'.[25] So when Charles wrote to his queen in May 1645 that Fairfax was the 'rebels new brutish general', Fairfax's identification with popular parliamentarianism had been a staple of the royalist press for years. In contrast to the earl of Essex who pledged himself 'to repressing the audacity of the people', Fairfax's reputation was built upon championing popular activism. The King's disparagement of Fairfax was well known enough for Clement Walker to adopt it in 1661, calling Fairfax 'the brutish general' of the Independents.[26]

In February 1644 Parliament ordered another thanksgiving in London's

churches for Fairfax's victory at Nantwich.[27] Further thanksgivings were
ordered for the victory at Selby that April, at which time Thomas Juxon also
referred to the northern parliamentarian army as 'Fairfaxian'.[28] Joseph Caryl's
thanksgiving sermon for Selby addressed Ferdinando: 'Will not your late
Victorie memoriz'd this day become the history of Christ's raigne? While I
remember how that noble Northerne-light was insulted in wanton-witted
rimes, as burnt downe into the socket, yea as quite extinct.' Caryl was flattering the Fairfaxes with comparisons to Gustavus Adolphus, depicting both
as protestant warlords of the north, fighting against heavy odds to preserve
true religion. This allusion would have pleased Sir Thomas who had formerly
been eager to join the Swedish army. He certainly emulated Gustavus in
leading from the front and was undoubtedly familiar with the corantos celebrating the Swedish king's victories. *Mercurius aulicus* mocked the endeavours
of the London press to elevate the Fairfaxes to similar adulation, writing on
23 September 1643 that 'the Lord Fairefax is the comfortable shining planet of
the North (truly he is a fixed starre in Hull)'. On 20 October 1645 Juxon noted
how the people were still comparing Sir Thomas Fairfax with Gustavus.[29] The
motif persisted in 1647 when Fairfax was hailed as the 'northern star' by Josiah
Ricraft, appearing as the first non-peer in his *Survey of Englands champions*,
while his cousin Sir William Fairfax and brother Charles Fairfax were named
as third and fifth respectively on Ricraft's list of slain parliamentary worthies.[30]
Ultimately, Fairfax's national reputation was forged through the London press
associating popular anti-royalist activism and military success with devout,
even millenarian protestantism.

II

In an age when generals were expected to lead from the front, expose themselves to danger and inspire their forces with gallantry, Fairfax's reputation
required his personal courage to be conspicuous. Often risking his life, at
times apparently needlessly, Fairfax was seriously wounded at least four times
and was extremely fortunate to survive the wars. Charles Carlton reckoned
that Fairfax had fought in ten battles, three skirmishes and eleven sieges.
Table 3 suggests this is a conservative estimate.[31] Performing acts of valour
and sustaining wounds was an integral part of Fairfax's style; maintaining
credibility with his soldiers and chaplains required he show himself unafraid
to do 'the Lord's work'. A brief review of the acts that forged Fairfax's personal
reputation for courage is therefore necessary.

On 25 November 1642 Sir Thomas Glemham with 250 cavalry attacked
Fairfax's quarters at Wetherby. Despite being taken by surprise, Fairfax demonstrated the reckless courage that forged his reputation. Rallying a handful of
followers, he shot Sergeant-Major Carre and twice struck Glemham with his

Table 3 *Sir Thomas Fairfax's military record, 1640–8*

Battles	Skirmishes	Sieges
Newburn Ford, 28 Aug 1640	Bradford, 21 Oct 1642	York, Nov 1642
Tadcaster, 6 Dec 1642	Wetherby, 25 Nov 1642	Leeds, Apr 1643
Leeds, 23 Jan 1643	Sherburn, 13 Dec 1642	Bradford, Jul 1643
Seacoft moor, 30 Mar 1643	Selby, 2 Jul 1643	Hull, Sep 1643
Wakefield, 21 May 1643	Beverley, Aug 1643	York, Apr–Jul 1644
Adwalton moor, 30 Jun 1643		Helmsley castle, Aug 1644
Winceby, 11 Oct 1643		Oxford, May 1645
Nantwich, Jan 1644		Bridgwater, Jul 1645
Selby, 11 Apr 1644		Sherborne castle, Aug 1645
Marston moor, 2 Jul 1644		Bristol, Sep 1645
Naseby, 14 Jun 1645		Dartmouth, Jan 1646
Langport, 10 Jul 1645		Exeter, Jan–Apr 1646
Torrington, 18 Feb 1646		Colchester, Jun–Aug 1648
Maidstone, 1 Jun 1648		

Principal sources: BL, Add. MS 18979; Bod., MS Fairfax 36; R. Bell (ed.), *The Fairfax correspondence: memorials of the civil war* (2 vols, London, 1849).

sword. Wounded in the head, he was lucky to survive. Defeat was averted only when a musketeer accidentally ignited a powder barrel, upon which the royalists took fright and retreated. The following month his horse was killed under him at Sherburn-in-Elmet.[32] Fairfax was almost captured at Wakefield in May 1643. He allowed himself to become separated from his men, escaping only through daring horsemanship. During the retreat from Leeds to Hull in July 1643, he was wounded again at Selby, recalling: 'I received a shott in ye wrest of my Arme, wch made ye Bridle fall out of my hand, wch being among ye nerves & veines, suddainely let out such a Quantity of Blood, yt I was ready to fall from my horse.' He remembered 'I had beene at least 20 houres on Horseback (after I was shot) without any Rest or Refreshmt: & as many houres before.' Upon his eventual arrival in Hull he was half-naked having lost his clothes, his shirt unfit to wear, shredded and bloodstained.[33] Even royalist antiquarian sources admired this remarkable ride from Bradford, through Leeds, Selby, Carlton ferry, Thorne, Hatfield, Crowle, Barton-upon-Humber, and from there by ferry to Hull. This ride forged his reputation as a commander who would fight to the last.[34]

His face was slashed open at Marston moor, leading a royalist pamphleteer to jibe 'thou art mark'd for a Roague'.[35] Scarcely recovered, Fairfax was again wounded besieging Helmsley in August 1644, this time more dangerously. He was shot at extreme range by a sniper in the garrison. The bullet was removed from his shoulder and initially his recovery was doubtful.[36] At the siege of Pontefract in January 1645, Fairfax was felled by the wind from a cannon ball, which so disfigured the officer stood next to him that he was thereafter known as Colonel 'Blowface' Forbes.[37] Braving such dangers inspired the officers of Colonel Matthew Alured's regiment to petition Fairfax that they might accompany him southward in 1645, offering to relinquish their commands and serve him as troopers.[38] As general, Fairfax employed all his powers of self-effacing magnanimity; in May 1645, when his own regiment of foot refused to take its turn marching as the army's rearguard, instead of disciplining them, he dismounted and walked with them himself, at a stroke transforming complaint at lost privileges into discussion of his exemplary act.[39]

Although Fairfax frequently suffered from the stone, gout, fever and sickness, he never seems to have allowed illness to prevent him from fighting. Late in 1645 he confided to his father: 'I am exceedingly troubled with rheumatism and a benumbing coldness in my head, legs and arms, especially on that side I had my hurts.'[40] His chaplain, Joshua Sprigge, detailed Fairfax's ailments but then noted: 'when he hath come upon action, or been near an engagement, it hath been observed, another spirit hath come upon him, another soul hath lookt out at his eyes; I mean he hath been so raised, elevated, and transported, as that he hath been not only unlike himselfe at other times, but indeed more like an Angell, then a man'.[41] Many civil war commanders believed in leading from the front, but Fairfax's attraction to danger was persistent, and he paid for it. In the House of Commons in 1659, Sir Arthur Hesilrige, sitting next to Fairfax, described him as so riddled with wounds that he blessed God Fairfax was still there. Fairfax's conviction in his elect status and trust in God's providence no doubt steeled him, but his continual inclination to conspicuous displays of courage at times surely hampered him from discharging the full responsibilities of command.[42]

III

By 1646 Fairfax's reputation became more contested within the fracturing parliamentarian coalition. Some former allies were jealous of Fairfax's success. A delegation from both Houses waited upon Fairfax at his residence in Queen Street when he returned to London in November 1646 and Speaker Lenthall orated: 'And surely the Honour of the late Lord General was not, while he lived, any way Eclipsed by the Succession of your Excellency in his Command, but rather augmented, while each retained the Brightness of his own Honour.'[43] These official remarks would hardly have been necessary if Fairfax was not being regularly compared to Essex to the detriment of the latter's memory. Fairfax attracted increasing hostility from Essex's old protégés and political Presbyterians. As public affection for the army plummeted during 1647, one of Fairfax's chaplains, Joshua Sprigge, wrote a glowing account of the New Model's victorious campaign. Entitled *Anglia rediviva: England's recovery*, it attempted to utilise Fairfax's reputation to bolster the army's flagging popularity but hardly won over MPs when it hailed Fairfax in its dedicatory, declaring that Parliament 'must die your Debters'.[44] Fairfax's presence on state occasions such as dining with the Prince Elector or receiving the French ambassador aroused further resentment, as did his broadly tolerant approach to religion within the army.[45] Polemicists such as Thomas Edwards failed to appreciate that Fairfax's much despised tolerance embraced Presbyterians as well as Independents among his officers. Edwards campaigned to maximise religious and political divisions within the parliamentarian ranks, the very eventuality Fairfax strove so hard to prevent. He regretted that Fairfax, 'that valiant and well-affected Gentleman, should have such kind of Chaplains and Preachers upon all occasions to preach before him as Mr Dell, Mr Saltmarsh, Mr Peters, Mr Cradock, Mr Symonds, Mr William Sedgwick and such like'. It was typical of Edwards to ignore that many of Fairfax's chaplains were Presbyterians; yet it is illuminating that Edwards remained guarded and uncharacteristically moderate in his criticism of the general.[46]

As a political settlement proved elusive, royalists and political Presbyterians increasingly shared fears of the potentially revolutionary nature of Fairfax's soldiers. Some even viewed him as personifying the impending demise of the old order. The newsletter penned by 'John Lawrans' to Secretary Nicholas reported that on 19 December 1648 the earls of Pembroke, Salisbury and Denbigh and Lord North humbled themselves before Fairfax, offering to surrender their privileges as peers if such were thought 'prejudiciall to ye publike interest'. Lawrans claimed Fairfax's officers jeered at them, but that Denbigh 'stooped a degree lower, & proffered his hand toward the stirrop as his Ex. mounted on horsebacke; for wch unworthy prostituting his honor, he deserves to be cashiered for ever, out of the nobility'.[47] Such an incident may well have occurred as Lord Grey of Groby had held Fairfax's stirrup a fortnight earlier and it certainly reflects the realities of Westminster power politics that December. The suggestion of Lawrans that Denbigh and the rest had devalued the peerage by such grovelling before a commoner played on royalist fears that the social hierarchy was on the point of collapse. None of the English peerage would have accepted Fairfax as a social equal, and many were surely sensitive to allegations that he had unmanned them by usurping their traditional military role from them.

These depictions of Fairfax as a threat to the social order, unlikely as they seem now, enjoyed some contemporary currency. As early as March 1646 an engraving of Fairfax had been published depicting him as the scourge of monarchy, with an axe cleaving through a crown.[48] The image of 'the Rider of the White Horse' as a champion of God's chosen people pitted Fairfax against the forces of worldly authority and power. In April 1650, when the prophet George Foster published his vision of a rider on a white horse, he drew upon the popular imagination of the millenarian image from seven years earlier. Foster's 'rider':

> cutting down all men and women that he met with that were higher than the middle sort, and raised up those that were lower than the middle sort, and made them all equal; and cried out, 'Equality, equality, equality' ... I the Lord of Hosts have done this ... I will ... make the low and poor equal with the rich ... I said Lord, what is this Generals name? And the Lord said, his name is Fairfax.[49]

In Foster's dreams, Fairfax was the rider, the instrument of God's vengeance, who would avenge the Leveller martyrs Lockyer and Thompson. This seems strange, especially given that Fairfax had overruled Cromwell in insisting upon Lockyer's execution. Foster was one of many who interpreted the egalitarian overtones in parliamentary propaganda further than Parliament intended. Imagining Fairfax and 'the Rider of the White Horse' as the grand leveller was not too dissimilar from Gerard Winstanley hopefully dedicating his book *The Law of Freedom* to Cromwell.

IV

Another important facet of the Fairfax family's reputation was their famed lenience towards defeated enemies. William Vavasour wrote to his cousin on 25 December 1644, that after the fall of York he had resolved to go overseas: 'which I had not attained but that poor Fairfax was the civilest in the world to me'. On 2 May 1646, a letter from Fairfax moved the Commons 'vehemently that the Lord Paulet might have that favour as to be admitted to make a composition'. Sir George Wentworth also thanked Ferdinando for protecting his 'poor broken family at Woodhouse'.[50] Fairfax offered Oxford and Exeter decent terms of surrender in 1646 and recommended to the House of Lords on 8 July that further generosity would be 'the most hopeful Course to take away the Seeds of War, or future Feuds among us for Posterity'.[51] Despite his hardened attitude after the second civil war, in February 1649 he still pleaded for the earl of Holland's life. He also protected the lukewarm royalist Sir Thomas Gower, receiving revenue in trust for him from 1649. During the 1650s he held the duke of Buckingham's estates in trust and paid the earl of Derby's sequestered Manx rents to his widow, despite her earlier discourtesies to him at the siege of Lathom.[52] His secretary, Rushworth, saved the estates of several northern catholic gentry by acting as their agent. Relations with the catholic branch of the Fairfaxes at Gilling became more gracious as Fairfax defended their household from unruly troops. He even arranged a catholic marriage for the sister of Charles, fifth viscount Fairfax. By his instigation, all charges of recusancy against the family were dropped.[53] Maintaining discipline among his soldiers often obliged Fairfax to protect the property of other royalist landowners. On 21 December 1648, Fairfax ordered his soldiers to refrain from interfering with the earl of Arundel's property at Selhurst park in Surrey.[54]

However, Fairfax was rarely represented with kindness by the royalist press. On the contrary, the values of humility and non-ambition that his stoic notions of honour had showcased in the parliamentarian press were mocked as puritan hypocrisy in royalist pamphlets. In 1643 *Mercurius aulicus* sarcastically quipped that Fairfax 'intreats supplyes of Money and Ammunition in such an humble way, and so reasonable are his demands, that it would move any heart to contribute to his supply'.[55] During the second civil war, several tracts eagerly reported his death. In June 1648, one claimed that his 'smoakie countenance' had made him look 'like the picture of Doomsday'. In a mock elegy, it condemned him for his ambition, rejoicing that he had been shot in Kent and predicting that he would join his father in hell.[56] Another published a satirical version of Fairfax's will that suggested he had suffered from venereal disease, adding that he had perjured himself and deceived the King over the failed settlement of 1647. One pamphlet addressed him as 'King Tom, the Arch-Traytor of England'. Recommending that he be beheaded, it declared his 'name shall be an hissing to Posterity'.[57]

Understandably the venom of royalist polemic intensified after the regicide. Despite Fairfax's withdrawal from the trial, he remained very visibly linked with the King's death. Immediately after the execution, rather than being credited for his efforts to spare Charles, Fairfax was widely depicted as the King's murderer in pamphlets, prints and paintings. *Mercurius pragmaticus* denounced him in verse:

> Thou senseless block, hold up thy head,
> Black Tom it is I meane,
> Thou mayst be hang'd when CHARLES is dead,
> and so conclude the Seane[58]

Several Dutch engravings of the execution illustrated Fairfax in an inset above the proceedings, implying his personal responsibility.[59] He was even presented in one engraving as the King's actual executioner, holding Charles's bloody severed head.[60] A similar image occurred in the top right inset of Weesop's famous painting of the execution.[61] Such exposure played on his guilt and compelled Fairfax to distance himself from what had been done. On 16 February 1649 John Langley remarked that 'Gen. Fairfax is melancholy mad, troubled in mind three or four times a week, yet hath not taken the engagement.'[62] The play *The second part of crafty Cromwell* stirred such gossip, depicting 'a guilt ridden Fairfax', 'pursued by Furies'.[63] John Crouch portrayed Fairfax as haunted by guilty nightmares to delight the readers of his newsbook in April 1649:

> His Excellency having businesse late in Whitehall, and coming out hastily to take Coach in the muckish of the Evening, it happened, that his Coach stood just on the place where the King was murdered, and Mr. *Miles Corbet* a Parliament man standing by the boot of the Coach, to sollicite him about something concerning the Navy, who making towards *Fairfax*, his *Excellency* turned suddenly about, mistaking *Corbet* (being of a black Complexion,) for the Devill; left his Coach, and run home into Queen-street in a great agony, and was so frighted, that he would eate nothing in two or three dayes after.[64]

Depicting Fairfax as distraught with guilt likened him to Judas Iscariot and was a very effective royalist device to highlight the King's divinity. As we shall see in Chapter 10, the other most damaging theme in royalist depictions of Fairfax after 1648 was that he was ruled by his wife.

Although Fairfax lived for much of the 1650s in relative obscurity, he was remembered in some unlikely quarters. When the ship *The Marigold* put into harbour at Derifar on the Icelandic fishery in June 1654, the locals enquired whether the Protector or Lord Fairfax was in the greater authority.[65] For a brief moment in early 1660 Fairfax was again the talk of the three kingdoms. The enduring power of his name was utilised when some of Robert Lilburne's soldiers seized a church in York to cries of 'a Fairfax', during the old general's takeover of the city on New Year's Day 1660. On 19 January 1660 Thomas Gower reflected that the Irish brigade, Lambert's forces and Monck's army had all waited upon news of Fairfax, while 'London had their eye principally upon him'. Few could comprehend why he retired home so quickly after this, his last triumph. Gower reflected: 'Some ascribe it to dullness, others that an order of Parliament hath more power upon him then all reason; some to farther design yet ripe, some to one thing, some to another.'[66] An excited series of entries in the diary of Samuel Pepys that January and February reported his actions and speculated on his plans.[67] Yet after his defeat in the Yorkshire election of 1661, Fairfax quickly faded into obscurity. He intimated his consciousness of the eclipse of his public reputation to Horatio, baron Townshend in November 1664, writing that 'my retirement makes me seem dead to the world'.[68]

V

Fairfax's acts of bravery did much to shape his popularity with his soldiers, but the bookish Fairfax seems to have understood well the importance of print in promulgating his reputation to a wider public. As early as 1643, Thomas May was attached to Fairfax's retinue to publish an account of the defence of Hull. By 1647 Fairfax clearly appreciated his soldiers' need for their own printing press to counter the increasing invective published against the army. He may even have been involved in the army's secretive financial support for Sprigge's *Anglia rediviva*.[69]

Much of Fairfax's wider reputation was shaped for him by his close connections in the London press, in particular the licensers John Rushworth and Gilbert Mabbott. Jason Peacey has recently shown that parliamentary propaganda was as often concerned with factional infighting as it was about defaming royalists. It was therefore critical that Rushworth and Mabbott were friends to the pro-Fairfax political Independents at Westminster. Rushworth was a distant kinsman of the Fairfaxes and Ferdinando signed off letters to Rushworth as 'your affectionate cosen'.[70] From 1642 Rushworth acted as emissary between the Fairfaxes and the Committee of Safety and in 1645 he was appointed secretary to Sir Thomas Fairfax and the New Model Army. From then, he reported frequently to Ferdinando on the progress of his son's campaigns.[71] Rushworth was concerned to deny Fairfax's enemies among Westminster's political Presbyterians any share of credit for the victory in 1646, and his position as licenser of newsbooks from April 1644 to March 1647 placed him in a good position to do so. Developing closer relations between the New Model and London's newsbooks, Rushworth ensured several weekly serials focused on Fairfax, including the *Perfect diurnall*, which he used to advertise Sprigge's glowing account of Fairfax in *Anglia rediviva*.[72]

Rushworth also shaped perceptions of Fairfax by writing letters to Parliament reporting the army's victories.[73] As army secretary, Rushworth was increasingly importuned over access to Fairfax, in particular over the granting of commissions, suggesting that the general's influence was valued more by contemporaries than by recent historians.[74] Rushworth's assistant, Gilbert Mabbott, was restored as licenser at Fairfax's insistence in September 1647, and although Mabbott became one of the individuals behind *The Moderate*, a journal sympathetic to the Levellers, as late as September 1648 this work still acclaimed Fairfax as 'Black *Tom* (the Conqueror)'.[75]

Both Gibb and Wilson claimed this curious nickname of 'Black Tom' was applied to Fairfax from his youth owing to his dark, swarthy looks.[76] Neither cited any evidence to support this, and although it has been suggested the appellation was an affectionate one applied to him by his troops, among primary sources, *The Moderate* excepted, it appears most frequently in hostile royalist sources.[77] Often it was employed pejoratively, after all Fairfax shared this appellation with the earl of Strafford, who was derisively known during his lieutenancy in Ireland as 'Black Tom Tyrant'.[78]

The crafting of Fairfax's reputation among parliamentarians was initially driven by his personal valour, military success and the self-representation of his religion and honour discussed in Chapter 8. Much of this would have been spread by oral communication, but the reporting of his conduct and demeanour by others in newsbooks, eulogies and works such as Sprigge's *Anglia rediviva* did much to develop this for him.[79] Such reporting presented a variety of images of Fairfax, deepening the enigmas and apparent contradictions in his character. Between 1642 and 1661 groups as far apart as royalists, sectaries, Presbyterians, Independents, Levellers and even Diggers all projected their hopes and fears upon him, praying that he would intervene in their interest. Individual royalists may have benefited from his supposed lenience towards the vanquished, but even his own wife's brother-in-law, Mildmay Fane, earl of Westmoreland, condemned him as 'Prince Tomaso alias Black Tom', depicting him as a warmonger that had ruined his country.[80] There was still less sympathy for him in the underground press, and royalist polemic savaged him as a puritan hypocrite, cuckold, apostate and murderer. This demonstrates that 'Black Tom' was a much more politically divisive figure than that suggested by his biographers, questioning their confident assertions of the universal esteem among contemporaries for his decency and heroism.[81]

NOTES

1 R. Cust, 'The "Public Man" in late Tudor and early Stuart England', in P. Lake and S. Pincus (eds), *The Politics of the Public Sphere in Early Modern England* (Manchester, 2007).

2 G. Burnet, *History of his own time*, 6 vols (Oxford, 2nd edn, 1833), vol. 1, p. 53; J. Peacey, *Politicians and Pamphleteers: Propaganda During the English Civil Wars and Interregnum* (Aldershot, 2004), p. 187.

3 P. R. Newman, *The Old Service: Royalist Regimental Colonels and the Civil War, 1642–1646* (Manchester, 1993), p. 23; P. R. Newman, 'Principle and sacrifice in armed royalism', in J. Morrill, P. Slack and D. Woolf (eds), *Public Duty and Private Conscience in Seventeenth-Century England* (Oxford, 1993), p. 235.

4 T. May, *The history of the parliament of England which began Nov. 3 M.DC.XL* (London, 1812), p. 197; BL, E88(23), *The rider of the white horse and his army, their late good successe in Yorke-shiere* (London, 1643); J. Raymond, *The Invention of the Newspaper: English Newsbooks, 1641–1649* (Oxford, 1996), p. 41.

5 BL, E88(23), *The rider of the white horse.*

6 C. Hill, *The English Bible and the Seventeenth-Century Revolution* (London, 1994), p. 304; J. Shaw, 'The life of master John Shaw', in C. Jackson (ed.), *Yorkshire diaries and autobiographies in the seventeenth and eighteenth centuries* (Surtees Society, 65, 1877), appendix, 367; BL, Add. MS 11743, fo. 16r–v.

7 Worcester College, Oxford, Wing 2251A: *The pindar of Wakefield* (London, 1643), pp. 1–2.

8 BL, E55(13), *Sions memento and Gods alarum in a sermon at Westminster before the honourable House of Commons on 31 May* (London, 1643).

9 *The parliamentary or constitutional history of England, being a faithful account of all the most remarkable transactions in parliament from the earliest times to the restoration of King Charles II, by several hands* (London, 1753), vol. 12, pp. 268–9.

10 D. Underdown, *Revel, Riot and Rebellion: Popular Politics and Culture in England, 1603–1660* (Oxford, 1985), p. 137.

11 J. Jones, 'The war in the north: the northern parliamentary army in the English civil war, 1642–1645' (Ph.D. thesis, York University, Canada, 1991), pp. 242–3.

12 J. Vicars, *God in the mount or England's parliamentarie-chronicle* (London, 1644), pp. 240–6, 272.

13 BL, E86(5), *The kingdoms weekly intelligencer*, 17–24 January (London, 1643), p. 29; BL, E246(2), *A perfect diurnall of the passages in Parliament*, 30 January–6 February (London, 1643).

14 J. H. Turner (ed.), *The autobiography and diaries of Rev. Oliver Heywood, 1630–1702* (Brighouse, 1882), vol. 1, pp. 96–7.

15 Worcester College, Oxford, Wing 2251A: *The pindar of Wakefield.*

16 Vicars, *God in the mount*, p. 343.

17 J. Ricraft, *A survey of England's champions and truths faithful patriots* (London, 1647), p. 42.

18 BL, E247(21), *A perfect diurnall of the passages in parliament*, 3–10 April (London, 1643); BL, Add. MS 18980, fo. 33v.

19 BL, E249(10), *A perfect diurnall of the passages in parliament*, 22–29 May (London, 1643).

20 BL, Add. MS 40883, fo. 104r.

21 BL, Add. MS 18980, fo. 102r.

22 *The parliamentary or constitutional history of England*, vol. 12, pp. 268–9, 326.

23 BL, Add. MS 40883, fo. 126r.

24 P. W. Thomas (ed.), *The English Revolution III. Newsbooks I. Oxford Royalist* (London, 1971), vol. 1, pp. 174, 357; Raymond, *The Invention of the Newspaper*, p. 227.

25 Thomas (ed.), *The English Revolution III. Newsbooks I. Oxford Royalist*, vol. 2, pp. 693–4.

26 BL, E292(27), *The King's cabinet opened* , 14 July (London, 1645), pp. 3–4; A. B. Hinds (ed.), *Calendar of State Papers Venetian, 1643–7* (London, 1926), p. 162; S. Barber, ' "A bastard kind of militia", localism, and tactics in the second civil war', in I. Gentles, J. Morrill and B. Worden (eds), *Soldiers, Writers and Statesmen of the English Revolution* (Cambridge, 1998), p. 143.

27 BL, E252(19), *A perfect diurnall of some passages in Parliament*, 29 January–5 February (London, 1644), p. 223.

28 BL, E252(29), *A perfect diurnall of some passages in Parliament*, 15–22 April (London, 1644); K. Lindley and D. Scott (eds), *The Journal of Thomas Juxon, 1644–1647* (Camden Society, 5th series, 13, 1999), p. 51.

29 YML, CWT, *The Saints thankful acclamation at Christs resumption of his great power and the initials of his kingdome: a sermon of thanksgiving preached by Joseph Caryl at Westminster* (London, 1644), p. 35; A. Gill, *The new starre of the north, shining upon the victorious king of Sweden* (London, 1632); Thomas (ed.), *The English Revolution III. Newsbooks I. Oxford*

Royalist, vol. 2, p. 534; Lindley and Scott (eds), *The Journal of Thomas Juxon*, pp. 88–9.

30 Ricraft, *A survey of England's champions*, pp. 37, 155.

31 C. Carlton, *Going to the Wars: The Experience of the British Civil Wars, 1638–1651* (London, 1994), p. 189.

32 BL, E128(28), *Speciall passages*, 22–29 November (London, 1642), pp. 135–6; YML, CWT, 42–12–16, *A true relation of the fight at Sherburn in the county of Yorke* (London, 1642), p. 1.

33 Bod., MS Fairfax 36, fos. 9v–10r.

34 T. Gent, *Gent's History of Hull reprinted in fac-simile of the original of 1735* (Hull, 1869), p. 152.

35 BL, E560(9), *A tragi-comedy, called New-market-fayre* (London, 1649).

36 BL, E254(28), *Perfect occurrences of Parliament*, 30 August–6 September (London, 1644).

37 My thanks to Robin Greenwood for kindly sharing with me his private research on William Forbes: BL, E24(23), *Mercurius civicus*, 9–16 January (London, 1645), p. 790.

38 BL, Add. MS 18979, fo. 194.

39 J. Sprigge, *Anglia rediviva* (London, 1647), p. 19.

40 R. Bell (ed.), *The Fairfax correspondence: memorials of the civil war* (London, 1849), vol. 1, p. 251.

41 Sprigge, *Anglia rediviva*, p. 42.

42 T. Burton, *Diary of Thomas Burton, esq*, ed. J. T. Rutt (London, 1828), vol. 3, p. 56; R. B. Manning, *Swordsmen: The Martial Ethos in the Three Kingdoms* (Oxford, 2003), pp. 57, 66.

43 J. Rushworth, *Historical collections* (London, 1721), part 4, vol. 1, pp. 388–9.

44 Sprigge, *Anglia rediviva*, opening dedicatory.

45 BL, Add. MS 18979, fo. 245.

46 J. Wilson, *Fairfax* (New York, 1985), pp. 92–3; A. Hughes, *Gangraena and the Struggle for the English Revolution* (Oxford, 2004), p. 215.

47 Bod., MS Clarendon 34, fo. 12r.

48 I. Gentles, *The New Model Army in England, Ireland and Scotland, 1645–1653* (Oxford, 1992), p. 141.

49 BL, E598(18), *The sounding of the last trumpet*, 24 April (London, 1650), pp. 17–18, 42, 46, 50–2. Foster was identified as the prophet of the Levellers by the Warboys Baptist church book, and even Christopher Hill argued that Foster suffered from the occasional 'partial lapse from sanity': C. Hill, *The World Turned Upside Down* (Harmondsworth, 1975), pp. 127, 223–4, 279.

50 *CSP dom. 1644–5*, p. 198; BL, Add. MS 10114, fo. 14v; Bell (ed.), *The Fairfax correspondence*, vol. 1. p. 176.

51 L. Daxon, 'The politics of Sir Thomas Fairfax reassessed', *History*, 90:4 (2005), 496.

52 R. Ashton, *Counter-Revolution: The Second Civil War and its Origins, 1646–8* (New Haven, 1994), p. 409; TNA, SP 23/88/953; M. Wilding, *Dragon's Teeth: Literature in the English*

Revolution (Oxford, 1987), p. 154; Bell (ed.), *The Fairfax correspondence*, vol. 1, pp. 86–7; E. Chisenhall, *A journal of the siege of Lathom House* (London, 1823), pp. 16–17.

53 H. Aveling, *Northern Catholics: The Catholic Recusants of the North Riding of Yorkshire, 1558–1790* (London, 1966), pp. 306, 316; H. Aveling, *The Handle and the Axe: The Catholic Recusants in England from Reformation to Emancipation* (London, 1976), pp. 172–3.

54 By permission of His Grace, the Duke of Norfolk, Arundel Castle, MD 1048, fo. 133.

55 Thomas (ed.), *The English Revolution III. Newsbooks I. Oxford Royalist*, vol. 2, p. 705.

56 BL, E448(9), *A case for Nol Cromwell's nose, and the cure for Tom Fairfax's gout*, 17 June (1648), pp. 1–6.

57 BL, E451(38), *The last will and testament of Tom Fairfax, and the army under his command*, 9 July (London, 1648), pp. 1–4; BL, E449(39), *A winding-sheet for the rebels at Westminster. A grave as deep as hell for Fairfax and his army*, 27 June (1648), pp. 1–4.

58 BL, E540(15), *Mercurius pragmaticus*, 16–30 January (London, 1649).

59 BL, Thomason 669, f.12(87), Engraving after Weesop, *Execution of Charles I* (1649); Ashmolean Museum, Oxford, CIII 198.

60 W. Emberton, *The English Civil War Day by Day* (Stroud, 1995), p. 199.

61 Reproduced in M. Ashley, *The Battle of Naseby and the Fall of King Charles I* (Stroud, 1992), pp. 80–1.

62 *Sutherland MS*, HMC, 5th report, appendix (London, 1876), p. 180.

63 L. L. Knoppers, *Constructing Cromwell: Ceremony, Portrait and Print, 1645–1661* (Cambridge, 2000), p. 17.

64 BL, E551(10), *The man in the moon*, 16–23 April (London, 1649), p. 16.

65 *CSP dom. 1654*, p. 350.

66 *Sutherland MS*, HMC, 5th report, appendix, pp. 193–4.

67 H. B. Wheatley (ed.), *The diary of Sir Samuel Pepys, with Lord Braybrooke's notes* (London, 1897), vol. 1, pp. 5–6, 9, 58.

68 Beinecke Rare Book and Manuscript Library, Yale University, Osborn files, folder 17645.

69 Peacey, *Politicians and Pamphleteers*, pp. 36, 109, 176.

70 *Ibid.*, p. 27; BL, Harleian MS 7001, fo. 194.

71 BL, Add. MS 18979, fos. 127, 218, 238, 247; BL, Add. MS 21506, fo. 41; BL, Add. MS 29747, fos. 14–16.

72 Raymond, *The Invention of the Newspaper*, pp. 38, 197; Peacey, *Politicians and Pamphleteers*, pp. 191, 225.

73 BL, Add. MS 31116, fos. 239r, 260r.

74 My thanks to Dr David Scott for raising this point: BL, Harleian MS 7001, fo. 198.

75 Raymond, *The Invention of the Newspaper*, pp. 54, 66; BL, E464(39), *The moderate*, 19–26 September (London, 1648).

76 J. Wilson, *Fairfax* (New York, 1985), p. 14; M. A. Gibb, *The Lord General: A Life of Thomas Fairfax* (London, 1938), p. 4.

77 BL, E447(19), *The cuckoo's nest at Westminster* (1648), p. 7; BL, E540(15), *Mercurius*

pragmaticus, 16–30 January (London, 1649); BL E602(21), *Mercurius elencticus*, 27 May–3 June (London, 1650).

78 W. Kelly, 'James Butler, twelfth earl of Ormond, the Irish government, and the bishops' wars, 1638–1640', in J. R. Young (ed.), *Celtic Dimensions of the British Civil Wars* (Edinburgh, 1997), p. 42.

79 Sprigge, *Anglia rediviva*, pp. 321–3.

80 Westmoreland had married Mary Vere, sister of Anne Fairfax, in 1638: *Earl of Westmorland's MS*, HMC, 10th report, part 4 (London, 1885), pp. 44–5; G. E. Cokayne, *Complete Peerage*, vol. 12, part 2 (London, 1959), pp. 567–70.

81 Wilson, *Fairfax*, p. 189; Gibb, *The Lord General*, p. xv.

Chapter 10

Gender and literature:
Anne Fairfax and Andrew Marvell

Recent historiographical trends have broken down old boundaries between social and political history through examining broader notions of what constitutes politics. By exploring 'the social depth of politics', historians no longer confine political history to the operation of a state's institutions, power and authority.[1] Social historians have emphasised political activity among individuals once regarded as incapable of political consciousness, while historians examining gender have extended the political realm into sexual relations. In particular, Richard Cust has argued that political historians need to 'integrate issues relating to sexual behaviour into their account of early modern political culture'.[2] This politics of gender is particularly important for a study of Sir Thomas Fairfax, because his troublesome marital relationship was frequently discussed by contemporaries. Seventeenth-century conduct books emphasised that England was a patriarchal society in which women remained in the private sphere of the domestic household, where they were supposed to be subordinate to men and aspire to be chaste, silent and obedient. Men were to inhabit the public sphere outside the household and work to provide for their families. In practice few women confined themselves entirely to the household, public and private spheres overlapped and both were prone to the rumour and gossip that shaped an individual's standing in the community. Those men that held public office were extremely susceptible to anxiety over how perceptions of their married lives might reflect upon their public honour and reputation.[3] A man who failed to govern his wife, children and servants was held to be unfit for public office. After the first civil war, Fairfax and his wife's political and religious views clashed, and Fairfax fell victim, like the earl of Essex before him, to the common contemporary discourse that a dysfunctional family suffered from an inversion of gender roles, with the women in control.[4]

I

This supposedly unnatural, womanly inversion of authority had little impact upon Sir Thomas Fairfax's upbringing; his mother, Mary, daughter of the earl of Mulgrave, died in childbirth in 1619, freeing him from what contemporary moralists feared was the effeminising influence of mothers. Ferdinando did not marry again until 1646, and although the youthful Sir Thomas had five sisters, he grew up in a masculine, martial environment dominated by his grandfather, the first baron Fairfax. Sir Thomas's wife also belonged to a military family: Anne, daughter of Horace, baron Vere of Tilbury. After months of intricate negotiations, Thomas and Anne wedded in Hackney, Middlesex, on 20 June 1637. Their marriage did not enjoy an auspicious start. Within three weeks, Thomas, 'after a fitt of ye stone fell into an ague ... ye fitts beginning with cold & then hott'. Lady Mary Vere remarked that her daughter 'wth watching & colde she gott is fallen into a fever, wch is ye more to her, because she hath never had any sicknes'.[5] It was not until December that Lady Vere announced 'I am glad to find by their letters they are both so well recovered. God graunt they may use their health to Gods glory.'[6]

The root of the couple's future differences was Anne's religion. Clarendon recalled: 'Having been bred in Holland, she had not the reverence for the Church of England that she ought to have had, and so had unhappily concurred in her husband's entering into rebellion.' Like many English families serving the protestant cause abroad, the Veres were particular about their reformed faith, educating their family in the English church at the Hague. Despite the Fairfaxes' reputation for godliness, Lady Vere troubled Lord Fairfax over provision of chaplains for her daughter.[7] In March 1648 the royalist newsbook *Mercurius elencticus* alleged that the first baron Fairfax had prophesised ill of their marriage, saying of Anne: 'that Anabaptist, whom he is now in Love with, and intends to make his Wife', would 'seduce him from his Religion and Loyalty'. As so often with civil war propaganda, their story was not without foundation, for the first baron had warned Thomas's uncle Charles Fairfax: 'such is Tom's pride (led much by his wife) that he, not contented to live in our rank, will destroy his house.'[8]

Life for the newly wed couple at Denton was subject to the imposing patriarchal authority of the ageing first baron, who eventually died on 2 May 1640. Sir Thomas wrote to Ferdinando in March 1642 that life in York did not agree with Anne who was 'often extreame il in her head'.[9] The Fairfaxes' espousal of stoic notions of honour, discussed in Chapter 8, included belief in decency and kindness towards one's spouse. Several writers of conduct books recommended that the husband might best meet wifely disobedience with patience, protecting his wife's reputation by not admonishing her in public. Patrick Collinson has remarked that the 'Stoics advocated mutuality and parity in marital relations', while Sir Richard Grosvenor advised his son in 1628: 'carry your selfe temperately & sweetly towards your wife. Love her hartely, use her with all respect, banish farr from you all harshness.'[10] Sir Thomas extended his humility to his mother–in-law, Lady Vere, informing her that he held 'more by obligation than merit the honour of being' her son. In his retirement Fairfax wrote a poem berating bad husbands, and another praising his wife as a 'machless creature' after her death in 1665.[11]

While Anne could hardly have chosen a royalist allegiance, her strong parliamentarianism was not entirely dictated by her husband's family. In 1642 and 1643 she remained with her husband, riding with his soldiery in their first campaigns. Although seventeenth-century field armies often depended upon female camp followers, this behaviour in a lady of Anne's status was highly conspicuous. After the defeat of Adwalton moor, Anne was among her husband's shattered forces besieged in Bradford by the earl of Newcastle's army. With the town's fall imminent, she accompanied her husband and his officers in a daring escape attempt, riding through the royalist lines at night. Sir Thomas recalled the episode: 'I must not forget to mention my wife who ran as great hazards with us in this Retreat, as any others, and with as little expression of feare (Not for any zeale or Delight, (I must needs say) in ye war, but) through a willing & patient suffering of this undesireable Condition.' Remembering for posterity, Sir Thomas downplayed suggestions of his wife's unwomanly, bellicose nature and military background, rather emphasising her stoic capacity for enduring suffering. Anne was captured while mounted behind one of Fairfax's officers, and Sir Thomas excused his failure to rescue her by explaining that he broke through the royalist positions alone, separated from his companions.[12]

Anne was taken prisoner to Newcastle's headquarters at nearby Bolling Hall. Bradfordians feared that the royalists would avenge themselves upon the town for its notoriety during the 'club-law'. The London press, hearing rumours of Anne's capture and foretelling Bradford's ruin, published shocking accounts of cavalier atrocities. One newsbook claimed that Anne was shot in the shoulder, her maidservant killed by 'barbrous and mercilesse Popish Souldiers', and Bradford's maidens stripped and ravished. Nehemiah Wallington noted with horror how 'those cruel enemies of God' had overrun the north.[13] Instead, on the first night of Anne's imprisonment, Newcastle rescinded his order that Bradford should be denied quarter, indirectly connecting Anne to the birth of a local legend. Joseph Lister recalled how, seeking an explanation for Newcastle's unexpected change of heart, Bradfordians established the legend of the white lady as an angel of mercy:

> But oh! what a night and morning was that in which Bradford was taken! what weeping, and wringing of hands! none expecting to live any longer than till the enemies came into the town, and to give them all Bradford quarter, for the brave Earl

of Newport's sake. However, God so ordered it, that before the town was taken, the Earl gave a different order, (viz.) that quarter should be given to all the townsmen. It was generally reported that something came on the Lord's Day night, and pulled the clothes off his bed several times, and cried out with a lamentable voice, 'pity poor Bradford!' that then he sent out his orders that neither man, woman, nor child, should be killed in the town; and that then the apparition which had so disturbed him, left him, and went away; but this I assert not as a certain truth; but this is true, that they slew very few in the town.[14]

The legend was retold in the 1820s by John Nicholson's play, *The siege of Brad-ford*, with a serving girl as the heroine, disguising herself as a ghostly maiden in Newcastle's chamber. This striking legend was long cherished in the neighbourhood; pictures of the ghost were bequeathed in wills from nearby Idle in the nineteenth century.[15] The story caught the imagination so effectively because its gendered portrayal of Bradford as a fearful, helpless victim of war deflected attention from the town's notorious, anti-royalist past. It also offered an explanation that minimised the credit due to the royalists for granting mercy.

On 27 July 1643 the House of Commons required Lord Fairfax to write to Newcastle to inform him that if Anne was not released 'order shall be taken for seizing and making Prisoners of all the Ladies, Wives to any Lords or others that are in actual War against the Parliament'.[16] Newcastle had no intention of holding Anne indefinitely, and he delivered her safely to Hull. Sir Thomas recalled Newcastle's generous act, but begrudged giving him credit: 'not many days after ye E. of Newcastle sent my wife back agn: in his Coach, with some Horse to Guard her. (Wch Generosity gained more yn any Reputation he could have gotten by detaining a Lady prisoner upon such tearmes)'.[17]

By the time of her release, Anne was the first lady of the parliamentarian cause in the north. The war presented her with an exciting opportunity for political involvement. In the cause's darkest days, she risked her life, endured capture and played her part encouraging the troops. According to William Harlakenden, in September 1643 she gave to one of Cromwell's captains a motto in a lady's favour, with the words: 'wrather dye yn truth deny'. Soon after, Anne was in London where Sir Thomas wrote to her of his victory at Nantwich on 28 January 1644.[18] In April 1645 Anne rejoined her husband on campaign and his anxieties over her health soon intensified his stress. Sir Thomas wrote to Ferdinando on 10 January 1646: 'I stayed on a day behind the army to see my wife a little better before I left her (which I thank god) I left in a good way of recovery.' On 31 January he commented that Anne had recovered, 'god be thanked', and that she intended to travel to London.[19]

Like many supporters of the parliamentary cause, by the end of the first civil war, Anne Fairfax was having misgivings. These doubts led her into conflict with her husband. Lucy Hutchinson claimed that when Lady Fairfax accompanied the army towards London after the siege of Oxford, Presbyterian ministers turned her against the army and her husband's chaplains with:

> such a bitter aversion against them that they could not endure to come into the General's presence while she was there; and the General had an unquiet, unpleasant life with her, who drove away from him many of those friends in whose conversation he had found such sweetness ... At Nottingham they had gotten a very able minister into the great church, but a bitter Presbyterian; him and his brethren my Lady Fairfax caressed with so much kindness that they grew impudent to preach up their faction openly in the pulpit, and to revile the others, and at length would not suffer any of the army chaplains to preach in the town.[20]

Sarah Mendelson and Patricia Crawford have argued that religion was 'the most common site of women's political engagement' during the 1640s, and Anne Fairfax was no exception. During the 1630s, Anne's mother, Lady Vere, had corresponded with a group of clergy who admired her godliness and courted her patronage. She became known as 'Delicia Cleri', 'the ministers' delight'. When Anne was about sixteen, Lady Vere even censured one of her husband's military chaplains, Stephen Goffe. In holding and expressing such strong religious opinions Anne was merely emulating her mother's example. From 1647 Anne grew torn between loyalty to her husband's army and allegiance to her inner Presbyterian convictions. She grew actively involved in politics despite her sex's theoretical exclusion from such matters. Furthermore, her status enabled her to engage conspicuously in high politics, which was regarded as even more of a male preserve.[21]

During 1647 Fairfax's army was increasingly attacked by Presbyterian ministers as being a nest of dangerous sectarians whose aim was to destroy hierarchy and subvert all church government. Thomas Edwards, among others, condemned Fairfax for failing to enforce religious discipline among his men. Fairfax's abhorrence of acrimony over what he perceived as minor differences steeled him against his army's detractors. While Sir Thomas was busy in his employments, Anne was spending much time in the company of Presbyterian ministers. Such religious and intellectual relationships were among the few male friendships permissible for elite married women. This was an important political act in itself, but when it became known that the men who reflected and shaped Anne's position were attacking her husband and his army, it undermined the patriarchal order. It suggested that all was not harmonious in the Fairfax household and that Anne was seeking spiritual compensation for unsatisfactory aspects of her marriage, a union that had failed to produce a male heir. The concerns of the army and Independents that Anne might influence Fairfax were heightened by the couple's public displays of unity, such as on 7 August 1647 when Anne accompanied Fairfax in his coach as he departed London. Cromwell hinted at these divisions between Anne and the army, writing to Fairfax on 7 March 1648: 'I most humbly begg my service may be prosecuted to your Lady, to whom I wish all happinesse, and establishment in the truth.'[22] Although Cromwell's subordinate position tempered his criticism of Anne into a polite concern for her well-being, he clearly understood she was at odds with the army.

In June 1648 John Crouch's *Mercurius melancholicus* made political capital out of this conflict, humorously depicting Lady Fairfax quarrelling for supremacy with Mrs Cromwell in *The cuckoo's-nest at Westminster*. This pamphlet satire began with the two ladies worried over recent reports of their husbands' deaths. Then it portrayed their infidelity and profiteering from the war in the absence of their cuckolded, 'Deer ab-hor'ed Husbands'. When Anne said 'if my Tom but recovers and thrives in his enterprise, I will not say tush to be Queen of England', Mrs Cromwell replied 'your husband is counted a fool, and wants wit to reign: every boy scoffs at him', adding 'come up, Mother Damnable, Joan Ugly; must you be queen! Yes, you shall: Queen of Puddledock or Billingsgate; that is fittest for thee.' Their argument concluded at news of a royalist rising, leaving them in panic, fleeing the consequences of their treachery.[23] Although Crouch's satire was for the amusement of royalists, part of his purpose may also have been to deepen any perceived discord within the army command.

By the politically charged time of the King's trial, some soldiers turned violent against Anne, believing her their enemy. In January 1649, Sir Thomas's sister Elizabeth Fairfax informed her uncle Charles Fairfax of Menston that as she passed Doncaster her uncle's soldiers mistook her for Anne and threatened her life, holding a pistol to her breasts.[24] The army's political enemies certainly sought Anne's support. Stephen Marshall and Obadiah Sedgwick organised London's Presbyterian clergy into sending two letters addressed not just to Sir Thomas but Anne also, on 17 January 1649. Sedgwick had known Anne since she was a child, having been a chaplain under her father in the Low Countries. Although Marshall and Sedgwick compromised the patriarchal order by sending political advice to a woman, they could theorise that a wife had the right to disobey her husband if his commands violated God's law. They expected Anne to influence her husband into restraining the army according to their wishes. Their letters expressed opposition to the purge of Parliament, reminding Thomas and Anne that legislation of 1641 forbade the arrest of MPs.[25] Other ministers such as John Geree approached Anne directly with complaints about Pride's purge. Dedicating his pamphlet to Anne and her mother, Lady Vere, on 15 January 1649, Geree implored them to 'with-draw him (whom you so dearly respect) from society in actions so contrary to the honour of God and our Religion. Oh study, that it may never be said, That any person of Honor, and of the Protestant Religion, had any hand in so unworthy an action, as the deposing or destroying of a King.'[26] These clergymen, who were effectively petitioning Anne, implicitly recognised she performed an important public role which would only be legitimate once channelled towards their political ends.

Anne's most famous political intervention was during the King's trial. When Fairfax was named as a commissioner, Clarendon later reported that a masked Anne called out from the public gallery: 'he had more wit than to be there'. This threw the court into disorder, as it was demanded who made the interruption.[27] Although actually present, John Rushworth reported a longer and less convincing interruption from Anne, 'being above in a Window', on 19 January 1649: 'the Lord Fairfax was not there in Person, that he never would sit among them and therefore they did him wrong to name him as a sitting Commissioner'.[28] Whitelocke noted another interruption on 22 January: 'Some who sat on the scaffolds about the Court at the tryall (particularly the Lady Fairfax the L. Generalls wife) did not forbeare to exclaime aloud agt the proceedings of the High Court, & the irreverent usage of the king by his subjects, in so much that the court was interrupted & the soldiers & officers of the Court had much to doe to quiet the ladyes & others.'[29] When sentence was passed on 27 January and Bradshaw declared that the King had been tried in the name of 'all the good people of England', Anne interjected 'no, nor the hundredth part of them!'[30]

During Daniel Axtell's trial in October 1660 several witnesses recalled Anne's interruptions of the King's trial. Edward Cook recalled her interruption as 'it is a lie, where are the People? Or their Consents? Cromwell is a Traitor.' Axtell was accused of ordering his musketeers to shoot her after having bellowed 'What Drab is that that Disturbs the Court?' Holland Simpson recalled a masked lady saying 'Oliver Cromwell is a Rogue and a Traitor', adding that 'it was the common Report' that it was Lady Fairfax. Sir Purbeck Temple affirmed that Anne was the woman in question, and that she had attended the trial with his sister, Mrs Nelson.[31]

Clarendon and Rushworth, published long after 1660, do not indicate that the identity of the lady was ever doubted, and Whitelocke recorded it was Anne, but evidence from Axtell's trial suggests that it might not have become common knowledge until years later.[32] A reference to Lady Fairfax's interruption was removed in the licensed edition of Gilbert Mabbott's *King Charls his tryal* in February 1649. When a second edition of this work that included the interruption was published in November 1649, the Council of State ordered its seizure.[33] Cromwell would have recognised her voice and although her disguise suggested she acted without her husband's knowledge, the ill feeling between her and the Cromwells had become notorious. John Crouch stirred these rumours in another comedy pamphlet play, entitled *A tragi-comedy called New-market fayre*. Written after June 1649, it amusingly depicted Fairfax, Cromwell and their wives quarrelling at an auction of the King's goods. Crouch's Mrs Cromwell upbraided Lady Fairfax, while making horns in a rude gesture:

Call me Mistris brazen-face ... thou Rotterdam slut, thou; call me brazen-face? Thou looks more liker a Mistris foolsface, or like thy husbands-face ... Come, come; I never had a Bastard by another man when my husband was at the Leaguer before Breda; nor do I keep company with Cavaliers at Taverns; nay at Bawdy Taverns too, when thy Tom Innocent has been in fight. Gorge me that Madam Turn-tayle.

Mrs Cromwell's pejorative use of the term 'thou' to her social superior also suggested there was something inherently socially subversive about the Cromwells' increasing prominence. Having decisively intervened in the political arena by urging her husband to withdraw from the King's trial, the charge of Anne's infidelity became a staple of the royalist press.[34]

How far Fairfax's eleventh-hour retreat from regicide was due to his wife remains open to question, but her opinions were the talk of London. One secluded MP, Edward Stephens, implored Fairfax to prevent the trial. He compared Fairfax to Pontius Pilate, reminding Fairfax to listen to his wife's exhortations:

The message of Pilates wife to her husband, in the behalf of Gods most holy Son, will be the best conclusion and advertisement to your Lordship touching his Royall Lieuetenant and your dread Sovereigne Charles: *Have thou nothing to do with that just man*: suffer anything, sleeping or waking, for his preservation, but let his life be the Jewell of your care, from that infallible and grounded principle of David: destroy him not for who can stretch forth his hand against the Lords Anointed, and bee innocent![35]

The royalist press chose to depict Anne as entirely responsible for changing her husband's mind in order to undermine Fairfax's legitimacy as a military and political leader. *Mercurius pragmaticus* reported that Anne had dreamed of a man entering her room with Fairfax's head in his hand, and taking this as a 'merciful admonition from Heaven', she urged her husband against the King's trial.[36] Anne's opposition to the King's trial has long been erroneously attributed to her increasingly royalist leanings. Yet even in 1649, Anne was far from a royalist. It would be a mistake to view such committed Presbyterians as Anne and her clergymen associates as lukewarm parliamentarians or closet royalists because of their opposition to the regicide. As Eliot Vernon has shown, numerous tracts were published by London's Presbyterian clergy and laity in opposition to the regicide. These asserted that unlike the faith breakers in the army, they were the true parliamentarians who had remained loyal to the Protestation and the Solemn League and Covenant.[37] Anne's husband's army had trampled on her hopes for a limited monarchy and a godly national church. Despite the claims of some newsbooks, she was no closet royalist and remained devoted to Parliament's war aims of 1642.[38] Cromwell's sister, Katherine Whitstone, would have sympathised with her predicament; for harbouring misgivings over the King's execution, she too was denounced as a royalist.[39]

By 1649 Fairfax became 'Tom Ladle', or 'his Ladleship' in John Crouch's royalist newsbook *The man in the moon*, mocked for his inability to control his wife.[40] In January 1650 Crouch invented a fictional skimmington where two fairground performers impersonated Fairfax and his wife. He described: 'a Riding at Smithfield-Barres: where, one that acted Sir Thomas, a horseback, with a Ladle in his hand, two Baskets of Prides Graines before him, and his Doxie, riding with her face to the horse tayle behind; one of them flung a Ladle of Graines in our Commanders face'.[41] Later, Crouch depicted Lady Fairfax playing '*In* and *In* in good earnest with Mr. T.W. an impoverished Cavalier'. When Fairfax upbraided her for it, she replied 'WEE will not be thought a W___ my Lord' and ran in a rage to her chamber. Crouch depicted Lady Fairfax as unable to master her passions, implying that as her political views had clashed with her husband's, then it naturally followed she had been sexually unfaithful as well. Crouch's tracts became doubly wounding for Fairfax because they depicted him not only as an impotent cuckold, but as a wittol too. A wittol was a man that knew of his wife's infidelity but who did nothing about it. This was just about the worst insult that could be directed against any man.[42] *Mercurius pragmaticus* went even further, portraying Anne as an '*Anabaptistian* Lady' who 'doth Queane it with her Soveraignes Jewels'. The crude symbolism here was that with the King dead, Lady Fairfax sought to emasculate the male political order. The tract also accused Mrs Cromwell of adultery, adding that Lady Fairfax and Mrs Cromwell 'regard no stones like those of their own chusing', for 'Mistriss *Cromwell* shee vowes (to delight her) she had rather have one of her man Cressits st___s, to touch her flesh, then all the Diamonds in Frank Allens Jewellrie.'[43]

By claiming that Lady Fairfax defied her husband's authority by sexual infidelity, Crouch and other royalist pamphleteers branded Fairfax a cuckold general. This neatly complemented previous royalist attacks on Fairfax's predecessor, the earl of Essex, whose two wives had both proved adulterous. Several royalist cavalry cornets had mocked Essex, sporting the motto 'Cuckold we come'.[44] This made the usual point that any man who could not dominate his wife sexually had no right to public authority.[45] Crouch utilised this image to mock Fairfax further in referring to the Leveller women petitioning for Lilburne's release: '*Fairfax* look to thy head, for *Judeth* is a coming, the women are up in armes, and vow they will tickle your *Members*.' This sort of propaganda generated the unlikely legend that Moll Cutpurse, despite being aged 65, robbed Fairfax on Hounslow heath in 1650.[46]

Anne's opposition to the King's trial and influence over her husband were later blamed for Thomas's resignation in June 1650. On 23 October 1649 Lord Lisle remarked that with Cromwell absent in Ireland, the influence of Anne and her ministers was prevailing upon Fairfax. Yet on 9 April 1650 he commented that Fairfax would command against the Scots, 'notwithstanding

the solliscitations of the Ladyes and ministers to the contrary'.[47] Retrospectively, Lucy Hutchinson portrayed Anne's unwarranted interference as responsible for Fairfax's fall from greatness:

> My Lord Fairfax, persuaded by his wife and her Presbyterian chaplains, threw up
> his commission at such a time, when it could not have been done more spitefully
> and ruinously to the whole Parliament interest ... But this great man was then as
> immovable by his friends as pertinacious in obeying his wife; whereby he then died
> to all his former glory, and became the monument of his own name, which every
> day wore out.[48]

Bulstrode Whitelocke believed that Fairfax initially favoured plans to invade
Scotland and agreed with Ludlow that Anne with her Presbyterian ministers
persuaded him to resign.[49] When Fairfax was presented as having resigned
owing to ill health, one preacher exhorted the army: 'though your old Lord
General be not with you, he is not against you ... You have his heart still in
the camp, though his spouse has persuaded his weary body to take rest in her
bosom.'[50] To minimise political embarrassment, official publications refashioned Lady Fairfax's persuasions away from the high political sphere to her
more proper feminine role as a domestic comforter.

In his 1808 edition of Lucy Hutchinson's memoirs, Reverend Julius
Hutchinson set out to reclaim Fairfax's religious identity for the Congregation-
alists, and to rescue his memory from the supposed damage done by Anne.
He asserted that despite claims that Fairfax was a Presbyterian, his chaplains
were Independents, and 'nor does it appear that he ever *changed his opinion*,
but only that he suffered himself to be over-ruled by his wife'. He represented
Fairfax's resignation as the beginning of the republic's downfall, opening the
way for a devious and power-hungry Cromwell. Shifting the responsibility for
Fairfax's resignation from husband to wife, enabled the Reverend to honour
his own denomination at the expense of another. He wrote 'if the Presbyterians have nothing else to answer for, the perverting the judgment of this
excellent man was a fault never to be forgiven'.[51]

Having seen how marital discord was held to have affected her husband's
reputation, we might pause to consider further how it affected her own. Anne
and her daughter Mary were not endowed with the wit or visual charms to win
popularity at Cromwell's court,[52] while marrying her daughter to the duke of
Buckingham appeared to confirm old slurs about Anne's social pretensions
and self-aggrandisement (Figure 6). Sir Henry Slingsby was even said to have
delivered a letter from Charles II to Anne in 1654.[53] Politically distanced from
the Protector's courtiers, Anne's personal piety was seen as spiritual pride
while her lack of physical beauty attracted further snide remarks. When Anne
and Mary attended court at Whitehall in November 1657 to plead for Buckingham's release, William Dugdale reported their frosty reception among

Lady Fairfax

Figure 6 Sir Thomas's wife, Anne. Not known for her beauty, she was clearly a formidable character.

'the great ladies there', adding 'but alas now, all this is not regarded, for I am told that the females there do say, Proud tits! Are their stomachs now come down?' Anne had also been mocked for her stout frame by Henry Neville, who unkindly remarked 'he that meanes to board her, must put off his doublet and swim'.[54]

Anne Fairfax demonstrated that her marital relationship was not entirely based on the subordination recommended in contemporary conduct literature, suggesting that although the ideal of gender relations shaped reality to some extent, in practice some relationships played out differently. Anne utilised her social rank, notions of her elect status, commitment to godliness and relationships with clergymen to implicitly challenge patriarchy and step outside protestant gender roles that emphasised the husband and father as the unquestioned spiritual head of the household. Unable to effectively challenge Fairfax's military reputation, by 1649 royalist pamphleteers changed tack and ridiculed him as a cuckold. This was so important because, as Elizabeth Foyster points out, 'without the core of a worthy sexual reputation, all other contributing facets to male reputation could be meaningless'. Fairfax's enemies sought to link his sexual conduct with his political decisions, and that Fairfax did not lose office in response to these rumours suggests that the republican regime saw them for the vindictive fabrications they almost certainly were. Yet the royalist press could dishonour Fairfax effectively just by airing them. No adultery needed to have taken place if they could inspire Fairfax to be jealous and suspicious of his wife, as Iago did to Othello.[55] The case of Anne Fairfax suggests that some women, especially among the elites, were not as powerless as was once believed, retaining the power to persuade, influence or shame their menfolk into reconsidering their positions. Even at the core of male high politics, issues of gender remained of critical significance. The civil war offered some women an 'unprecedented opportunity for political and religious expression', and Anne Fairfax was among the many who embraced it. Women could become more heavily engaged in politics despite their theoretical exclusion from such matters, suggesting that the mid-seventeenth century represents an important if ultimately short-lived period in gender history.[56]

II

A consensus has emerged among recent historiography, which has seen a linguistic turn among historians coincide with a growing acknowledgement among literary scholars of the necessity of interpreting seventeenth-century poetry within the context of a broader cultural analysis that takes closer account of contemporary historical events. Sir Thomas Fairfax's own literary endeavours and his employment of Andrew Marvell as tutor to his only surviving child, Mary, provide a promising context for an interplay between these disciplines that can examine the attempted literary justifications of Fairfax's retirement.

By 1650 Marvell had become well known to the Fairfaxes. His father, Reverend Andrew Marvell, had been master of the Charterhouse Hospital in Hull, and had married into the Alured family. The poet's father had also been curate at Flamborough, the seat of Fairfax's uncle Sir William Constable, and he had dedicated a sermon to Anne Sadleir of Standon, Hertfordshire, a friend of Ferdinando Fairfax.[57] Andrew Marvell spent much of the civil war overseas, not returning to England until 1647. In June 1650 he penned 'An Horatian ode upon Cromwell's return from Ireland', which not only declared Cromwell's pre-eminence but advocated the forthcoming campaign against Scotland over which Fairfax resigned. Nevertheless, Fairfax subsequently employed him as Mary's tutor at the recently renovated Nun Appleton. During his tenure there from autumn 1650 to autumn 1652, Marvell taught Mary several languages and wrote two poems celebrating the Fairfaxes: 'Upon the Hill and Grove at Billborow' and 'Upon Appleton House'.[58] The latter in particular offered a political defence of the general's withdrawal from state affairs into a country retirement, and perhaps an endorsement of his impending return to arms to counter the Scots invasion of August 1651.

Probably written in July–August 1651, 'Upon Appleton House' was part of a genre of country house poems emerging at this time, beginning with Ben Jonson's 'To Penshurst', that embraced the new idea of peace and solitude in the country house.[59] Another purpose of the country house poem was to represent the owner through a description of the house. Marvell reminded his readers that Fairfax's estate at Nun Appleton was not built on deforestation or economic exploitation, but on the righteous taking over of a corrupt old nunnery. Therefore the house's 'foundation myth' eulogised masculine, protestant valour vanquishing feminine superstition and 'restoring the house to its proper function as a Puritan seat'. As a reminder of this, part of the gardens of the house, laid out like an artillery battery, were aimed towards nearby Cawood castle, lately a 'bastion of prelacy' and residence of the Archbishop of York.[60]

Sometimes the poet's purpose in describing a country house was extended to offer visions of 'perfect moral commonwealths'. Marvell asserted that the qualities of Nun Appleton as a house were modesty, moderation, sobriety and Englishness, all reflective of a 'primitive Christian virtue'. He complemented the predictable emphasis upon Fairfax's illustrious, protestant military ancestry, with a description of Fairfax's family as a 'Domestick Heaven' with Mary growing up under a 'Discipline severe'. This refashioning of Fairfax as the stern family patriarch challenged his recent depiction as 'Tom Ladle' and 'his ladleship' in the royalist press.[61] Indeed Anne Fairfax's virtual absence from the poem avoided raising awkward questions about Fairfax's patriarchal authority, and the rumours of Anne's involvement in Presbyterian plots against the republic, for which the minister Christopher Love had recently been executed.[62]

Marvell underlined how Fairfax's conscience and lack of ambition, qualities which formed the very basis of his integrity, had compelled his resignation from command.[63] Marvell's praising of the honour of a quiet private life in part anticipated the 'country' identity that emerged in the 1690s, while his lauding of Fairfax's modesty and humility as 'the lowliest but the highest of all Christian qualifications'[64] gave literary form to Fairfax's ideals of honour. Derek Hirst and Stephen Zwicker have observed how Marvell and Fairfax 'provided refuge for one another' in 1651, Fairfax offering 'sustenance and sociability' and Marvell providing 'a vision of estate and history within which Fairfax might take moral shelter'.[65]

In 1654 John Milton echoed Marvell's literary treatment of Fairfax, praising him for blending 'the highest modesty and purity of life with the most consummate courage'. Milton likened Fairfax's retirement to that of 'Scipio Africanus of old' who 'conquered not the enemy alone, but also ambition'. Having penned a sonnet during the siege of Colchester that praised Fairfax to the skies, during the 1650s Milton was naturally concerned to represent Fairfax as approving of the following regimes. He did this by justifying Fairfax's retirement as 'that most delightful and glorious rest', deserved 'by the ancient heroes after wars', and refuting speculation that Fairfax's resignation had been political, espousing the official line that attributed it to poor health.[66] Fairfax would have been pleased by such literary representations of his retirement that praised his lack of personal ambition. In contrast, soon after, Cromwell became particularly sensitive to charges of ambition; from 1656 the Protector became fearful that his own faults, self-interest and private gain had turned God's providence against England.[67]

Although most famous in the literary world for his patronage of Marvell, Fairfax employed his retirement with gardening and writing his own literature and poetry. This refashioning of his self-image echoed Wentworth's explanations of his withdrawal from court and office in 1623–4. Wentworth had praised the fresh air and peaceful merits of a country life in Yorkshire, recommending this course of action to Sir George Calvert in 1623 as 'a wanting sometimes to Persons of greater Eminency in the Administrations of Commonwealths'. A country retirement from public duty supposedly instilled virtue, enhancing religious and philosophical understanding. Like Wentworth, Fairfax presented himself as having spurned the corruption of high politics, to turn to spiritual reflection and learning. However, unlike Wentworth, he harboured no great yearning to return to high office. Whereas Wentworth had sought to dominate south Yorkshire by making Wentworth Woodhouse the grandest house in the locality, Fairfax's Nun Appleton was still modest enough in 1651 for Marvell to write of its 'dwarfish confines'.[68]

Fairfax had been raised from an early age to consider scholarship an integral part of his religious duty and sense of honour. His grandfather's brother Edward Fairfax had also been a poet, and during the 1650s Sir Thomas enjoyed the company of his scholarly uncles Charles Fairfax, at Menston, and Henry Fairfax, rector at Bolton Percy. Among several scholarly endeavours, he translated into English the 'History of Barlaam and Josaphat, King of India'. This medieval Christianised version of an Indian legend narrated how Josaphat, the son of an Indian king, was converted to Christianity by the holy man Barlaam. Jospahat then converted his father, but abandoned the kingdom once he succeeded to the throne, dying as a humble hermit. Fairfax was comforted by the story's religious emphasis on the virtues of solitude, patience, contemplation and retirement from worldly affairs, which he no doubt hoped was mirrored by his own circumstances.[69] Philip Major has recently argued that Fairfax was more than 'a modest dabbler in literary trifles', and that we should not underestimate his scholarly aptitude and linguistic confidence.[70] Fairfax translated several chapters of François de Foix's French edition of 'Hermes Trismegistus'. To these writings of ancient philosophy he appended his own accompanying commentary, and he translated from Latin some of the works of the ancient Roman military author Vegetius.[71] He also wrote a history of the church prior to the Reformation.[72]

A volume of his literary work survives entitled 'The Imployment of my Solitude'. In this he translated the Psalter into English in addition to numerous songs from the Old Testament, as well as penning several hymns.[73] Thereafter entitled 'The Recreations of my Solitude', Fairfax composed poems that reflected his stoic ideas about honour. Praising patience, temperance and virtue, he wrote poems denouncing anger, envy and ill husbands. He also noted several sayings as 'vulgar proverbs' that reflected his continuing attraction to stoic principles of honour:

> By Doges & Hawkes, by Loves & Armes
> For one delight comes thousand harmes
>
> When Pride on horseback getteth upp,
> Loss & shame sits on the croup.
>
> Human praise is a vain blaze.
>
> Nature made nothing so sublime.
> But Virtue to the top will climb.[74]

Fairfax also penned a treatise on horse breeding and provided Charles II with the mount for his coronation.[75] Uneasy at the prospect of the restoration of unrestrained Stuart despotism, he wrote:

Hence then Dispaire my hopes why should bury itt
Sence this brave steed Bredd first was in my Query
Now thus advanc't with highest honors Laden
While his that bredd him on by most mens trodden
But tis noe matter seing tho' hast gott th'Advance
Then please the Royal Rider with thy Prance
Soe may thy Fame much rayse thy Prayses higher
Then Chestnut that begot thee or Brid La-dore his sire.[76]

Fairfax has never been highly rated for his literary endeavours and much of what he wrote was translated or borrowed from other sources. Yet through his antiquarian pursuits and his employment of Marvell, he clearly endeavoured to further his family's reputation for learning. Much like his sermon notes, discussed in Chapter 6, his writings reflected a meticulous concern for godliness and scholarship, inseparable qualities in his conception of honour.

NOTES

1 P. Collinson, 'De Republica Anglorum: or, history with the politics put back', in P. Collinson, *Elizabethan Essays* (London, 1994), p. 13; K. Wrightson, 'The politics of the parish in early modern England', in P. Griffiths, A. Fox and S. Hindle (eds), *The Experience of Authority in Early Modern England* (Basingstoke, 1996), pp. 10–46.

2 R. Cust, 'Honour and politics in early Stuart England: the case of Beaumont v. Hastings', *Past and Present*, 149 (1995), 58.

3 E. Foyster, 'Gender relations', in B. Coward (ed.), *A Companion to Stuart Britain* (Oxford, 2003), pp. 111–29.

4 Cust, 'Honour and politics in early Stuart England', 82–3.

5 Bod., MS Fairfax 31, fo. 112.

6 *Ibid.*, fo. 126.

7 G. Huehns (ed.), *Selections from the History of the Rebellion and Civil Wars and the Life by Himself* (London, 1953), pp. 314–15; Bod., MS Fairfax 31, fo. 124; J. Anderson, *Memorable women of the puritan times* (London, 1862), vol. 1, p. 242.

8 BL, E433(14), *Mercurius elencticus*, 15–22 March (London, 1648), pp. 128–9; G. W. Johnson (ed.), *The Fairfax correspondence: memoirs of the reign of Charles I* (London, 1848), vol. 1, p. 314.

9 Bod., MS Fairfax 32, fo. 30.

10 A. Fletcher, 'The protestant idea of marriage in early modern England', in A. Fletcher and P. Roberts (eds), *Religion, Culture and Society in Early Modern Britain: Essays in Honour of Patrick Collinson* (Cambridge, 1994), p. 172; P. Collinson, 'Sir Nicholas Bacon and the Elizabethan via media', in P. Collinson, *Godly People: Essays on English Protestantism and Puritanism* (London, 1983), p. 140; R. Cust (ed.), *The Papers of Sir Richard Grosvenor, 1st Bart.* (The Record Society of Lancashire and Cheshire, 134, 1996), p. 27.

11 Johnson (ed.), *The Fairfax correspondence*, vol. 1, p. 387; Bod., MS Fairfax 40, fos. 571–2, 598–600; BL, Add. MS 11744, fo. 45v.

12 Bod., MS Fairfax 36, fo. 9r–v.

13 B. Donagan, 'Codes and conduct in the English civil war', *Past and Present*, 118 (1988), 82; BL, E61(16), *Certaine informations*, 17–24 July (London, 1643), pp. 209–10; BL, Add. MS 40883, fo. 126r

14 T. Wright (ed.), *The autobiography of Joseph Lister of Bradford in Yorkshire* (London, 1842), p. 23.

15 J. Nicholson, *The siege of Bradford, with notes* (Bradford, 2nd edn, 1831), pp. 19–20; J. H. Turner, *Idle or Idel in olden times: a lecture delivered in the old chapel* (n.p., c.1886).

16 *JHC*, vol. 3, p. 183.

17 Bod., MS Fairfax 36, fo. 10r.

18 BL, Egerton MS 2647, fo. 286; *Lowndes MS*, HMC, 7th report, appendix (London, 1879), p. 564; R. Bell (ed.), *The Fairfax correspondence: memorials of the civil war* (London, 1849), vol. 1, pp. 74–5.

19 BL, Add. MS 18979, fos. 214, 219.

20 L. Hutchinson, *Memoirs of the Life of Colonel Hutchinson*, ed. N. H. Keeble (London, 1995), pp. 209–10.

21 S. Mendelson and P. Crawford, *Women in Early Modern England* (Oxford, 1997), p. 403; D. Willen, 'Godly women in early modern England: puritanism and gender', *Journal of Ecclesiastical History*, 43 (1992), 570, 574–6.

22 A. Fraser, *Cromwell Our Chief of Men* (London, 1973), p. 205; BL, Sloane MS 1519, fo. 158.

23 BL, E448(9), *A case for Nol Cromwells nose, and the cure of Tom Fairfax's gout. Both which rebells are dead, and their deaths kept close, by the policy of our new states*, 17 June (London, 1648); BL, E447(19), *The cuckoo's-nest at Westminster, or the Parlement between the two lady-birds, Quean Fairfax, and Lady Cromwell, by Mercurius melancholicus*, 15 June (London, 1648), pp. 7–8.

24 BL, Add. MS 36996, fo. 143.

25 G. Edwards, *The Last Days of Charles I* (Stroud, 1999), p. 115; Willen, 'Godly women in early modern England', 564, 574–5; A. Laurence, *Parliamentary Army Chaplains, 1642–1651* (Woodbridge, 1990), p. 172.

26 YML, CWT: FAI 1644–9(20), *Might overcoming right* (London, 1649).

27 Clarendon, *History of the rebellion and civil wars in England*, ed. W. Dunn Macray (Oxford, 1888), vol. 4, p. 486.

28 J. Rushworth, *Historical collections* (London, 1721), part 4, vol. 2, p. 1395.

29 BL, Add. MS 37344, fo. 248v.

30 Clarendon, *History of the rebellion and civil wars in England*, ed. Dunn Macray, vol. 4, p. 486.

31 *A complete collection of state trials* (London, 1730), vol. 1, p. 944, vol. 2, pp. 366–9.

32 C. V. Wedgwood, *The Trial of Charles I* (London, 1964), pp. 175–6.

33 J. Peacey, 'Reporting a revolution: a failed propaganda campaign', in J. Peacey (ed.), *The Regicides and the Execution of Charles I* (Basingstoke, 2001), pp. 175, 180.

34 Bod., Wing T2018B, *A tragi-comedy called New-market fayre* (London, 1649), p. 5.

35 BL, E536(38), *A letter of advice, from a secluded member of the House of Commons, to his excellency, Thomas Lord Fairfax, to admonish him of the Kings danger, his own duty, and the sad consequence of oppression and tyranny.* 30 December 1648 (London, 1649), p. 5.

36 Anderson, *Memorable women of the puritan times*, vol. 1, p. 255.

37 BL, E539(9), *An apologeticall declaration of the conscientious Presbyterians of the province of London*, 24 January (London, 1649); BL, E540(11), *A vindication of the ministers of the Gospel in, and about London* (London, 1649).

38 A. Hughes, *Gangraena and the Struggle for the English Revolution* (Oxford, 2004), p. 406; E. Vernon, 'The quarrel of the Covenant: the London Presbyterians and the regicide', in Peacey (ed.), *The Regicides*, pp. 202–24.

39 Mendelson and Crawford, *Women in Early Modern England*, p. 416.

40 L. Potter, *Secret Rites and Secret Writing* (Cambridge, 1989), pp. 15, 35.

41 BL, E590(12), *The man in the moon*, 23–31 January (London, 1650), p. 314.

42 BL, TT E601(5), *The man in the moon*, 10–26 April (London, 1650), pp. 390–1; E. A. Foyster, *Manhood in Early Modern England: Honour, Sex and Marriage* (Harlow, 1999), pp. 7, 109.

43 Francis Allen was a wealthy Independent and alderman of London: BL, E594(7), *Mercurius pragmaticus*, 19–26 February (London, 1650).

44 D. Underdown, *A Freeborn People: Politics and the Nation in Seventeenth-Century England* (Oxford, 1996), p. 102; I. Gentles, 'The iconography of revolution', in I. Gentles, J. Morrill and B. Worden (eds), *Soldiers, Writers and Statesmen of the English Revolution: Essays Presented to Austin Woolrych* (Cambridge, 1998), pp. 99, 101.

45 Foyster, *Manhood in Early Modern England*, pp. 4, 115.

46 BL, E551(10), *The man in the moon*, 16–23 April (London, 1650), p. 11; H. Speight, *Upper Wharfedale* (London, 1900), p. 78.

47 BL, Add. MS 18738, fo. 82v; G. Dyfnallt Owen (ed.), *De L'Isle and Dudley MS, vol. 6, 1626–98*, HMC, 77 (London, 1966), p. 477.

48 Hutchinson, *Memoirs of the Life of Colonel Hutchinson*, ed. Keeble, pp. 240–1.

49 BL, Add. MS 37345, fo. 81r; C. H. Firth (ed.), *The memoirs of Edmund Ludlow* (Oxford, 1894), vol. 1, pp. 242–3.

50 BL, E604(5), *A sermon preached in the chapel at Somerset House* (London, 1650).

51 L. Hutchinson, *Memoirs of the life of Colonel Hutchinson*, ed. Reverend Julius Hutchinson (London, 2nd edn, 1808), pp. 270n, 315–16n.

52 Anderson, *Memorable women of the puritan times*, vol. 1, p. 62.

53 D. Underdown, *Royalist Conspiracy in England* (New Haven, 1960), p. 121.

54 *Sutherland MS*, HMC, 5th report, appendix (London, 1876), p. 177; BL, E590(10), *Newes from the New Exchange, or the commonwealth of ladies*, 30 January (London, 1650), p. 5.

55 Foyster, *Manhood in Early Modern England*, pp. 10, 134.

56 *Ibid.*, p. 209; Mendelson and Crawford, *Women in Early Modern England*, pp. 346, 418.

57 N. Murray, *World Enough and Time: The Life of Andrew Marvell* (London, 1999), p. 47; W. H. Kelliher, 'Andrew Marvell', *Oxford DNB*; Bod., MS Fairfax 32, fo. 15.

58 N. Smith (ed.), *The Poems of Andrew Marvell* (Harlow, 2003), pp. 203–41, 267–80.

59 Murray, *World Enough and Time*, p. 54.

60 *Ibid.*, p. 57; L. S. Marcus, 'Pastimes with a court', in T. Healy (ed.), *Andrew Marvell* (London, 1998), pp. 74, 78.

61 A. D. Cousins, 'Marvell's "Upon Appleton House, to my Lord Fairfax" and the Regaining of Paradise', in C. Condren and A. D. Cousins (eds), *The Political Identity of Andrew Marvell* (Aldershot, 1990), pp. 53, 56–9, 62, 74.

62 D. Hirst and S. Zwicker, 'High summer at Nun Appleton, 1651: Andrew Marvell and Lord Fairfax's occasions', *Historical Journal*, 36:2 (1993), 255–6, 260–2.

63 P. Griffin, *The Modest Ambition of Andrew Marvell: A Study of Marvell and his Relation to Lovelace, Fairfax, Cromwell and Milton* (Newark, University of Delaware Press, 1995), p. 63.

64 C. Hill, *A Turbulent, Seditious, and Factious People: John Bunyan and his Church* (Oxford, 1988), p. 279.

65 Hirst and Zwicker, 'High summer at Nun Appleton', 266.

66 D. Masson, *The Life of John Milton* (London, 1877), vol. 4, pp. 601–2; Markham, p. 362.

67 B. Worden, 'Oliver Cromwell and the sin of Achan', in D. L. Smith (ed.), *Cromwell and the Interregnum* (Oxford, 2003), pp. 38, 52, 58.

68 D. Howarth, *Images of Rule: Art and Politics in the English Renaissance, 1485–1649* (Basingstoke, 1997), pp. 192–3; R. Cust, 'Wentworth's "change of sides" in the 1620s', in J. F. Merritt (ed.), *The Political World of Thomas Wentworth, Earl of Strafford, 1621–1641* (Cambridge, 1996), p. 71; Smith (ed.), *The Poems of Andrew Marvell*, p. 217.

69 *The Fairfax Library and Archive, Sotheby's Sale Catalogue* (London, 1993), lot 480.

70 P. Major, 'Jumping Josaphat', *Times Literary Supplement* (28 July, 2006), p. 13.

71 BL, Add. MS 25447.

72 I. Gentles, 'Thomas, third baron Fairfax', *Oxford DNB*.

73 Bod., MS Fairfax 40, fos. 1–551. Parts of this volume also appear in BL, Add. MS 11744.

74 *Ibid.*, fos. 616, 618, 628, 633.

75 YML, Typescript of Thomas Fairfax, 'A treatise touching the breeding of horses' (c.1660).

76 Bod., MS Fairfax 40, fo. 612.

Chapter 11

Fairfax and Cromwell

Oliver Cromwell has always personified the English revolution. His name labels the period, submerging other individuals into becoming Cromwellians. Parliamentarians and republicans are frequently defined in relation to him, rendering attempts at comparisons with him problematic and unequal. This is because, as J. C. Davis has suggested, Cromwell has become 'a defining exemplar (for better or for worse) of the national character', and 'a central figure in the shaping of English – and British – historical destinies'.[1] Fairfax was probably more closely involved than any other individual in Cromwell's rise to prominence so the nature of their relationship invites more detailed attention. After an analysis of their wartime relationship, this chapter charts the emergence of depictions of Fairfax as the honest, unwitting tool of Cromwell, questioning this image by focusing in particular upon the occasions when serious differences arose between the two men. The chapter then examines their contrasting impressions upon popular memory before concluding with an assessment of their respective impacts on the English revolution.

I

Fairfax and Cromwell were two of the civil war's most important personalities and both might claim to be the war's most successful general.[2] Until 1649 their careers appear to show remarkable similarities. Yet their backgrounds and wartime experiences contrasted greatly. Thirteen years Fairfax's senior, Cromwell was far less secure in his social status and during the early 1630s he temporarily slipped below the ranks of gentility.[3] Unlike Cromwell, Fairfax was from a family with intense martial traditions. Bred for horsemanship and soldiering, Fairfax travelled abroad and received a military education from Lord Vere, the leading English captain of the age. In contrast Cromwell's soldiering began in 1642 and was largely self-taught. Despite these differences they appear to have formed a close, almost fraternal relationship, built upon shared masculine identities of puritan godliness and military comradeship. From the outset Fairfax perceived himself as the senior partner; his commission under his father both predated and outranked Cromwell's. In some ways Fairfax endured a harder war than Cromwell, sustaining several severe wounds, and, until 1645, usually heavily outnumbered in his engagements. While Cromwell lost his son during the wars, Fairfax lost his father, brother and cousin.

Cromwell's first involvement with Fairfax did not prove an auspicious start. On 23 May 1643, as Newcastle's army was preparing to finish the Fairfaxes, Lord Fairfax specifically requested reinforcement from Cromwell, warning Parliament that otherwise he would 'be forced to accept of dishonourable conditions'.[4] As Fairfax's army was abandoned to face Newcastle alone, Cromwell warned Colchester's corporation that aid for the heavily outnumbered Fairfax needed to be swift. Yet on 2 June 1643 Cromwell signed John Hotham's treacherous letter that claimed Newcastle's army, 'so weak and in such a distraction', was in no condition to defeat the Fairfaxes.[5] This explanation was clearly untrue, so along with other parliamentarian commanders gathered at Nottingham, Cromwell must share the blame for the defeat on Adwalton moor. He can hardly have been comfortable when he first met Sir Thomas Fairfax in Hull on 26 September 1643. Drawing twenty troops of horse out of Hull, Fairfax then accompanied Cromwell south into Lincolnshire. Upon arriving in Boston, Cromwell wept when he found that a consignment of money from East Anglia had not arrived.[6] Yet many of Fairfax's men had fought without pay for a full year. The Fairfaxes had experienced enormous difficulties in raising cavalry, and received no aid from elsewhere in doing so. The geographical areas and social strata that they had controlled and recruited from were not conducive to mustering cavalry. The Pennine urban clothing districts yielded few skilled riders and serviceable horses; at Adwalton moor they fielded only thirteen under-strength troops. Fairfax's few horsemen became exhausted from the continual scouting, patrolling and raiding required against their more numerous and rested enemy counterparts. The Fairfaxes' small base of gentry support hampered cavalry recruitment further. In 1643–4 there were at least twenty-six yeomen and tradesmen serving as captains under the Fairfaxes – many more than under Cromwell. This confounded military theory but until recently its significance has passed unnoticed.[7]

In inspiring their officers to fight without pay and keeping an outnumbered army in the field, the Fairfaxes contrasted sharply with Parliament's other noble generals. Sir William Constable remarked in September 1643 that Lord Fairfax 'is not scanted of officers that have suffered much'. Many such as John Asquith of Leeds had crippled themselves raising troops at their own charges. Others such as Lieutenant Thoresby had received no pay by December 1643, despite having been imprisoned by the enemy.[8] Captain John Hodgson was stripped to his shirt after his capture at Bradford in July 1643, while such was 'the heate of imployemt in the north under ye Lord Fairefax', that John Hudchen claimed that despite being wounded, he had been mutilated by royalists after his surrender.[9]

When Fairfax met Cromwell in September 1643, most of his officers' estates were under enemy control, as were his family residences at York, Denton and Nun Appleton. With the Eastern Association largely free of enemy troops, Cromwell had no such experience. Faced by the royalists' strongest army, the Fairfaxes were compelled to adopt a more demanding strategy. Some newsbooks recognised this; one praised Ferdinando for having 'prosecuted the warre like a politick Generall, and for being too weake to encounter his enemy in the field, he hath frequently assaulted him in his Quarters with good success, and defended the places most considerable, and repulsed the enemy, suffering few of his fast friends to become a prey to the cruell enemy'.[10]

From 1642–4 the Fairfaxes were heavily outnumbered and the heartland of their support was endangered. This dictated what military theorists now call a 'Fabian' strategy, or a 'war of attrition by strategic defence'. Their hopes for victory lay in avoiding conventional battle, hoping that a series of smaller attacks and retreats would surprise, weaken and demoralise Newcastle's army. Their small, incremental victories, such as at Leeds and Wakefield, not only harassed royalist supply and communications, but were intended to build confidence among their forces and protect their supporters' home region from royalist occupation. Their strategy required speed and surprise, civilian support and sustenance, and a bold, aggressive spirit when opportunities occurred.[11] Clarendon described how frustrating this strategy became for the royalists, remarking that the Fairfaxes':

> courage, vigilance and insuperable industry, was not inferior to any who disquieted his Majesty in any part of his dominions, and who pursued any advantage he got further, and recovered any loss he underwent sooner, than any other in the kingdom: So that there were more sharp skirmishes and more notable battles in that one county of York, than in all the Kingdom besides ... the Lord Fairfax and his son with incredible activity reducing towns when they had an army, and when they were defeated in the field, out of small towns recovering new armies.[12]

This strategy changed from September 1643, when Cromwell offered Fairfax his first opportunity to command cavalry on equal terms with the enemy. During the following Lincolnshire campaign Cromwell proved himself an effective and trustworthy ally, a welcome change from Cholmley and the Hothams. After their successful collaborations at Winceby and Marston moor, Fairfax was keen to maintain this relationship and despite the Self-Denying Ordinance he was determined to appoint Cromwell lieutenant-general of the

New Model's cavalry. Fairfax argued for Cromwell's appointment on religious grounds, stressing 'the constant presence and blessing of God that have accompanied him'.[13] Fairfax was attracted by Cromwell's professions of religion and faith in providence, beliefs that Fairfax shared, as well as by Cromwell's record of military successes. There was a political dimension too; as seen in Chapter 3, Cromwell had recently been teller for those MPs voting in favour of Sir John Hotham's execution. Both men shared similar allies in Parliament, and both were committed to a decisive victory over the King before negotiating a settlement. On 10 June 1645, the House of Commons granted Fairfax's request to appoint Cromwell as lieutenant-general and the next day Fairfax summoned Cromwell, remarking: 'you cannot expect but that I make use of so good an advantage as I apprehend this to be to the publick good'. Fairfax added that the enemy 'make their Horse their Confidence. Ours shall be in God.'[14]

Fairfax knew Cromwell would appreciate this last remark. From 1643 both generals had won reputations for piety, godly rhetoric and trust in providence. In his 'Short memorials', Sir Thomas cherished his father's remarks that the victory at Wakefield in 1643 had been 'more a miracle yn a victory; more ye effect of Gods Divine power then Humane force'.[15] Much of the language in his official dispatch to Parliament reporting the victory at Nantwich in January 1644, was echoed in a personal letter to his wife, where he wrote that 'God is to have the glory, who put them so happily into our hands.'[16] Fairfax and Cromwell's language of victory was almost indistinguishable. Both perceived God as an active force in their lives, believing God ordained their victories and that diehard royalists were defying providence. After Naseby Cromwell commended Fairfax to Speaker Lenthall: 'The Generall served you with all faithfulnesse and honour, and the best recommendation I can give him, is, I daresay he attributes all to God, and had rather perish then assume it to himselfe, which is an honest, and a thriving way.'[17] Where Cromwell differed from Fairfax was his readier extension of this rhetoric into politics. Repeatedly during 1647 Cromwell justified controversial political events as occurring through providence. Cromwell's search for signs of God's blessing was the one constant of his political career. Davis has summed up that what set Cromwell apart from Fairfax and Lambert was that for Cromwell 'military activity was always subordinate to the claims of religion and politics and that in both of these spheres he also established claims to pre-eminence'.[18]

Prior to 1649 when Cromwell intervened politically he felt he did so to assist rather than undermine Fairfax. When he granted covert support to Cornet Joyce he was in London while Fairfax was at Bury St Edmunds. Knowing Fairfax was ill, Cromwell probably felt he should ease Fairfax of the burden of giving such an audacious order, confident that Fairfax could be placated afterwards. In March 1648 Cromwell assured Fairfax: 'I putt a high and true valew upon your love, which when I forget I shall cease to be a gratefull and an honest man.'[19] Here Cromwell reflected new Renaissance ideas about the virtues of same-sex friendships, suggesting that they had forged a close, fraternal relationship.[20] Cromwell's high regard extended to Fairfax's family, especially his uncle Charles Fairfax, whom he assured in November 1648: 'Sir I all waies approve of what comes from you.'[21]

II

Memoirists such as Denzil Holles, Richard Baxter and Sir Philip Warwick had other ideas about Fairfax and Cromwell's relationship. To advance their retrospective portrayal of Cromwell as ambitious, corrupted and conspiratorial, Fairfax was consigned to the role of stooge. Clarendon claimed that by April 1647 Cromwell was controlling Fairfax 'purely by his dissimulation, and pretence of conscience and sincerity', effectively replacing him as commander 'though Fayrefax continued general in name'.[22] Denzil Holles also claimed that Fairfax was in thrall to Cromwell and his supporters as 'if he had been hewed out of the block for them, fit for their turns, to do whatever they will have him, without considering, or being able to judge'. He claimed Fairfax knew nothing of Joyce's seizure of the King, because Fairfax 'must have no more than what they are pleased to carve and chew for him'. He described Fairfax's promotion to command all English forces in 1647 as 'otherwise signifying Mr. Oliver Cromwell, of whom Sir Thomas was the shadow'.[23] Although Holles was warped by hatred of Cromwell, other contemporaries reached similar conclusions. In November 1647 one intelligence report commented that Cromwell's 'advice and co-operation have hitherto directed the action of Fairfax'.[24] Richard Baxter reflected that Fairfax was appointed general 'because they supposed to find him a man of no quickness of parts, of no elocution, of no suspicious plotting wit, and therefore one that Cromwell could make use of at his pleasure'. Sir Philip Warwick echoed that Fairfax was a man of 'a very common understanding' and 'of a worse elocution; and so a most fit tool for Mr. Cromwell to work with'.[25] This literary device deflected blame and was intended to exonerate the simpleton or illustrate the deceiver's depth of cunning; it certainly aided retrospective depictions of a conspiratorial Cromwell, commanding events from an early stage.[26]

This image has proved so enduring because it was particularly well suited to explaining the regicide. In September 1648 Cromwell was depicted in *Mercurius pragmaticus* as plotting to make himself great at Fairfax's expense. Soon after, a play portrayed Fairfax as an honourable moderate outwitted by the Machiavellian Cromwell intent on undermining his master's interest in the army.[27] In June 1649 a refined satirical attack upon Cromwell was printed as a mock-up of a sermon Cromwell supposedly preached at Sir Peter Temple's lodgings in Lincoln's Inn Fields. In it, Cromwell described Fairfax as 'fitter farre to bee passive then active in the Affaires of State, hee is fitter for a Charge then a Councell: and the truth is ... he wants braines to doe any thing of moment ... willing allwaies to submit to better judgements then his owne'. This 'Cromwell' added that Fairfax had naively revealed to him that Mr Sedgwick had written to Lady Fairfax advising her to compel her husband to prevent the King's execution. In response on 28 January 1649, 'Cromwell' rode to Fairfax's house with two troops of horse to 'secure him by force'.[28] This account built upon royalist rumours that Cromwell had accused Fairfax of intending to rescue the King and had confined him to his house so that the execution could proceed.[29] It increased Cromwell's culpability and trans-formed Fairfax from the honourable moderate to the dull-witted nonentity represented by Clarendon's remarks: 'out of the stupidity of his soul he was throughout overwitted by Cromwell, and made a property to bring that to pass which could hardly have been otherwise effected'.[30]

The memoirs of Thomas Herbert have also been used to suggest that Fairfax was easily cozened. Immediately after the King's execution, Herbert encoun-tered Fairfax in the Long Gallery at Whitehall and Fairfax supposedly asked him 'how the King did'. Herbert suggested that Fairfax was resolved to prevent the execution by force of arms, but that he had been deliberately distracted with a prayer meeting in Colonel Harrison's apartment when the blow was struck, and was therefore unaware that Charles had been dispatched.[31] This contention seems far–fetched, but David Hume and Anthony Wood elaborated upon it to claim that Harrison had deceived Fairfax, hypocritically passing off news of the King's death as a miraculous answer to their prayers. Such fabrica-tions later annoyed William Godwin and Sir Clements Markham intensely,[32] but Herbert's story supported attempts to accuse Cromwell of deceiving Fairfax over the regicide, thereby mitigating Fairfax's guilt and enhancing Cromwell's culpability. Baxter also held that Cromwell kept Fairfax '(as it was said) in praying and consulting till the stroke was given and it was too late to make resistance'. Baxter explained that Fairfax resigned soon after because he 'would have no more of the honour of being Cromwell's instrument or mask, when he saw he must buy it at so dear a rate'.[33] The clergyman John Thomlinson echoed this explanation, entering it in his diary on 1 November 1718: 'Fairfax, who had the command of the army, was detained by Oliver to seek the Lord in prayer while they took the king's head of[f]. When he came out and enquired after the king etc., he gave up his commission, which was what Oliver Cromwell wanted.'[34] By erroneously presenting his resignation as an immediate response to the regicide, Fairfax was refashioned with stronger royalist principles and less culpability for the regicide. This refashioning also wrongly depicted Fairfax as uninvolved with the foundation of the republic.

While Fairfax was not reduced to being Cromwell's stooge there is little doubt that the King's execution fundamentally transformed their relationship.

Until then Cromwell had been Fairfax's key enforcer in the army with Fairfax expecting Cromwell to support his opposition to regicide. When Cromwell changed his mind so late, Fairfax probably felt betrayed, a notion that subsequently ripened in a troubled mind haunted by the King's death. The regicide corroded Fairfax's authority within the army, isolating him from Cromwell and other key officer–regicides such as Ireton, Okey, Whalley and Harrison. On 11 March 1649 foreign diplomats struggled to gain access to Fairfax 'who was surrounded in his chamber' by many officers. When the ambassadors wished to speak with Fairfax alone, he withdrew with them into another room, but Cromwell reportedly entered soon after with several officers, without permission or 'any act of civility'.[35]

The idea of Fairfax as Cromwell's cipher has a long pedigree but it depends upon a negative view of Cromwell as conspiratorial, devious and ambitious. It distances Fairfax from responsibility for his actions and accepts his 'Short memorial' too much at face value. It draws heavily upon rumours, hostile royalist sources, embittered retrospective commentators and the satirical contemporary press.

As John Morrill has pointed out, the events of 1647 to 1649 were told and retold by the contemporary press, linking the names of Cromwell and Ireton as the true leaders of the army, and fashioning Fairfax as 'their stooge', and 'the other officers their lackeys'.[36] Cromwell and Ireton were far more decisive than Fairfax in shaping the King's fate but Cromwell never questioned Fairfax's status as his superior officer. The image of the puppet Fairfax and the crafty Cromwell have become mutually dependent figures. There is increasing recognition of this among recent historians and a concern not to ascribe to Cromwell too much importance before 1649; among them Davis has highlighted Cromwell's obedience to Fairfax and his strenuous efforts to prevent his resignation.[37] When Cromwell succeeded to command, he inherited what was still essentially Fairfax's army. He emulated Fairfax's style of leadership and was obliged to retain much of his predecessor's practices. These included promotion by seniority rather than through patronage and the tradition of the general engaging in debate with senior officers over important decisions.[38]

When the two men differed, Cromwell frequently could persuade Fairfax, but equally, Bulstrode Whitelocke observed Fairfax overrule Cromwell in councils of war, remarking that although Fairfax talked little, 'he was the only judge', and 'hath ordered things expressly contrary to the judgement of all his council'.[39] The two most significant occasions on which Cromwell failed to persuade Fairfax were the regicide and the projected invasion of Scotland in 1650. Ironically, these are the very episodes so frequently used to illustrate Fairfax's subjection to Cromwell. Lucy Hutchinson recalled that despite rumours to the contrary, Cromwell argued with Fairfax all night to dissuade him from resigning in June 1650.[40] Ludlow remarked that Cromwell said he would rather serve under Fairfax 'than command the greatest army in Europe'.[41] Yet Fairfax remained immovable and his rejection of Cromwell's invitations to sit in the Nominated Assembly and the first Protectorate Parliament indicated further estrangement. Their final disagreement occurred over the duke of Buckingham's imprisonment.[42] In late August 1658, Fairfax, accompanied by his cousin Brian Fairfax, waited on Cromwell at Whitehall to intercede for Buckingham's release, only to receive an infuriating lecture from the ailing Protector. Fairfax walked out, rather rudely as Brian recalled: he 'turned abruptly from him in the gallery at Whitehall, cocking his hat, and throwing his cloak under his arm, as he used to do when he was angry'. Although his story remains plausible, Brian probably exaggerated it to distance Fairfax from Cromwell for a post-Restoration audience. Indeed, he suspiciously referred to Cromwell as Fairfax's 'old acquaintance' rather than friend.[43] The quarrel had clearly arisen because of Buckingham's royalism, not, as the duke later claimed, because Cromwell was jealous of Fairfax's 'greater interest in the Army'.[44]

III

Another contrast in their relationship came in their engagement with popular politics. More secure in his social status than Cromwell, Fairfax feared slipping from it less than Cromwell did. Consequently he appears to have been less alarmed than Cromwell at challenges from social 'inferiors'. Fairfax clearly opposed the Levellers but was not so vilified by them, and does not seem to have dreaded them to the same extent as Cromwell. On occasions, his personal charisma, humility and tact won over groups as disparate as royalists, clubmen and mutineers. When Cromwell impatiently denounced the western clubmen of 1645 as malignants, Fairfax displayed greater political and diplomatic skills to defuse their opposition. Meeting the Dorset clubmen's leaders, he treated them civilly and promised them justice against plunderers in Parliament's forces.[45] Similar contrasts occur between their approaches and reactions to the army mutiny of May 1649. Fairfax often showed himself a stricter disciplinarian than Cromwell, but not in the case of the Burford mutineers. On 12 May 1649 Fairfax published an astute declaration that tackled these mutineers' grievances and expressed considerable enthusiasm for the republic. It approved the regicide as 'that great act of justice which was by good men so called for', praised the abolition of the House of Lords and assured the mutineers that their concerns would be addressed. He promised nobody would be forced to serve in Ireland and that proposals were in hand for a new and more representative Parliament. He offered pardon to all who returned to obedience, but threatened force against those who defied providence by continuing in mutiny.[46]

So many mutineers still held such personal respect for Fairfax that this declaration crumbled their resolve. Colonel Whalley's regiment sought to demonstrate their loyalty by replacing their sea-green Leveller ribbons with blue – Fairfax's colour. When Scroop's regiment mutinied at Salisbury on 10 May, they declared 'their esteem and respects to my Lord General, but for any other they had nothing to say to them'.[47] Fairfax was prepared to negotiate with the mutineers. On 12 May he pleaded: 'when did I ever refuse you, in referring any just desire of the Armies to the Parliament?' On 13 May he argued they had been 'abused' by 'false suggestions'. He appointed the former Leveller Major Francis White to treat with them on his behalf. However, these negotiations were primarily intended to sow dissension among the mutineers; despite Cromwell's pledge not to pursue with force, the generals closed in upon the mutineers rapidly.[48] Having covered forty-five miles, Fairfax's force entered Burford at midnight on 14/15 May, capturing most of the surprised mutineers with minimal resistance.

Ian Gentles has contrasted the reactions of Fairfax and Cromwell to this episode. To Cromwell, crushing the mutiny was a triumphant relief, 'like waking from a bad dream'. Blaming the likes of John Lilburne, Cromwell believed reports that if the Levellers had gained control of the army, all government would have been dissolved, clergy and lawyers murdered, and all men's estates apportioned 'by way of Community'. In contrast, Fairfax acknowledged the mutineers as his soldiers, 'understood their frustration and recognised the justice of many of their demands'.[49] After threatening the mutineers with death, Fairfax became inclined to mercy, moved by their sorrow and submission. Although they had numbered several hundred, he made an example of just three: Cornet Thompson, Corporal Perkins and Corporal Church. They were shot in Burford churchyard on 17 May. Cromwell was intent on executing another, Cornet Denne, but Fairfax overruled him.[50] Fairfax ensured little punitive action was taken against the rest; they were even given debentures for their pay arrears.[51]

Dismayed that his army had divided against itself, Fairfax asked Major White how the mutineers' 'affections were towards him'. White replied that they had spoken well of Fairfax and that the affair might have been resolved without violence. This saddened Fairfax, but it angered Cromwell who reprimanded White, saying he should be 'ashamed to inform my Lord things so ridiculous, as to talk of a composure'.[52] Fairfax's report to Speaker Lenthall reflected regret, a sense that such an affair should never be permitted to recur, and that the Rump should learn from it to settle the republic 'upon foundations of Justice and Righteousness'.[53] He urged Parliament to aid the deluded poor so 'they may see you will improve your power for their good, and then your Enemies shall be found lyars'. A little later he wrote of his hopes that 'unity will be the subject of every mans desires'.[54] As Peter Gaunt has pointed out, amid the annual commemorations still held at Burford it is often forgotten that the executed mutineers 'were sacrificed by Fairfax to the cause of army discipline, not by Cromwell to an alleged conservative reaction'.[55]

IV

The remainder of this chapter will briefly consider how Cromwell's name has largely eclipsed Fairfax from popular memory. The nineteenth-century renewal of interest in the parliamentary cause reflected by Thomas Carlyle focused on Cromwell, and Carlyle did not consider Fairfax as worthy of much comment.[56] While some oral memories of Fairfax survived, most were restricted to Yorkshire. Among them was the recollection of Jacob Sands. Aged ninety in 1800 Sands claimed his grandfather opened the gate for Fairfax at Oakwell Hall after Adwalton moor and offered him directions. Fairfax supposedly hid from royalist pursuers in 'Black Tom's well' at Newton Kyme. Around 1900 locals still claimed the well was haunted and that no one could be sure Fairfax was buried at Bilbrough. On Halloween, Fairfax's ghost is said to gallop down the avenue of trees at Newton Kyme.[57] Yet even in Fairfax's West Riding heartlands, the phrase 'in Oliver's days' became a nineteenth-century term for times of exceptional prosperity.[58] In John Nicholson's play for Bradford's theatre, *The siege of Bradford*, one character referred to Fairfax in 1643 as 'Cromwell's general'.[59] Cromwell, not Fairfax, stood in statuary or stained glass in the nonconformist chapels of Bradford, Leeds and Harrogate, while Bradford's own dramatic history was forgotten by the *Bradford Observer*'s report in 1845 that Cromwell had armed 'the people' against 'the divine right of the nobility'. Early nineteenth-century romantic Cromwellianism was embedded in Fairfax's home parish of Otley, where Walter Fawkes of Farnley Hall collected civil war relics that allegedly included swords belonging to Fairfax, Lambert and Cromwell, along with Cromwell's hat and Fairfax's chair. Yet it was Cromwell that Fawkes was keenest to celebrate, commenting that 'there are Cromwells in all lands and ages'.[60] Likewise, the antiquarian Norrison Scatcherd of Morley heaped admiration upon Cromwell for the victory at Dunbar, 'the most glorious of his incomparable feats'. Scatcherd relished how Cromwell sang Psalm sixty-eight on the field, forgetting that Fairfax's armed ministers had done so before only four miles away at the taking of Leeds in 1643.[61]

Glenn Foard's study of the commemoration of Naseby reveals how Cromwell's name has dominated the battle's memory both locally and nationally. One explanation for this was the strong identification of later nineteenth-century nonconformists and radical politicians with Cromwell's name. When Joseph Arch, leader of the Agricultural Labourer's Union, spoke at a political rally at Naseby in 1876 he was introduced as 'Our Cromwell'.[62] Yet outside the world of dissenters and political radicals, the memory of Cromwell held most deeply in the popular psyche is that of Cromwell the destroyer: demolisher of castles and desecrator of churches. John Byng remarked in 1781 that 'Whenever I enquire about ruins, I always get the same answer, that it was some popish place and destroyed by Oliver Cromwell.' Almost every English parish church claims that Cromwell stabled his horses there or damaged the building. This legendary Cromwell personifies the parliamentary cause as iconoclastic, destructive of heritage, an aberration from English good sense, unfairly embracing the deeds and attitudes of many of Cromwell's fellow parliamentarians.[63]

In contrast to Cromwell the destroyer, Fairfax is often remembered as a preserver. This partially accounts for Cromwell's memory overshadowing Fairfax's in folklore and tradition; villains are remembered longer and more intensely than champions of moderation. Flora Thompson's *Lark Rise to Candleford* described how Oxfordshire mothers threatened naughty children with 'Old Crumell'll have 'ee'. Even in twentieth-century England, children have been brought up to hate Cromwell.[64] In contrast, the Fairfaxes enjoyed a reputation as preservers of culture and guardians of the estates of defeated royalists. After York's surrender, in July 1644, the corporation thanked Lord Fairfax with 'a butt of sack and a tunn of French wine' for 'the great love and affection he hath shewed to the Citty'. The surrender articles prohibited the defacement of churches and left the administration of justice to the city's magistrates.[65] One puritan minister addressed a poetical dedication of Fairfax to Sir Thomas Widdrington, that Ferdinando:

> Did save our Minster too, Lantherne restore
> Both rescued from ye Caledonian Boar.[66]

Sir Thomas Fairfax was held to have saved the Minster's windows by taking them down for safekeeping soon after York's surrender. In 1700 Samuel Gale praised Sir Thomas Fairfax for this 'Honourable and Noble Act', while James Torre concurred in 1719 by lauding the 'generous and tender regard' of Lord Fairfax, for 'his saving the City, as well as its Cathedral'. In 1932 the twelfth baron Fairfax unveiled a tablet commemorating this in the Minster's Chapter House. Sir Thomas ensured that Roger Dodsworth was permitted to transcribe the monastic records in St Mary's Tower, York, before that building was exploded.[67] Sir Thomas is remembered as 'merciful and civilized' for saving Oxford's treasures after its surrender, for which his name is commemorated on a monument in the Bodleian. John Aubrey remarked that Fairfax 'was a lover of learning', who guarded the Bodleian well, adding that the royalist garrison had caused more damage than Fairfax's men. Recently, *The Guardian* newspaper contrasted Fairfax's care for cultural treasures with the American capture of Baghdad in 2003. Fairfax later donated valuable manuscripts to Oxford University, and in 1674 a Latin verse honoured him among its patrons.[68] For all these reasons, Fairfax is often remembered as an opposite of Cromwell: restrained, moderate, decent, a preserver rather than destroyer. As seen in Chapter 4, some royalists surprisingly even attempted to explain away Fairfax's severity at Colchester.

Until 1649 the similarities between Fairfax and Cromwell are more striking than their differences. Both began their military service as cavalry commanders and went on to generate successful reputations as generals. Both were consumed with concern for signs of God's providence and both were inclined to tolerate a broader range of 'godly' protestant religious opinion than many of their contemporaries. Both were fully embedded in the factional politics within the parliamentary cause, sharing connections in the 'war party' and among Westminster's political Independents. From 1645 to 1649 their careers were so interwoven that for a time they became mutually dependent figures. Cromwell and the parliamentarian cause needed Fairfax as the military figurehead popular with the soldiers. Increasingly reticent in political matters, Fairfax depended on Cromwell as his closest deputy, key enforcer and political man of business in the army. Both men were concerned to stifle political radicalism and social levelling, although Fairfax did not attract the same intense enmity from frustrated radicals as Cromwell. The two men appear to have developed a close friendship that was only shattered by Cromwell's eleventh-hour decision to support the execution of the King. With Fairfax unable to fully reconcile himself to this revolutionary act, contemporary commentators naturally considered his subordinate had somehow duped him. Like these contemporaries, historians have rightly been preoccupied with Cromwell because he went on to become head of state in 1653. Owing to this prominence, in the popular imagination Cromwell has personified many of the most negative aspects of the parliamentary cause, whereas Fairfax, opting for withdrawal and retirement, has rightly or wrongly been considered a champion of decency, moderation and a very English disdain for revolutionary politics.

NOTES

1 J. C. Davis, *Oliver Cromwell* (London, 2001), p. 1.

2 Alfred Burne considered Fairfax a considerably superior general to Cromwell: A. H. Burne, 'Generalship in the first civil war, 1642–1644', *History Today*, 1 (1951), 63–9.

3 B. Coward, *Oliver Cromwell* (Harlow, 1991), pp. 11–12.

4 E. Peacock, 'On some civil war documents relating to Yorkshire', *YAJ*, 1 (1870), 102.

5 T. Carlyle (ed.), *Oliver Cromwell's letters and speeches: with elucidations* (London, 3rd edn, 1857), vol. 1. pp. 120–1; BL, Add. MS 18979, fo. 141r.

6 J. Rushworth, *Historical collections* (London, 1721), part 3, vol. 2, p. 280; Coward, *Cromwell*, pp. 30–1.

7 J. Jones, 'The war in the north: the northern parliamentary army in the English civil war, 1642–1645' (Ph.D. thesis, York University, Canada, 1991), pp. 242–3; I. Gentles, 'The civil

wars in England', in J. Kenyon and J. Ohlmeyer (eds), *The Civil Wars: A Military History of England, Scotland, and Ireland, 1638–1660* (Oxford, 1998), p. 110.

8 BL, Egerton MS 2647, fo. 211; TNA, SP 28/265/57–65; 'Extracts from a manuscript book written or possessed by Ralph Thoresby' (Publications of the Thoresby Society, 28, 1923), p. 433.

9 J. H. Turner (ed.), *The autobiography of Captain John Hodgson of Coley Hall, near Halifax* (Brighouse, 1882), p. 25; TNA, SP 19/84/28.

10 BL, E85(9), *Speciall passages*, 10–17 January (London, 1643), p. 189.

11 S. D. M. Carpenter, *Military Leadership in the British Civil Wars, 1642–1651: 'The Genius of this Age'* (London, 2005), pp. 59, 63–4, 75.

12 Clarendon, *History of the rebellion and civil wars in England*, ed. W. Dunn Macray (Oxford, 1888), vol. 3, p. 102n.

13 C. Hill, *God's Englishman: Oliver Cromwell and the English Revolution* (London, 1970), p. 132.

14 Coward, *Cromwell*, p. 39; Rushworth, *Historical collections*, part 4, vol. 1, p. 39.

15 Bod., MS Fairfax 36, fo. 8r; YML, CWT, 43–05–29, *A fuller relation of that miraculous victory which it pleased God to give unto the parliaments forces under the command of the right honourable Lord Fairefax, against the earle of New-castles army at Wakefield in Yorkshire* (London, 1643), pp. 4–5.

16 *Captain Stewart's MS*, HMC, 10th report, part 4 (London, 1885), p. 65; R. Bell (ed.), *The Fairfax correspondence: memorials of the civil war* (London, 1849), vol. 1, pp. 74–5.

17 BL, E288(26), *An ordinance of the Lords and Commons assembled in Parliament*, 17 June (London, 1645), p. 1.

18 Davis, *Cromwell*, p. 111.

19 BL, Sloane MS 1519, fo. 158.

20 E. A. Foyster, *Manhood in Early Modern England: Honour, Sex and Marriage* (Harlow, 1999), p. 126.

21 BL, Add. MS 36996, fo. 131.

22 Clarendon, *History of the rebellion and civil wars in England*, ed. Dunn Macray, vol. 4, pp. 219–24.

23 D. Holles, 'Memoirs of Denzil, Lord Holles, Baron of Ifield in Sussex from the year 1641 to 1648', in F. Maseres (ed.), *Select tracts relating to the civil wars in England* (London, 1815), pp. 188, 210, 246, 287.

24 A. B. Hinds (ed.), *Calendar of State Papers Venetian, 1647–1652* (London, 1927), p. 30.

25 R. Baxter, *The Autobiography of Richard Baxter*, ed. N. H. Keeble (London, 1974), p. 46; P. Warwick, *Memoires of the reign of King Charles I with a continuation to the happy restauration of King Charles II* (London, 1701), p. 246.

26 B. Worden, *Roundhead Reputations: The English Civil War and the Passions of Posterity* (London, 2001), pp. 236, 324.

27 BL, E462(8), *Mercurius pragmaticus*, 29 August–5 September (London, 1648); University of Cambridge Library, Wing 491:33, *The famous tragedie of King Charles I basely butchered* (London, 1649), p. 20.

28 BL, E561(10), *A most learned, conscientious, and devout-exercise; held forth the last Lords-day, at Sir Peter Temples, in Lincolnes-Inne-Fields*, 25 June (London, 1649), pp. 7–8.

29 T. Carte (ed.), *A collection of original letters and papers, concerning the affairs of England from the year 1641 to 1660. Found among the duke of Ormonde's papers* (London, 1739), vol. 1, p. 212.

30 Clarendon, *History of the rebellion and civil wars in England*, ed. Dunn Macray, vol. 4, p. 487.

31 T. Herbert, *Memoirs of the last two years of the reign of King Charles I* (London, 1813), p. 194.

32 W. Godwin, *History of the commonwealth of England* (London, 1824), vol. 2, p. 681; Markham, p. 351.

33 Baxter, *Autobiography*, p. 66.

34 J. C. Hodgson (ed.), 'The diary of Rev. John Thomlinson', *Six North Country Diaries* (Surtees Society, 118, 1910), p. 145.

35 Hinds (ed.), *Calendar of State Papers Venetian 1647–1652*, p. 90.

36 J. Morrill, 'Cromwell and his contemporaries', in J. Morrill (ed.), *Oliver Cromwell and the English Revolution* (Harlow, 1990), p. 263.

37 Davis, *Cromwell*, pp. 90–1, 96.

38 S. R. Gardiner, *History of the commonwealth and protectorate, 1649–60* (London, 1894), vol. 1, p. 288; A. Woolrych, 'Cromwell as a soldier', in Morrill (ed.), *Oliver Cromwell and the English Revolution*, p. 104; A. Marshall, *Oliver Cromwell, Soldier: The Military Life of a Revolutionary at War* (London, 2004), p. 280.

39 B. Whitelocke, *Memorials of English affairs* (Oxford, 1853), vol. 2, p. 20.

40 L. Hutchinson, *Memoirs of the Life of Colonel Hutchinson*, ed. N. H. Keeble (London, 1995), p. 241.

41 C. H. Firth (ed.), *The memoirs of Edmund Ludlow* (Oxford, 1894), vol. 1, p. 243.

42 A. Woolrych, *Commonwealth to Protectorate* (Oxford, 1982), pp. 138–9; B. D. Henning (ed.), *The House of Commons, 1660–1690* (London, 1983), vol. 2, p. 292.

43 B. Fairfax, *A catalogue of the curious pictures of George Villiers, duke of Buckingham, in which is included the valuable collection of Sir Peter Paul Rubens with the life of George Villiers, duke of Buckingham, the celebrated poet written by Brian Fairfax, esq* (London, 1758), p. 31.

44 BL, Egerton MS 2146, fo. 45.

45 Marshall, *Cromwell*, p. 154; Rushworth, *Historical collections*, part 4, vol. 1, pp. 52–3.

46 BL, E555(6), *A declaration from his excellencie with the advice of his councel of war concerning the present distempers of part of Commissary Generall Iretons and of Colonel Scroops Regiments*, 12 May (London, 1649), pp. 4–6.

47 BL, E555(16), *The moderate*, 8–15 May (London, 1649).

48 BL, E574(26), Francis White, *A true relation of the proceedings in the business of Burford*, 27 September (London, 1649), pp. 1–5.

49 BL, E530(25), *Perfect occurrences*, 25 May–1 June (London, 1649), p. 1054; I. Gentles, *The New Model Army in England, Ireland and Scotland, 1645–1653* (Oxford, 1992), p. 349.

50 BL, E556(1), *A declaration of the proceedings of his excellency the lord general Fairfax in the reducing of the revolted troops*, 23 May (London, 1649), pp. 10–15.

51 A. Woolrych, *Britain in Revolution, 1625–1660* (Oxford, 2002), p. 447.

52 BL, E574(26), *A true relation*, p. 8.

53 Bod., MS Tanner 56, fo. 40.

54 BL, E555(27), *A full narrative of all the proceedings betweene his excellency the Lord Fairfax and the mutineers*, 18 May (London, 1649), p. 2; BL, E530(28), *A perfect diurnall*, 28 May–4 June (London, 1649), p. 2544.

55 P. Gaunt, *Oliver Cromwell* (Oxford, 1996), p. 111.

56 Carlyle (ed.), *Oliver Cromwell's letters and speeches*, vol. 1, p. 163.

57 J. W. Walker (ed.), *Our local portfolio* (Halifax Reference Library: extracts from *Halifax Guardian*, 1856–62), p. 5; H. Speight, *Lower Wharfedale* (London, 1902), p. 364; G. B. Wood, *Yorkshire Villages* (London, 1971), p. 122.

58 A. Smith, 'The image of Cromwell in folklore and tradition', *Folklore*, 79 (1968), 20.

59 J. Nicholson, *The poetical works of John Nicholson: the Airedale poet, carefully edited from the original editions with additional notes and a sketch of his life and writings by W. G. Hird* (London, 1876), p. 365.

60 Worden, *Roundhead Reputations*, pp. 248, 250, 306; M. Sharples, 'The Fawkes-Turner connection and the art collection at Farnley Hall, Otley, 1792–1937', *Northern History*, 26 (1990), 136.

61 BL, Add. MS 41071, fo. 36; BL, E88(23), *The rider of the white horse and his army* (London, 1643), p. 6.

62 G. Foard, *Naseby: The Decisive Campaign* (Barnsley, 2004), pp. 342–88.

63 Smith, 'The image of Cromwell', 23, 26, 38; *The Observer*, 27 February 2005.

64 Smith, 'The image of Cromwell', 18, 32.

65 City of York Archives, House Books B36, fos. 102–3.

66 BL, Add. MS 11743, fo. 21r.

67 J. Spraggon, *Puritan Iconoclasm during the English Civil War* (Woodbridge, 2003), p. 192; P. Wenham, *The Siege of York, 1644* (York, 1994), pp. 92–3, 118; T. Gent, *The Ancient and Modern History of the Ancient City of York* (York, 1730), pp. 54–5.

68 Bod., MS Aubrey 8, fo. 60r; Bod., MS Fairfax 32, fos. 145–6; Markham, p. 445.

Conclusion

———◆———

The 'Short memorials' and the battle for the memory of Black Tom

The battle for the memory of Black Tom Fairfax began even before he was interred at Bilbrough church near York on 22 November 1671. His funeral sermon was given by Richard Stretton, a Presbyterian minister who had been his personal chaplain since the Restoration. Stretton knew Fairfax extremely well and had been allowed to read much of the general's writing, including his manuscript memoirs, the 'Short memorials'. Stretton's sermon was based on Acts 13:36 and its theme was how Fairfax had served his generation according to the will of God. Stretton made no apologies to royalists for Fairfax's civil war conduct and he immediately tackled Fairfax's role in the King's execution. He orated that Fairfax 'ever had a high esteem and reverence for his Majesty of Blessed Memory, King Charles the 1st, and always thought him the mirror of the Princes of his age. I have often heard him sadly bewail the misapprehensions ... that that excellent Prince had of him.' Stretton was concerned to distance Fairfax further from the unnamed regicides: 'As for the horrible act of theirs in murthering of their sovereign he ever detested it, and used all the means that possibly he could for the preventing of it.' Stretton even claimed Fairfax had told him that his brooding over the King's fate worsened his health more than the wounds he endured in the wars. Stretton then reminded his audience of Fairfax's vital role in the Restoration, and how the many others who claimed credit for it would scarcely have prospered without him.[1]

Having asserted Fairfax's innocence of regicide, Stretton praised him as a paragon of puritan civic virtue. Supposedly, Fairfax had 'served his generation according to the will of God', with faith, piety, modesty, benevolence, generosity and love of learning. Despite his entire public career being based on military service, Stretton commemorated him as a man of peace. He nevertheless aggressively defended Fairfax's memory from his enemies. Stretton's censures of the Restoration regime and vengeful royalists were scarcely veiled; he declared it was 'a great trouble and a presage more, when God takes away such men of honour and integrity in such a corrupt age. If there be any such vile and degenerate spirit, as can make this subject of our lamentation an occasion of rejoicing let them see their sin and folly.'[2]

I

Fairfax intended to shape his own memory, at least among his own family, by writing two brief memoirs during the 1660s in his own hand. The first was entitled 'Short memorials of some things to be cleared during my command in the Army'. Its style was awkward, stilted and brief, running to only nine sides. In it, he explained his conduct, as Gardiner succinctly observed, 'not as it had actually been, but as he fancied it ought to have been'.[3] The audience of Fairfax's 'Short memorials', to some extent, was himself. He denied responsibility for the revolutionary events of 1647–9, but encountered difficulties in explaining his involvement in the purge, regicide and republic. The second memorial was entitled: 'A Short Memoriall of ye Northerne Actions during the war there, from the yeare 1642 Till the yeare 1644'. This was a happier affair for him; it was twice as long, ran to seventeen sides, and reflected upon his northern campaigns of 1642–4 with a pride that his modesty struggled to suppress. According to his cousin Brian, Fairfax did not intend the 'Short memorials' to be published, but rather 'to remain for the Satisfaction of his own Relations'.[4] Fairfax intended the memorials to assist his family's defence of their honour on occasions when his memory and reputation proved troublesome.

At least four manuscript versions of these memorials survive. Markham identified the version now held at Yale University to be the original, in Fairfax's own hand, while the British Library now holds the copied manuscript Brian Fairfax prepared for publication, with his erasures sometimes indicated. However, another autograph version survives in the Bodleian Library, which is also in Fairfax's own hand. This is the version favoured by recent scholars and it is the one that at present can be most reliably cited although a very similar manuscript copy, suggested by John Adamson to be the original, is held in the Clark Memorial Library, Los Angeles.[5]

There is no doubt that the 'Short memorials' were the product of a tired and troubled mind, and a recent student of Fairfax's politics has aptly described them as a 'self-inflicted wound'.[6] Fairfax was writing around twenty years after the times he described. Horace Walpole remarked: 'One can easily believe his having been the tool of Cromwell, when one sees, by his own memoirs, how little idea he had of what he had been about.'[7] He was either unable or unwilling to recall his role in specific events and offered excuses rather than explanations. His aim in writing the first memorial was to blame treacherous officers, agitators and a 'levelling faction' for the purge of Parliament, the

King's death and establishment of the republic. Few historians today would accept this case. Still fewer would credit his claim that from the time of Triploe Heath onwards he never gave his free consent to anything the army did, and that the agitators set his name to their papers without his permission: 'So here, hath a Generalls power beene broken & Crumbled into a Levelling Faction.' In a blatant falsehood he claimed that his officers 'were placed & Displaced by ye will of ye new Agitators, who with violence so carried all things as it was above my power to Restraine it'. These passages suggest he may even have deluded himself into accepting such untruths. He even appropriated the language which had been used against him and his soldiers by his enemies; he claimed that he stalled the soldiers' first petition for their arrears at Nottingham in 1646, by his 'Cutting off of Hydrays Head'.[8] Moving swiftly from the King's death to his resignation, he neglected to mention his role in establishing the republic and gave no explanation for why he did not resign his command until seventeen months after the King's execution. This set the agenda for future sympathetic commemorations of him, all of which passed over this period in silence.

Despite Fairfax's wishes, in 1698 his cousin Brian began considering publishing the 'Short memorials' and secured the consent of Thomas, fifth baron Fairfax for the enterprise. Brian wrote an epistle dedicatory for them on 22 April 1699 in which he explained that although the fifth baron never consented to copies being taken, some imperfect ones had fallen into the hands of an editor who had recently published another civil war memoir, 'wherein his Lordship is scarce ever Nam'd but with Reproach'. Brian was almost certainly referring to the memoirs of Denzil Holles which were also published that year; the publisher's note of Holles's memoirs had intimated that a similar publication concerning Fairfax was 'in good hands', and was hoped to 'be shortly exposed to public view'. Holles's memoirs were scornful of Fairfax and compared him unfavourably with the earl of Essex. Holles suggested that within the army Cromwell 'was to have the power, Sir Thomas Fairfax only the name, of General; he to be the figure, the other the cypher'. Brian Fairfax tackled this directly in his epistle dedicatory, declaring that his cousin had governed the army 'not as a Cypher, but with great Prudence and Conduct'.[9]

Both Fairfax and Holles's memoirs were Whig publications. Reflecting a 1690s' Whig view of the civil wars, they warned of the dangers of military tyranny. Holles's publisher remarked that his memoirs were to honour those who 'took up arms, not to destroy the King, or alter the Constitution, but to restore the last, and oblige the former to rule according to the Law'.[10] These publications followed John Toland's recent editions of Algernon Sidney's *Discourses concerning government* and Edmund Ludlow's *Memoirs* in 1698. The latter of these had been extensively rewritten by Toland, and was intended to remind its audience that liberty was incompatible with a large standing army.

It spearheaded a literary campaign against the Whig Junto for abandoning true Whig principles.[11] The publication of Fairfax's *Short memorials* the following year suggests that Brian Fairfax may well have been writing from a similar standpoint. In 1987 Austin Woolrych hinted that 'the gross inaccuracies and confusions' in Fairfax's published *Short memorials* threw doubt over how much of them was Fairfax's own work.[12] Woolrych was right to be suspicious.

In his epistle dedicatory Brian Fairfax attempted to use his cousin's military reputation, humility and modesty to rescue his memory from the taints of regicide and revolution. He had a delicate task to balance these conflicting concerns. He sought to absolve his cousin from complicity in the King's death, but to defend him from charges of having been Cromwell's pawn. Brian claimed his edition was printed from the originals in his cousin's own hand, left by the general in his study at Denton 'without any Material Alterations from the Original, but only by placing them in the natural order of Time'. Brian did not rewrite them to the extent that Ludlow's memoirs and Baxter's autobiography were altered, both of which Blair Worden points out were adjusted to 'reduce their religious dimension' for a 1690s' audience.[13] Nevertheless, he did significantly alter the *Short memorials*. He shortened and removed the religious language in the original manuscript. He chose to omit his cousin's very first sentences of the 'Short memorials of some things to be cleared during my command in the Army.' These lines resounded with a providential puritanism that Brian deemed unsuitable for an eighteenth-century commemoration of Fairfax:

> Now when God is visiting ye Nation for ye Transgressions of their ways; As formerly he did to our sort of men, so doth he it to another sort; so that all may see their errors & his Justice. And as we have cause to Implore his Mercy, having sinned against him, so must we still vindicate his Justice, who is always cleare when he Judgeth.[14]

Similarly, Brian excluded this first sentence of Fairfax's memorial of the northern war, deeming it unsuitable: 'I did not think to have taken up my pen any more to have written on this subject, but yt my silence seemed to accuse me of ingratitude to God.'[15] Brian was anxious to protect his cousin from charges of having gloried in rebellion, and Fairfax's outpourings of puritan piety were carefully removed from the published version, along with anything remotely critical of kingship.

In explaining his supposed eclipse from power by the army agitators, Fairfax claimed that 'in to such failings all authority may fall'. Attempting to mitigate his perceived faults, he remarked that other powers had also failed the people: 'sometimes Kingly Authority may be abused to their, & ye Kingdoms pr[e]judice; sometimes under a parliamentary Authority, much injury hath been done'. Brian excised Fairfax's remark about abuse of kingly power while allowing the remark about injuries inflicted by parliamentary authority to remain.[16] This piece of editing served two purposes: it denounced the 1690s' Junto Whigs as well as shielding his cousin from his own anti-royalism. Brian also eliminated the concluding passage from the published version. This is so important because it contained the very core of Fairfax's defence of his parliamentarian allegiance:

> Hoping also that God will, one day, cleere this Action we undertooke so far as concerns his honour, & ye integrity of such as faithfully served in it; For I cannot believe yt such wonderfull successes shall be given in vaine. Though cunning & Deceitfull men must take shame to ymselves, yet ye purposes & Determinations of God shall have happy effects to his Glory, and the Comfort of his people.[17]

Here, Fairfax's providential protestantism was struggling to reconcile his army's many battlefield victories with the parliamentarian coalition's failure to provide a stable settlement and godly reformation. He was not alone in his confusion; many puritans in the 1660s struggled to understand why God had shown them such mercies to no avail.[18] With his faith in providence and the English people challenged, Fairfax responded in the same way as he did to the King's execution; he attributed it to the will of God, and soldiered on in the hope that God would once more smile upon his chosen people. Surely Fairfax would have been distraught had he known that his cousin felt such a crucial passage unworthy of inclusion in the published version.

Even in the less politically sensitive narrative of his northern campaigns, Brian felt some of his cousin's remarks should not be included in his published edition. The general wrote of his defeat at Adwalton moor: 'But yn, agn:, it pleased God to mix water with our wine, & to bringe us into a better Condition by ye Brinks of Ruine & Destruction.' Brian felt this providential explanation out of place in the published edition; it was erased along with his cousin's remembrance of the royalist Colonel Skirton as 'A wild & Desperate man'.[19] Fairfax's remarks concerning his military nadir were also withheld from publication. Fairfax described his exhausted ride from Bradford to Hull after having been in the saddle for over forty hours. He had been shot in the wrist and his clothes were reduced to rags with sweat and blood. He had seen his wife captured by the enemy and his little daughter left for dead in a farmhouse along the way. His thankfulness for God's mercy in preserving him and his family, expressed in Biblical terms, was also excised by his cousin:

> Considering wch, In all Humility & Reverence I may say I was in Jobs Condition wn he said, naked came I ought of my mothers womb, & naked shall I returne thither, The Ld gave, ye Ld gave, & ye Ld hath taken away, blessed be ye name of ye Ld. But, God, who is a God of mercy & Consolation, doth not always leave us in Distresse.[20]

To aid him in writing the epistle dedicatory, Brian borrowed a copy of

Fairfax's funeral sermon from Richard Stretton, and on 10 November 1698, transcribed his own copy from it.[21] He drew heavily from Stretton's passage about Fairfax during the 1650s, rewording it to stress how Fairfax spent that decade 'earnestly wishing and praying for the Restitution of the Royal Family' and how this 'made him always lookt upon with a jealous eye by the Usurpers of that time'.[22] Both men knew that Fairfax abstained from royalist conspiracy throughout the 1650s, but their refashioning of his image advanced suggestions that this was not so.

Another prime concern of Fairfax's 'Short memorials' was the preservation of his reputation as a successful general. In commemorating his first campaigns, Fairfax did this at the expense of others. In 1643 he became preoccupied with fears of treachery among his fellow officers. When Sir Thomas headed the committee at Hull to seek out traitors and turncoats, he arrested one of its members, Captain Bladen, for giving intelligence to the enemy.[23] Fears of treachery during the Fairfaxes' defence of Hull led to the arrest of Major-General John Gifford for having received letters that attempted to persuade him to change sides. After the Fairfaxes, Gifford was the highest ranking soldier in their army. A professional soldier from Darlington, he had held an important command during the bishops' wars before serving under the Hothams from March to December 1642.[24] Despite having forged the Fairfaxes' Yorkshire infantry, he was stripped of command on 3 October 1643 and sent to the Tower of London. Wittily described by *Mercurius aulicus* as the only soldier the Fairfaxes had, he was still awaiting trial in June 1644, but was eventually exonerated when Lord Fairfax signed his arrears claim on 27 February 1646.[25] Gifford subsequently served in Ireland and became captain of Cromwell's lifeguard, but Sir Thomas Fairfax ignored this in his 'Short memorials' and chose to blame Adwalton moor on 'some ill affected officers, chiefly Major Gen: Gyffard'. He blamed Gifford for delaying their deployment which was 'not without some suspition of Trechery'. Having explained that Gifford commanded the left wing at Adwalton, Fairfax then altered his account to claim that Gifford commanded the reserves that failed to intervene. In referring to similar royalist recriminations after Marston moor, P. R. Newman remarked that 'stories such as this should always be treated with the gravest suspicion as indicating less a reality than a frame of mind among the defeated'.[26] Twenty years later, for all Fairfax's studied modesty, he remained a jealous guardian of his military reputation. His story successfully deflected blame for the defeat and was readily accepted by other memoirists and antiquarians.[27] When explaining other reverses in his 'Short memorials', Fairfax again blamed subordinates rather than accept responsibility. John Hodgson recollected that the defeat on Seacroft moor arose from Fairfax's mistake, but Fairfax's memoirs blamed his soldiers for their own capture, claiming they were 'careless in Keeping Order' and desperate for drink 'being an exceeding hot Day'. In July 1643 with his infantry besieged in Bradford, encircled by an enemy host over ten times larger, including thousands of cavalry, he again blamed subordinates. While he broke out with a few horsemen leaving his garrison to its fate, Fairfax gave Colonel Rogers the impossible task of extricating the infantry from the encircled town. To assuage his guilt at abandoning them, he explained their capture by accusing Rogers of 'a cowardly Fear'. Such remarks surely underline Newman's observation that 'Sir Thomas Fairfax was partial to blaming everyone and anyone if he were ever discomfited.'[28] This was especially the case when the defence of his military reputation was at stake at a time when there was little else he had left. Again, concerning Marston moor Fairfax's 'Short memorials' played down the rout of his wing of cavalry so effectively that Alfred Burne believed that Fairfax was the allied general who did most to win the battle.[29]

II

Differing commemorations of Fairfax have been driven by rival memories of the civil wars and contrasting political and religious identities. The Fairfax family's continued friendliness to protestant dissenters and opposition to Stuart absolutism maintained some of the principles of their famous forbear. By the 1680s they were firm Whigs. Fairfax's memory was long cherished by Yorkshire dissenters who appropriated his principles and qualities to their identities, from late seventeenth-century admirers such as Ralph Thoresby, Oliver Heywood and Jonathan Priestley, through to the Victorian antiquaries Joseph Hunter, Norrison Scatcherd and John Horsfall Turner. In contrast, royalist and Tory memories saw him as the weak-willed man who failed to save Charles I and prevent Cromwellian tyranny.

Fairfax's successors honoured his memory by emulating their perception of his politics. His cousin Henry succeeded him as fourth baron in 1671. Henry was regarded as the leader of Yorkshire's Presbyterians and became a leading Whig in all three Exclusion Parliaments. He received much support from dissenters and courted the votes of Sheffield's cutlers, complained of as 'sectarys and fanatics' by the court candidate Sir John Reresby in circumstances reminiscent of civil war allegiances.[30] The fourth baron's friend the antiquarian Ralph Thoresby noted of his funeral at Denton in April 1688 that 'the poor wept abundantly, a good evidence of his charity'. His son, Thomas, fifth baron Fairfax, was another Whig MP and a supporter of the Williamite seizure of York in 1688. Brian Fairfax dedicated the *Short memorials* to the fifth baron, reminding him of the family's reputation for protestantism and liberty: 'Your Lordship had the good fortune to be born after the Storms and Tempests of that Age: But you have had the Honour to appear eminently in defence of our Religion, and Civil Rights, in this last happy Revolution, as your Noble

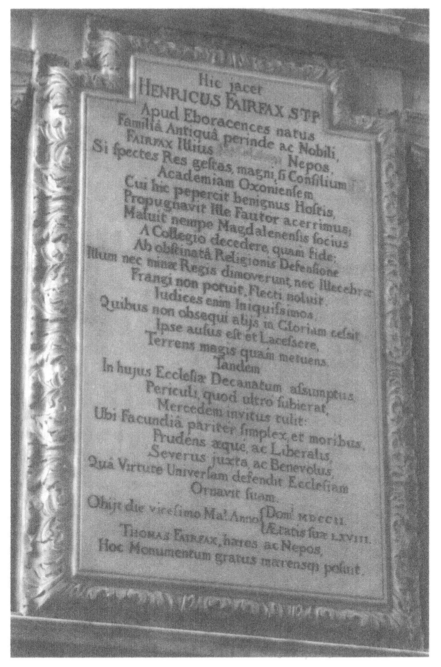

Figure 7 The memorial to Dean Henry Fairfax in Norwich Cathedral,
with the word 'Nasebiani' erased

Predecessor did at the Restoration.'[31] In vain, Brian hoped General Fairfax would be remembered for his more acceptable peaceful role in the Restoration rather than his more divisive and warlike part in the civil wars.

In 1687 another of the general's cousins, Henry Fairfax, was abused by Judge Jeffreys as fit for a madhouse for opposing James II's choice of a catholic president for Magdalen College, Oxford. In 1689 Henry became dean of Norwich, where he is commemorated by a memorial in the cathedral. A translation of the Latin inscription reads: 'He preferred as a Fellow of Magdalen to abandon his college rather than his faith; from his determined defence of his religion ... neither the threats nor the blandishments of the king moved him; he could not be broken, he refused to bend.' In 1703 the monument was covered with a cloak until the offending word 'Nasebiani', connecting him to his parliamentarian cousin, was erased (Figure 7). It was feared that the monument's commemoration of the general gloried in rebellion and would provoke a riot by a Tory mob. Another Tory riot was directed against the sixth baron's brother, Henry Culpepper Fairfax, who was among the Whig members of Oriel College threatened by an Oxford mob in October 1715.[32]

Among the dissenters who cherished Fairfax's memory was Ralph Thoresby, author of the antiquarian work *Ducatus Leodiensis*. Thoresby justified the parliamentarianism of his forbears by associating them with Fairfax, under whom they had served as army officers. He explained that the Thoresbys 'had from Similarity of Principles, religious and political, been long devoted' to the Fairfaxes. He claimed his father and uncle were 'like the old General of the Parliament', as 'moderate Presbyterians, but without any violent Animosity to the Church'. He added 'like him they were never undevoted to the Person of King Charles the first'. Thoresby even purchased the jewel that Parliament had awarded Fairfax after Naseby from the general's executors.[33] In other places, the memory of Fairfax was not so guarded. Even after the Restoration, every 11 May Taunton's inhabitants held riotous festivities and sang a song that celebrated Fairfax's army relieving the town in 1645.[34]

By the eighteenth century, the dictionary *Biographica Britannica* freely discussed Fairfax's shortcomings: 'His boundless ambition, and his great desire to rule, made him weakly engage, with the utmost zeal, in the worst and most exceptionable parts of our unhappy civil wars ... Happy would it have been for the nation, happy would it have been for him' if he had 'retired sooner'.[35] Such accusations of ambition and overzealousness are comparatively rare in observations upon Fairfax and are far more familiarly applied to Cromwell.

By the early nineteenth century the parliamentary cause was at last winning more scholarly admirers such as William Godwin and Thomas Carlyle.[36] Although Carlyle's idolising of Cromwell thrust Fairfax into the background, Fairfax's reputation was commemorated by the Airedale poet John Nicholson.

Nicholson opposed catholic emancipation and produced the play, *The siege of Bradford*, in 1821, which portrayed Fairfax and his officers as 'filled with the purest patriotism', and 'fired with stern religious enthusiasm'. The play depicted Fairfax inspiring Bradford's defenders with tales of the Marian martyrs.[37] In 1830 the nonconformist antiquarian Norrison Scatcherd, who was descended from one of Fairfax's officers, celebrated how it was still 'a matter of notoriety' that the people of the West Riding cloth towns 'detested the Royalists in these parts, and did them all the injury imaginable on their marches'.[38]

All three of Fairfax's biographers echo Brian Fairfax's rebuttal of Holles's charge that Fairfax was Cromwell's cipher, suggesting the potent longevity of this negative image of Fairfax. Fairfax's first biographer was a distant relative, the Victorian naval officer, explorer and civil servant Clements Markham. Markham was born in Stillingfleet, within two miles of Nun Appleton. Markham asserted that Fairfax's delay in retiring arose from his selfless duty, arguing that if he had 'consulted his own ease ... every personal consideration would have led him to throw up his command'. Markham argued that Fairfax's notion of patriotic service endured under 'whatever form of government the ruling powers might introduce'. He credited Fairfax with 'unswerving uprightness' and immunity to 'extraordinary temptations', with a life led 'without a stain upon his honour' or 'taint of self-seeking'. These were the very qualities the *Biographica Britannica* said had fallen to his ambition.[39] The second Fairfax biography by Mildred Ann Gibb was published in 1938, and the third in 1985 by another naval officer and diplomat, John Wilson.[40] All are narratives which shower praise on Fairfax's 'English' virtues: his military ability, gentlemanly conduct and discomfort with politics. None criticise Fairfax; all avoid the difficult questions of his involvement in the army's revolution, just as Fairfax would have wished. Gibb's eulogising conjures up images of the Spitfires of 1940. She wrote:

> During the first stages of the war in Yorkshire, [Fairfax] was quickly credited with almost supernatural powers; peasants and townsfolk took heart when the news spread abroad that 'the Rider of the White Horse' was coming to their relief, and the psychological effect of his fame upon the enemy was incalculable ... It was this spirit, this legend almost, which kept Yorkshire from falling during the early part of 1643. The forces were too unevenly matched for Fairfax to have a sporting chance in any encounter ... this makes his prolonged and finally successful resistance something of a miracle.[41]

Fairfax was reinvented to stand for the supposed English principles of fair play and sympathy for the underdog. Ann Hughes has characterised Gibb as part of an 'older generation of radical and liberal historians', comparable in views to Brailsford, and the above quote captures neatly the adoring tone of all three biographies.[42]

Fairfax's monuments at the Bodleian, York Minster and Bilbrough church applaud Fairfax for his moderation and integrity. In 1808 Julius Hutchinson considered that these values would 'distinguish Fairfax to the end of time', and that his resignation dashed hopes for a settled republic that 'would have rendered the nation great and happy'.[43] This representation of Fairfax's moderation, gentility and decency has proved enduring among his biographers and admirers but it sits uneasily alongside royalist images of him as the dull, brutish general who was too cowardly or incompetent to prevent the King's death.[44] Fairfax's championing of popular insurgency, his fervent, but broadly tolerant puritan temperament, and his attachment to notions of humility and duty in serving the commonwealth all suggest he was a more implacable opponent of Stuart divine-right monarchy than has hitherto been supposed. Despite his family's initial reluctance to go to war, they provided northern parliamentarianism with an energetic and committed leadership that helped turn the war in Parliament's favour. Sir Thomas's appointment as general of the New Model intensified the prosecution of the war and further hastened the royalists' defeat. Although his political leadership of the army thereafter was not so decisive, his sympathy for his soldiers' grievances facilitated the politicisation of the army, purge of Parliament and execution of Charles I. Yet, depending on one's perspective, Fairfax might be criticised both for failing to lead the revolutionaries of 1648–9 more decisively and for failing to moderate their course. Although his self-representation of modesty, restraint and stoic forbearance was to some degree a propaganda construct calculated to appeal to puritan concepts of honour, rarely in the seventeenth century did such a major figure choose to retire from such a position of power as Fairfax did in 1650. Yet his resignation might be considered as the action of a man broken by self-doubt, or at least indicative of his failure to live with the consequences of his actions. Fairfax would no doubt like to be remembered as the most successful general of his day, with a religious temperament forged by humility, scholarship and the conviction of the elect; that he had served his people according to the will of God.

Despite the historiographical perception of 1640–60 as a watershed in British history, from Fairfax's perspective the English revolution achieved little of permanence. The failure to establish the godly reformation and limited monarchy for which he had fought deeply challenged but did not overcome his belief in providence. He prayed that his failings would not cause him to be remembered among the unscrupulous and ambitious statesmen of the interregnum. Yet Fairfax and his 'Short memorials' provide us with a telling example of the pitfalls of trying to spin fresh interpretations upon one's past actions to suit changed circumstances. A close biographical study of Fairfax indicates the dangers of ascribing inevitability to either Cromwell's rise or the King's death. It also reveals something of how the fractures within parliamentarianism rendered a stable settlement so elusive from 1646 to 1660. The rival memories of Fairfax remind us how the political and religious divisions that emerged during the civil wars have never entirely receded from British identities.

Like Cromwell, Fairfax clung to his belief that he had served God's cause; his 'Short memorials' lamented 'I cannot believe yt such wonderfull successes shall be given in vaine': a fitting epitaph for both Fairfax and the English revolution.[45]

NOTES

1 Bod., MS Fairfax 33, fos. 19v–21v.

2 *Ibid.*, fo. 28v.

3 S. R. Gardiner, *History of the commonwealth and protectorate, 1649–60* (London, 1894), vol. 1, p. 293.

4 Bod., MS Fairfax 36, fo. 1r; B. Fairfax (ed.), *Short memorials of Thomas, lord Fairfax* (London, 1699), p. ii.

5 Bod., MS Fairfax 36; Beinecke Rare Book and Manuscript Library, Yale University, Osborn shelves b168; BL, Harleian MS 6390; William Andrews Clark Memorial Library, University of California, Los Angeles, MS 95041; Markham, p. 393n.

6 L. Daxon, 'The politics of Sir Thomas Fairfax reassessed', *History*, 90:4 (2005), 487.

7 H. Walpole, *A catalogue of the royal and noble authors, with list of their works* (London, 2nd edn, 1759), vol. 2, p. 223.

8 Bod., MS Fairfax 36, fo. 4v.

9 Fairfax (ed.), *Short memorials*, pp. iii–v; D. Holles, 'Memoirs of Denzil, lord Holles, baron of Ifield in Sussex from the year 1641 to 1648', in F. Maseres (ed.), *Select tracts relating to the civil wars in England* (London, 1815), p. 210.

10 Holles, 'Memoirs of Holles', p. 188.

11 B. Worden, *Roundhead Reputations: The English Civil War and the Passions of Posterity* (London, 2001), pp. 95, 131; C. Rose, *England in the 1690s: Revolution, Religion and War* (Oxford, 1999), p. 95.

12 A. Woolrych, *Soldiers and Statesmen: The General Council of the Army and its Debates, 1647–1648* (Oxford, 1987), p. 103n.

13 Bod., MS Fairfax 36; Fairfax (ed.), *Short memorials*, p. ii; Worden, *Roundhead Reputations*, pp. 39, 63.

14 Bod., MS Fairfax 36, fo. 1r.

15 *Ibid.*, fo. 5r.

16 *Ibid.*, fo. 4v.

17 *Ibid.*, fo. 5r.

18 Worden, *Roundhead Reputations*, p. 49.

19 Bod., Fairfax MS 36, fo. 8r–v.

20 *Ibid.*, fo. 10r.

21 Bod., MS Fairfax 33, fos. 18–34.

22 *Ibid.*, fo. 21v; Fairfax (ed.), *Short memorials*, p. vii.

23 The Bladens had been servants of the first baron Fairfax, and Ferdinando had sent Captain Bladen to aid Sir Thomas in January 1643: HRO, BRS/7/19, BRS/7/53; Bod., MS Fairfax 30, fo. 129; R. Bell (ed.), *The Fairfax correspondence: memorials of the civil war* (London, 1849), vol. 1, p. 35.

24 At Hull in 1642 and during his career in Ireland he was often referred to as 'Jefford': College of Arms, London, Curia Militaris, 5/83; Durham University Library, Mickleton-Spearman MS 2/469; J. A. Atkinson et al. (eds), *Darlington Wills and Inventories* (Surtees Society, 201, 1993), pp. 13, 85; M. C. Fissel, *The Bishops' Wars* (Cambridge, 1994), p. 43; TNA, SP 28/138/4; BL, E107(12), *An extract of all the passages from Hull, York, and Lincolnshire*, 19 July (London, 1642), p. 8; Bod., MS Tanner 62A, fos. 103–4; J. Rushworth, *Historical collections* (London, 1721), part 3, vol. 2, pp. 126, 271.

25 P. W. Thomas (ed.), *The English Revolution III. Newsbooks I. Oxford Royalist* (London, 1971), vol. 1, pp. 465–6; BL, E252(41), *A perfect diurnall of some passages in Parliament*, 3–10 June (London, 1644), p. 355; *JHC*, vol. 3, pp. 285, 518, 704; TNA, SP 16/513/part i/107–8.

26 BL, E121/4/8, no. 13; C. H. Firth and G. Davies, *The Regimental History of Cromwell's Army* (2 vols, Oxford, 1940), vol. 2, pp. 639–41; *CSP dom.* 1653–4, p. 66; Bod., MS Fairfax 36, fo. 8r–v; TNA, SP 16/513/part i/107–8; T. T. Wildridge (ed.), *The Hull letters* (Hull, 1886), p. 160; P. R. Newman, *The Battle of Marston Moor, 1644* (Chichester, 1981), p. 67.

27 T. Wright (ed.), *The autobiography of Joseph Lister of Bradford in Yorkshire* (London, 1842), p. 19; W. Grainge, *The battles and battlefields of Yorkshire* (York, 1854), p. 161; L. Huntley, *The Fairfaxes of Denton and Nun Appleton* (York, 1906), p. 23; N. Scatcherd, *The history of Morley, in the parish of Batley, and West-Riding of Yorkshire* (Leeds, 1830), p. 273.

28 J. H. Turner, *The autobiography of Captain John Hodgson of Coley Hall, near Halifax* (Brighouse, 1882), p. 24; Bod., MS Fairfax 36, fos. 7r, 9r–v; TNA, SP 28/1A/176; P. R. Newman, 'The defeat of John Belasyse: civil war in Yorkshire, January–April, 1644', *YAJ*, 52 (1980), 132.

29 A. H. Burne, 'Generalship in the first civil war, 1642–1644', *History Today*, 1 (1951), 63–9.

30 D. R. Lacey, *Dissent and Parliamentary Politics in England, 1661–1689* (Rutgers University Press, 1969), pp. 117, 393.

31 B. D. Henning (ed.), *The House of Commons, 1660–1690* (London, 1983), vol. 2, p. 291; Fairfax (ed.), *Short memorials*, p. x.

32 G. Webb, *Fairfax of York: The Life and History of a Noble Family* (York, 2001), p. 23; I. Atherton, C. Harper–Bill and V. Morgan (eds), *Norwich Cathedral* (London, 1996), pp. 477–8; BL, Lansdowne MS 987, fo. 239; Bod., MS Fairfax 35, fo. 94.

33 R. Thoresby, *Ducatus Leodiensis* (Leeds, 2nd edn, 1816), p. vii; C. Fairfax Dover, 'The Fairfax jewel', *Journal of the Fairfax Society*, 3:4 (2001), 79.

34 Here Fairfax was remembered as 'one of the first characters of his times for integrity and military accomplishments': J. Toulmin, *History of Taunton in the county of Somerset* (Taunton, 1822), pp. 415, 423.

35 Worden, *Roundhead Reputations*, p. 184.

36 W. Godwin, *History of the commonwealth of England* (4 vols, London, 1824); T. Carlyle, (ed.), *Oliver Cromwell's letters and speeches: with elucidations* (3 vols, London, 1857).

37 J. Nicholson, *The poetical works of John Nicholson: the Airedale poet, carefully edited from the original editions with additional notes and a sketch of his life and writings by W. G. Hird* (London, 1876), pp. xii–xv.

38 Scatcherd, *The history of Morley*, p. 247.

39 Worden, *Roundhead Reputations*, p. 242n; Markham, pp. 361–2, 385, 401.

40 J. Wilson, *Fairfax* (New York, 1985).

41 M. A. Gibb, *The Lord General: A Life of Thomas Fairfax* (London, 1938), p. 40.

42 A. Hughes, 'Gender and politics in Leveller literature', in S. D. Amussen and M. Kishlansky (eds), *Political Culture and Cultural Politics in Early Modern England: Essays Presented to David Underdown* (Manchester, 1995), p. 162.

43 L. Hutchinson, *Memoirs of the life of Colonel Hutchinson*, ed. Rev. J. Hutchinson (London, 2nd edn, 1808), pp. 315–16n.

44 J. D. Legard, *The Legards of Anlaby and Ganton* (London, 1926), p. 77; S. E. Prall (ed.), *The Puritan Revolution: A Documentary History* (London, 1968), p. 310; G. Edwards, *The Last Days of Charles I* (Stroud, 1999), p. 185.

45 Bod., MS Fairfax 36, fo. 5r.

Select bibliography

PRIMARY SOURCES

Manuscript sources

BEINECKE RARE BOOK AND MANUSCRIPT LIBRARY, YALE UNIVERSITY

Osborn files, folder 5119: Brian Fairfax, 'Reasons for taking ye oath of Abjuration', c.1702

Osborn files, folder 5122: Letter of Sir Thomas to Ferdinando, 2nd baron Fairfax, 13 February 1645/6

Osborn files, folder 17645: Thomas, 3rd baron Fairfax to Horatio, 1st viscount Townshend, 10 November 1664

Osborn shelves b101: The commonplace book of Ralph Assheton of Kirkby Grange

Osborn shelves b165: Thomas, 1st baron Fairfax, 'A Discourse of Court and Courtiers Digested into Sundrie Heads and Chapters written in the Year of our Lord 1633'

Osborn shelves b168: Short Memorials of Thomas, 3rd baron Fairfax

Osborn shelves b233: Poems of Lady Jane Cavendish

Osborn shelves fb25: 'The Coppie of the Challenge sent by the Earle of Northumberland to Sir Francis Veare And Sir Francis Veare his answere on St Georges day the last yeare of Queen Elizabeth anno dom 1602'

Osborn shelves fb94: The Pym Correspondence

Osborn shelves fb155: The commonplace book of John Browne

BODLEIAN LIBRARY, OXFORD

MS Aubrey 8

MS Clarendon 34

MS Fairfax 30–7, 40

MS Tanner 56–62

MS Top Yorks C14

BRISTOL CITY RECORD OFFICE

8029(9) Original letter from Sir Thomas Fairfax to his father, Bristol, 12 September 1645

41084/6: *A true relation of the storming Bristoll and the taking the town, castle, forts, ordnance, ammunition and arms, by Sir Thomas Fairfax's army, on Thursday the 11 of this instant Septemb. 1645* (London, 1645)

BRITISH LIBRARY, LONDON

Additional MS 4929: Psalm and sermon notes by Thomas, third baron Fairfax and Lady Fairfax

Additional MS 5832, fo. 209b: The case of Colonel Christopher Copley

Additional MS 10114: Parliamentary diary of John Harrington, 1646–53

Additional MS 11692: Manuscripts presented by the Hon. P. P. Bouverie

Additional MS 11743: Poetry collected by the Fairfax family

Additional MS 11744: Poems by Thomas, Lord Fairfax

Additional MS 15858: Original letters and correspondence of Sir Richard Browne and John Evelyn

Additional MS 18738: Autograph letters, 1433–1817

Additional MS 18979: Fairfax correspondence, 1625–88

Additional MS 18980: Original letters, relating to the civil wars; addressed principally to Prince Rupert, 1642–58

Additional MS 21417–27: Baynes correspondence

Additional MS 21506: Original letters and autographs of eminent persons, 1587–1835

Additional MS 25447: Translation of the Pimander of Hermes Trismegistus, by Thomas, 3rd baron Fairfax

Additional MS 28326: The Highway to Heidelberg, 1622

Additional MS 29747: Autograph letters

Additional MS 31116: Parliamentary journal of Lawrence Whitacre, 1642–7

Additional MS 32096: State papers, historical documents, and official and private letters, 1086–1760, vol. 6.

Additional MS 33770: The examinations of the Farnley Wood plotters, 1663

Additional MS 34195: Collection of original letters, warrants and papers, 1576–1763

Additional MS 34274: Miscellaneous autograph letters

Additional MS 34727: West papers, miscellaneous letters, 1532–1734

Additional MS 36996: Fairfax papers, transcripts, 1645–8

Additional MS 37344: Whitelocke's annals, vol. 4, 1645–9

Additional MS 37345: Whitelocke's annals, vol. 5, 1649–53

Additional MS 40883: Diary of Nehemiah Wallington, 1641–3

Additional MS 41071: Hone papers

Additional MS 44848: Historical letters and papers of the sixteenth and seventeenth centuries

Additional MS 71448: Correspondence and papers of James Chaloner

Additional MS 71449: Daniel King's monuments of the family of the Veres

Egerton MS 1048: Collection of historical and parliamentary papers, 1620–60

Egerton MS 2145: History of the life of Philippe du Plessis-Mornay, translated by Brian Fairfax and dedicated to the Prince of Orange, 2 Feb 1687/8

Egerton MS 2146: Manuscripts and poems by Brian Fairfax

Egerton MS 2618: Historical letters and papers, 1556–1753

Egerton MS 2647: Correspondence of Sir Thomas Barrington, 1643

Harleian MS 162–6: Parliamentary journal of Sir Simonds D'Ewes

Harleian MS 252, fo. 33: 'An Historicall Diarie of the Militarie Proceedings ... of Sir Thomas Fairfax ... by John Rushworth'

Harleian MS 6390: The memorial of Thomas Lord Fairfax, prepared for the press by Dr Brian Fairfax

Harleian MS 7001: Original letters from several considerable persons

Lansdowne MS 987: Bishop Kennett's collections, vol. 53

Select bibliography

Sloane MS 1519: Original letters, 1574–1667
Stowe MS 152, fo. 69: Petition of the northern officers
Stowe MS 744: Dering correspondence, 1640–67

BRYNMOR JONES LIBRARY ARCHIVE, UNIVERSITY OF HULL
DDHO: Hotham MS
DDCY: Cholmley MS

CITY OF HULL RECORD OFFICE
BRS/7: Papers relating to the Hothams and the civil wars

CITY OF YORK ARCHIVES
House Books B36

COLLEGE OF ARMS, LONDON
Curia Militaris: Records of the High Court of Chivalry, 1633–41

DURHAM UNIVERSITY LIBRARY ARCHIVE
Mickleton-Spearman MS

EAST RIDING OF YORKSHIRE RECORD OFFICE, BEVERLEY
DDRI 43/8: Documents of the Bethell Family of Rise Park

FOLGER SHAKESPEARE LIBRARY, WASHINGTON DC
V.a.14 Sermon notes of Thomas, 3rd baron Fairfax, c.1661–7
V.a.15 Sermon notes of Thomas, 3rd baron Fairfax, c.1661–7
Bennet MS, X.d.483 (198), copy of letter from Edward Sexby, William Allen and Thomas
    Shepheard, gentlemen soldiers, to Sir Thomas Fairfax, Major General Skippon and
    Lieutenant General Cromwell, 28 April 1647
Cavendish-Talbot MS, X.d.428 (79), letter of Sir George Savile to Avery Copley, 26
    January 1593

THE NATIONAL ARCHIVE, KEW
ASSI 45: Clerks of the assizes records, northern circuit
E121: Certificates for the sale of crown lands
SP 16: State papers of the reign of Charles I
SP 19: Papers of the committee for advance of money
SP 22: Papers of the committee for plundered ministers
SP 23: Papers of the committee for compounding
SP 24: Papers of the committee for indemnity
SP 28: Commonwealth exchequer papers

WEST YORKSHIRE RECORD OFFICE, CALDERDALE CENTRAL LIBRARY, HALIFAX
Brearcliffe MS, MISC 182: Manuscripts of John Brearcliffe, apothecary and antiquary,
    1618–82
FW:14/1: Association of the parish of Halifax, April 1643

Papers of Nathaniel Waterhouse of Halifax, 1559–1650, MIC:7
'Our local portfolio': cuttings from the *Halifax Guardian*, 1856–62, collected by J. W. Walker

WEST YORKSHIRE RECORD OFFICE, WAKEFIELD
Minute book of the parliamentarian army's council of war, 1647–8: C469/1
West Riding Quarter Sessions, QS

WORCESTER COLLEGE, OXFORD
Clarke MS, 4/2 Accounts of Christopher Copley's troop of horse

YORK MINSTER LIBRARY
Additional MS 258: James Lumsden's plan of Marston moor
Typescript of Thomas Fairfax, 'A treatise touching the breeding of horses' (c.1660)

YORKSHIRE ARCHAEOLOGICAL SOCIETY LIBRARY AND ARCHIVE, CLAREMONT, LEEDS
MS 205a: Letter to the constable of Mirfield

Printed primary sources

The contemporary tracts and newsbooks cited in the endnotes are too numerous to be listed again here, but they were principally drawn from among the Thomason Tracts, Early English Books Online, and the Civil War Tracts at York Minster Library.

Barber, F. (ed.): 'West Riding sessions rolls', *YAJ*, 5 (1879)
Baxter, R., *The Autobiography of Richard Baxter*, ed. N. H. Keeble (London, 1974)
Bell, R. (ed.): *The Fairfax correspondence: memorials of the civil war* (2 vols, London, 1849)
Bickley, F. (ed.): *Report on the manuscripts of the late Reginald Rawdon Hastings*, HMC, 78 (4 vols, London, 1928–47)
Binns, J. (ed.): *The Memoirs and Memorials of Sir Hugh Cholmley of Whitby, 1600–1657* (YASRS, 153, 2000)
Birch, T. (ed.): *A collection of the state papers of John Thurloe, esq* (7 vols, London, 1742)
Boyle, J. R. (ed.): *Memoirs of Master John Shawe, sometime vicar of Rotherham, minister of St Mary's, lecturer at Holy Trinity church, and master of the Charterhouse, at Kingston-upon-Hull. Written by himself in the year 1663–4* (Hull, 1882)
Burnet, G., *History of his own time* (6 vols, Oxford, 2nd edn, 1833)
Burton, T., *Diary of Thomas Burton, esq*, ed. J. T. Rutt (4 vols, London, 1828)
Calendar of state papers domestic
Carlyle, T. (ed.): *Oliver Cromwell's letters and speeches: with elucidations* (3 vols, London, 1857)
Cartwright, J. J. (ed.): 'Papers relating to the delinquency of Lord Savile, 1642–1646', *Camden Miscellany*, vol. 8 (Camden Society, 2nd series, 31, 1883)
Cary, H. (ed.): *Memorials of the great civil war in England from 1646 to 1652* (2 vols, London, 1842)

Cholmley, H., *The memoirs of Sir Hugh Cholmley, knt. and bart., addressed to his two sons* (London, 1787)

Civil War Tracts, York Minster Library

Clarendon, *History of the rebellion and civil wars in England*, ed. W. Dunn Macray (6 vols, Oxford, 1888)

Clarendon, *State papers collected by Edward, earl of Clarendon* (2 vols, Oxford, 1767–73)

Clarendon, *The history of the rebellion and civil wars in England* (3 vols, Oxford, 1717)

Clay, J. W. (ed.): *Abstracts of Yorkshire wills* (YASRS, 9, 1890)

Cooper, J. P. (ed.): *Wentworth Papers, 1597–1628* (Camden Society, 4th series, 12, 1973)

Cowper MS, HMC, 12th report, appendix, part II (London, 1888), vol. 2

Cust, R. (ed.): *The Papers of Sir Richard Grosvenor, 1st Bart, 1585–1645* (The Record Society of Lancashire and Cheshire, 134, 1996)

Dugdale, W., *The visitation of the county of Yorke* (Surtees Society, 36, 1859)

Dyfnallt Owen, G. (ed.): *De L'Isle and Dudley MS, vol. 6, 1626–98*, HMC, 77 (London, 1966)

Eyre, A., 'A dyurnall or catalogue of all my accions', in C. Jackson (ed.): *Yorkshire diaries and autobiographies of the seventeenth and eighteenth centuries* (Surtees Society, 65, 1877)

Fairfax, B., *A catalogue of the curious pictures of George Villiers, duke of Buckingham, in which is included the valuable collection of Sir Peter Paul Rubens with the life of George Villiers, duke of Buckingham, the celebrated poet written by Brian Fairfax, esq* (London, 1758)

Fairfax, B. (ed.): *Short memorials of Thomas, lord Fairfax* (London, 1699)

Firth, C. H. (ed.): *The life of William Cavendish, duke of Newcastle to which is added the true relation of my birth breeding and life by Margaret, duchess of Newcastle* (London, 1906)

Firth, C. H. (ed.): *The Clarke papers, vols 1–4* (Camden Society, new series, 41, 54, 61, 62, 1891–1901)

Firth, C. H. (ed.): 'Papers relating to Thomas Wentworth, first earl of Strafford', in *Camden miscellany*, vol. 9 (Camden Society, 3rd series, 53, 1895)

Firth, C. H. (ed.): *The memoirs of Edmund Ludlow* (2 vols, Oxford, 1894)

Firth, C. H., and Rait, R. S. (eds): *Acts and ordinances of the interregnum, 1642–1660* (3 vols, London, 1911)

Green, M. A. E. (ed.): *The letters of Queen Henrietta Maria* (London, 1857)

Hackett, J. *Scrinia reserata: a memorial offered to the great deservings of John Williams D.D.* (London, 1692)

Herbert, T., *Memoirs of the last two years of the reign of King Charles I* (London, 1813)

Hinds, A. B. (ed.): *Calendar of State Papers Venetian, 1642–1652* (3 vols, London, 1925–7)

Holroyd, A. (ed.): *Collectanea Bradfordiana: a collection of papers on the history of Bradford and the neighbourhood* (Saltaire, 1873)

Hope, E. (ed.): *A puritan parish clerk: a commentary on current events made in the registers of St. Mary's church, Beverley, by Nicholas Pearson, parish clerk 1636–1653* (Beverley, n.d.)

House of Lords MS, HMC, 4th report, part 1, report and appendix (London, 1874)

House of Lords MS, HMC, 5th report, appendix (London, 1876)

Hutchinson, L., *Memoirs of the Life of Colonel Hutchinson*, ed. N. H. Keeble (London, 1995)

Johnson, G. W. (ed.): *The Fairfax correspondence: memoirs of the reign of Charles I* (2 vols, London, 1848)

Journals of the House of Commons (JHC)

Journals of the House of Lords (JHL)

Lindley, K., and Scott, D. (eds): *The Journal of Thomas Juxon 1644–1647* (Camden Society, 5th series, 13, 1999)

Lisles, *The pindar of Wakefield, or a true narration of the unparallell'd victory obtained against the Popish army at the taking in of Wakefield in Yorkshire by the Lord Fairfaxe his forces, May 20. 1643. As it was sent in a letter from one in that army to his friend here in London, not altering it from his native tone, more like Chaucer's English, then ours here* (London, 1643)

Lister, J. (ed.): *West Riding Sessions Records: Orders 1611–1642, Indictments 1637–1642* (YASRS, 53, 1915)

Lomas, S. C. (ed.): *Leyborne Popham MS*, HMC, 51 (London, 1899)

Macfarlane, A. (ed.): *The Diary of Ralph Josselin, 1616–1683* (Oxford, 2nd edn, 1991)

Margaret, duchess of Newcastle, *The life of the thrice noble, high and puissant prince William Cavendishe, duke, marquess, and earl of Newcastle* (London, 1667)

Marvell, A., *The Poems of Andrew Marvell*, ed. N. Smith (Harlow, 2003)

Maseres, F. (ed.): *Select tracts relating to the civil wars in England* (London, 1815)

May, T., *The history of the parliament of England which began Nov. 3 M.DC.XL* (London, 1812)

Parsons, D. (ed.): *The diary of Sir Henry Slingsby of Scriven, bart* (London, 1836)

Peacock, E., 'On some civil war documents relating to Yorkshire', *YAJ*, 1 (1870)

Portland MS, HMC, 29, 13th report, appendix, part 1 (London, 1891), vol. 1

Priestley, J., 'Some memoirs concerning the family of the Priestleys written at the request of a friend by Jonathan Priestley, 1696, aetatis suae 63', in C. Jackson (ed.): *Yorkshire diaries and autobiographies of the seventeenth and eighteenth centuries* (Surtees Society, 77, 1883)

Raymond, J. (ed.): *Making the News: An Anthology of the Newsbooks of Revolutionary England, 1641–1660* (Moreton-in-Marsh, 1993)

Ricraft, J., *A survey of England's champions and truths faithful patriots* (London, 1647)

Rushworth, J., *Historical collections* (4 parts, London, 1721)

Rushworth, J., *The trial of Thomas, earl of Strafford* (London, 1721)

Scott, W. (ed.): *The original memoirs written during the great civil war being the life of Sir Henry Slingsby and memoirs of Captain Hodgson, with notes* (Edinburgh, 1806)

Shaw, J., 'The life of Master John Shaw', in C. Jackson (ed.): *Yorkshire diaries and autobiographies in the seventeenth and eighteenth centuries* (Surtees Society, 65, 1877)

Sprigge, J., *Anglia rediviva; England's recovery: being the history of the motions, actions, and successes of the army under the immediate conduct of his excellency Sir Thomas Fairfax, Kt. captain general of all the parliaments forces in England* (London, 1647)

Sutherland MS, HMC, 5th report, appendix (London, 1876)

Thomas, P. W. (ed.): *The English Revolution III. Newsbooks I. Oxford Royalist* (4 vols, London, 1971)

Thomason Tracts, British Library

Thoresby, R., *Ducatus Leodiensis: or, the topography of the ancient and populous town and parish of Leedes and parts adjacent in the West Riding of the county of York*, ed. T. Dunham Whitaker (Leeds, 2nd edn, 1816)

Tibbut, H. G. (ed.): *The Letter Books of Sir Samuel Luke, 1644–1645* (Publications of the Bedfordshire Historical Records Society, 42, 1963)

Turner, J. H. (ed.): *The autobiography and diaries of Rev. Oliver Heywood, 1630–1702* (4 vols, Brighouse, 1882)

Turner, J. H. (ed.): *The autobiography of Captain John Hodgson of Coley Hall, near Halifax* (Brighouse, 1882)

Vicars, J., *God in the mount or England's parliamentarie-chronicle* (London, 1644)

Warwick, P., *Memoires of the reign of King Charles I with a continuation to the happy restauration of King Charles II* (London, 1701)

Whitelocke, B., *Memorials of English affairs from the beginning of the reign of Charles I to the happy restoration of King Charles II* (4 vols, Oxford, 1853)

Wildridge, T. T. (ed.): *The Hull letters* (Hull, 1886)

Wright, T. (ed.): *The autobiography of Joseph Lister of Bradford in Yorkshire* (London, 1842)

SECONDARY SOURCES

Books

Adair, J., *By the Sword Divided: Eyewitnesses of the English Civil War* (London, 1983)

Amussen, S. D., and Kishlansky, M. (eds): *Political Culture and Cultural Politics in Early Modern England: Essays Presented to David Underdown* (Manchester, 1995)

Anderson, J., *Memorable Women of the Puritan Times* (2 vols, London, 1862)

Ashton, R., *Counter–Revolution: The Second Civil War and its Origins, 1646–8* (New Haven, 1994)

Atkinson, D. H., *Ralph Thoresby, the topographer: his town and times* (2 vols, Leeds, 1885)

Aveling, H., *The Handle and the Axe: The Catholic Recusants in England from Reformation to Emancipation* (London, 1976)

Aveling, H., *Northern Catholics: The Catholic Recusants of the North Riding of Yorkshire, 1558–1790* (London, 1966)

Bennett, M., *The Civil Wars in Britain and Ireland, 1638–1651* (Oxford, 1997)

Binns, J., 'A Place of Great Importance': Scarborough in the Civil Wars* (Preston, 1996)

Carlton, C., *Going to the Wars: The Experience of the British Civil Wars, 1638–1651* (London, 1994)

Carpenter, S. D. M., *Military Leadership in the British Civil Wars, 1642–1651: 'The Genius of this Age'* (London, 2005)

Cliffe, J. T., *Puritans in Conflict: The Puritan Gentry During and After the Civil Wars* (London, 1988)

Cliffe, J. T., *The Yorkshire Gentry from the Reformation to the Civil War* (London, 1969)

Collinson, P., *Elizabethan Essays* (London, 1994)

Collinson, P., *Godly People: Essays on English Protestantism and Puritanism* (London, 1983)

Collinson, P., and Craig, J. (eds): *The Reformation in English Towns, 1500–1640* (Basingstoke, 1998)

Condren, C., and Cousins, A. D. (eds): *The Political Identity of Andrew Marvell* (Aldershot, 1990)

Coward, B. (ed.): *A Companion to Stuart Britain* (Oxford, 2003)

Coward, B., *Oliver Cromwell* (Harlow, 1991)

Cust, R. P., *Charles I: A Political Life* (Harlow, 2005)

Cust, R. P., and Hughes, A. (eds): *Conflict in Early Stuart England: Studies in Religion and Politics 1603–1642* (London, 1989)

Davis, J. C., *Oliver Cromwell* (London, 2001)

Dransfield, J. N., *History of Penistone* (Penistone, 1906)

Edwards, G., *The Last Days of Charles I* (Stroud, 1999)

English, B., *The Great Landowners of East Yorkshire, 1530–1910* (Hemel Hempstead, 1990)

Farr, D., *John Lambert, Parliamentary Soldier and Cromwellian Major-General* (Woodbridge, 2003)

Fincham, K. (ed.): *The Early Stuart Church, 1603–1642* (Basingstoke, 1993)

Firth, C. H., and Davies, G., *The Regimental History of Cromwell's Army* (2 vols, Oxford, 1940)

Fissel, M. C., *The Bishops' Wars* (Cambridge, 1994)

Fletcher, A., and Roberts, P. (eds): *Religion, Culture and Society in Early Modern Britain: Essays in Honour of Patrick Collinson* (Cambridge, 1994)

Foard, G., *Naseby: The Decisive Campaign* (Barnsley, 2004)

Fox, G., *The Three Sieges of Pontefract Castle, Printed from a Manuscript Compiled and Illustrated by George Fox* (Leeds, 1987)

Foyster, E. A., *Manhood in Early Modern England: Honour, Sex and Marriage* (Harlow, 1999)

Gardiner, S. R., *A History of the Great Civil Wars* (4 vols, London, 1904)

Gaunt, P., *Oliver Cromwell* (Oxford, 1996)

Gentles, I., *The New Model Army in England, Ireland and Scotland, 1645–1653* (Oxford, 1992)

Gentles, I., Morrill, J., and Worden, B. (eds): *Soldiers, Writers and Statesmen of the English Revolution* (Cambridge, 1998)

Gibb, M. A., *The Lord General: A Life of Thomas Fairfax* (London, 1938)

Godwin, W., *History of the commonwealth of England* (4 vols, London, 1824)

Heal, F., and Holmes, C., *The Gentry in England and Wales, 1500–1700* (Basingstoke, 1994)

Healy, T. (ed.): *Andrew Marvell* (London, 1998)

Heaton, H., *The Yorkshire Woollen and Worsted Industries* (Oxford, 2nd edn, 1965)

Henning, B. D. (ed.): *The House of Commons, 1660–1690* (3 vols, London, 1983)

Hey, D., *Yorkshire from A.D. 1000* (London, 1986)

Hill, C., *The English Bible and the Seventeenth-Century Revolution* (London, 1994)

Hill, C., *A Turbulent, Seditious, and Factious People: John Bunyan and his Church* (Oxford, 1988)

Hill, C., *The World Turned Upside Down: Radical Ideas During the English Revolution* (London, 1980)

Select bibliography

Hill, C., *Antichrist in Seventeenth-Century England* (London, 1971)

Hill, C., *God's Englishman: Oliver Cromwell and the English Revolution* (London, 1970)

Hirst, D., *England in Conflict, 1603–1660: Kingdom, Community, Commonwealth* (London, 1999)

Holstun, J., *Ehud's Dagger: Class Struggle in the English Revolution* (London, 2000)

Hughes, A., *Gangraena and the Struggle for the English Revolution* (Oxford, 2004)

Hughes, A., *The Causes of the English Civil War* (Basingstoke, 2nd edn, 1998)

Hughes, A., *Politics, Society and Civil War in Warwickshire, 1620–60* (Cambridge, 1987)

Huntley, L., *The Fairfaxes of Denton and Nun Appleton* (York, 1906)

Hutton, R., *The Royalist War Effort, 1642–6* (London, 2nd edn, 1999)

Hutton, R., *The Restoration: A Political and Religious History of England and Wales, 1658–1667* (Oxford, 1985)

James, M., *Social Problems and Policy during the English Revolution, 1640–1660* (London, 1966)

Johnson, D., *Adwalton Moor, 1643: The Battle that Changed a War* (Pickering, 2003)

Jones, P., *The Siege of Colchester, 1648* (Stroud, 2003)

Kelsey, S., *Inventing a Republic: The Political Culture of the English Commonwealth, 1649–1653* (Stanford, 1997)

Kenyon, J., and Ohlmeyer, J. (eds): *The Civil Wars: A Military History of England, Scotland and Ireland, 1638–1660* (Oxford, 2002)

Kishlansky, M., *The Rise of the New Model Army* (Cambridge, 1979)

Kyle, C., and Peacey, J. (eds): *Parliament at Work: Parliamentary Committees, Political Power and Public Access in Early Modern England* (Woodbridge, 2002)

Laurence, A., *Parliamentary Army Chaplains, 1642–1651* (Woodbridge, 1990)

Legard, J. D., *The Legards of Anlaby and Ganton* (London, 1926)

MacInnes, A. I., *The British Revolution, 1629–1660* (Basingstoke, 2005)

Maltby, W. S., *The Black Legend in England: The Development of Anti-Spanish Sentiment, 1558–1660* (Durham, North Carolina, 1971)

Manning, B., *1649: The Crisis of the English Revolution* (London, 1992)

Manning, B., *The English People and the English Revolution* (London, 2nd edn, 1991)

Manning, B. (ed.): *Politics, Religion and the English Civil War* (London, 1973)

Manning, R. B., *Swordsmen: The Martial Ethos in the Three Kingdoms* (Oxford, 2003)

Manning, R. B., *Hunters and Poachers: A Social and Cultural History of Unlawful Hunting in England, 1485–1640* (Oxford, 1993)

Marchant, R. A., *The Church under the Law: Justice, Administration and Discipline in the Diocese of York, 1560–1640* (Cambridge, 1969)

Marchant, R. A., *The Puritans and the Church Courts in the Diocese of York, 1560–1642* (London, 1960)

Markham, C. R., *The life of Robert Fairfax of Steeton, 1666–1725* (London, 1885)

Markham, C. R., *A life of the great lord Fairfax* (London, 1870)

Marshall, A., *Oliver Cromwell, Soldier: The Military Life of a Revolutionary at War* (London, 2004)

Mendelson, S., and Crawford, P., *Women in Early Modern England, 1550–1720* (Oxford, 1997)

Merritt, J. F. (ed.): *The Political World of Thomas Wentworth, Earl of Strafford, 1621–1641* (Cambridge, 1996)

Miall, J. G., *Congregationalism in Yorkshire* (London, 1868)

Morrill, J., *Revolt in the Provinces: The People of England and the Tragedies of War, 1634–1648* (London, 1999)

Morrill, J., *The Nature of the English Revolution* (London, 1993)

Morrill, J. (ed.): *Oliver Cromwell and the English Revolution* (Harlow, 1990)

Morrill, J., Slack, P., and Woolf, D. (eds): *Public Duty and Private Conscience in Seventeenth-Century England* (Oxford, 1993)

Murray, N., *World Enough and Time: The Life of Andrew Marvell* (London, 1999)

Newman, P. R., *The Old Service: Royalist Regimental Colonels and the Civil War, 1642–1646* (Manchester, 1993)

Newman, P. R., *Marston Moor* (Chichester, 1981)

Ollard, R., *This War Without An Enemy: A History of the English Civil Wars* (London, 1976)

Peacey, J., *Politicians and Pamphleteers: Propaganda During the English Civil Wars and Interregnum* (Aldershot, 2004)

Peacey, J. (ed.): *The Regicides and the Execution of Charles I* (Basingstoke, 2001)

Pennington, D. H., and Roots, I. A. (eds): *The Committee at Stafford* (Manchester, 1957)

Potter, L., *Secret Rites and Secret Writing: Royalist Literature, 1641–1660* (Cambridge, 1989)

Purdy, D., *Yorkshire Hearth Tax Returns* (Studies in regional and local history, 7 , University of Hull, 1991)

Reckitt, B. N., *Charles the First and Hull, 1639–1645* (London, 1952)

Reilly, T., *Cromwell: An Honourable Enemy: The Untold Story of the Cromwellian Invasion of Ireland* (Dingle, co. Kerry, 1999)

Richardson, R. C. (ed.): *Town and Countryside in the English Revolution* (Manchester, 1992)

Russell, C., *The Fall of the British Monarchies, 1637–1642* (Oxford, 1991)

Saltmarshe, P., *History and Chartulary of the Hothams of Scorborough in the East Riding of Yorkshire, 1100–1700* (York, 1914)

Scatcherd, N., *The history of Morley, in the parish of Batley, and the West-Riding of Yorkshire* (Leeds, 1830)

Scott, D., *Politics and War in the Three Stuart Kingdoms, 1637–49* (Basingstoke, 2004)

Seaver, P. S., *Wallington's World: A Puritan Artisan in Seventeenth-Century London* (Stanford, 1985)

Sharpe, K., *Remapping Early Modern England: The Culture of Seventeenth-Century Politics* (Cambridge, 2000)

Sharpe, K., and Lake, P. (eds): *Culture and Politics in Early Stuart England* (London, 1994)

Smith, D. L., (ed.): *Cromwell and the Interregnum* (Oxford, 2003)

Speight, H., *Lower Wharfedale* (London, 1902)

Speight, H., *Upper Wharfedale* (London, 1900)

Spraggon, J., *Puritan Iconoclasm during the English Civil War* (Woodbridge, 2003)

Stirling, A. M. W., *The Hothams: Being the Chronicles of the Hothams of Scorborough and South Dalton from their hitherto unpublished family papers* (2 vols, London, 1918)

Stoyle, M., *Soldiers and Strangers: An Ethnic History of the English Civil Wars* (New

Haven, 2005)

Stoyle, M., *West Britons: Cornish Identities and the Early Modern British State* (Exeter, 2002)

Stoyle, M., *Loyalty and Locality: Popular Allegiance in Devon during the English Civil War* (Exeter, 1994)

Sunderland, F. H., *Marmaduke, Lord Langdale* (London, 1926)

Trease, G., *Portrait of a Cavalier: William Cavendish, First Duke of Newcastle* (London, 1979)

Underdown, D., *A Freeborn People: Politics and the Nation in Seventeenth-Century England* (Oxford, 1996)

Underdown, D., *Revel, Riot and Rebellion: Popular Politics and Culture in England* (Oxford, 1985)

Underdown, D., *Somerset in the Civil War and Interregnum* (Newton Abbot, 1973)

Underdown, D., *Pride's Purge: Politics in the Puritan Revolution* (Oxford, 1971)

Walker, J. W., *Wakefield: Its History and People* (Wakefield, 2nd edn, 1966)

Walter, J., *Understanding Popular Violence in the English Revolution: The Colchester Plunderers* (Cambridge, 1999)

Wanklyn, M., and Jones, F., *A Military History of the English Civil War, 1642–1646: Strategy and Tactics* (Harlow, 2005)

Warmington, A. R., *Civil War, Interregnum and Restoration in Gloucestershire, 1640–1672* (Royal Historical Society, studies in history, new series, 1997)

Webb, G., *Fairfax of York: The Life and History of a Noble Family* (York, 2001)

Wedgwood, C. V., *The Trial of Charles I* (London, 1964)

Wedgwood, C. V., *The King's War, 1641–1647* (Manchester, 1958)

Wenham, P., *The Siege of York, 1644* (York, 2nd edn, 1994)

Wheater, W., *A history of Sherburn and Cawood* (London, 2nd edn, 1882)

Wilding, M., *Dragon's Teeth: Literature in the English Revolution* (Oxford, 1987)

Wilson, J., *Fairfax: A Life of Thomas, Lord Fairfax, Captain-General of all the Parliament's Forces in the English Civil War, Creator and Commander of the New Model Army* (New York, 1985).

Wood, A., *Riot, Rebellion and Popular Politics in Early Modern England* (Basingstoke, 2002)

Woolrych, A., *Britain in Revolution, 1625–1660* (Oxford, 2002)

Woolrych, A., *Soldiers and Statesmen: The General Council of the Army and its Debates, 1647–1648* (Oxford, 1987)

Woolrych, A., *Commonwealth to Protectorate* (Oxford, 1982)

Worden, B., *Roundhead Reputations: The English Civil War and the Passions of Posterity* (London, 2001)

Worden, B., *The Rump Parliament, 1648–1653* (Cambridge, 1974)

Articles

Adamson, J. S. A., 'The baronial context of the English civil war', *TRHS*, 5th series, 40 (1990)

Addy, J., 'The uncontrollable and ungovernable parish of Halifax in the seventeenth century', *THAS*, new series, 1 (1993)

Aylmer, G. E., 'Collective mentalities in mid-seventeenth-century England: II. Royalist attitudes', *TRHS*, 5th series, 37 (1987)

Aylmer, G. E., 'Collective mentalities in mid-seventeenth-century England: I. The puritan outlook', *TRHS*, 5th series, 36 (1986)

Binns, J., 'Scarborough and the civil wars, 1642–1651', *Northern History*, 22 (1986)

Black, V., 'In search of Black Tom Fairfax', *York Historian*, 3 (1980)

Clay, C. T., 'The Protestation of 1641: Halifax signatories', *THAS* (1919)

Clifton, R., 'Popular fear of catholics during the English revolution, 1640–1660', *Past and Present*, 52 (1971)

Cross, C., *Urban Magistrates and Ministers: Religion in Hull and Leeds from the Reformation to the Civil War* (University of York, Borthwick Papers, 67, 1985)

Cust, R., 'Catholicism, antiquarianism and gentry honour: the writings of Sir Thomas Shirley', *Midland History*, 23 (1998)

Cust, R., 'Honour and politics in early Stuart England: the case of Beaumont v. Hastings', *Past and Present*, 149 (1995)

Cust, R., 'News and politics in early seventeenth-century England', *Past and Present*, 112 (1986)

Dale, B., 'Cromwell in Yorkshire', *Bradford Antiquary*, new series, 1 (1900)

Dale, B., 'Ministers of the parish churches of the West Riding during the puritan revolution', *Bradford Antiquary*, new series, 1 (1900)

Daxon, L., 'The politics of Sir Thomas Fairfax reassessed', *History*, 90:4 (2005)

Donagan, B., 'The web of honour: soldiers, Christians, and gentlemen in the English civil war', *Historical Journal*, 44:2 (2001)

Donagan, B., 'Atrocity, war crime, and treason in the English civil war', *American Historical Review*, 99 (1994)

Donagan, B., 'Did ministers matter? War and religion in England, 1642–1649', *JBS*, 33 (1994)

Donagan, B., 'Codes and conduct in the English civil war', *Past and Present*, 118 (1988)

Duckett, G., 'Civil war proceedings in Yorkshire', *YAJ*, 7 (1882)

French, H., 'The search for the "middle sort of people" in England, 1600–1800', *Historical Journal*, 43:1 (2000)

Gentles, I., 'The choosing of officers for the New Model Army', *Historical Research*, 67 (1994)

Hanson, T. W., 'Three civil war notes', *THAS* (1916)

Hanson, T. W., 'Halifax parish church, 1640–1660, part 1', *THAS* (1915)

Heumann, J. M., 'Fairfax and the lifeguard's colors', *Albion*, 26:3 (1994)

Hirst, D., 'The fracturing of the Cromwellian alliance: Leeds and Adam Baynes', *EHR*, 108 (1993)

Hirst, D., and Zwicker, S., 'High summer at Nun Appleton, 1651: Andrew Marvell and Lord Fairfax's occasions', *Historical Journal*, 36:2 (1993)

Hopper, A., 'The Farnley wood plot and the memory of the civil wars in Yorkshire', *Historical Journal*, 45:2 (2002)

Hopper, A., ' "Fitted for desperation": honour and treachery in Parliament's Yorkshire command, 1642–1643', *History*, 86:2 (2001)

Hopper, A., 'A directory of parliamentarian allegiance in Yorkshire during the British civil wars, 1638–60', *YAJ*, 73 (2001)

Hopper, A., 'The clubmen of the West Riding of Yorkshire during the first civil war: "Bradford club-law"', *Northern History*, 36:1 (2000)

Hopper, A., ' "The popish army of the north": anti-catholicism and parliamentary allegiance in Yorkshire, 1642–6', *Recusant History*, 25:1 (2000)

Hopper, A., *'The Readiness of the People': The Formation and Emergence of the Army of the Fairfaxes, 1642–3* (University of York, Borthwick Papers, 92, 1997)

James, M., 'English politics and the concept of honour, 1485–1642', *Past and Present*, supplement, 3 (1978)

Kelsey, S., 'Constructing the council of state', *Parliamentary History*, 22:3 (2003)

Kelsey, S., 'The ordinance of the trial of Charles I', *Historical Research*, 76 (2003)

Kelsey, S., 'The trial of Charles I', *EHR*, 118:477 (2003)

Kelsey, S., 'The death of Charles I', *Historical Journal*, 45:4 (2002)

Kendall, H. P., 'The civil war as affecting Halifax and the surrounding towns', *THAS* (1910)

Kishlansky, M., 'The case of the army truly stated: the creation of the New Model Army', *Past and Present*, 81 (1978)

Lindley, K. J., 'The impact of the 1641 rebellion upon England and Wales, 1641–1645', *Irish Historical Studies*, 18 (1973)

McDonald, F. M. S., 'The timing of General George Monck's march into England, 1 January 1660', *EHR*, 105:415 (1990)

Marston, J. G., 'Gentry honour and royalism in early Stuart England', *JBS*, 13 (1973)

Morrill, J., 'The ecology of allegiance in the English revolution', *JBS*, 26 (1987)

Morrill, J., 'Mutiny and discontent in English provincial armies, 1645–1647', *Past and Present*, 56 (1972)

Newman, P. R., 'The defeat of John Belasyse: civil war in Yorkshire, January–April, 1644', *YAJ*, 52 (1980)

Peacey, J., 'Marchamont Nedham and the Lawrans letters', *Bodleian Library Record*, 17:1 (2000)

Scott, D., ' "The northern gentlemen", the parliamentary Independents, and Anglo-Scottish relations in the Long Parliament', *Historical Journal*, 42 (1999)

Scott, D., ' "Hannibal at our gates": loyalists and fifth-columnists during the bishops' wars – the case of Yorkshire', *Historical Research*, 70:173 (1997)

Smith, A., 'The image of Cromwell in folklore and tradition', *Folklore*, 79 (1968)

Temple, R. K. G., 'The original officer list of the New Model Army', *Historical Research*, 59 (1986)

Underdown, D., 'The problem of popular allegiance in the English civil war', *TRHS*, 5th series, 31 (1981)

Underdown, D., 'Party management in the recruiter elections, 1645–1648', *EHR*, 83 (1968)

Willen, D., 'Godly women in early modern England: puritanism and gender', *Journal of Ecclesiastical History*, 43 (1992)

Withington, P., 'Views from the bridge: revolution and restoration in seventeenth-century York', *Past and Present*, 170 (2001)

Wood, A., 'Beyond post-revisionism?: the civil war allegiances of the miners of the Derbyshire "peak Country" ', *Historical Journal*, 40 (1997)

Woolrych, A., 'Yorkshire and the Restoration', *YAJ*, 39 (1958)

Woolrych, A., 'Yorkshire's treaty of neutrality', *History Today*, 6 (1956)
Wootton, D., 'From rebellion to revolution: the crisis of the winter of 1642–1643 and the origins of civil war radicalism', *EHR*, 105 (1990)

Literature

Marshall, B., *The Siege of York in the days of Thomas, Lord Fairfax* (London, 1902)
Nicholson, J., *The poetical works of John Nicholson: the Airedale poet, carefully edited from the original editions with additional notes and a sketch of his life and writings by W. G. Hird* (London, 1876)
Nicholson, J., *The siege of Bradford, with notes* (Bradford, 2nd edn, 1831)
Sutcliffe, R., *The Rider of the White Horse* (London, 1959)

Unpublished theses

Bates, D., 'The honour culture of royalist officers in the north during the first civil war, 1642–1646' (M.Phil. thesis, University of Birmingham, 2002)
Bennett, R., 'Enforcing the law in revolutionary England: Yorkshire, 1640–1660' (Ph.D. thesis, University of London, 1988)
Cambers, A., 'Print, manuscript and godly cultures in the north of England, c.1600–1650' (Ph.D. thesis, University of York, 2003)
Coster, W., 'Kinship and community in Yorkshire, 1500–1700' (Ph.D. thesis, University of York, 1992)
Hopper, A., 'The extent of support for parliament in Yorkshire during the early stages of the first civil war' (Ph.D. thesis, University of York, 1999)
Jones, J., 'The war in the north: the northern parliamentary army in the English civil war, 1642–1645' (Ph.D. thesis, York University, Canada, 1991)
Newman, P. R., 'The royalist army in the north of England, 1642–5' (Ph.D. thesis University of York, 1978)
Newton, J., 'Puritanism in the diocese of York, 1603–1640' (Ph.D. thesis, University of London, 1956)
Rogerson, D., 'Popular politics in the West Riding during the English civil war, 1640–1648' (MA thesis, University of Warwick, 1991)

Index

Literary works can be found under authors' names. Page numbers in italic refer to illustrations.

Lightning Source UK Ltd.
Milton Keynes UK
UKOW06f2223120216

268283UK00005B/75/P